# SketchUp:
# A Design Guide for Woodworkers

## Complete Illustrated Reference

Joe Zen

POPULA R
WOODWORKING

# SketchUp:
## A Design Guide for Woodworkers

Complete Illustrated Reference

Joe Zeh

## ABOUT THE AUTHOR

Joe Zeh, an accomplished woodworker, is an electrical engineer with more than 35 years of experience in the computer and graphics industry, ranging from computer design to executive management, including being vice president of 3D graphics at ATI Technologies Inc. He teaches SketchUp both in video and live courses, and offers free SketchUp advice on his blog. You can view his web site and blog, or contact him via email.

E-mail: jpz@srww.com
Web site: www.srww.com
Blog: www.srww.com/blog

## DEDICATION

This book is dedicated to my sister Betty, to whom I owe all that I accomplished in life.

# CONTENTS

Introduction: About SketchUp: A Design Guide for Woodworkers                 07

**PART ONE**   **SKETCHUP'S WORKBENCH & ITS TOOLS**                          **19**

01   The SketchUp Workspace                                                  20

02   The SketchUp Toolbox                                                    37

**PART TWO**   **THE APPRENTICE & THE BEDSIDE TABLE**                        **57**

03   Drawing Tapered Legs                                                    58

04   Adding Joinery                                                          73

05   Using Joinery to Define Parts                                           84

06   Modeling a Traditional Drawer                                           95

07   Adding Cock Bead & Pull                                                 122

08   Ruby Script Extensions                                                  140

09   Creating Shop Drawings                                                  150

10   Texturing the Bedside Table                                            163

| PART THREE | THE JOURNEYMAN & NONRECTILINEAR PIECES & COMPLEX CURVES | 177 |
|---|---|---|
| 11 | Splayed Pieces: The Dough Box | 178 |
| 12 | Splayed Pieces: The Shaker Shop Stool | 194 |
| 13 | Modeling a Clock Hood with Two-Dimensional Circular Curves | 217 |
| 14 | Tabletop Edges with Noncircular Curves | 236 |
| 15 | Bracket Feet with Bézier Curves | 243 |
| 16 | Cabriole Legs with Bézier Curves | 256 |
| Appendix A | Mac OS X User Help | 270 |
| Appendix B | Preferences | 272 |
| Appendix C | Model Info | 275 |
| Appendix D | Component-related Dialog Boxes | 280 |
| Appendix E | SketchUp Viewers | 283 |
| Appendix F | The Warehouse | 284 |

# ABOUT SKETCHUP: A DESIGN GUIDE FOR WOODWORKERS

*My brother-in-law frequently admonishes me to "Plan your work and work your plan." The origin of this quote is unknown but can be found in church sermons as early as 1880. "Plan your work," succinctly describes the role SketchUp plays for woodworkers. "Work your plan," is the role of the woodworker.*

*The role of "SketchUp: A Design Guide for Woodworkers" is to teach SketchUp to woodworkers in a language that is familiar, and in a manner that is conducive to learning. I am confident that when you finish reading this book you will be a better woodworker and will more quickly and precisely "Plan your work and work your plan."*

*—Joseph P. Zeh (A.K.A. Chiefwoodworker)*

"SketchUp: A Design Guide for Woodworkers" is a book with a target audience of woodworkers, cabinetmakers and furniture builders (both hobbyists and professional). There are a number of SketchUp books on the market that cater to the architect, landscaper, marketing and advertising professional, and modeler. However, at the time of this writing, there was no other book on the market that focused specifically on the woodworker. And that's ironic, since there is no other tool so completely compatible with the woodworker's needs in designing, planning and completing a furniture piece.

However, while the theme of "SketchUp: A Design Guide for Woodworkers" is woodworking, this book will also appeal to a larger audience, including designers and architects, because SketchUp is the fastest growing application for creating 3D drawings and rendered models. This book starts by teaching the basic tools available in SketchUp and proceeds through sketching, drawing, dimensioning, producing shop drawings and texturing for photorealistic rendering. The vehicle for teaching SketchUp is real furniture projects that I have designed and crafted (including frequent explanations of joinery and crafting techniques). A companion web page, www.srww.com/sketchup_a_design_guide_for_woodworkers.html, will direct you to complete SketchUp drawings and models for all furniture pieces used in examples and exercises.

This book is intended to be thorough, technically accurate, compelling and a good source for future reference. The examples and techniques used, while not basic and simple, should be completely familiar to the woodworker and architect alike. While beginners

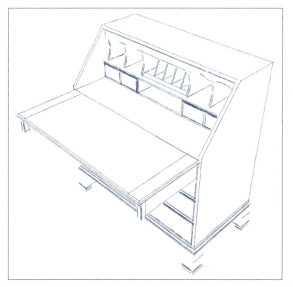

**Figure 1** | SketchUp sketch of a secretary

**Figure 3** | X-ray view; notice internal joiner

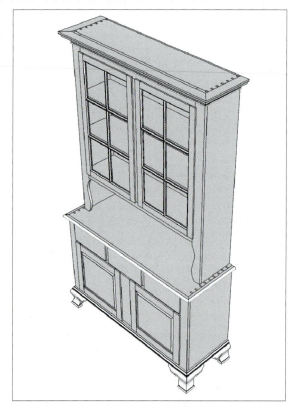

**Figure 2** | SketchUp drawing of a six-pane oak hutch

with no prior knowledge of SketchUp will find this book the appropriate starting point, and indeed the only one they need to learn SketchUp, the experienced SketchUp user will also find it challenging and informative.

## OVERVIEW OF SKETCHUP

So what is SketchUp? Simply put, SketchUp is a 3D sketching, modeling, rendering and design documentation tool. However, SketchUp is much more powerful than this simple description implies. SketchUp derives its name for a task it does quite well, drawing sketches, as can be seen in **Figure 1**.

SketchUp comes in two versions: SketchUp Pro and SketchUp Make. The major difference between the two is in their ability to save/open/export/import files from/to other CAD applications such as Auto-CAD and TurboCAD; and of course, their price. SketchUp Pro is richly supported in exporting and importing features, sells for $590 and is used commercially. SketchUp Make is free and targeted at the general public to encourage its use and the sharing of creative 3D models. Both are available for download directly from the SketchUp site sketchup.com. I use both versions because I teach SketchUp and write

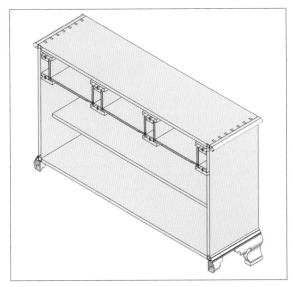

**Figure 4** | Section view of the hutch base

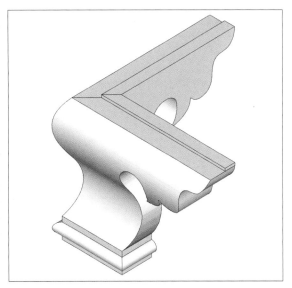

**Figure 5** | Ogee bracket foot drawn with a Bézier Ruby script

Ruby script plugins. SketchUp Make is all the non-professional woodworker needs to create dimensioned shop drawings, cut lists and photorealistic renderings. Moreover, SketchUp Make is easy to learn due to its intuitive user interface.

To get an idea of the power of SketchUp, look at the completed drawing of a six-pane oak hutch I designed and crafted and rendered without texturing (shown in **Figure 2**). This image is shown in perspective view, but SketchUp allows you to switch between parallel projection and perspective view with a single mouse click.

Another nice feature is the X-ray capability; **Figure 3** shows the hutch base only in X-ray view. Selecting the X-ray view is essentially displaying a line drawing. However, SketchUp weights the line drawing so that you get a feeling of depth. Notice that you can see the construction within the unit. X-ray view also aids in the design of a piece by allowing you to attach geometry to inside intersections, making connections to parts that are difficult to reach.

Sometimes we need a cross section of a model, called "sectioning" in engineering drawing parlance. To section the hutch base all I have to do is define a sectioning plane and move it into position as shown in **Figure 4**. This is a section in the vertical front plane,

but sections can be made in any plane, including complex sections, by simply rotating the sectioning plane in one or two axes. Sections can be saved as a view and can be dimensioned just like any other view.

One thing you may notice if you look at this section in detail is that you can see inside the pieces that make up the structure. For example, you can see inside the draw bottoms and runners. This is because SketchUp is a surface modeler, not a solid modeler – more on this later.

SketchUp's native curve features are limited to circles or arcs that are portions of a circle. At first blush you may think this very limiting because it is impossible to draw cabriole legs, for example, with just circular curves. But that couldn't be further from the truth. If you are an experienced user of high-end tools such as AutoCAD, you must learn to let SketchUp provide a more intuitive and simpler way. If I had to describe SketchUp in one word it would be *intuitive*. The way it works is more natural and akin to the way people draw when they draw by hand. This requires AutoCAD, and other CAD tool users, to come down the learning curve a bit and re-climb it. But once you do, you will find SketchUp is more comfortable and faster.

**Figure 5** shows the ogee bracket foot I designed for the six-pane oak hutch. The curves are produced

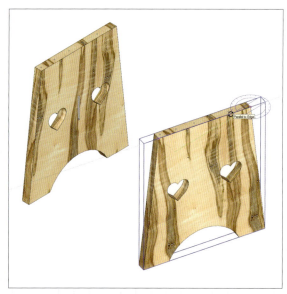

**Figure 6** | Rotating a component with the Rotate tool

using a free plugin that provides a variety of Bézier-spline curve tools, much like French curves when drawing by hand. Ruby script plugins are an ingenious feature of SketchUp, which I will get to later.

One example of SketchUp's more intuitive approach can be demonstrated by rotating a part. In **Figure 6** you can see that I simply selected the part (outlined in blue), grabbed the Rotate tool and began rotating. If I wish to rotate it to a standard angle such as 30° the built-in inference engine will let me know when I am there so I can click to complete the rotation. If I want an unusual angle such as 13.99°, I simply type 13.99 into the Value Control Box (VCB) and press *Enter*. But I don't have to place my cursor in the VCB; it is context sensitive. The VCB knows that if I type a number at this stage it must be an angle. So I simply type 13.99. The inference engine and VCB are very powerful features of SketchUp; they free you from having to place your cursor for input or worry about viewing planes and world coordinate systems. I can draw a complete piece of furniture without ever moving the axis or thinking about a work plane or even a coordinate system. Try that with TurboCAD or AutoCAD!

SketchUp's presentation style, simple dimensioning and inference engine make it easy to create exploded and dimensioned views. **Figure 7** is an exploded view of a grandfather clock's hood. Notice the assembled hood on the left of the image and the exploded hood on the right. Each component, or part, is labeled with the component name. The modeler doesn't need to type the component name in; simply click with the labeling tool.

Dimensioning is equally easy. **Figure 8** is a dimensioned view of a trundle bed finial that is turned on the lathe. This view can be printed at a 1:1 scale (full scale) so the turner can set calipers with it. The dimensioning tool, like the labeling tool, requires no input from the modeler. Simply click on two points representing the dimension line and place the dimension. Note that the labeling tool can also be used to add notes to the drawing.

As mentioned earlier, SketchUp is a surface modeler, not a solid modeler. This means it represents solids as surfaces. For example a cube is constructed by creating six connected surfaces. In a solid modeler if you were to section or slice a cube you would have two new cubes. In SketchUp you are left with two halves of an enclosure and you can see inside each half – like cutting a closed cardboard box in half. This is a real problem if you are designing and modeling mechanical parts, especially if you have to derive such things as weight, center of gravity and mass from your drawing. But for furniture or architectural design this is not a problem. It can easily be solved with a plugin, which I will describe shortly.

When comparing SketchUp with big brother CAD tools, it also falls short in other areas such as logical operations and splines (complex curves). Logical operations give you the ability to add parts to create a new one or to subtract two parts. For example, suppose you drew the sides of a drawer complete with tails and now wanted to draw the back with pins. Rather than draw the pins, start with the drawing of a rectangular board sized correctly for the back. Copy one of the sides and place it at right angles to the board. Then subtract the copied side from the board and voilà! You now have the board with pins on one end. Repeat the step on the other end and you're done. This is slightly more difficult in the free version of SketchUp. However, one of the nice parts of SketchUp

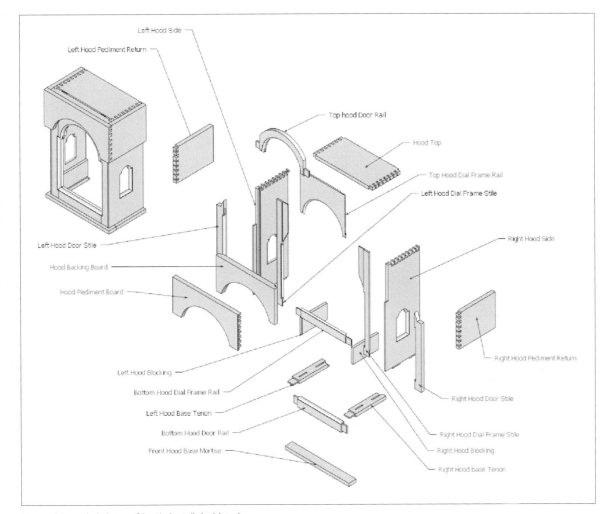

**Figure 7** | An exploded view of the Shaker tall clock hood

is that it allows plugins that enhance its feature set, and there is a worldwide community out there generating free, downloadable, plugins called Ruby scripts. Almost any feature you want to add can be found on the web. The Pro version of SketchUp has these logical operations natively, six of them in fact.

As an example of adding features with plugins, recall the earlier section of a hutch base, where you could see inside the drawer bottoms and runners. You can download a Ruby script called SectionCutFace.rb written by TIG ©, which places a command on the context menu (right mouse click). This command

restores the faces on the exposed ends. A little cleanup is required, but the results produce a much more readable picture. Compare **Figure 9** with the previous base section in **Figure 4**.

Another example of a SketchUp plugin is one that I wrote called CutList Bridge. This plugin lets you create a cut list with three simple mouse clicks. CutList Bridge exports the cut list to a CSV (comma separated value) file, which can then be imported into Microsoft Excel, OpenOffice Calc or CutList Plus fx. **Figure 10** is a cut list for the Shaker tall clock pictured above. In this case the cut list is shown in CutList Plus fx,

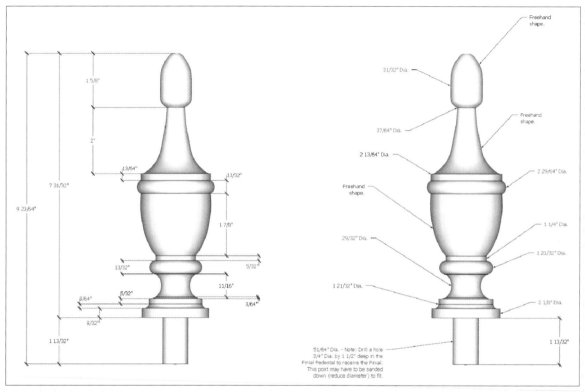

**Figure 8** | Turning drawings for a trundle bed finial

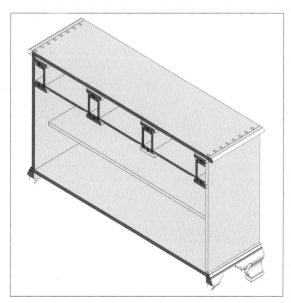

**Figure 9** | Section view of the hutch base with restored faces

a professional cut list and materials optimization application.

There are hundreds (perhaps thousands) of Ruby scripts for SketchUp on the Internet and most of them are free. I have a few favorites that I have downloaded and use frequently. I have also written a number that I provide for free on my website (srww.com) and blog (srww.com/blog).

I find new scripts on the Internet every few weeks. Ruby scripts can be found in a number of places. The SketchUp team maintains a warehouse of extensions that can be accessed through a SketchUp tool icon. In addition, this same warehouse can be used to access thousands of SketchUp models or to contribute your own models to the warehouse. There are many other places on the internet where you can access Ruby script plugins too numerous to mention here, but a simple Google search will uncover them.

**Figure 10** | A CutList Plus fx cut list produced by CutList Bridge

If I haven't convinced you of the power of SketchUp yet, perhaps the photorealistic rendering of a cherry chest, shown in **Figures 11** and **Figure 12**, will. This is a SketchUp model. I took images of finished grain from a previous project using a digital camera. Will Manning of IDX took these image files and my SketchUp model and using the IDX Renditioner plugin for SketchUp rendered these images. Notice the real cherry grain, the end grain on the pins, the shadows on the floor and the bricked walls. The shading can be adjusted for region, time of year and time of day based on world averages.

By now I hope I've impressed upon you just how robust and powerful a tool SketchUp can be for woodworking. I find the presentation style of the rendered drawings are much more readable and pleasing than the staid presentations of more expensive solids modelers. **Figure 13** is a

**Figure 11** | A cherry chest of drawers rendered by SketchUp and the IDX Renditioner plugin

**Figure 12** | A cherry chest of drawers rendered by SketchUp and the IDX Renditioner plugin

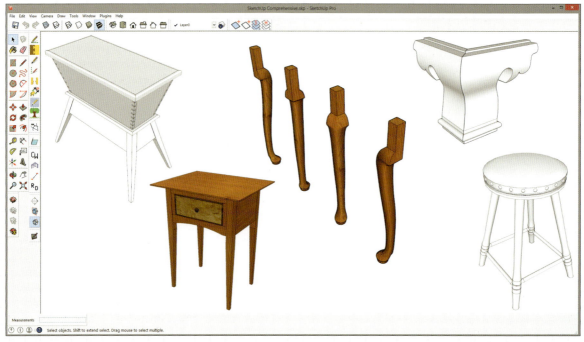

**Figure 13** | A sample of SketchUp models taught in this text

sample of the models and shapes you will learn to draw in this text.

## HOW TO USE THIS BOOK

This text is written in a linear fashion and is best used by going through it from beginning to end. However, if you are already a knowledgeable and experienced user of SketchUp you might choose to skip around – just be cautious as some of the chapters build upon each other, such as in Part Two of the book.

You should not begin reading a chapter and draw as you read. I highly recommend that you first read the chapter, study all the figures and read the captions. Then go back and re-read the chapter and draw as you go along. This two-step approach will reduce confusion considerably.

In the earlier sections of this text you'll find step-by-step instructions including tool icons. I will include these until I feel I have repeated myself enough that you should have learned the use of a tool and its associated icon or command. The training wheels have to come off at some

point. In Part Three, I assume you are a knowledgeable user and no longer need the step-by-step directions and icons. If at any time you need to refresh yourself on a tool's use, command or icon you can return to the Chapter Two section on Selecting & Using Tools. Also, later in this Introduction is a section called Other Helpful Sources. Of course, no text is the complete and final word on a subject, so please feel free to supplement your study of SketchUp with other sources of information.

### Organization

This book is organized in parts. Each part is self-contained and can stand alone as a reference. Parts progress in difficulty and functionality. Part One: SketchUp's Workbench & Its Tools, focuses on the basic SketchUp window environment and the tools that come with SketchUp. It does not use or refer to any functionality that might be added with a Ruby script. Nor does it cover the environments of LayOut or Style Builder, which come with SketchUp Pro. In Part One, the basic tools are explained, but there is no drawing or modeling presented. This part can stand alone as a reference for the Workspace, the basic toolbars and tools. If you feel comfortable with the SketchUp environment and tools you can skip Part One and go directly to Part Two.

## Conventions Used

There are a few conventions used in this text that will aid in understanding and learning. This section is invaluable and should be read by all.

## Icons

Throughout the text you will encounter occasional icons. The 📁 icon will show up in a yellow shaded box to provide the reader with important and general information that applies to a specific topic or tool. The ✏ icon will appear in a blue shaded box and instructs the reader to take note of an important point. These two icons are points of emphasis. The reader should pay close attention to them.

> When beginning a new chapter first read through it without attempting to model anything. Instead, as you read look at and study each figure, read the captions, and relate what is being accomplished in each figure to the text you are reading. If the figure has dimensions follow them and do the arithmetic to relate them to one another. For the most part, the figures build on one another; imagine the steps needed to fill in between consecutive figures. Then, and only then, begin the chapter again and model as you read. This procedure will eliminate a lot of frustration.

In Part Two, I assume you are using each SketchUp tool for the first time. When a new tool is introduced, its tool icon will be shown. For example, in text I might say "Using the Move ✛ tool, move the leg 14" to the right along the Red axis." I will continue to use its icon until I feel that you should have committed it to memory. After that I will no longer use the icon. In Part Three, I assume you have mastered the tools and

know how to locate new ones, so I will rarely use tool icons in Part Three.

Many users prefer using shortcut keys to icons. I don't use short cut keys in this text. However, SketchUp supplies a Quick Reference Card in PDF format for both Microsoft Windows and Mac OS X. At the time of this writing you could download it by going to help.sketchup.com/en/article/116693. If that hyperlink doesn't work simply Google "SketchUp Quick Reference Card."

## Key Definitions

There are a few words and phrases I use throughout this text that you may not see in other SketchUp texts, including SketchUp's own. It is important you understand these.

The word *primitive*, or *primitive*s, when used in this text means points, lines, faces, rectangles, circles, polygons and arcs including construction lines and points. In short, a primitive is any drawn object except a solid, group or component. They are the most fundamental of drawing objects from which all other geometry is drawn. A part is in its primitive state unless it is made into a group or component.

> It is very important to understand that when two primitives touch, even when they are on different layers, they stick together. This is a source of real frustration for new SketchUp users. Fortunately, there are mechanisms to avoid this and a set of drawing rules to eliminate frustration. The mechanism is to make primitives into components. The rules are the "Six Rules for Modeling in SketchUp," which will be presented in Part One.

The word *entity*, or *entities*, is any object or collection of objects: whether drawn, such as primitives, solids, groups or components; or placed such as a dimension or text. The reverse is also true; the word *object* or *objects*, is any entity or collection of entities.

The words *line* and *edge* can be confusing. An edge is a drawing primitive shown as a black line of finite length and drawn with a Drawing tool. A line is a construction aid usually drawn with Construction or Edit tool. It may be infinite or finite in length and is shown as stippled and not solid. Unfortunately, single edges are drawn with a Line tool, which confuses the terminology. In the text I will sometimes use the term *line* to mean an edge. It will usually be clear from the context what I intend. But be aware of the difference.

The word *context* or the phrase *in context* refers to the state of a tool, or where in the use of a tool the user is. When a tool is selected its context begins. A tool may require the user to proceed through a number of steps. When the tool is left by selecting another tool, its context ends. While in the tool's context, its parameters can be changed or corrected any number of times; generally by typing a number in the VCB (Value Control Box). But when its context is left or changed its parameters can only be changed by editing, deleting or re-drawing.

There are a few tools that when selected do not change the first tool's context. The Camera tools such as Pan, Zoom, Previous and Next are good examples. If a second tool is selected and it does not deselect the first tool's icon, but rather grays it out, then the first tool's context is temporarily suspended. After using the second tool, immediately reselect the grayed out first tool and its context will be restored. However, if you select a third tool after the second tool, the first tool's context is lost.

There is also a Context menu accessed with the right mouse button. The word *context* in this instance refers to the state of the model and the tool currently selected. For example, if the Select tool is used to select a component and the mouse is right clicked while over the component a menu will pop up. Here one of the available tools is Edit Component. The tool Edit Group will not appear as an option because the selected entity is a component not a group. The Context menu is one that changes depending on the state of the model and the tools used; you can only learn all

its capabilities by selecting it frequently under various conditions and experimenting with its choices.

*Drawing* and *modeling* are used interchangeably in this text, as were drawing and drafting in the old days of hand drawn 2D prints. Modeling is perhaps the more in vogue word since 3D is still relatively new, and it permits modeling something much like building a prototype or mock-up. But I find that limiting this text to either word doesn't cover the full spectrum of 3D. Further, if it weren't for the Push/Pull tool, all SketchUp models would be drawn in 2D; and all 3D components start as 2D shapes.

## REFERENCES TO TOOLS & MENUS

References to menu items, buttons, boxes, windows etc. will generally be capitalized indicating that you should expect to find it exactly as written. For example, under the Window menu the first item is Model Info. If you click on this, a Model Info dialog box will appear. Both the command Model Info and the Model Info dialog box will appear capitalized.

Throughout this book I will refer to menus and submenus. For example, Intersect Faces is an oft used command. There is no tool icon or shortcut for this command. When I wish to instruct the reader to use the command Intersect Faces I will write it as Edit/Intersect Faces/With Selection. This tells the reader that the command Intersect Faces is found by going to the Edit menu first, then the submenu Intersect Faces, which has an arrow indicating there are further submenus, and finally selecting With Model.

## GETTING HELP FOR "SKETCHUP: A GUIDE FOR WOODWORKERS"

I maintain a companion web site in support of "SketchUp: A Design Guide for Woodworkers." You can find it at the following hyperlink: srww.com/sketchup_a_guide_for_woodworkers.html

Throughout this book I will refer to files to download. You will find them on this page in the Downloads section organized by book part and chapter. I will post errata to this page when a user points out a problem or I discover a mistake. I will also provide short videos that will cover issues and topics in this book in more detail. Be sure to visit this page when you begin reading this book and come back often to check for changes or helpful information. Should you find a problem in the text or figures I would appreciate a report emailed to jpz@srww.com.

## OTHER HELPFUL SOURCES

There are many helpful sources in addition to this book that the reader should be familiar with. To begin with you should bookmark the SketchUp Knowledge Center at help.sketchup.com/en. If you wish to learn more about the Move tool for example, type "Move Tool" into the Knowledge Center's search box and click the Search icon.

I often go straight to Google and type in the subject I am interested in, but I prefix it with SketchUp. For example, I type "SketchUp Move Tool" into the Google search box and enter. Generally the first item on the return search is what I want.

Both the free and the Pro versions of SketchUp have an Instructor that will give you information about the selected tool. You can open Instructor by selecting the menu Window/Instructor. I find this to be one of the most useful tools for learning the function of an individual tool. If you are a beginner, leave Instructor open. As you select various tools it will update to give you information for that tool. **Figure 14** shows this for the Move tool.

You should also check out the SketchUp home page where you will find many helpful resources. Go to www.sketchup.com. There, at the bottom of the page, you will find hyperlinks for Plugins, Knowledge Center and Forum. You will find the Forum is another good place to go for help.

My own web site and blog also have numerous articles, tutorials and models. You can access any post I ever wrote on my blog by going to srww.com/blog/?tag=sketchup. My website and blog have a top level menu item called – drum roll please - SketchUp. You can access this page directly by going to srww.com/google-sketchup.htm. Lastly go to srww.com/sketchup_a_design_guide_for_woodworkers.html to access My Book page where you will find information specific to, and in support of, "SketchUp: A Design Guide for Woodworkers." At the risk of sounding vain, these links should be on your browser's Favorite list as well.

**Figure 14** | The Instructor dialog box explaining how to use the Move tool

## MICROSOFT WINDOWS & MAC OS X

This book is written using the Microsoft Windows version of SketchUp Make. I have chosen to use the Windows version because of its much larger installed base. However, the differences between Microsoft Windows and Mac OS X versions of SketchUp are finite and relatively minor. To assist the Mac user I have included a Mac OS X User Help section in Appendix A. If you are a Mac OS X user I highly recommend reading that section before beginning Part One.

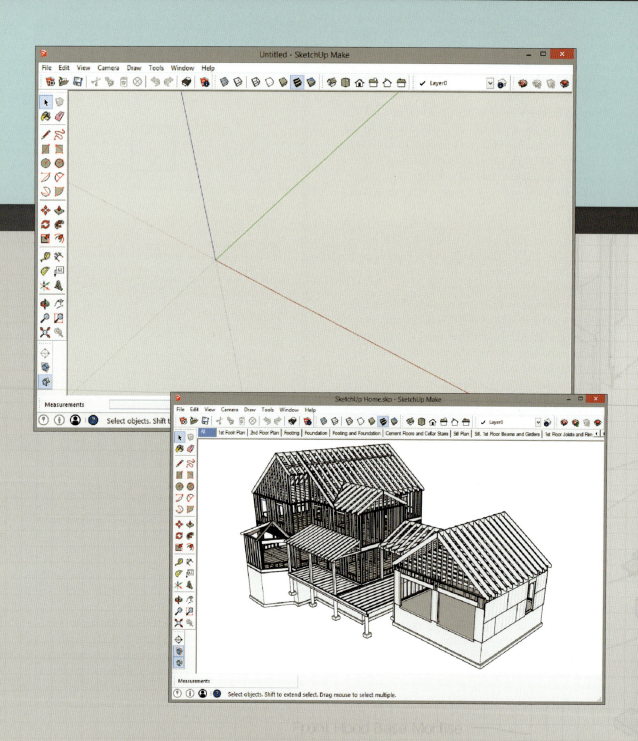

# PART ONE:
# SKETCHUP'S WORKBENCH & ITS TOOLS

Before we begin drawing or modeling we need to discuss SketchUp's workbench and its tools.

SketchUp's workbench is more precisely called its Workspace. The SketchUp workspace is highly customizable, allowing you to create a unique workspace configured to the way you work.

Within the workspace are a number of toolboxes; more precisely toolbars and tools. These too are customizable. In fact, you can add user-defined tools to the tools bars and menus through SketchUp's Ruby API. But let's not jump too far ahead.

# THE SKETCHUP WORKSPACE

*The SketchUp Window is your workbench or more precisely workspace.*
*You should become as familiar with it as you would your woodshop.*

Before we begin our study of SketchUp we must first install it, customize the toolbars for woodworking and configure our workspace. Once this is completed, I will give you a quick tour of the workspace so you will be familiar with it and able to navigate around it.

In this book I will use SketchUp and SketchUp Make to refer to the free version of SketchUp. SketchUp Make is the focus of this book and is all the hobbyist woodworker needs. Occasionally I will point out differences between SketchUp Make and SketchUp Pro; when I refer to the professional version I will always refer to it as SketchUp Pro and not SketchUp.

## INSTALLING SKETCHUP MAKE

You can download the free version from the SketchUp home page, which, at the time of this writing is sketchup.com. Follow these download and installation instructions:

1. On the home page click the Download SketchUp button.
2. This will bring you to a page titled "You're about to download SketchUp." Answer the prompt "I plan to use SketchUp for:" with "Personal Projects."
3. This will set up the page to download SketchUp Make. Fill in the remaining fields shown in **Figure 1** as follows:
   a. Your e-mail address.
   b. "Other"
   c. Your operating system.
   d. You must check this box.
   e. Check only if you wish this information.
4. Click the Download SketchUp Make button.
5. A dialog box similar to **Figure 2** will appear. Click *Save File*. This will save the installation file in your Downloads folder (or whatever folder you designate).
6. Go to your Downloads folder, locate and click on "SketchUpMake-en-x64.exe" (or "SketchUp-Make-en-x32.exe" if you downloaded the 32-bit version). This will start the SketchUp installer.
7. The next dialog box to appear is titled "Welcome to the SketchUp Make 2015 (64-bit) Setup Wizard." Click *Next*.
8. The dialog box will update with the "Trimble SketchUp Make License." Check the "I accept the terms in the License Agreement" checkbox and click *Next*.
9. The dialog box will again update to "Destination Folder." You can change the destination folder if you are an experienced user, but I highly

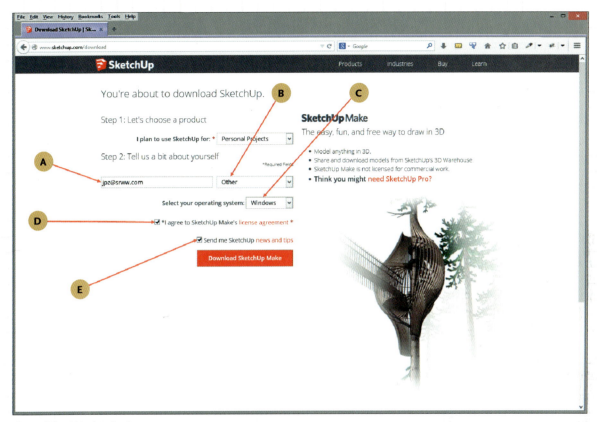

**Figure 1** | SketchUp download page

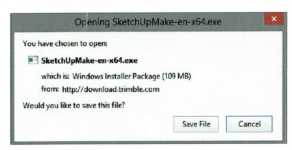

**Figure 2** | Save File dialog box

recommend that you accept the suggested folder by simply clicking *Next*.

10. In the next dialog box update, "Ready to install SketchUp Make 2015 (64-bit)," click *Install*.

11. The installer will proceed to install SketchUp. A dialog box titled "Files In Use" may appear (similar to **Figure 2A**. I strongly recommend you

choose "Do not close applications. A reboot will be required." Click *OK*.

12. When the installer is completed, a dialog box will appear titled "Completed the SketchUp Make 2015 (64-bit) Setup Wizard." Click *Finish*.

13. A dialog box will appear informing you that a restart is required. Close all applications and then click *Yes*.

After the restart is completed you should see three new icons on your desktop: LayOut 2015, Style Builder 2015 and SketchUp 2015. LayOut and Style Builder are applications that come with the Pro license. For the first 30 days of a first-time installation of SketchUp Make your license is a full Pro license. This is Trimble's way of letting you sample the Pro license hopefully so you decide to purchase it. After the first 30 days the license will revert to a Make

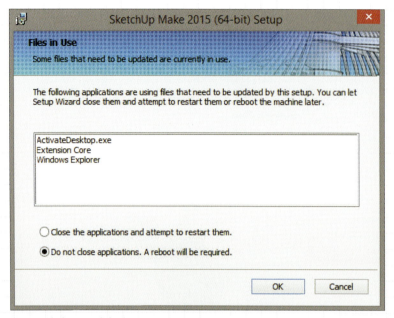

**Figure 2A** | File in Use dialog box

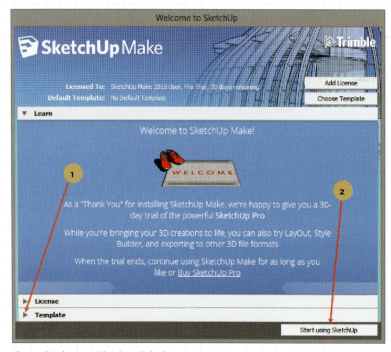

**Figure 3** | Welcome to SketchUp dialog box

license. This text does not cover LayOut or Style Builder, nor does it cover the added functionality to SketchUp offered by the Pro license. So if you choose to try either of these applications, you are on your own. I suggest deleting their icons and ignoring them unless or until you decide to purchase a Pro license. In any event, my advice is to learn SketchUp Make before upgrading to a Pro license.

Click on the SketchUp 2015 icon to get started. A dialog box opens titled "Welcome to SketchUp" shown in **Figure 3**. Notice near the top it says "Licensed To: SketchUp Make 2015 User, Pro Trial, 30 days remaining." This is again a reminder that for the first 30 days you have a Pro license. To proceed to using SketchUp follow these steps:

1.  Click the arrow to the left of Template in the lower left hand corner. The dialog box updates to a list of templates. Scroll down until you find "Woodworking – Inches" and choose it.
2.  Click the "Start Using SketchUp" button. The SketchUp window will now appear.

## SETTING UP THE TOOLBARS

When SketchUp opens for the first time it will look similar to **Figure 4**. This is the primary workspace. For now close the Instructor

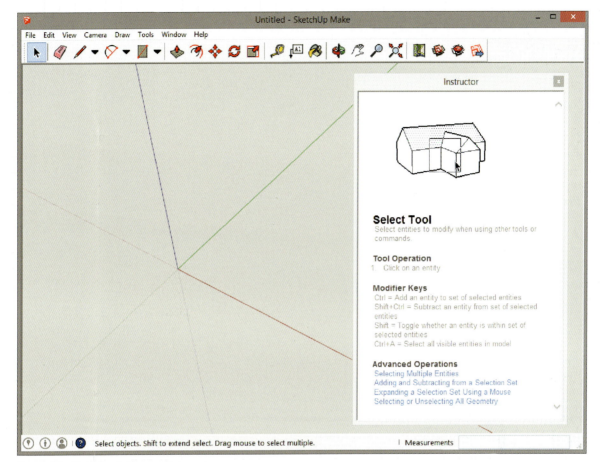

**Figure 4** | The SketchUp window upon first opening

dialog box. You can always get back to it using menu Window/Instructor.

We want to configure this window such that all tools we frequently use are at our finger tips. The toolbar shown in the initial installation configuration is called the Getting Started toolbar. You can verify this by clicking on the View/Toolbars menu to open the Toolbars dialog box. Choose the Toolbars tab and notice Getting Started is the only toolbar checked. We will not be using this toolbar, so uncheck it now. This should leave all toolbars as unchecked. Now we will check those that we will use and customize. Check the following toolbars:

1. Large Tool Set
2. Layers
3. Measurements
4. Section
5. Standard
6. Styles
7. Views
8. Warehouse

Leave the Toolbars dialog box open; it must be open to customize a toolbar. You can identify the name of a toolbar by checking and unchecking a toolbar in the Toolbars dialog box and observing which toolbar appears or disappears. You can locate a tool icon within a toolbar by hovering over it and reading the tool tip. Now identify the Large Tool Set. Within the Large Tool Set is a tool icon called Position Camera. With your mouse drag and drop this icon in an

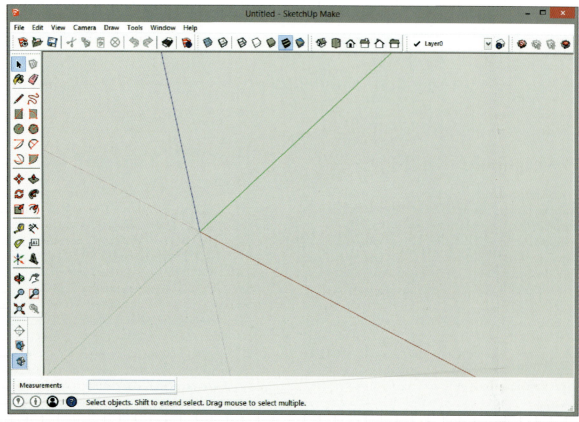

**Figure 5** | The SketchUp window after toolbar selection and customization

open area of the SketchUp window. It will disappear from the Large Tool Set toolbar. Do the same for the Look Around, Walk and Section Plane tool icons in the Large Tool Set.

> To delete a tool icon from a native SketchUp toolbar go to menu View/Toolbars. While the Toolbars dialog box is open, using your mouse drag and drop the icon you wish to delete onto an open space in the SketchUp window. When done close the Toolbars dialog box. Note: this does not work for Ruby Plugin Script toolbars. Mac OS X users should refer to Appendix A for toolbar customization.

While the Toolbars dialog box is still open choose the Options tab. I suggest unchecking Large Icons because we will want to preserve all the workspace real estate we can. If your vision requires it, leave Large Icons checked. Large and small versions of an icon can be slightly different from one another because of the difference in size, so get familiar with both. For now close the Toolbars dialog box. We will revisit it later when we create a custom toolbar.

With this toolbar selection and customization my SketchUp workspace looks like **Figure 5**. Set up your workspace by choosing these same toolbars and arranging them the way I have. This will make it easier for you to follow along in the text. You can change these at any time; this selection is not permanent. Take note that each toolbar has a grip, a vertical or horizontal dotted bar, which is available whenever a toolbar is docked to either the top, bottom, left or right ribbons. Grab a grip with the cursor and you can move a toolbar around; place it on another ribbon or on the workspace as a free floating toolbar. When you place it in the workspace undocked, its name appears along the top. Now you can resize the toolbar just as you would a window (though it will only snap to sizes that are integer rows by columns).

## CONFIGURING THE WORKSPACE

Configuring the workspace consists of choosing a viewing perspective, setting up preferences that are application wide, and setting up model specific information. The choice of viewing perspective is a wee bit controversial in the SketchUp community. Let's look at the choices.

Under the Camera menu, in the second section, you will see Parallel Projection, Perspective and Two-Point Perspective. The default after installing SketchUp is Perspective. Most books on SketchUp and most internet tutorials use Perspective view. This is due to the fact that SketchUp was initially considered an architectural sketching tool – not a design documentation tool. I am going to suggest you use Parallel Projection for all but photorealistic rendering. I will explain why in a moment, but first let me explain the differences.

## PARALLEL PROJECTION VERSUS PERSPECTIVE

There are actually three forms of parallel projection: Isometric, Diametric and Trimetric. SketchUp implements only isometric and uses the generic label Parallel Projection (except on the Views toolbar icon where it is labeled "Iso"). In this text *parallel projection* and *isometric view* are used interchangeably, though isometric is more technically correct.

Parallel projection is a view used widely in technical and engineering drawings. It represents a three-dimensional object on a two-dimensional plane with three axes 120° apart. There are two major benefits to parallel projection over perspective representations.

First, there is no vanishing point in parallel projections. As the name implies, all lines along a given axis are

parallel to all other lines along that same axis. Second, because there is no vanishing point, three dimensional drawings can be accurately scaled (e.g. 1"= 12').

The first benefit means that viewing a complex drawing is easier than perspective because you can immediately tell whether lines are parallel or orthogonal. Even lines off axis are easily recognizable for what they are (such as 45° lines). The second benefit means that measurements can be made directly from a scaled drawing. This is useful in the shop or the field if you have a scaled drawing and a 6" scale handy.

The major disadvantage of a parallel projection is that it does not appear realistic, that is it does not appear the way the human eye sees things. When we look at a building or a train we tend to see it diminish in size the further it is from our eyes. A train, if long enough, will disappear to a point. When we see a drawing of a very long object – such as a train – that does not diminish in size with distance, we have the sense that something is amiss.

There are four perspective projections: Zero-point, One-point, Two-point and Three-point. SketchUp implements Three-point and Two-point and calls them Perspective and Two-Point Perspective respectively. Without going into the technical details of each, suffice it to say that one of the four choices is better suited to an object depending on what the object is. For example, Zero-point is well suited to mountain ranges, which are larger by far than any other object in a drawing and have no parallel lines. It would look unnatural to see the Rocky Mountains vanish to a single point in a landscape rendering.

SketchUp implements the two perspectives that are most easily represented and which are most useful to architectural drawing. The major advantage of perspective drawing is that they look more natural to the human eye. The major disadvantage is that you cannot produce a scaled drawing from a perspective drawing. You will see later that SketchUp does not allow printing to scale of a perspective view, because it is simply not possible.

My suggestion is to use Parallel Projection for all but photorealistic renderings. Many drawing mistakes have been made simply because one did not recognize when lines were parallel in a perspective drawing. In an isometric drawing it is obvious. Shop drawings are most useful if all line lengths maintain relative size – even if they are not to any useful scale – because equally sized lines, dados and tenons are immediately recognizable.

Fortunately, no matter what projection we use for drawing, in SketchUp we can immediately switch to another with the click of a mouse. With that somewhat long winded explanation, go ahead and select Camera/Parallel Projection; that is what I will use in this text and setting Parallel Projection will make it easier to follow along.

## PREFERENCES

Preferences can be found in menu Windows/ Preferences. To simplify matters I have included in Appendix B all pages of the System Preferences dialog box for reference. We will deal here with only changes we wish to make to the default selections set during installation. Refer to Appendix B, Preferences, as I describe the changes.

In the Applications page you may wish to specify an image editor. I have specified my favorite: Tech-Smith's Snagit editor. When I wish to edit an image in SketchUp it will automatically open Snagit for editing. You may never use this option, so there is no need to specify an editor.

I have a lot of Ruby script plugins I use. At this point you may only have those that came with SketchUp as it was downloaded and installed. To enable these plugins, in the Extensions page check any that appear. You can disable them at a later date by unchecking them. We will discuss installing plugins available through the internet at a later point in this text.

In the Files page you will notice that I customized the file locations to my user directory. This is not necessary, but it does make things easier to find. For example, my Models are saved to the default folder C:\ Users\Joe\Dropbox\SketchUp Files\Models.

In the General page be sure to check Create backup, Auto-save and specify 5 for "Every _ minutes." Nothing is more frustrating than creating a large drawing or making a lot of changes only to have a system crash or power failure resulting in all work being lost.

If you have hardware acceleration on your system and your driver supports OpenGL, be sure to check "Use hardware acceleration" in the OpenGL window. Almost all systems manufactured over the last few years now have hardware acceleration.

Notice in the Template page that I have selected "Woodworking – Inches" as my default template. I will explain how to make a personalized custom template shortly. At that time you may wish to do the same and come back to the Template page to select it. For now leave it as we set it up earlier in the text.

That's it for the System Preferences changes. Next we will set up model preferences using menu Window/Model Info.

 System Preferences settings are system and application wide. They are model independent and persist through closing and opening SketchUp.

## MODEL INFO

Model wide preferences are accessed through the menu Window/Model Info. I have included in Appendix C all pages of the Model Info dialog box for reference. Again, we will deal here with only changes we wish to make to the default selections set during installation. Refer to Appendix C, Model Info, as I describe these changes.

In the Credits page you will notice that I took credit as author for a model by clicking the Claim Credit button. This is useful if you are going to share your models in 3D Warehouse or retrieve models from 3D Warehouse. Each time a model is downloaded the owner's nickname will be visible in the Contributor's section along with the name of the model. Before you can claim credit for a model you have to set up a Google account, log into it and set up your personal information. To set up an account go to google.com/accounts/NewAccount and follow the instructions.

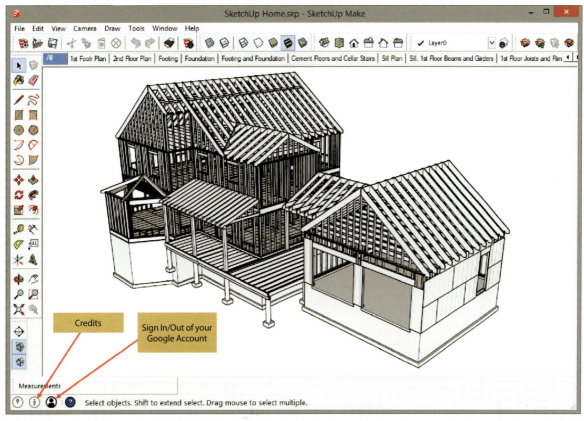

**Figure 6** | Credits and Google sign-in icons

Once you have your account set up you can log in by clicking the Google account icon in the lower left hand corner of your SketchUp workspace denoted by an upper body icon. You can access the Credits page through menu Window/Model Info or by clicking the little person icon in the lower left hand corner of the SketchUp workspace. See **Figure 6**. You must open your saved model before you can claim credit.

In the Dimensions page, I have changed the font color to red and selected Slash for the Leader Lines/Endpoints. This is a matter of taste, but I find they make a dimensioned drawing less black and less crowded. Change the font color by clicking on the color patch next to the Fonts button. This brings up the Choose Color dialog box. In the Picker drop-down box choose RGB. Select the color red by typing 255, 0 and 0 in the input fields as shown in **Figure 7**.

On the Text page, I have changed the Screen Text and Leader Text fonts to red. Follow the same procedure used to change the Dimensions font color.

On the Units page, in the Format drop-down box choose Fractional. Also, in the Precision drop down box choose ⅟₆₄", the highest available precision. Important: uncheck "Enable length snapping" to allow the Inference Engine to connect lines precisely (we will discuss the Inference Engine in some detail later). Leaving this option checked may result in lines not being connected when they should be and creating troublesome modeling errors.

Throughout this text we will refer to individual System Preferences and Model Info pages. But for now we will leave all remaining options in the System Preferences and Model Info sections as selected by installation defaults.

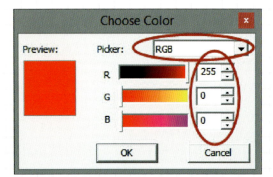

**Figure 7** | Dimensions' page Choose Color dialog box

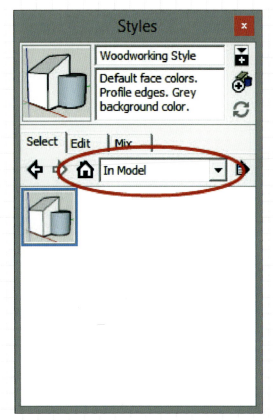

**Figure 8** | Styles dialog box

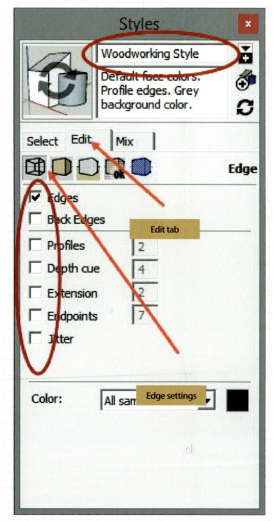

**Figure 9** | Styles Edge Settings page

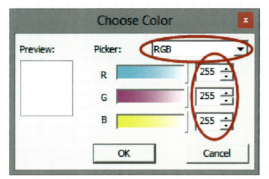

**Figure 10** | Styles Background Settings Choose Color dialog box

Model Info settings are specific to the current active model. They do not persist across models as you open a new or existing model. Rather, they are part of a model's file. We will learn shortly how we can make one set of Model Info settings apply to all new models using a custom Template file.

## STYLES

The Styles dialog box can be accessed through the Window/Styles menu. In this set up section we will be interested in the In Model styles only. To display the In Model styles in the Styles dialog box first choose the Select tab and then click the little house icon or use the drop down box to choose In Model as shown in **Figure 8**.

With the In Model styles selected there is only one style at the moment and it is called Woodworking Style. We are going to modify this style for our purposes. Select the Edit tab and then the Edge Settings icon; the icon on the left immediately under the Select tab. Check the Edges check box and make sure all other check boxes are unchecked. See **Figure 9**.

While the Styles dialog box is still open and the Edit tab selected, choose the Background Settings icon (located immediately under the Edit tab). Make sure Sky and Ground are unchecked; we are draw-

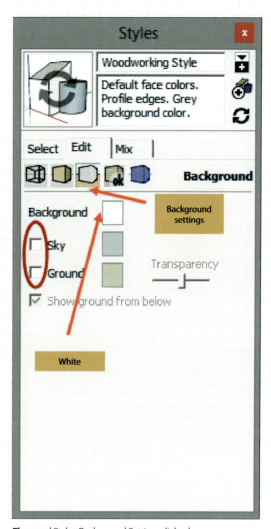

**Figure 11** | Styles Background Settings dialog box

ing furniture, not a house. Click on the color patch next to Background and change the color to white by choosing RGB in the drop down box and typing 255, 255 and 255 into the input fields as shown in **Figure 10**.

The Background Settings should now appear as shown in **Figure 11**. The white background will save on inkjet ink when printing shop drawings. The lack

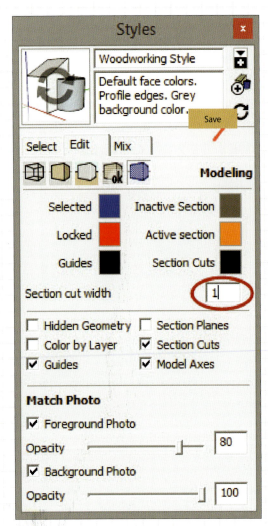

**Figure 12** | Styles Modeling Settings dialog box

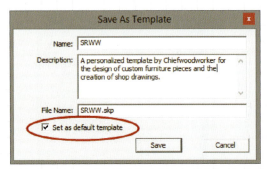

**Figure 13** | Save As Template dialog box

of sky and ground will help you avoid distraction while navigating the model.

Our final Styles dialog box change is on the Modeling Settings page accessed by clicking on the last icon on the right just under the Mix tab. Enter 1 in the field called Section cut width. The Modeling Settings page should look like **Figure 12**. You are now ready to save all your Styles changes, and this step is

necessary to preserve all the changes you have made. Click the icon marked *Save* in red shown in **Figure 12**. Close the Styles dialog box.

One final procedure before we make a personalized custom Template. The workspace in SketchUp has no dimension scale visible to the user, so in a blank model we have no way of knowing how large the blank screen is. Is it a mile wide, 100 feet wide, 1 foot wide or 1 inch wide? To help us know where we are starting off we want to set the window size. To accomplish this follow these instructions:

1.  Locate the Rectangle ⬛ tool and click on it with your cursor to select it. Your cursor will change to a red pencil with a small rectangle.
2.  Click on the axes origin and then drag the cursor out to form a rectangle. Do not worry how large the rectangle is; just make the rectangle fill most of the screen. Do not click a second time, but simply type 12,12 and then press *Enter*. You do not need a space between 12 and 12, just a comma. Our default dimensions are inches so this will make the rectangle 12" x 12".
3.  You may or may not be able to see the rectangle at this point; do not worry if you can't see it. With your cursor click on the Zoom Extents tool. This will fill your workspace with the rectangle.
4.  Choose menu Edit/Select All which will highlight the rectangle perimeter and its face. Now choose menu Edit/Delete and the rectangle will be deleted.

This procedure has calibrated your workspace to approximately 12" x 12". You are now ready to create a personalized custom Template.

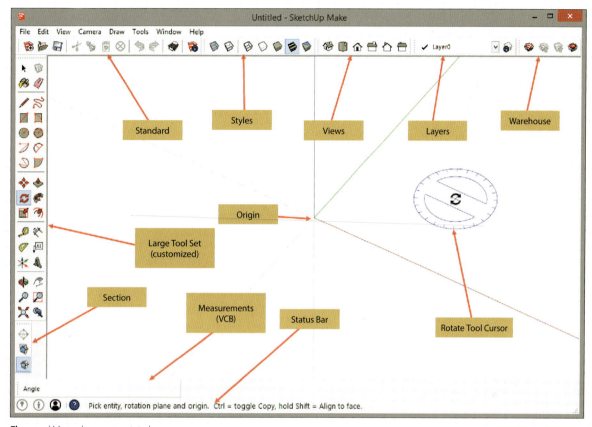

**Figure 14** | My workspace annotated

## CREATING A CUSTOM TEMPLATE

Creating a custom template is easy; simply choose menu File/Save As Template and fill in the missing information. Check the "Set as default template" check box and click the *Save* button. **Figure 13** shows this completed for my SRWW custom template. You can use a name that suits you and a description of your own. The file name will default to whatever is in the Name field with the suffix of .skp.

Notice that for my template the File Name is SRWW.skp. This is telling us that a custom template is nothing more than a blank model file with settings that we customized. When you choose File/New or open SketchUp by clicking on its icon it simply opens a model file called SRWW.skp. So every new model starts out the same way and with the same custom selections. You can, of course, change these for any given model, but at least you are always starting from the same place.

## A TOUR OF THE WORKSPACE

One of the first things a professional cabinetmaker does after hiring a new woodworker is to give the new employee a tour of the shop. A woodworker who is not intimately familiar with the shop is not an efficient employee and may make the difference between profit and loss. Sketching and drawing when using a CAD tool is similar in that if you are not intimately familiar with the workspace you will never be efficient. You will become frustrated and may even abandon the tool altogether, simply because you didn't take the time to become familiar

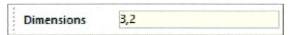

**Figure 15** | The Measurements toolbar

| Angle | 45.0 |
|---|---|

**Figure 16** | The Value Control Box (VCB)

with the environment. Don't let that happen to you. Refer back to this section as often as necessary in order to successfully acquaint yourself with the SketchUp workspace.

Individual tools are covered in Chapter 2. In this section you'll learn where to find them, including their supporting menus, boxes and windows. **Figure 14** shows the arrangement of the workspace as it is currently configured; it is annotated to point out the major toolbars.

## TOOLBARS

Toolbars can be displayed by going to menu View/Toolbars and checking the one you want displayed. I have already explained how to do this in the section on "Setting Up the Toolbars." Here I will describe each one shown in **Figure 14** starting at the bottom and going clockwise.

### Status Bar

 Pick entity, rotation plane and origin.  Ctrl = toggle Copy, hold Shift = Align to face.

The Status Bar is a strip along the bottom of the window. The first three icons are for online operations. The leftmost is called *Geolocation*. It is not pertinent to the focus of this book. The second icon, a picture of a little person, is used to set up Credits. The third icon, an upper body, is used to sign in and out of your Google account (if you have one). The second and third icons are explained in the Model Info section where the Credits page is explained.

The forth icon – the question mark – will show or hide Instructor, a context sensitive help box. Instructor information will change with each tool as a new one is selected.

What is of real interest in **Figure 14** is what follows the Instructor icon. Notice it says "Pick entity, rotation plane and origin. *Ctrl* = toggle Copy, hold *Shift* = Align to face." This is a little cryptic, but it is a very useful context sensitive set of instructions. Remember, we have the Rotate tool selected. This instruction is a helpful guide on what to do next to use the Rotate tool properly. This message will change with each tool and with each step as you progress through using the tool. Use this guidance information frequently; it is your guide to learning the tools. Even seasoned users need to refer to it at times.

## Measurements – More Commonly Called the Value Control Box or VCB

The Measurements toolbar consists of a value descriptor and a value box more commonly referred to as the Value Control Box or VCB. **Figure 15** shows a measurements toolbar as it is displayed when the Rectangle tool is selected. It is asking the user to supply a Dimensions value. The VCB is where the user can type in two values, length and width, separated by a comma; 3,2 has been entered meaning 3" x 2".

The VCB and its descriptor is context sensitive, meaning it will change to reflect the tool in use. **Figure 16** shows the VCB and its descriptor

## TOOLBARS

Any toolbar, including the VCB, can be moved around the workspace by grabbing its vertical (or horizontal) bar and moving it to the desired position. To enable a clean workspace, toolbars can even be placed outside the workspace. In addition they can be docked to either the top or bottom ribbon or to either the left or right side. When not docked their shape may be changed by grabbing an edge and pulling. The shape will change to an integer of numbers of icons per side.

when the Rotate tool is in use. The descriptor has changed to ask the user to supply an Angle value in the VCB. The value can be supplied in one of two ways; by typing a value or by moving the cursor until the desired value is displayed in the VCB. When typing a value there is no need to place your cursor in the VCB. SketchUp understands the context and whatever you type will be displayed in the VCB. You will discover that the VCB is very powerful and the focus of much of what happens while we draw. **Figure 16** shows the value 45.0 in the VCB which indicates 45˚. From this point forward I will use the term VCB to mean the Measurements toolbar, its descriptor and the value box.

## Section

The Section toolbar is used to create cross sections of a model. The tools in the Section toolbar allow you to create sections, show or hide section planes and show or hide section cuts. Sections can be helpful in shop drawings when you must communicate a difficult area of construction or dimension objects that are otherwise not visible. However, I have not used it much in my work.

## Large Tool Set

The Large Tool Set toolbar is a combination of smaller toolbars. While our workspace is set up with the Large Tool Set, I am actually going to explain it using its subset toolbars: Principal, Drawing, Edit, Construction and Camera. You can find each of these using menu View/Toolbars. This opens the Toolbars dialog box. Select the Toolbars tab and you will find them there.

### Principal

I am not sure why this toolbar is called Principal, but so be it. One tool contained in it – and indeed a principal one – is the Select tool, which is used to select an object or a collection of objects. Also in this toolbar are the Paint Bucket, Make Component and Eraser tools. These tools are used to texture or color faces, create a component, erase geometry and smooth edges. You will

use the Select and Eraser frequently. The Select tool is especially useful in the editing of geometry even though it is not designated an editing tool.

## Drawing

The Drawing toolbar is self-explanatory and contains the primary drawing tools: Line, Freehand, Rectangle, Rotated Rectangle, Circle, Polygon, Arc, 2 Point Arc, 3-Point Arc and Pie. You will discover later that SketchUp represents all geometric objects as a collection of points (invisible), lines and faces. A circle, for example, is an n-sided polygon where the user specifies n (the default is 24).

## Edit

The Edit toolbar contains tools that modify geometry. The Move and Rotate tools modify your model by repositioning objects. Both tools can also make additional copies of a geometric object. In fact the Move and Rotate tools are sometimes referred to as the Move/Copy and Rotate/Copy tools. The Push/Pull, Follow Me, Offset and Scale tools actually change or modify an object. These tools are described in detail later but suffice it to say they give 3D shape to an object as with the Push/Pull and Follow Me tools, or change its size as with the Offset and Scale tools. As you will see, the Push/Pull tool is very special; indeed without it SketchUp would not be a 3D modeler.

## Construction

The Construction toolbar is misnamed in my opinion. It would be better labeled Measuring & Marking, because that is the functionality it provides. The Tape Measure, Dimension and Protractor tools both measure and mark dimensions and angles. The Text and 3D Text tools label objects, and the Axes tool allows you to reposition an object's axis. The Tape Measure and Protractor tools also place construction lines and points, hence the Construction toolbar name.

### Camera

The Camera toolbar is a must in the workspace. It contains the tools needed to move around your drawing such as Pan and Orbit. Zooming tools such as Zoom, Zoom Window and Zoom Extents allow you to position the Camera closer or further away from an object or window. SketchUp saves past Camera positions; the Previous tool allows you to retrieve them. Note that I customized the Camera section of the Large Tool Set and removed the Position Camera, Look Around, Walk and Section Plane tools. In woodworking the Position Camera, Look Around and Walk tools are almost never used. I removed the Section Plane tool in favor of adding the Section toolbar to the workspace.

## Standard

The Standard toolbar contains the basic application tools found in almost all computer applications: New, Open, Save, Cut, Copy, Paste, Erase, Undo, Redo and Print. In addition is the Model Info tool which brings up the Model Info dialog box. Many of these tools are seldom used in woodworking and in my opinion are good candidates for removal from the Standard toolbar if you are in need of tool ribbon real estate.

## Styles

The Styles toolbar allows you to display your model in one of five standard 3D renderings, and to display any of those as an X-ray or exposed Back Edges. The standard renderings are Wireframe, Hidden Line, Shaded, Shaded With Textures and Monochrome. X-ray is a very powerful and useful tool when drawing complex models; it allows you to see inside a model and attach objects to points otherwise invisible. Back Edges, like X-ray, allows you to see hidden edges and in some situations is more useful than X-ray. In some situations you can expose otherwise hidden and hard to see geometry by using

Wireframe. In fact, I use this mode rendering style almost exclusively when adding joinery.

## Views

The Views toolbar allows you to quickly view your model in one of six standard views: Iso, Top, Front, Right, Back and Left. Iso is a little mis-labeled in that it is not necessarily an isometric view. If you have selected Camera/Perspective or Camera/Two-Point Perspective, Iso will show a view at an angle to two axes. If you select Camera/Parallel Projection, Iso will indeed show an isometric view. Notice that the Views toolbar does not have an icon for Bottom. However, you can access Bottom by selecting menu Camera/Standard Views/Bottom.

## Layers

The Layers toolbar is a drop-down box and an icon. The drop-down box is a list of all available layers with the active or selected object's layer checked. Note that when the drop-down box is displaying the active layer its background color is white; when it is displaying a selected object's layer its background is yellow. If the drop-down box is displaying a collection of selected objects' layer, and all those objects are on the same layer, its background color is yellow. If that collection of selected objects is on more than one layer, the drop-down box is blank and its background color is white.

In addition to displaying the active layer or the layer objects exist on, the drop-down box also allows the user to place an object or objects on any available layer. The Layer Manager icon to the right of the drop-down box brings up the Layers dialog box.

## Warehouse

The Warehouse has four tool icons: Get Models, Share Model, Share Component and Extension Warehouse. The Get Models tool will take you to an online warehouse of models. The

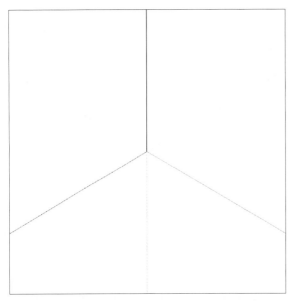

**Figure 17** | Red, Green and Blue axes in Parallel Projection mode

warehouse is populated by SketchUp users like you; people who wish to share their models. To share a model, use the Share Model tool. Likewise you can share a single component – such as a cabriole leg – with the Share Component tool. The Extension Warehouse tool will take you to a warehouse of Ruby script plugins. The Extension Warehouse is populated by SketchUp users who have a programming skill and wish to share their plugin with other users. This warehouse is not the only source for plugins, but it is a large resource and you should become familiar with it.

## Cursor

While not a toolbar or tool, the cursor is a necessary and handy resource. The cursor is context sensitive and will reflect the selected tool as a helpful reminder of what operation is being performed. Shown in **Figure 14** is the Rotate tool cursor. Some cursors, such as the Rotate, Protractor and Rotated Rectangle tool cursors, play a role in helping the user specify values or select edges or faces. Each tool has its own icon and many of them are modified with tool modifier keys. Learn to recognize each tool's cursor and its modified cursors. They can be very helpful.

## Origin

The Origin has no special marking but is simply the intersection of the three major axes: R(ed), G(reen) and B(lue). It's a handy place to begin all models but is not necessary for modeling.

## AXES

The 3D coordinate system in SketchUp is a simple three axes system labeled Red, Green and Blue (or R,G,B) representing the x, y and z axes respectively. Each axis has a solid line and a dotted line component. Solid lines represent positive values and dotted lines negative values. Where the axes intersect is the origin or (0,0,0) in (x,y,z) notation.

When viewed in the Back view and Camera/Parallel Projection mode the major (positive) axes are 120° apart as shown in **Figure 17**. Notice that when the negative portion of the axes are included there are 60° separating each axis. This scheme is the very definition of isometric parallel projection, which ensures that all lines parallel to a given axis are also parallel to all other lines parallel to that axis, making scaled drawings possible.

The plane created by the R(ed) and G(reen) axes is called the ground plane in SketchUp parlance. When designing furniture it is not critical that we construct our furniture models to sit on the ground plane; however, if we later want to render them in a house or on a landscape it is helpful to follow this convention.

One last comment about the axes; there is little need to be concerned about plus or minus signs when specifying an object size, such as the length of a line. As you draw an object, SketchUp takes note of the direction you are going and manages the sign itself.

## MENU BAR

Along the top of **Figure 14** you will see the menu bar with some typical menu names and some names that may be new to you: File, Edit, View, Camera, Draw, Tools, Window and Help. I will not describe every menu or submenu here. Many of them are self-explanatory to anyone who has ever used a personal computer. Some of them are new or unique to

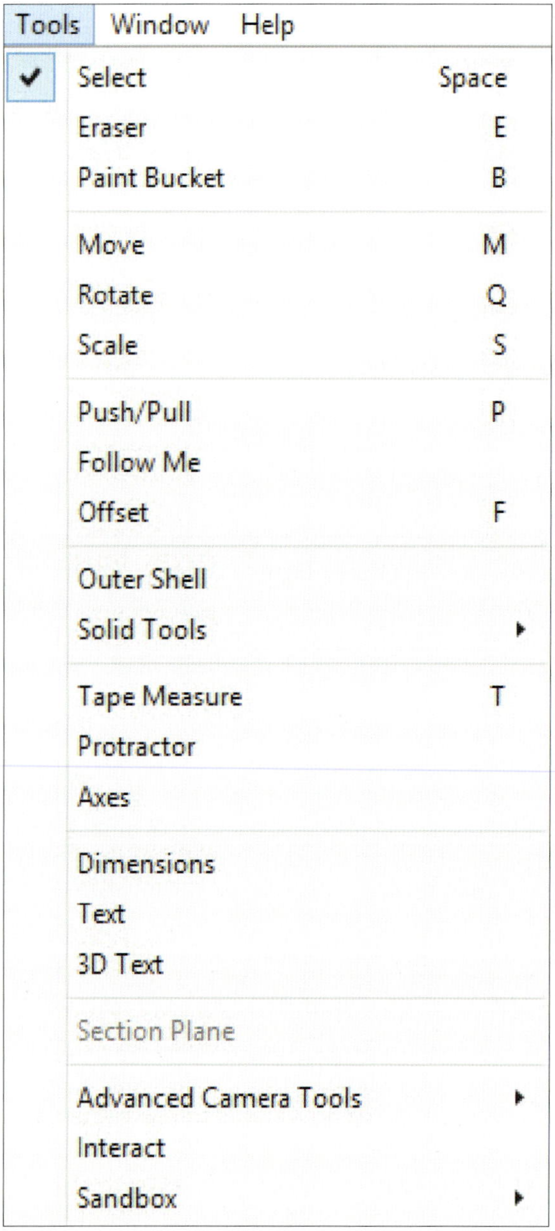

| Tools | Window | Help | |
|---|---|---|---|
| ✓ | Select | | Space |
| | Eraser | | E |
| | Paint Bucket | | B |
| | Move | | M |
| | Rotate | | Q |
| | Scale | | S |
| | Push/Pull | | P |
| | Follow Me | | |
| | Offset | | F |
| | Outer Shell | | |
| | Solid Tools | | ▶ |
| | Tape Measure | | T |
| | Protractor | | |
| | Axes | | |
| | Dimensions | | |
| | Text | | |
| | 3D Text | | |
| | Section Plane | | |
| | Advanced Camera Tools | | ▶ |
| | Interact | | |
| | Sandbox | | ▶ |

**Figure 18** | The Tools menu

SketchUp. A few of which I have already explained such as View/Toolbars. While the actual menu bar organization is not important, and in my opinion is often misleading, I will explain each tool in them as we use the tool in Parts Two and Three.

However, a quick look at the Tools menu in **Figure 18** shows a few SketchUp conventions. On the left of the tool names is a column that is mostly empty. However, note the check mark next to Select, indicating that the Select tool is the currently active tool. To the right of each tool name you may see a closed arrow head indication of a submenu with entries you must choose from. Also to the right of each tool may be a single letter or multiple letters and key names; these are the shortcut keys for tools that have them.

# THE SKETCHUP TOOLBOX

*In every woodshop there are commercially made tools, both power and hand tools. SketchUp has a set of tools that are part of the application; you might liken these to the commercially made tools in your shop.*

*Also in every woodshop are handmade tools, jigs and fixtures. SketchUp can also be extended with Ruby scripts called plugins – similar to the way you might customize your woodshop with handmade tools, jigs and fixtures.*

*Chapter 2 covers the tools supplied in SketchUp. Chapter 10 will introduce Ruby scripts and plugins. Together they make SketchUp the powerful and popular 3D drawing application that it is.*

Before launching into a description of SketchUp tools, we need to understand two semi-tools that come to the aid of all tools: the VCB (Value Control Box) and the Inference Engine. Mastering these tools will make drawing more precise, faster and more efficient.

## VCB – THE VALUE CONTROL BOX

The VCB is located in the lower right hand corner of the workspace (unless the Measurements toolbar is checked in menu View/Toolbars, in which case it is located wherever the user places it). The VCB is always visible and is critical to the use of many of SketchUp's tools. The VCB is context sensitive and will display appropriate information as you draw. The information displayed depends on the tool currently selected.

In addition to displaying values the user can type values into the VCB to exactly specify a value. When doing so, the user must press *Enter* to have the value accepted. It is not necessary to put your cursor in the VCB. The VCB is always awaiting input from the keyboard and knows the context of your typing.

In Chapter 1, in the section "Model Info," we selected "Format: Fractional," which in turn specified default dimensions of inches. If the value typed into the VCB is unitless the VCB will default to the template for units, in this case inches. However, you can specify other units by simply including them after the value, for example 3cm for three centimeters. No space is necessary between the value and the unit. The VCB cannot be explained fully on its own,

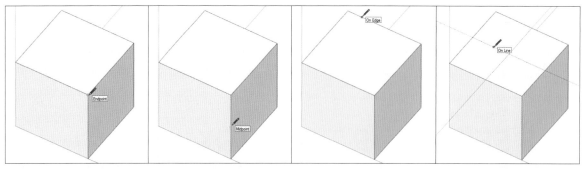

**Figure 1** | Typical Inference Engine tool tips when a cursor is moved along a line

but only in the context of each tool (which we will do as we introduce each tool). However, here are VCB behaviors common to all tools:

- You do not need to place your cursor in the VCB to enter a value. The VCB understands the context of each tool and is waiting for user input; simply type a value.
- You can type a value in the VCB either before or after using a tool, but before selecting another tool.
- After entering a value in the VCB you must press the *Enter* or *Return* key before it is accepted.
- The time between selecting tool *A* followed by selecting tool *B* is called tool *A*'s context. As long as you are in a tool's context you can change a value by retyping it in the VCB; you can do this as many times as needed.
- Once you have changed context (chosen a new tool) you cannot use the VCB to change geometry created by the previous tool.
- Values that are typed with no units are interpreted by the VCB as default units. With SketchUp set up as we have done 9.5, 11 1/8 typed into the VCB will be interpreted as nine and one half inches by eleven and one eighth inches (9½" x 11⅛"). Notice you can mix fractions and decimals. If you wish to specify a unit other than the default unit you can simply type the unit after the value. For example: 3',9 will be interpreted as 36" by 9". You can even mix imperial units and metric units. For example: 3',2.54cm will be interpreted as 36" x 1" (one inch being the equivalent of two point five four centimeters).
- There is no need for a space to separate values, though if one is supplied the value will still be interpreted correctly.

- The VCB will prefix a value with the tilde (~) symbol if the value is not precise, that is, not an integer factor of the value specified in the Precision field on the Units page of the Model Info dialog box. That number is ¹⁄₆₄" in our case. Any value that is not an integer multiple of ¹⁄₆₄" will be preceded by a tilde (~). This is almost always an indication of an undesirable value since we wish to draw precisely.

## INFERENCE ENGINE

In my mind there are four aspects of SketchUp that place it head and shoulders above all other drawing packages when used for woodworking. A shallow learning curve and intuitive interface are two of them. But the most impressive, and the two that are most outstanding, are the Inference Engine and the Push/Pull tool. Together these features make drawing natural, easy and fun.

The Inference Engine, like its name implies, infers what you are attempting to do and helps you do it. It does this in the context of the tool in use and the geometric points surrounding the current position of the cursor. With that knowledge the Inference Engine will give you cues, or hints, with tooltips. As you move the cursor, the surrounding geometric points change as will the tooltips.

## SNAPPING TO INFERRED POINTS

**Figure 1** shows examples of tooltips that will appear when the cursor is moved along a line. Accompanying a tooltip is a colored dot that highlights a point that can be snapped to with the click of the mouse. The Inference Engine snap behavior only requires that your mouse be close to, not exactly on, a point. If you are close enough for the tooltip to appear, the VCB will hold a value that is precise and can be used for exact drawing. All that the user need do is a simple click to instruct the VCB to accept this precise point.

> Remember, Inference Engine tooltips and highlighted points are inferred suggestions of what the user may intend. Use them wisely and be sure they are what you desire before clicking to accept the suggestion.

> All edges have three points that the Inference Engine will snap to: two endpoints and a midpoint. If two edges are on the same plane and cross each other, each edge will split into two edges at their intersection forming an intersection and new endpoints and midpoints.

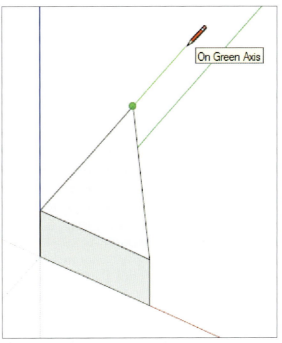

**Figure 2** | Another form of On (R,G,B) Axis tooltip

> Note the terminology difference between *line* and *edge*. An *edge* is a drawing primitive shown as a black line of finite length and drawn with a Drawing tool. A *line* is a construction aid usually drawn with Construction or Edit tool. It may be infinite or finite in length and is shown as stippled and not solid. Unfortunately, single edges are drawn with a Line tool, which confuses the terminology.
>
> In the text I will sometimes use the term line to mean an edge. It will usually be clear from the context what I intend. But be aware of the difference.

## Endpoint

The first drawing in **Figure 1** shows the Line tool cursor close to the intersection of three edges of a cube. An Endpoint tooltip appears and a green circular dot highlights the precise point of inferred interest.

## Midpoint

The second drawing in **Figure 1** shows the Line tool cursor close to the midpoint of an edge on the cube. A Midpoint tooltip appears and a blue circular dot highlights the precise point of inferred interest.

## On Edge

The third drawing in **Figure 1** shows the Line tool cursor close to a point on an edge on the cube. Note that the point is not the midpoint or an endpoint. An On Edge tooltip appears and a red square highlights a point on the line of inferred interest.

## On Line

The fourth drawing in **Figure 1** shows the Line tool cursor close to a construction line. An On Line tooltip appears and a red square highlights a point on the construction line of inferred interest.

**Figure 3** | Snapping on faces, construction line intersections, points projected from a point and arcs

### Red (Green or Blue) Axis or On Red (Green or Blue) Axis

The fifth drawing in **Figure 1** shows the Line tool cursor close to the Red axis. The black circular dot at the origin was produced by first hovering over the origin and then moving the cursor along the Red axis to encourage the Inference Engine into producing the Red Axis tooltip and red square. This is the technique used to begin an edge on the Red axis.

If you wish to begin an edge at the origin, first hover over the origin with the Line tool; you will see a yellow circular dot. Click to accept the Inference Engine origin precisely and then move your cursor along the Red axis or to any other position in 3D space. If you move along the Red axis to place the endpoint of an edge, you will see either a Red Axis tooltip with a red square or an On Red Axis tooltip with no red square. The tooltip indicates that if you click to end the edge or use the VCB to enter an exact length, the drawn edge will lie on the Red axis. In either case the VCB will continuously indicate the length of the edge.

the cursor is moved away from the first point and is near an imaginary line parallel to the Green axis an On Green Axis tooltip will appear and a green line will extend from the starting point to the cursor, indicating the inferred position of the intended line. If the user clicks to accept the point or types a precise number into the VCB and presses *Enter*, an edge is produced with the appropriate length extending from the starting point in a direction parallel to the Green axis.

### On Face

The first drawing in **Figure 3** shows the Line tool cursor close to the face of a cube. An On Face tooltip appears and a blue diamond highlights a point on the face of inferred interest.

### Intersection

The second drawing in **Figure 3** shows the Line tool cursor close to the intersection of two construction lines. An Intersection tooltip appears and a red X highlights the inferred point of intersection.

> In this section, any operation involving the Red axis can be used on the Blue or Green axis with appropriate results. The tooltips will of course be adjusted for the axis such as On Blue Axis or On Green Axis.

> Recall from high school geometry that for lines (or edges) to intersect they must reside on the same plane. A corollary of seeing an Intersection tooltip for two lines is that those lines (or edges) reside on the same plane.

Another form of tooltip On Red (Green or Blue) Axis is shown in **Figure 2** which shows the Line tool selected and the first point of an edge already established at the corner of a solid right triangle. As

The Intersection tooltip can appear in other situations. Consider **Figure 4**. Two independent objects have been moved into an overlapping position. The top face of the cylinder and the front face

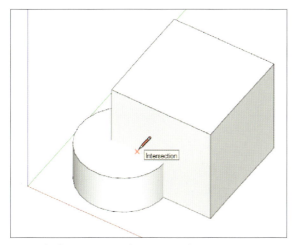

**Figure 4** | Inference Engine and intersecting planes

of the cube share no edges. However, their planes do intersect. Moving the cursor near a point of intersection causes an Intersection tooltip to appear along with a red X. I should point out that the cylinder and cube are in primitive form (consisting entirely of primitives and not groups or components), which is why the color of X is red and the tooltip reads Intersection. If one or both of these objects were either a group or a component, the color of X may be purple and the tooltip would read Intersection in Group or Intersection in Component.

## From Point

The third drawing in **Figure 3** shows the Line tool cursor nearly perpendicular to the midpoint of the cube's edge. The blue dotted line indicates the extension line is also parallel to the Blue axis, which in this case also means it is on the face of the cube. A From Point tooltip appears and a black dot highlights the inferred point of extension.

The fourth drawing in **Figure 3** shows the Line tool cursor near the center of the face. Notice the black dots at the center of the two edges and their extension lines meeting near the Line tool cursor. This is an easy way to find the center of a rectangular face.

## Half Circle

The fifth drawing in **Figure 3** is a little more complex. I have selected the Arc tool, which requires a start point, an end point and a bulge value. In **Figure 3** I have used the endpoints of the cube's lower edge as the start and end points indicated by the green dots. As the cursor is moved up the face of the cube arcs are formed starting with arcs that are less than a semicircle and increasing to arcs greater than a semicircle. In-between there is a point where an exact semicircle is formed. When the cursor is close to that point a Half Circle tooltip appears and a blue diamond or black dot may appear depending on the surrounding geometry. In this case a black dot indicates the point of inferred interest; it is also a point along a line parallel to the Red axis and passing through the center of the left edge. A simple inspection of the geometry will tell you that the face is a square and the circle's radius is equal to one-half the face's edge length.

## Parallel to Edge

To demonstrate the Parallel to Edge Inference Engine tooltip, I made use of two Inference Engine tooltips. In the first drawing in **Figure 5** I used the Line tool and From Point tooltip to establish the first point of a line. Note the starting point is extended from the midpoint of the lower edge of the 3D object. The dotted line indicating the From Point origin remains while I locate the endpoint of the line. As the cursor moves in a direction nearly parallel to the edge of the 3D object, a Parallel to Edge tooltip appears with a magenta line extending from the start point to the cursor indicating the inferred parallel line of interest.

The Parallel to Edge tooltip can be used in another way that is similar to From Point. From Point appears when an extension from a point is made parallel to an axis. But suppose we want to extend the edge of an object that is not parallel to any of the three axes? In **Figure 6** the Line tool is used to establish the starting point of a line at the upper right corner of a pie shaped wedge. Notice none of the edges are parallel to an axis. As the cursor is moved away from the starting point in a direction that is nearly an extension of the edge, a Parallel to Edge tooltip appears with a magenta line extending from the starting point to the cursor, inferring the intended extension. Also notice that the cursor is some distance from the magenta line demonstrating that you don't have to be accurate

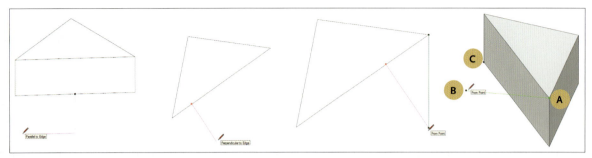

**Figure 5** | Inference Engine tooltips for parallel and extension lines

with the cursor in order to draw precisely. But a word of caution: Be sure you don't move your cursor in the process of clicking to accept the inferred point. Use a steady hand and gentle clicks.

In each of these tooltip explanations I have used the words nearly or close. Your job is to get in the area of what you intend to draw. The Inference Engine will do the rest, allowing you to draw precisely.

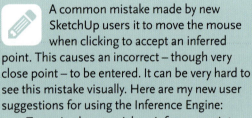

A common mistake made by new SketchUp users it to move the mouse when clicking to accept an inferred point. This causes an incorrect – though very close point – to be entered. It can be very hard to see this mistake visually. Here are my new user suggestions for using the Inference Engine:

- Zoom in close to pick an inference point.
- Approach the desired point slowly and watch for the Inference Engine to appear; then get a little closer.
- Gently click the mouse button to select the inference point.
- Always use smooth and gentle movements.

You will eventually master these moves and perform them very quickly.

## Perpendicular to Edge

The second drawing in **Figure 5** shows the Line tool drawing a line from a point on the bottom edge. This is the same object shown in all four drawings

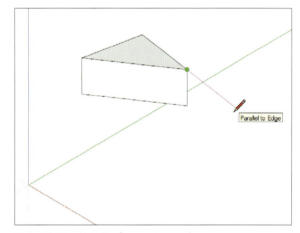

**Figure 6** | Extending a line from an on-axis edge

of **Figure 5** but viewed from the top. As the cursor is moved away from the starting point in a direction nearly perpendicular to the edge, a Perpendicular to Edge tooltip appears with a magenta line extending from the starting point to the cursor inferring the desired line.

If we continue to move the cursor out from the starting point, keeping the Perpendicular to Edge tooltip and magenta line visible, we will eventually get a From Point tooltip as shown in the third picture in **Figure 5**. This indicates that not only is the inferred line perpendicular to the edge, but it terminates at a From Point extension. The From Point is an extension line from the end of the edge and parallels an axis, in this case the Green axis. This is another example of how Inference Engine tooltips can combine to assist in drawing complex shapes. It is not unusual to see three tooltips combine to lend assistance.

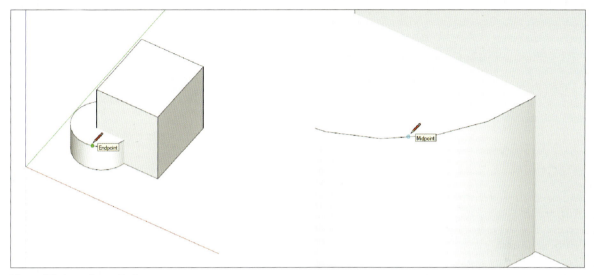

**Figure 7** | Circles are formed by line segments

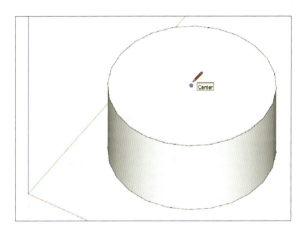

**Figure 8**

Sometimes Inference Engine tooltips can be difficult to interpret. The fourth image in **Figure 5** is a case in point. In this example, I clicked on point A with the Line tool and moved the cursor along the Green axis until I got a From Point tool tip at point B and an extension line from point C to B. The student might ask, "Why an extension line at point B from point C and not at other points along line AB?" The line CB is special; it is perpendicular to line AB, indicating the shortest distance form point C to line AB. The Inference Engine is powerful and very useful to the modeler; the modeler being you, the woodworker, as you design your fine furniture pieces.

Since we introduced circles (cylinders are extruded circles) I should point out that SketchUp does not actually draw circles, but rather many sided polygons to represent circles. In fact, SketchUp only draws edges or lines; all shapes are approximated with a number of line segments. The default case for a circle is a 24-sided polygon. If you move the cursor around a circle as shown in **Figure 7** you will see these line segments have endpoints and midpoints which can be located with the help of the Inference Engine. We will get into this more in Part Two and in detail in Part Three.

### Center

In **Figure 8**, as the Line tool cursor is moved around the face of the circle forming the top of the cylinder, and near its center, a Center tooltip appears along with a purple dot to indicate the inferred desired point, the circle's center. The object shown in **Figure 8** is a primitive object. If it were a group the tooltip would read Center in Group or Center in Component if the object were a component.

I have not covered all Inference Engine tooltips in this section (nor will I cover all of them in this book). But as we get into drawing, new Inference Engine tooltips will appear and those discussed here will be encountered. It is by actually drawing that you will discover the power of the Inference Engine and learn how to use it effectively. Here I have introduced many of them and provided examples that will help you to interpret new ones you run across. You may find yourself referring to this section frequently while you get a few models under your belt.

## ENCOURAGING THE INFERENCE ENGINE

Sometimes the Inference Engine needs help in order to assist you. Finding the center of a circle is a good example. If you simply place your cursor on the face of a circle and move around where you expect the center to be you may get frustrated when the Inference Engine does not willingly produce the expected Center tooltip. In this case you can encourage the Inference Engine by moving your cursor to the perimeter until you locate an Endpoint and then move slowly to the center and the tooltip will "magically" appear.

Another case where you frequently need to encourage the Inference Engine is when drawing a line that starts at one point and you intend it to end with the use of a From Point tooltip. This is demonstrated in the third drawing in **Figure 5**. The line starts at a point on the edge of the triangular object. You wish to extend it perpendicularly (using the Perpendicular to Edge tooltip) until we get a From Point tooltip indicating an extended line from an endpoint and parallel to the Green axis in this case. In a perfect world we would simply click on the desired starting point with the Line tool selected, move out in a perpendicular direction keeping the Perpendicular to Edge tooltip visible, stop when we see the From Point tooltip and click again. The world is not perfect, and sometimes the From Point tooltip never appears. When this happens, simply move the cursor to the endpoint that you wish to extend from and then move slowly in the extended direction until you get the results shown in **Figure 5**.

There are a number of cases where the Inference Engine needs encouragement but they are too numerous to list here with instructions for doing so. In gen-

eral, encouraging the Inference Engine is accomplished by hovering your cursor over another point that hints to the Inference Engine what you are trying to accomplish. When hovering pause for a second or two and move the cursor slowly. You will almost always provide encouragement to the Inference Engine.

## LOCKING THE INFERENCE ENGINE

As you will soon see when we describe each tool in detail, you can often lock the inferred direction, for example Perpendicular to Edge, by holding the Shift key down after you obtain the Inference Engine tooltip. When doing so the line indicating the inferred direction will be thickened and the cursor will move only along that direction. This can be of tremendous value to the Inference Engine when your motion is unstable. Releasing the Shift key releases the lock.

Cursor locking to an axis direction can also be done with the Arrow keys. The Up and Down Arrow keys lock the Blue axis, the Right Arrow key locks the Red axis, and the Left Arrow key locks the Green axis. Push any of the Arrow keys to lock on an axis or push the Shift key to release the lock.

## CONTEXT MENU

The context menu is always readily available by pressing the right mouse button. As its name implies, the context menu will change depending on the tool selected and where you are in the sequence of events to complete the tool operation. **Figure 9** shows the context menu after selecting a group object. Notice the sequence of tools Edit Group, Explode and Make Component. Because the object selected is a group already, a Make Group tool is not included. However, you have the option of exploding the group into its primitives using the Explode tool or changing it to a component using the Make Component tool.

The context menu is hard to explain in text because it is always changing with changing context, and the combinations are quite numerous. The best way to learn the context menu is to view it frequently

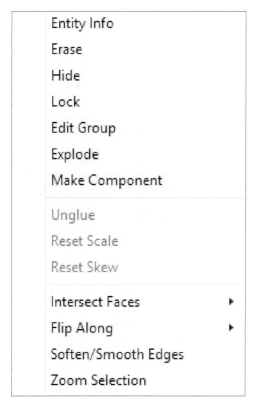

**Figure 9** | The Context menu with a group entity selected

and observe the various tools available. Some tools may be available only on the context menu; this is especially true of tools added by Ruby scripts.

The context menu is your friend and always nearby. Learn its capabilities and use it to speed drawing.

## SELECTING & USING TOOLS

Just as it is in the woodshop, it is important to select the right tool for the job and use it correctly. Here I am going to point out how to recognize them and where to get them. Some tools only exist in one place while others are available in several locations and through different methods.

## MENU BAR

The Menu Bar is located at the top of the SketchUp work area. When first installed SketchUp will have eight menus: File, View, Camera, Draw, Tools, Window and Help. Later, when we add Ruby script plugins, there will be another menu added called Extensions. This menu was called Plugins in all versions of SketchUp prior to 2015. The folder the plugins reside in on your hard drive is still called Plugins, but the menu has been renamed to Extensions to be consistent with the Preferences dialog box. I will explain each menu briefly below.

### File

Under the File menu you should find all tools pertinent to the current model file; I will sometimes call this your SKP file. Choose menu File on your computer and peruse the entries. You will find many of them familiar because almost all applications have these base File menu items. Some of them however are specific to SketchUp and particularly useful to woodworkers and I will point them out here. Others are obvious or will be typically accessed through other means and I will not discuss them here.

### Save As Template

We have already discussed the Save As Template item in Chapter 1 under the section called "Creating a Custom Template." You can modify your custom template at any time as follows:

1. Open a blank or new model using menu File/New. This blank model will use your old custom template.
2. Make any changes to the Preferences, Model Info or Styles dialog boxes you wish. Make any other changes you wish; for example menu Camera/2-Point Perspective.
3. Choose menu File/Save As Template and follow the procedure discussed in Chapter 1 section Creating a Custom Template.

### 3D Warehouse

3D Warehouse has three submenus: Get Models, Share Model and Share Component. The 3D

Warehouse is an online repository maintained by SketchUp. However, you can add any of your own models to it with the menu File/3D Warehouse/Share Model. You can also share an individual component with the Share Component submenu. Perhaps the submenu you will most use is Get Models. There are thousands of SketchUp models and components that you can access and bring into your own models with the Get Models submenu.

## Import

File/Import is a tool you may find very useful as a woodworker. I often take digital images of antiques with my camera or phone. With judicious framing of a picture and noting actual measurements of a piece, you can import the JPG image into SketchUp and scale it to actual size. Then you can "trace" it with tools such as Line, Rectangle, Arc or Bézier Curves and create a 3D model. Not all file types under Import or its companion Export are available to SketchUp Make users, but importing JPG images is one you should become very familiar with.

## Edit

In general the tools in the Edit menu are used to change objects. Many of the Edit tools can also be found in the Context menu too, or with tool icons of their own. Some of them are basic to any application such as Undo and Redo. Here I will describe a few that are particularly important for modeling fine furniture pieces.

## Copy

You might ask, "Why explain the Edit/Copy function? Isn't it obvious?" Well yes, in its normal use. However, it is not obvious to those new to SketchUp that you can copy a component from one SketchUp model file using Edit/Copy and paste it into another SketchUp model file using either Edit/Paste or Edit/Paste In Place.

There are a couple of things to note about the Edit/Copy command. When you perform a Copy command every aspect of the objects copied are also copied. For example, materials or textures and the layers they reside on, as well as the component definition if the object(s) are groups or components.

## Paste

You can paste an object copied with the Copy command into the same SketchUp file or another SketchUp file. In either case when you paste the object with the Paste command you will need to choose where you place it in the model; you will place the object's origin at a point you choose. Remember that when you copied the object using the Copy command you also copied the layer it resided on and other aspects such as its material or texture image. When you paste the object using the Paste command into another model those objects will now be part of that model; layers and materials will be added to the destination model.

## Paste In Place

The Paste In Place command is identical to the Paste command except for one very important difference. When using the Paste command the user must choose where to place the object's origin. When using the Paste In Place command the object's origin is placed at the same (R,G,B) point in the destination model as it existed in the source model. This can be useful if, for example, you are creating models with some variants but wish the major components be the same in all variants.

## Delete Guides

When you are modeling you may add construction lines and construction points to assist you. If you wish to delete them when you no longer need them you can use the Delete Guides command. Be careful, however. This command deletes all guide lines and points. You may think you have protected some by placing them on a layer that is not visible, but that does not inhibit the Deleted Guides command. All guides will be deleted. It is often best to select the guides you wish to delete and use the Context tool Erase.

## Hide and Unhide

The Hide command is used to hide selected geometry from view. Typically Hide is used to hide edges to unclutter a face (surface). But it can also be used to hide a component or group from view.

Its companion command, Unhide, is used to unhide an edge or other selected object and make it visible again. You might ask how you select an invisible object. You must first use the View/Hidden Geometry command to expose all hidden geometry, and then select the desired objects before using the Unhide command. You can then go back to View/Hidden Geometry and uncheck it to once again make invisible the hidden geometry.

## Lock and Unlock

The Lock command is often used to further protect a component or group. Select a component or group and choose menu Edit/Lock. The selection color will change from blue to red indicating that this object is now protected from change. You cannot delete a locked component or group nor can you place it in Edit Component or Edit Group mode. In fact you cannot even move a locked component or group. To make a change you must first select it and use menu Edit/Unlock/Selected. Alternatively you can unlock all locked objects without selecting them by using Edit/Unlock/All.

## Intersect Faces

The Intersect Faces tool can be used on two or more objects to logically create a third object. A little cleanup is almost always required. Intersect Faces is fundamental to complex shapes, such as dovetailed joints, and especially curved components such as cabriole legs. We will run into this tool a lot.

## *View*

The View menu has a lot of check style commands. Check style commands are commands you either check, and the check mark is visible in front of the command, or uncheck. When visible the check mark indicates that the command is active.

## Scene Tabs

Scene Tabs, when checked, displays any Scenes created in the model as tabs horizontally aligned just below the top tool icon ribbon. Uncheck it to hide the Scenes Tabs. We will discuss Scenes in detail in Chapter 9, "Creating Shop Drawings."

## Hidden Geometry

When checked the View/Hidden Geometry command will make visible all geometry that has been hidden. Geometry can be hidden with the Edit/Hide tool or by other tools automatically. For example, when a circle is extruded with the Push/Pull tool is vertical lines are smoothed and hidden. They can be exposed when Hidden Geometry is checked.

## Axes

When checked the Red, Green and Blue axes are visible. Uncheck View/Axes to hide the Red, Green and Blue axes.

## Guides

When checked the guidelines (a.k.a construction lines) and construction points are visible. Uncheck View/Guides to hide guide lines and construction points.

## Component Edit

Component Edit does not place a component or group in edit mode. Rather it allows you to choose whether or not you want other components visible while you are editing a component or group. When checked View/Component Edit/Hide Rest Of Model will hide all other components and groups while you are editing a component or group in Edit Component or Edit Group mode. It will leave other instances of the same component visible however.

If you wish to make other instances of the same component you are editing invisible while in Edit Component mode, use menu View/Component Edit/Hide Similar Components. Component Edit and its submenus are used to remove clutter while you are editing a component or group.

## *Camera*

The Camera menu will be our least-used menu primarily because the tools on it are more readily and easily accessible through tool icons, shortcuts or the Context menu; but also because, as woodworkers, many of these tools are not terribly useful. For example, Position Camera, Walk and Look Around are very useful if you are a home or building architect and wish to do a 3D walkthrough, but as woodworkers we would unlikely do a walkthrough of a furniture piece.

## Draw

Like the Camera menu, the Draw menu is seldom used because it is well covered with tool icons and some shortcut keys.

## Tools

Like the Camera and Draw menus, the Tools menu is seldom used because it too is well covered with tool icons and shortcut keys.

## Window

The Window menu is where you will find most of the dialog boxes you will use while modeling. In Chapter 1 we discussed the Preferences, Model Info and Styles dialog boxes.

### Entity Info

Entity Info is a dialog box you will use often and should always be open or readily available on your desktop. If you select a single object the Entity Info box will give you all the pertinent information about that object. For example, type of object and the number in the model, the layer it resides on, its name and definition name, whether it is locked or hidden and whether it casts or receives shadows. You can also move an object to a different layer by choosing it from the Layer drop-down box. In fact, any of the fields shown in the Entity Info dialog box can be edited to reflect desired changes.

If you select multiple objects and they have a common attribute, such as the layer they reside on, the Entity Info box will reflect that. However, if even one selected object has a different value for a given attribute that field will be blank.

The Entity Info box can be used to place a number of selected items on the same layer by selecting it from the Layer dropdown box.

### Materials

The Materials dialog box is primarily used when texturing a model, which we will get to in Chapter 10, "Texturing the Bedside Table." Until texturing has begun this dialog box can remain closed. From this dialog box you can choose from a large library of materials supplied by SketchUp and bring those mate-rials into the model for use, or you can select and edit a material already in the model. Editing a material includes changing its size, color, opacity, name and source file. Textures are often JPG images of wood grain or pictures taken of finished wood. They can be large in size and will consequently bloat your file size, something you may wish to pay attention to.

### Components

Like Materials, the Components dialog box exposes a library of components (more technically correct: a library of component definitions). From the Components dialog box you can access a library of components supplied by SketchUp and bring them into the model, or select a component already in the model and place another instance of it, for example three additional legs from a leg in the library as a result of the first leg being drawn.

Like the Entity Info dialog box, the Components dialog should always be open or readily available on your desktop. You will use it frequently though not as frequently as the Entity Info dialog box.

### Layers

The Layers dialog box is the third box that should always be open or readily available on your desktop. It might be the most frequently used dialog box. The Layers dialog box lists all the layers used in the model. Each layer has a name with a radio button on the left to indicate which layer is active, a checkbox on the right to indicate which layers are visible, and a color patch that can be used to color object in the model according to the layer they reside on.

Here is something you will hear frequently in this text: Layer0 should always be the active layer. At no time should any other layer be active. That means Layer0's radio button should be black in the center indicating it is the active layer.

You can add and delete layers from the Layers dialog box, though later on in this course you will install one of my plugins to use better tools for adding layers. The primary purpose of layers is to provide a mechanism for choosing which components or objects are visible at any point in time or in any particular scene.

You will see in Chapter 9, "Creating Shop Drawings," how well Layers, Scenes, Styles and dimensioning work together to produce the shop drawings you need to build a piece.

## Scenes

The Scenes dialog box is similar to the Layers dialog box. It lists all the available scenes in the model. Each scene has a name and to the left of the active scene is a small pencil icon indicating it is active; meaning it is the one being currently displayed. From the Scenes dialog box you can add or delete scenes and move a scene up or down in the list. If the Scene Tabs are visible (menus View/Scene Tabs is checked) the tabs will be aligned along the top in the same order as they appear in the Scenes dialog box list.

A scene is nothing more than a collection of visible layers, a rendering style, a rendering view, a drawing style and some other drawing attributes such as sections, shadows, lighting, and parallel projection or perspective. When you have a scene composed as desired, you update a Scene Tab to remember all the previously mentioned attributes (and more). Then, each time you go back to that scene it is composed identically as you updated it. I will cover much more on scenes in Chapter 9, "Creating Shop Drawings."

## Instructor

The Instructor dialog box is one that may prove very helpful to those new to and just learning SketchUp. When open its contents change with each selection of a new tool to instruct the user on how to use that tool. The instructions are accompanied with a short video that visually demonstrates the tool's use. In addition the modifier keys for each tool are explained. This is a dialog box the new user may want to have available on the desktop for reference.

## Extensions

The Extensions menu will only appear on the menu bar if one or more Ruby script plugins is installed and has a command that resides on the Extensions menu. Otherwise it will not be visible. In older versions of SketchUp prior to 2015 this menu was called Plugins. With release 2015 the name was changed to Extensions to be compatible with the Preferences dialog box.

## Help

The Help menu is similar to most applications' Help menu. There is one menu item I wish to touch on.

### Knowledge Center

Clicking on the Knowledge Center opens your default web browser to the SketchUp Help web page. From there you can type a topic of interest into the Search field and get quick answers. In addition, while on that page look under Learn More for the User's Guide and Release Notes. Both are a wealth of information, especially for the beginner.

## TOOL ICONS

Not all tool icons will appear in this section. I am going to list only those we will use in Part One. By the time you get to Part Two you should be familiar enough with SketchUp that you can locate the tools on your own.

### Select Tool

Select is the active tool when SketchUp opens. It is the tool we will use most often. The Select tool is used to select a single object or multiple objects. You can select a single object with a click; or multiple objects by dragging a bounding box. You will learn that the Select tool is far more powerful than its simple icon implies.

### Eraser Tool

The Eraser tool is used to erase (delete) a single object by clicking on it or multiple objects by dragging the Eraser cursor across them. It can also be used to hide lines or soften them.

### Line Tool

The Line tool is used to draw lines or, more correctly, edges. It is used whenever a single line or multiple connected lines are needed.

## Rectangle Tool

The Rectangle tool is used to draw rectangles. Next to the Select tool this is probably the second most used tool. Almost all 3D objects used in furniture pieces begin with a rectangle, which is then extruded to a 3D object. You will become very familiar with this tool.

## Circle Tool

The Circle tool is used to draw circles of a given radius. However, as we've already discussed, SketchUp cannot draw curved lines; rather it represents all curves as a series of connected straight lines. SketchUp default circle is a symmetrical polygon with 24 sides. The user can specify fewer or more sides, but more sides will cost in performance and file size. The sides in the circle are not only connected but are "welded," meaning they are polylines. Polylines do not form visible orthogonal lines when extruded. Instead they form hidden and softened lines so that, when extruded, they appear as smooth curves.

## 2-Point Arc Tool

The Arc tool is used to draw a circle segment. It is specified by choosing the arc's end points and then its bulge. Like the Circle tool, the Arc tool creates a polyline arc. The default is 12 sides, but the user can specify fewer or more sides. We will use the 2-Point Arc tool in Part Two, and you will learn much more about arcs, circles and noncircular curves in Part Three.

## Move Tool

The Move tool is used to move one or more objects in 3D space. Most often it is used to pick up one or more objects and attach them to an existing point, for example an apron to a leg. The move tool can also be used to copy one or more objects and move the copy to a point in 3D space. In fact, it can be used to copy and replicate multiples of an object or group of objects. An example is creating a picket fence from one picket component. Hence, the Move tool is often referred to as the Move/Copy tool.

## Push/Pull Tool

If asked to choose just one tool to define SketchUp, I would choose the Push/Pull tool. Without it there is no SketchUp. The Push/Pull tool is used to extrude a face in a direction normal to it. The Push/Pull tool is what gives 3D shape to a 2D image. It can also be used to edit the shape of an object by further extruding a face or decreasing the amount it is already extruded. You will find that the Rectangle tool and Push/Pull tool combines to touch just about every part you model in a furniture piece.

## Rotate Tool

The Rotate tool is used to rotate an object, or group of objects, on a plane with the center of rotation at a point on the plane and around an axis normal to that plane. It is used by choosing an object, a plane, a point and an angle. The Rotate tool, like the Move tool, can be used to copy and replicate objects in a circular array. For example, you can create a set of wagon wheel spokes from one spoke component. Hence, the Rotate tool is often referred to as the Rotate/Copy tool.

## Follow Me Tool

The Follow Me tool is similar to the Push/Pull tool in that it is used to extrude a face. However, the Follow Me tool extrudes a face while following a path provided by a line, connected line segments, polyline or face periphery. It is mostly used to place trim around some surface such as a tabletop. The shape of the trim is defined by the face that is to be extruded.

## Scale Tool

The Scale tool is used to change the size of an object or objects. It can uniformly scale about a center or other point on the bounding box of the object. It can also scale along one axis of the bounding box or any two axes of the bounding box. The Scale tool has limited use in designing a furniture piece. This is because while you may want to scale a leg, you usually do not want its joinery scaled. However, it can be used in special cases and in Part Two you will be introduced to two of them.

## Offset Tool

The Offset tool is used to shrink or expand the periphery of a face. Shrink means to create a new periphery in the same shape but equidistant from the original on all edges. The new periphery is on the same plane as the face. This tool is particularly useful in woodworking, for example, when you wish to create a tenon with ¼" shoulders all around. It has many other applications as we'll discuss later in the book.

## Tape Measure Tool

The Tape Measure tool has three purposes: measuring, marking and creating construction lines. When measuring between two points the Tape Measure tool will indicate length in a tool tip and in the VCB.

When marking it places a construction point a specified distance from a point with a stippled line connecting the two; this line is not a construction line and the Inference Engine does not recognize it. The construction point, however, is recognized by the Inference Engine.

When creating a construction line parallel to a selected edge the Tape Measure places a construction line. This is a real construction line and is recognized by the Inference Engine.

When using the Tape Measure tool to measure the distance between two points pay close attention to the distance being reported by the tooltip or VCB. If a measurement is preceded by a tilde (~) symbol it is likely a modeling problem you need to correct.

When modeling furniture we almost always want dimensions that are an integer multiple of our chosen precision; $\frac{1}{64}$" in our case. If a measurement is not an integer multiple of $\frac{1}{64}$" the tilde symbol will appear. Ask yourself if this is what you intended. Sometimes such a dimension is unavoidable and does not need to be corrected. But in most cases it is an indication of a modeling inaccuracy and if not checked can created larger problems down the road.

## Dimension Tool

The purpose of the Dimension tool is to place dimensions in a scene; a collection of scenes combine to produce dimensioned and scaled shop drawings. The Dimension tool is used by selecting two endpoints and then moving the cursor to place the dimension where you wish. The Dimension tool is context sensitive and will place a dimension that is: a) the point-to-point straight line distance; b) the vertical or parallel to the Blue axis distance; c) the horizontal or parallel to the Red axis distance; or d) the depth or parallel to the Green axis distance. Depending on how you are viewing the model one of b, c or d will not be available. However, you can always orbit the model to obtain it.

Some new to SketchUp like to use the Dimension tool to measure the distance between two points. While you can do this, it is dangerous in one respect. If the distance you are trying to measure is not an integer multiple of $\frac{1}{64}$" the Dimension tool will round it to the nearest $\frac{1}{64}$" and report that distance with no tilde (~) symbol. The user will have no warning that something may be amiss with the measurement as discussed in the note above. Use the Dimension tool to dimension a scene and not to check dimensions.

## Protractor Tool

Like the Tape Measure tool, the Protractor tool is used to measure angles and create construction lines. The Protractor has a protractor for a cursor as does the Rotate tool and is used in a manner similar to the Rotate tool. The user chooses a plane, a vertex and two lines that pass through the vertex and are on the chosen plane. The angle between is shown in the VCB. Alternatively, the user can choose a plane, a vertex a starting line that passes through the vertex on the chosen plane and then specify an angle. A construction line will be placed at the specified angle from the starting line, passing through the origin on the chosen plane.

## Text Tool

The purpose of the Text tool is similar to the Dimension tool; it allows you to place text boxes with notes or text labels with leader lines in a scene. This is the tool you use for annotating shop drawings. It is particularly useful with exploded views because the default text for a label is the components part name. This saves a lot of typing time and prevents a lot of typos.

## Axes Tool

The Axes tool is used to change the drawing axes of the model. You use it by choosing a point for the new origin, then a point to specify a Red axis and finally a point to specify a Green axis. The Blue axis will run through the origin and normal to the Red/Green plane. Changing the model axis does not change the Ground plane, nor does it affect lighting or shadows. Further, if you choose a Red or Green axis that are not parallel to the current model axis, the new axis will not be reflected in the standard Front, Back, Top, Bottom, Right or Left views, nor the Iso view.

The Axes tool can also be used to change a component's axes, though I recommend you select the component and choose the Change Axes tool.

## Orbit Tool

The Orbit tool is used to orbit around the model. In reality it is the camera that is orbiting around the model and giving the user a different view. The Orbit tool, and its cousins Pan and Zoom tools, are essential to the process of modeling. Without them it would be very difficult to access connection points in the model.

## Pan Tool

The Pan tool is used to move the model right, left, up, down or diagonally without zooming in or out relative to the screen plane. This can be helpful when dimensioning a model that won't fit on screen and still have the detail the user desires. Remember, that for all the camera tools it is the camera that is actually moving, not the model.

## Zoom Tool

The Zoom tool is a camera tool used to enlarge or shrink the model image by zooming in or out. Again,

it is the camera that is getting closer or further away from the model.

## Zoom Extents Tool

The Zoom Extents tool is a camera tool used to fill the workspace viewing area with the model currently displayed. Zoom Extents is a frequently used tool. One of its uses is to find the model when you can't see it. Oft times the camera is too far back reducing the model image to something too small to see; or perhaps the camera is too far to the right, left, top or bottom. A simple click of the Zoom Extents tool will fill the screen with the model.

Another use of Zoom Extents is to move the camera back so it is not looking inside a model. Users new to SketchUp often get the camera in a position such that it is so close it is viewing the inside of a component. To the user it looks as if they have lost part of their model. A simple click of Zoom Extents saves the world.

## Section Plane Tool

Occasionally we need to show a cross section of a part or joinery. This is a job for the Section Plane tool. This tool permits orienting a plane in 3D space and moving it into position to expose the internal edges and faces of a cross section. We have discussed that SketchUp is a surface modeler, not a solids modeler, and therefore we may want to use a Ruby script plugin to assist the Section Plane tool, which we will discuss later.

## Display Section Planes Tool

When we use the Section Plane tool a section plane is created to indicate where the section is created. The Display Section Planes tool toggles the section plane; that is, makes it visible or invisible. The deselected state of this tool is an invisible section plane.

## Display Section Cuts Tool

When we use the Section Plane tool a section cut is created. The Display Section Cuts tool toggles the section cut; that is, makes it visible or invisible. The deselected state of this tool is an invisible section cut.

## STYLES (OR RENDERING) ICONS

There are seven Styles toolbar icons that we will use frequently in this text. Though they are called Styles icons they really determine how our model will be rendered on the screen. The first two style icons, X-Ray and Back Edges, modify the last five rendering modes. In Shaded, Shaded With Textures and Monochrome styles shading can be controlled by the sun if set up in the Window/Shadows dialog box, in which case shading is determined by location, time zone, time of day and date.

### X-Ray Style

When selected, the X-ray style will make all faces transparent to a degree depending on their depth from the front of the image. It is similar to taking an X-ray of a physical object.

### Back Edges Style

When selected, the Back Edges style is similar to X-ray except that the normally hidden edges will appear as lighter dashed lines through faces that are transparent to a degree depending on their depth from the front of the image.

### Wireframe Style

In Wireframe mode all edges are equally visible with no weighting by depth. Also, no faces are rendered, and therefore, both X-ray and Back Edges style icons are grayed out.

### Hidden Line Style

In Hidden Line mode only edges not hidden by other edges or faces are drawn. Faces are also drawn but not shaded or otherwise treated. Therefore, in Hidden Line mode you can use X-ray and Back Edges.

### Shaded Style

In Shaded mode only edges not hidden by other edges or faces are drawn. Faces are also drawn and they are shaded with an applied solid color. If no solid color is applied then either Front or Back color is used. In Shaded mode you can use X-ray and Back Edges.

### Shaded With Textures Style

In Shaded With Textures mode only edges not hidden by other edges or faces are drawn. Faces are also drawn, and they are shaded with an applied texture. If no texture has been applied this mode is the same as Shaded. In Shaded With Textures mode you can use X-ray and Back Edges.

### Monochrome Style

In Monochrome mode only edges not hidden by other edges or faces are drawn. Faces are also drawn and they are shaded with either the Front or Back color as appropriate. In Monochrome mode you can use X-ray and Back Edges.

## VIEWS (OR CAMERA STANDARD VIEWS) ICONS

There are six Views toolbar icons that we will use frequently in this text. Though they are called Views icons, they are really the standard camera views found in menu Camera/Standard Views. The Bottom standard view has no Views toolbar icon.

### ⌂ Front View

Displays the model with the camera positioned directly in front. By definition this is the Red/Blue plane view with the positive Green axis pointing into the screen.

### ⌂ Back View

Displays the model with the camera positioned directly in back. By definition this is the Red/Blue plane view with the positive Green axis pointing out of the screen.

### Left View

Displays the model with the camera positioned directly to the left. By definition this is the Green/Blue plane view with the positive Red axis pointing into the screen.

### Right View

Displays the model with the camera positioned directly to the right. By definition this is the Green/Blue plane view with the positive Red axis pointing out of the screen.

###  Top View

Displays the model with the camera positioned directly above. By definition this is the Red/Green plane view with the positive Blue axis pointing out of the screen.

### Iso View

The Iso view will render the model on isometric axes. The orientation of the axes will depend on the previous view of the model. It will render the model by moving the camera to the nearest isometric view.

## SHORT CUT MENU

I have listed here all the default assigned shortcut keys. Commands are on the left and shortcut keys on the right. You can use menu Window/Preferences and select the Shortcuts page to reassign or customize any command you wish.

### CAMERA COMMANDS

| | |
|---|---|
| Image Igloo | I |
| Orbit | O |
| Pan | H |
| Zoom | Z |
| Zoom Extents | Ctrl+Shift+E |
| | Shift+Z |
| Zoom Window | Ctrl+Shift+W |

### DRAW COMMANDS

| | |
|---|---|
| Arcs/2-Point Arc | A |
| Lines/Line | L |
| Shapes/Circle | C |
| Shapes/Rectangle | R |

### EDIT COMMANDS

| | |
|---|---|
| Copy | Ctrl+C |
| | Ctrl+Insert |
| Cut | Shift+Delete |
| | Ctrl+X |
| Delete | Delete |
| Make Component | G |
| Paste | Ctrl+V |
| | Shift+Insert |
| Redo | Ctrl+Y |
| Select All | Ctrl+A |
| Select None | Ctrl+T |
| Undo | Alt+Backspace |
| | Ctrl+Z |

### FILE COMMANDS

| | |
|---|---|
| New | Ctrl+N |
| Open | Ctrl+O |
| Print | Ctrl+P |
| Save | Ctrl+S |

### TOOLS COMMANDS

| | |
|---|---|
| Eraser | E |
| Move | M |
| Offset | F |
| Paint Bucket | B |
| Push/Pull | P |
| Rotate | Q |
| Scale | S |
| Select | Space |
| Tape Measure | T |

### VIEW COMMANDS

| | |
|---|---|
| Animation/Next Scene | PageDown |
| Animation/Previous Scene | Page/Up |
| Edge Style/Back Edges | K |

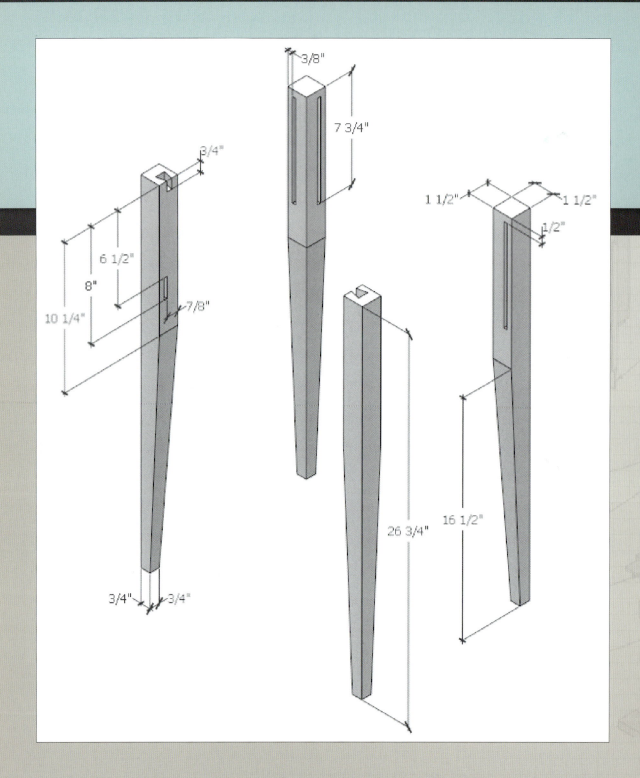

# PART TWO:
# THE APPRENTICE & THE BEDSIDE TABLE

Frank Klausz, a master cabinetmaker and premier dovetail guru, apprenticed in Europe under his father. I have on several occasions listened to Frank describe old Europe apprenticeships and marveled at the quality of training. As a beginner, an apprentice is not allowed to make cuts or handle a plane; he might start out fetching wood or sanding. Only with repetition and demonstrating a mastery of the fundamentals would an apprentice advance to the next level of woodworking.

In Part Two we begin with the very basics of modeling. Our goal is to model a simple Bedside Table consisting of four tapered legs, a curved apron, one dovetailed draw and a beveled top. I assume the reader is a beginner and I will therefore handhold the reader, guiding him/her keystroke-by-keystroke through the process. Unlike Frank's father, I can't stop you from proceeding to the next chapter before you have mastered the current one. But I strongly encourage you to discipline yourself in this regard. If you don't, you'll likely be doomed to frustration and may ultimately give up on SketchUp. That would be a big mistake.

# 03

# DRAWING TAPERED LEGS

*In this first chapter of Part Two you learn to draw or, if you prefer, model tapered legs. This may seem like a shallow goal for an entire chapter. But rest assured we will cover a lot of the tool set and functionality of SketchUp. And remember, it is best to keep an open mind and think of yourself as an apprentice. I'll play the role of the master, and you'll follow my lead — much as Frank Klausz did under his father.*

When approaching SketchUp as a beginner, here are six rules that will serve you well:

## SIX RULES FOR 3D MODELING IN SKETCHUP

1. ***Save your work frequently.***
   Under the Window menu choose Preferences. Select the General panel and under Saving make sure both Create Backup and Auto-Save check boxes are checked. Set Every to 5 minutes. In addition, get into the habit of saving your file frequently using the File/Save (or File/Save As if it is the first save). You must save your file once before Create Backup takes effect, so do it immediately upon beginning a model. 3D modeling is a lot of work and losing multiple hours of work can make you blood-curdling angry. Follow this basic rule to avoid hypertension.

2. ***Layer0 should always be active when modeling.***
   Make sure that Layer0 is always active. Access the Layers dialog box with menu Window/Layers and make sure the radio button to the left of Layer0 is selected. This should remain true through the entire modeling phase. This ensures that all primitives reside on Layer0. More importantly, it means that the primitives of a given group or component are not on different layers which would make using Layers to view and hide individual parts nearly impossible.

3. ***Draw one part at a time.***
   Never allow a part in its primitive state to touch another part in its primitive state. The word *primitive*, or *primitives*, means points, lines, faces, rectangles, circles, polygons and arcs including construction lines and points. In short, a primitive is any drawn object except a solid, group or component. Primitives are the most fundamental of drawing objects from which all other geometry

is drawn. A part is in its primitive state unless it is made into a group or component. It is very important to understand that when two primitives touch, even when they are on different layers, they *stick* together.

4. ***As soon as a part takes 3D shape make it a component.***

   Components save time and frustration. In addition, they dramatically reduce the file size of your model. Groups are similar to components but components have several advantages, most importantly reducing file size and increasing efficiency in editing. Avoid groups if possible. A part doesn't have to be completed before making it a component; in fact it should be made a component as soon as it takes on a 3D shape. Further modeling of the part or edits to it can be made later using the protective Edit Component or Edit Group tools.

5. ***As soon as a component is created move it to the layer where it will reside.***

   The best way to move a component to a different layer is by using the Entity Info box. If the desired layer does not exist, use the Layers box to create it, and then move the desired component onto the layer. Both the Layers and Entity Info box can be found on the Window menu.

6. ***Draw a complete model before creating scenes, texturing or dimensioning.***

   Draw a complete model first, including joinery. Be sure all parts are components. All components must have a unique and descriptive Definition Name. All component instances should have a unique instance (part) name. This I call the modeling phase. Only when the 3D model is complete should you move on to creating scenes, texturing or dimensioning.

Later in the text I will describe a better and more trouble-free method to create a new layer than using the Layers box. However, it requires the use of a Ruby script, which we haven't discussed yet.

Rules 2 through 4 are important because in SketchUp primitives are "sticky." That is, if they touch one another they stick together, more accurately they share points, edges and faces. Therefore, if table legs and a table-top are drawn in their correct position relative to each other, and are in their primitive state, they would be touching. Separating them onto different layers or making them individual components or groups becomes, at best, frustrating and, at worst, near impossible. In fact if you tried to move a leg the top would move; worse it would become totally distorted.

SketchUp's sticky nature is one of its most difficult aspects to deal with, unless you follow these rules. Once mastered, drawing parts and converting them to components will become second nature. You will also discover that this sticky nature of SketchUp's primitives was not perpetrated on the unsuspecting beginners by its developers to inflict hypertension and a nervous breakdown. Rather there is an overriding useful purpose that will be evident as you continue learning SketchUp.

## PREPARING TO DRAW

A completed SketchUp model of the Bedside Table can be downloaded at srww.com/sketchup_a_guide_for_woodworkers.html. You will find it under Downloads, Part Two, Chapter 3. Before we begin modeling, familiarize yourself with its design and dimensions. For this chapter we are especially interested in the tapered legs. You may want to print out the BedsideTable.pdf file for reference.

Since this is a SketchUp text and not a course in furniture design, several stages of furniture design (architecture, style, rough sketch, joinery selection and over all dimensioning) will be deferred to later in the text. To that end, the detail design criteria and dimensions will be given as needed. The mortises and dovetails in the tapered legs will be covered in Chapter 4 when we draw the aprons. It will become more clear in time why we are leaving the mortises and dovetails until Chapter 4.

Throughout Part Two of this text I will be feeding you keystroke-by-keystroke instructions. In order that you might follow along it is imperative that our work-

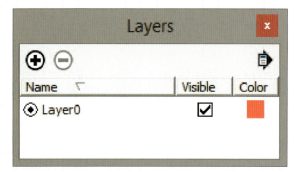

**Figure 1** | Make sure Layer Zero is active

spaces are configured the same. We walked through the correct configuration in Chapter 1 – if you didn't configure your workspace then, you should do so now (see page 25).

When you have your workspace configured, click the Front ⌂ , Iso 🍥 and Zoom Extents ✖ tool icons, in that order. Click the Shaded 🔵 tool icon in the Styles toolbar. I also recommend that you configure your toolbars as described in "Setting Up the Toolbars" in Chapter 1.

Let's review the rules above to see if we are ready to draw. Rule 1 instructs us to save our file immediately so that the Create Backup and Auto-Save functions will begin. Use menu File/Save As to save your file in a folder of your choice and name it Bedside Table. Rule 2 instructs us to make sure Layer0 is the active layer throughout the modeling phase. Menu Window/Layers will open the Layers dialog box. Be

sure Layer0 is active as shown in **Figure 1**. Now we are ready to draw a leg.

## CREATING A 3D COMPONENT

Refer to the detailed dimensions given in **Figure 2**. Notice that the overall dimensions of the leg are 1 ½ inch square by 26¾ inches long. The bottom of the leg is ¾ inches square and tapers from the floor to its overall thickness at 16½ inches up. Start drawing the left front left leg by selecting the Rectangle ▧ tool icon. Click on the origin, move the cursor diagonally across the Red/Green plane approximately 1" visually and click. Before doing anything else type ¾,¾ and hit *Enter*. This last step places the dimensions of a rectangle into the VCB (Value Control Box). You must include the comma separating the two dimensions, however, a space separating the comma and the second dimension is optional. For printed text clarity, I may include a space in the text, though to save key strokes I never include a space when entering values in the VCB. The second click in this operation is also optional provided the dimensions are typed into the VCB immediately, and then followed by *Enter*. Because the template we chose specifies inches as the default units, the units do not need to be included. If, however, these dimension's units were any other than the specified default, the unit would need to be included (e.g. a 2mm square rectangle would be typed as 2mm,2mm).

I should mention two other points about entering these dimensions: First if you enter them in the wrong order don't worry, simply retype them in the correct order (this is a square so entering them in the wrong order is difficult). Second, these values can be entered in decimal form if desired by typing .75, .75 and pressing *Enter*.

At this point the drawn square may appear very small, perhaps even invisible, or very large. In either case select the Zoom Extents ✖ tool icon to bring the square into view. It now fills the screen. To zoom out select the Zoom 🔍 tool icon, drag the cursor vertically downward anywhere in the screen area until you have zoomed out the desired amount. Drag the cursor

### CENTERING THE MODEL

It often occurs that your model seems too large, missing sections as though they were sliced off. Or you may find yourself disoriented and don't know what you are looking at. Don't panic! Use the Zoom Extents ✖ tool to center your model on screen; or alternatively the Zoom 🔍 tool to zoom out and bring the complete model into view.

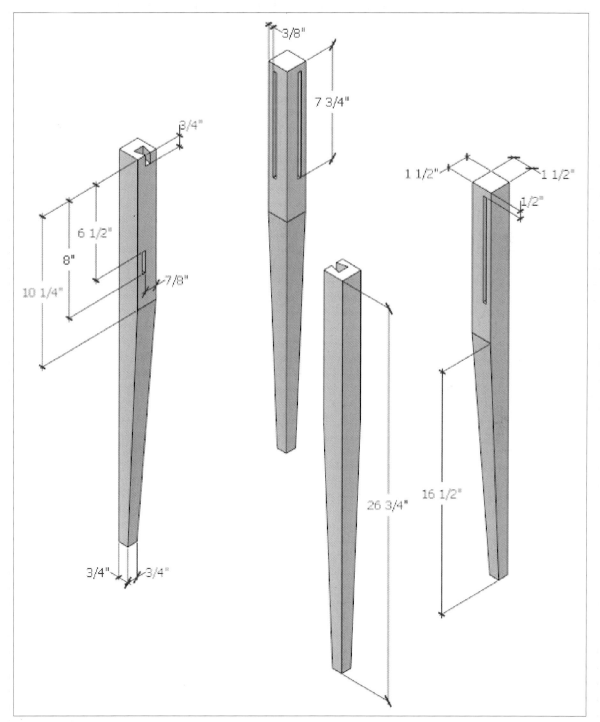

**Figure 2** | Detailed leg dimensions

vertically upward to zoom in. You can also use the mouse thumb wheel for this purpose.

Next, using the Push/Pull ✦ tool icon, click the rectangles face. Notice this fills the face with blue dots indicating the face being operated on. Move the cursor upward approximately 20" and click (optional). Type 16.5 and *Enter*. You may need to use the Zoom Extents ✕ and Zoom 🔎 tools again to bring the entire object onto the screen. You will find this procedure necessary frequently throughout this text. I will not instruct you on this procedure again and leave it to you to execute as needed.

If you did everything as instructed your picture should now look like **Figure 3**. It doesn't really matter where the origin and axis are. However, if you started your initial rectangle somewhere other than at the origin, do the following so that we are both viewing the same picture.

We will orient the origin at the lower left front corner of the leg, with the red axis along the X direction, the green axis along the Y direction and the blue axis along the Z direction. To accomplish this click the X-Ray ⬖ tool icon (you can also use the Back Edges ⬖ tool icon if it makes things clearer to you). You should now be able to see the lower left back corner. Selecting the Axes ✳ tool icon, click on the lower left front corner of the leg, move the cursor right along the

In SketchUp, much like in the shop, there are numerous ways to do things. I have done and will do things throughout this text that I believe either introduces the most new tools or presents things is a manner that is easy to learn. In so doing I may instruct you to do things in a way that is less efficient. This is a tradeoff. I believe that when exposed to numerous tools and methods you will choose the method most comfortable and efficient for you. For example, I use tool icons throughout the text. Most professionals use keystroke shortcuts. In the more advanced sections of this text I will try to point out what I believe to be best practices, but in the end the choice is yours.

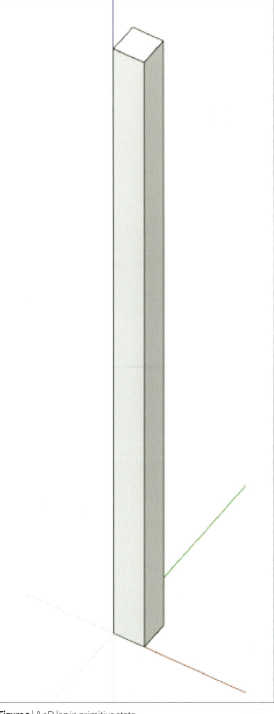

**Figure 3** | A 3D leg in primitive state

bottom edge to the endpoint, and click. Endpoint will show up as a tooltip when you are over it. Now move back along the lower left side edge to endpoint and click. Deselect the X-ray ◍ tool by selecting the Select ⭢ tool, or pressing the *Space Bar*. Your picture should now look like the one shown in **Figure 3**. If your picture still does not look like **Figure 3** start over and follow every direction carefully.

We now have a 3D shape and Rule 4 instructs us to make it a component. Thinking ahead a little (refer to **Figure 2**), we might guess that the back legs will be mirror images of one another and the front legs also mirror one another. However, the completed front and back legs will *not* be mirror images of one another. This is because the front and back of the table are different in that the joinery used is different. The front has a draw with top and bottom rails forming the drawer opening, and the back is just an apron. Hence the mortises in the front and back legs will be different. In addition the front top rail uses dovetail joinery. On the other hand, if we ignore the mortise and dovetail joinery, then all four legs are identical. Therefore, we can save ourselves a lot of work if we name the leg component "Leg"; use it for all four legs until we find it necessary to differentiate them.

> Thinking ahead is one of the most important skills you can develop to become proficient with SketchUp. Another is to draw only when absolutely necessary. I will frequently point out situations where you can apply these skills.

Using the Select ⭢ tool icon triple click any face of the leg. All lines and faces should turn blue and the faces filled with an array of blue dots. Right click on the selected entities and select Make Component from the Context menu. The Create Component dialog box will open. In the Name box the name Component#1 is highlighted and will be assigned if you don't rename the component.

Rename it Leg. Make sure the Replace selection with component check box in the lower left is checked. If you wish, you can enter a description for the Leg in the Description field. Click the Create button. The leg is now selected and outlined in blue. Leave it selected.

Now we want to create a Legs layer; recall Rule 5. The Layers dialog box should already be open. If not, under the Window menu choose Layers and the Layers dialog box will appear. Repeat this procedure to open the Entity Info and Components dialog boxes. If your screen is too cluttered you can minimize/maximize these boxes by clicking on the top bar next to the name of the box. Notice in the Entity Info dialog box that the name we assigned to this component, Leg, appears in the Definition Name box, not the Name box. I highly recommend you pause for a moment and read the section "Create Component" in Appendix D to avoid confusion on naming components. Come back when you fully understand it.

In the Layers box click the ⊕ icon. Layer1 is highlighted as a suggested name and will be assigned if you don't change it. Type Legs into the name box and press *Enter*. Notice the Visible check box next to Legs is checked meaning whatever resides on this layer will be visible in the screen area.

The Leg component should already be selected, but if not use the Select ⭢ tool to do so. In the Entity Info dialog box, use the Layer drop-down and choose Legs. At this point Layer0 should be void of any component and layer Legs should contain our leg. Check to be sure this is the case as follows. Using the Select tool deselect the leg by clicking anywhere in the drawing area except on the leg. In the Layers dialog box make sure the radio button is selected next to Layer0. Uncheck the Visible box next to the Legs layer. The leg should now disappear. Now select the radio button next to the Legs layer and the leg should reappear. Uncheck the Visible box next to Layer0 and the leg should still be visible. Now reselect the radio button next to Layer0 and leave the Legs layer Visible check box checked.

This little experiment indicates that the Leg exists only on the Legs layer and not Layer0. This is not entirely true, and the details I am about to explain are very important to understanding how SketchUp works. Using the Select ⬉ tool select the leg and right click on it to open the Context menu. Choose Edit Component. Triple click with the Select tool on a face of the leg. All lines and entities are now selected. Notice in the Entity Info dialog box that all lines and entities exist on Layer0, not the Legs layer. This is because we drew the primitives on Layer0, then we collected them all into a component with Make Component and placed the component on the Legs layer. If we closely follow the rules outlined in "Six Rules for 3D Modeling in SketchUp," no matter how many components we use in a model, their primitives will all reside on Layer0, but their component definitions (hence the Definition Name in the Entity Info dialog box) will reside on the layers we assign the component to.

Where beginners often get into trouble is by violating Rule 2. They switch active layers while modeling. Primitives of a given component end up spread across numerous layers. Then they are surprised when choosing the appropriate layer that not all of the primitives are visible in the component.

## EDITING A 3D COMPONENT

Now we have the Leg component protected by making it a component. If we should accidentally connect a primitive (or primitives) to a component, such as Leg, those primitives will not stick to it, though they may stick to each other. However, this means that all changes to Leg must be done in the Edit Component mode. This is a small price to pay for protection that could save us from a nervous breakdown.

With the Select ⬉ tool icon select the Leg and right click on it to bring up the Context menu. Choose Edit Component. Notice that the Leg is surrounded by a dotted bounding box. This means that all edits done inside this box will be to the Leg component only. This will become clear when we start to add joinery. As long as we see the bounding box we are in Edit Component mode. To exit Edit Component mode, click outside the box with the Select ⬉ tool. But stay in Edit Component mode until I instruct you to leave it.

We will now use the Scale ▦ tool icon to produce the taper. Recall that the leg starts with a dimension of ¾" square at the bottom and tapers to 1½" square at 16½" up. A scaling factor of 2 can be calculated by dividing 1.5 by 0.75. This is the factor we will use to get the taper. Using the Select ⬉ tool select the top surface of the leg. It should become highlighted with blue dots indicating that you have selected its face. Now select the Scale ▦ tool icon. Notice the eight small cubes that appear. These are for gripping and pulling. Place your cursor over the back right grip, the one diagonally farthest from the blue axis. Notice that a red line appears connecting the opposite corner and

## LAYER0 (LAYER ZERO) IS A SPECIAL LAYER

If you experiment with primitives and components spread across various layers, including viewing them under various configurations of visibility boxes checked, you will quickly discover that Layer Zero is special; it behaves different than all other layers. Here are the differences:

1. Layer Zero cannot be deleted or purged.

2. You cannot change the name of Layer Zero.

3. Primitives that reside on Layer Zero are available for SketchUp to configure and display a component or group even if Layer Zero's visibility box is not checked.

These differences are the primary reasons one should always draw on Layer Zero (meaning Layer Zero is always the active layer) and move groups or components to an appropriate layer. There is no need to make another layer active, and indeed you will get into trouble.

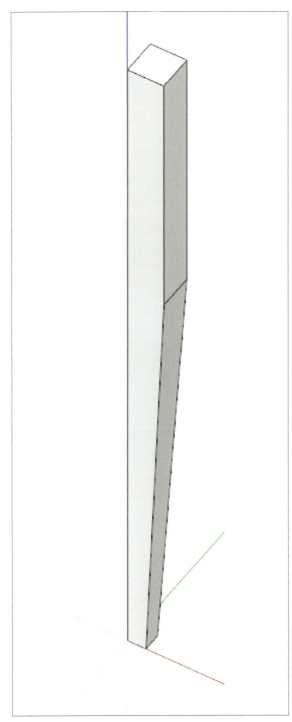

**Figure 4** | The tapered leg component

forming a hypotenuse relative to the sides. We are going to scale that hypotenuse by a factor of two. Drag the grip to the right approximately 1", then press *Enter* (optional). Now type 2 and *Enter*; we have our taper.

Referring back to the **Figure 2**, the distance between the end of the taper and the top of the leg is 26¾" minus 16½" or 10¼". Let's use this to stretch the leg. Select the Push/Pull ✦ tool, place the cursor over the top of the leg and Drag it up approximately 1" and press *Enter* (optional). Type 10¼ and press *Enter*. Select the Zoom Extents ✖ tool. With the Select ▸ tool, click outside the bounding box to exit Edit Component mode. Voilà! We have a tapered leg. It should look like **Figure 4**.

## CHECKING A 3D COMPONENT FOR PROPER CONSTRUCTION

Before we go any further, let's compare the dimensions of the leg we modeled to those in **Figure 2**. I will describe how to do the first one and then you can check the rest. Select the Tape Measure ✐ tool icon. Click on the origin. Move the cursor to the right along the Red axis until the bottom right front corner is reached. As you hover over the corner a tooltip will appear for a few seconds and indicate ¾"; that is, if you drew the original rectangle correctly. Do not click, but simply move the cursor to the top left front corner and hover over it. A tooltip will appear for a few seconds and indicate 26¾" (or 2' 2¾" depending on how units are set in the Model Info dialog box). From an anchored point you can check a number of dimensions using this technique. Press *Esc*. Now repeat this process to check the remaining dimensions.

While checking the dimensions of a component with the Tape Measure ✐ tool you may see a dimension such as ~10½". The tilde (~) symbol means approximately. Hence this measured dimension is approximately 10½". This is a very common problem for people just beginning with SketchUp. But it is one you have to nip in the bud quickly or you will get a long way along in a model before you realize you may have to redo the entire model. You will then become frustrated and unhappy with SketchUp. The tilde (~)

symbol should always cause you to question if you should see it. For more information on this potential problem see the Frequently Asked Questions (FAQ) section on this book's web page; srww.com/ sketchup_a_guide_for_woodworkers.html.

So here is what to look for and what you need to do to proceed. First, since every dimension we use in this model is exact e.g. 5 ½" not 5.4444449, we should never see a tilde symbol (~) before a measurement when using the Tape Measure tool or any other tool (the Dimension ✎ tool will never display a tilde symbol because it rounds dimensions). If you see a tilde symbol while checking a component your model has a problem, and you need to correct it.

I suggest using the Tape Measure tool frequently while learning SketchUp to check your steps, lest you get way down the road and find a problem that can't be easily repaired. If you see a tilde symbol zoom in close, and you will see that a line is not connecting to the point it should connect to; there is a gap. The solution to your problem is to keep a very close eye on the Inference Engine. The Inference Engine is the mechanism that produces those tooltips such as End-point, Midpoint, Midpoint in Component, On Edge, On Line, On Red Axis, etc. When you are trying to connect a line or polygon to a point, slow down with your mouse and be sure you click it only when you see the Inference Engine tooltip you desire. This will ensure you are connecting two points exactly.

Often, what new students do is locate the correct Inference Engine tooltip, but then when clicking do it with just enough force to move the mouse slightly off the desired point. Over time you will develop a motion that is reliable, but early on you have to be careful and conscious of clicking on the tooltip. Also, use the mouse wheel to zoom in close when trying to connect a line or polygon to a point. Don't try to connect things when the entire model is in the window because likely you are not close enough to get an exact attachment.

One other thing that may cause the problem you are seeing is a setting in Model Info. Go to Window; choose Model Info and then Units. Make sure that "Enable length snapping" is unchecked. If you have problems with your model and don't understand what

is going on, send me a copy of your SKP file, and I will tell you what your mistake is. Email the model file to jpz@srww.com.

## ADDING SIMILAR COMPONENTS TO THE MODEL

Select the Orbit ✥ tool and orbit around the leg by dragging the cursor anywhere in the viewing area. Take note at how the Orbit tool works. If you have a mouse wheel you can combine it with the Orbit tool to zoom in/out while orbiting. Notice that the leg is tapered only on two adjacent sides. This is because we used the Scale tool to drag a corner, that corner being common to two sides. We could have instead grabbed a side grip and drag, which would have tapered only one side. OK, let's get back to a common picture between us. Click the Front ⬆ , Iso ⬢ and Zoom Extents ✖ tool icons, in that order. I will use this sequence of tools frequently to get us back looking at the same image and view. So in the future, if I say "go home" or something of that nature you can take it to mean: Click the Front ⬆, Iso ⬢ and Zoom Extents ✖ tool icons, in that order.

Go Home – means click the Front, Iso and Zoom Extents tool icons, in that order. This is a signal from me to you that we need to synchronize our model view.

Using the Zoom 🔍 tool, zoom out to make room for three more legs. With the Rectangle ▱ tool click on the top left front corner of the leg. Move the cursor along a line approximately 30 degrees to the red axis. Notice a rectangle forms and is parallel to the Red, Green plane. Type 18, 13.5 and press *Enter*. This will place a rectangle on the top of the Leg 18" wide and 13½" deep. Make sure the 18" dimension is along the Red axis and the 13½" dimension is along the Green axis. This can be verified by checking the shape

**Figure 5** | Components In Model library with Leg component Shown

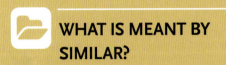

## WHAT IS MEANT BY SIMILAR?

The word *similar* in this section heading means components with the same Definition Name. I use the word *similar* as opposed to *identical* because it is consistent with Trimble's own documentation.

Components that are dragged-and-dropped into the work area from the Components Library are similar to others in the work area with the same Definition Name.

Components that are copied or copied and rotated or copied and mirrored (Flip Along) are also similar.

You may give any component a different instance name (Name in the Entity Info dialog box) and it is still similar to other components with the same Definition Name.

visually; the long side is along the red axis and the VCB says 18, 13.5. This rectangle serves only to provide a place to attach the other three legs, as you will see in a moment. We don't need the face of the rectangle, only its edges, and the face will obscure our visibility. To delete it select the rectangle's face with the Select ⬉ tool; this will fill the face with blue dots. Press the *Delete* key.

The dimensions 18" and 13½" were not given in **Figure 2** but they can be obtained from the completed BedsideTable.pdf file you printed out. They will appear on the Front View and Side View drawings as the outside edge spacing of the legs. Anytime I feed you a dimension and you are not sure where it came from you can refer to the BedsideTable.pdf file.

The rectangle we drew has four corners, one of which is located at the top left front corner of the leg. The other three corners will locate the outside corners of the other three legs. To get these additional legs we have a couple of choices. We could drag them one at a time from the Components In Model library, or we could just make a copy of the one already there and move it in place and repeat this process twice more. The latter is going to be our best option, but let me describe the former just so you know how it's done.

The Components dialog box should still be open from our earlier work. If not you can access it with menu Window/Components. When this dialog box opens initially, it may point to a fairly large library of components that come with SketchUp, for example windows and doors. Our Leg component is not in this library. It is in a library called In Model. To access it click on the In Model ⌂ icon in the Components dialog box. You should now see the Leg component as shown in **Figure 5**. Let me remind you that the leg name that appears in the Components dialog box is the Definition Name that appears in the Entity Info dialog box.

Look at the Components dialog box; next to the In Model ⌂ icon is a drop-down menu where you can access other libraries as well as the In Model library.

At this point we could drag and drop a Leg placing it close to a corner of the rectangle. With the

Move ✤ tool we could then place it and then drag and drop two more. But there is a better way we will use here that also makes use of the Move ✤ tool.

The Move tool is also the Copy tool and in fact is often called the Move/Copy tool. It has a number of modes and options for use. We will use just a couple of options here.

If the leg is selected in the viewing area deselect it by clicking the Select ⬈ tool in an empty space. Select the Move ✤ tool and hover over the top left back corner of the leg until it is outlined in blue, indicating selection, and click. Press the *Ctrl* key once and a + sign will appear in the cursor indicating the Move tool is now the Copy tool. Move the cursor in the direction of the Green axis to the back left corner of the rectangle until an Endpoint tooltip appears and click. The leg is now in place, but comparing this leg to its counterpart in **Figure 2** you will notice that the tapers are on the wrong sides. This is because the back leg needs to be a mirror image of the front leg, not merely a copy.

## MIRROR IMAGING A COMPONENT

To Mirror we use the Context menu Flip Along tool. Right click on the back Leg with the Select ⬈ tool and chose Flip Along. We have a choice to make. Recalling that we moved the copy of Leg along the green axis we will mirror the new Leg in the green direction, so choose Component's Green.

Whenever a component or group is mirrored, note the axis direction along which it was moved prior to mirroring. That axis is the color that should be chosen for the Flip Along tool. If you move at an angle to two axes you will need to note both and use the Flip Along tool twice. For example, suppose we moved the left front leg diagonally to the right rear leg position. The Flip Along tool must be used twice, once using the Component's Red and once using the Component's Green to correctly mirror the leg.

Mirroring a component or group does not constitute editing it. So a component's Definition Name in the Entity Info dialog box will not change, nor will a group's name change. Further, if several instances of a component exist in the model and several are mirrors of the others, editing any of them using Edit Component will still edit all instances.

Before we go any further, let's think ahead again. We now have a left front leg and a left back leg; each is a Leg component. We know the table's back apron and its front drawer opening are going to require different joinery and therefore the Leg component names must be different. We know the two front legs will be identical as will the two back legs. So let's rename the left front leg component to Front Leg and the left back Leg component to Back Leg. Remember, it is the component's Definition Name that we are changing, and we will do it in the Entity Info dialog box. But don't rush off and change these component names just yet. How we change them is very important.

With the Select ⬈ tool, select the left back leg and right click to bring up the Context menu. Choose Make Unique. Notice the Definition Name in the Entity Info box changed from Leg to Leg#1. SketchUp is trying to help us here but the assigned Definition Name is not very descriptive. Change it to Back Leg and press *Enter*. With the Select ⬈ tool, select the left front leg and rename the Definition Name for the left front leg to Front Leg. The Make Unique context tool can always be used on a component to create a new component that is identical but with a unique Definition Name. Subsequently that unique component can be edited for differences, in this case its different joinery.

We need two more legs. With the left front leg still selected select the Move ✤ tool, press *Ctrl* to switch to Copy. With the Copy cursor (Move cursor with a + sign) click on the top right front corner of the left front leg and move it in the red direction along the red axis until you see the

Endpoint tooltip on the right front corner of the rectangle and click. We need to mirror the right front leg. We note that we moved it along the red axis during the copy and placement procedure. With the right front leg still selected right click on it to bring up the Context menu. Choose Flip Along and Component's Red.

We need one more leg, the right back leg. We could use the same copy technique we used before on the right front leg to copy and move the left back leg to the right back leg position. But to demonstrate a different approach this time we will first use the Rotate ⟳ tool to mirror the leg.

Using the Rotate ⟳ tool in this way requires a little forethought as to the point and axis you want to use for rotation. When the right back leg is in place we want the two tapers to be facing front and left. A quick examination of the left back leg suggests we can accomplish this by copying and rotating it 90° clockwise. It also suggests that we want the axis of rotation to be the Blue axis and the point of rotation around the left back corner of the left back leg. Using the Select ⬉ tool, select the left back leg. Select the Rotate ⟳ tool and press *Ctrl* to switch to Copy. A + sign is added to the cursor.

Notice, if you hold the cursor in empty drawing area space, the cursor favors a blue color with the protractor lying parallel to the Red/Green plane. If you hold the cursor over any face of the leg it will change to a color orthogonal to the plane that face is in. If you hold it over a leg taper face it will turn black and lie in a plane parallel to the taper's plane. The color of the protractor indicates the axis it will rotate around. We want the Blue axis.

Place the cursor first over the very top of the left back leg and then move it to the top left back corner of the leg and click. Now move the cursor along the Red axis. Remain on the Red axis with an On Red Axis tooltip and click. If you prefer, you can click on the right back corner of the rectangle for this last step, but be sure you see the Endpoint tooltip before clicking. Now move the cursor to the left front corner of the rectangle until a purple dot appears and click. Notice a new copy of the Back Leg was created and rotated 90° clockwise.

The student should now be able to use the Select and Move tools to move the new leg into place. When you have done that, recall Rule 3. We need to delete the rectangle. If we were to leave this rectangle in place it may stick to the next part we want to draw in the following chapter. Select the Eraser ✐ tool and erase each of the rectangles' edges by clicking on them with the little circle in the Eraser tool's cursor. We don't need the rectangle anymore; it has served us well to locate the legs.

Before we go any further let's select each leg, one at a time, using the Select tool and give them each a unique name. Do not confuse this operation with the Make Unique context tool, which creates components with unique Definition Names. For each leg selected, look at the Entity Info box. You will see a blank Name field. In it type a unique name as follows:

- Select the left front leg and in the Name box type Left Front Leg
- Select the right front leg and in the Name box type Right Front Leg
- Select the left back leg and in the Name box type Left Back Leg
- Finally, select the right back leg and in the Name box type Right Back Leg

**Figure 6** shows the completed legs with four Entity Info boxes superimposed on it to indicate the naming convention used. It is important that you develop a naming convention of your own that is descriptive and uniquely names both component Definition Names and Instance Names. Think about what we have done here and remember the approach. This will help tremendously when it is time to create exploded views and parts lists.

Check that your drawing looks exactly like **Figure 6** (without the dialog boxes, of course). Save your file. In the next chapter we will add aprons and some joinery.

## THE OUTLINER TOOL

I want to introduce another dialog box I seldom use, but it is a good diagnostic tool to check naming and also a good tool for finding your way around complex models. Under the Window menu choose Outliner. The Outliner dialog box opens as shown in **Figure 7**.

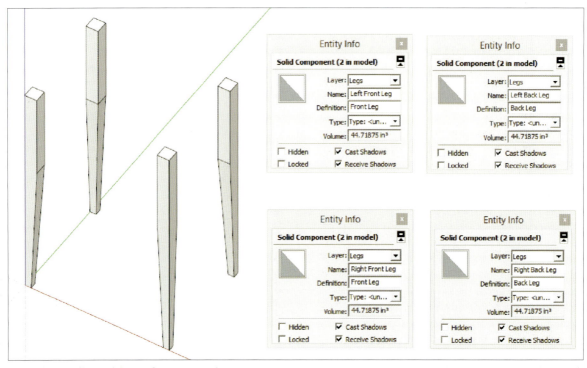

**Figure 6** | Finished legs with Entity Info superimposed

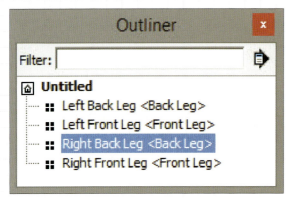

**Figure 7** | The Outliner dialog box

Examine it carefully. We will not go deeply into the use of the Outliner dialog box at this time, but notice how the list is organized. The name between the <> characters is the component's Definition Name, the name that is given in the Create Component dialog box and the In Model component library name. The name in front of the

<> characters is the part unique name. In the Filter box type "back" and notice what happens. Select one of the entries (e.g. Left Back Leg) and notice what happens in the drawing area. Notice that part is selected. Now type "left" in the Filter box and observe the changes. Select both entries in the box below the Filter box and notice two parts are selected. As this drawing grows or especially when working with a very large complex design, the Outliner dialog box becomes very useful.

## CHAPTER REVIEW

In SketchUp there are many ways to accomplish the same thing. But as far as tapered legs are concerned, the approach we used here is especially fast and easy. Let's review what we did. Upon opening SketchUp we checked that our application and model were both configured correctly. Following Rule 1 we saved our model and named it Bedside Table.

We started drawing a simple rectangle using the Rectangle tool, drawn at the axis with dimensions of the leg bottom. We used the Push/Pull tool to extrude this rectangle to the dimension where the taper begins.

Following Rule 4 we created our first component and gave it a Definition name of Leg. We also created a Legs layer and placed the leg on it per Rule 5. Realizing at this dimension the leg takes on its overall thickness, and knowing that we want the tapers always facing its neighbor leg, we entered Edit Component mode and used the Scale tool to resize the top of the leg component. This created tapers on two leg faces.

We again used the Push/Pull tool to give the leg its final length. At this point we exited Edit Component mode. Thinking ahead we created a rectangle at the top of the leg sized to aid us in placing the remaining three legs we needed for a table. We deleted the rectangle's face because it was not needed and would only serve to block our view.

Using the Move/Copy tool we copied the left front leg and placed it in the position of the left back leg. Like almost all woodworking projects, many parts are mirror images of one another. To mirror the back leg we used the Context tool Flip Along and taking note of the axis we moved the back leg along chose Component's Green.

At this point we realized that front and back legs would have different joinery, hence they are not exactly the same component. We saved ourselves work by renaming the back Leg's Definition Name to Back Leg using the Make Unique context tool. Likewise we renamed the front Leg's Definition Name to Front Leg in the Entity Info dialog box.

Again using the Move/Copy tool we copied and mirrored the left back leg to the right back leg position. This time when we opened the Context menu and selected Flip Along we chose Component's Red because we copied and moved the Front Leg along the red axis.

For a change of pace we used the Copy/Move tool with the Rotate tool to copy, move and mirror the Back Leg and placed it in the right back leg position. Using the Rotate tool for this purpose,

in my opinion, is less efficient and requires more planning. There are instances where the Rotate tool is the right tool for the job but mirroring is not one of them.

Lastly we selected each leg and gave it a unique part name by using the Entity Info dialog box and typing the parts name into the Name field. As instructed by Rule 3 we deleted our rectangle to avoid problems with the parts that will be drawn in the next chapter.

Along the way we always had Layer0 selected as the active layer per Rule 2. This will remain true for the entire text.

Because we added components to the model by using the copy feature of the Move and Rotate tools, we didn't have to concern ourselves with placing the three additional legs on the Legs layer. However, had we acquired the three additional legs by dragging them from the In Model Components library they would need to be moved from Layer0 to the Legs layer. Again we saved ourselves a little work and avoided mistakes.

In this chapter we introduced and used numerous tools; these might be considered the workhorse of furniture design. All counted this chapter made use of the following tools listed in the order they were used:

- ⌂ Front
- 📦 Iso
- ✖ Zoom Extents
- ◈ Shaded
- ▤ Rectangle
- 🔍 Zoom
- ◈ Push/Pull
- ◈ X-Ray
- ◈ Back Edges
- ✳ Axes
- ➤ Select
- ▦ Scale
- 🔍 Tape Measure
- ✦ Orbit
- ✦ Move/Copy
- 🔄 Rotate/Copy
- ▰ Eraser

In addition the following Context menu tools were introduced:
- Make Component
- Edit Component
- Flip Along
- Make Unique

And lastly we were introduced to the following dialog boxes:
- Layers
- Create Component
- Entity Info
- Components
- Outliner

## EXERCISES FOR THE STUDENT

1. Draw a cube on Layer0. Make it a component called Cube. Create a layer called Cube and place the cube on it. Create a layer called Random. Using Edit Component to edit the Cube component and choose a few of its primitives, such as a face and two lines, and place them on layer Random while still in Edit Component mode. Exit the Edit Component mode. Now choose as many combinations of active layer radio buttons and Visible check boxes as you can. In each combination orbit around the cube and see if the entire cube is visible. This demonstrates what can happen if you spread primitives over more than Layer0.

2. Repeat this entire chapter several times until you can draw the tapered legs without referring to the text. Don't be satisfied with just drawing the legs correctly. Place them on the correct layer and name them appropriately. It won't take as long as you think, and as you do this you will begin to understand what each of the tools is accomplishing. Only when you have been successful drawing the legs on your own should you move on to Chapter 4.

3. As you move your mouse around a model you may see tooltip text and additional shapes added to the cursor such as a purple circle or dot. What is the name of the engine producing them and what is the purpose of this engine? Should you ignore it?

4. What are primitives? What happens when two primitives touch? How do I protect a set of primitives from another primitive(s)?

5. Which layer should be active when drawing a tapered leg?

6. What should a modeler do when a part first takes three-dimensional shape?

7. What does right clicking bring up in SketchUp?

8. To make changes to a component (or group) what must I do?

9. The VCB (Value Control Box) is context sensitive. What does that mean?

10. To change the Move tool to Move/Copy what keyboard key must I hit? What corresponding change takes place on the cursor?

# 04

# ADDING JOINERY

*In this second chapter of Part Two you learn to use the placement of existing components to aid in drawing joinery. A tenet of modeling in SketchUp is to never draw unless absolutely necessary; that's why the SketchUp team created the Component library and the Move/ Copy tool. Another tenet is: if you must draw, use the surrounding components to aid in sizing and placement of geometry. In this chapter you will learn several techniques to accomplish this.*

When we left Chapter 3 we had four tapered legs placed such that the tapers were always facing another leg or inward. All four legs were on the Legs layer. The front legs were Front Leg components and the back legs were Back Leg components. Hopefully you saved your work. If not, it is a good exercise to reproduce the same state of the model, on your own, without following the detailed steps. You can also find the Bedside Table SKP file at srww.com/sketchup_a_guide_for_woodworkers. html web page in the Downloads section under book Part 2, Chapter 4. This file was saved at the end of Chapter 3.

In either case let's open the drawing and pick up where we left off. So that we are viewing the same screen image go home. Confirm that the Layer0 radio button in the Layers dialog box is selected and check the Legs layer Visible box.

Throughout this text I will continually ask you to do more and more on your own; after all you are

learning. If at any point you think you are making a mistake in the middle of a tool operation, just hit *Esc* (Escape) on your keyboard and you will be placed back to the beginning of that operation. If you have completed an operation and made a mistake, use the Undo ↶ tool as many times as you need to get back to a place that is correct.

Recall earlier we said all four legs are all identical until we consider joinery; which is why we changed the left front leg and left back leg component names from Leg to Front Leg and Back Leg respectively. Well, we require mortises and dovetail sockets in the legs as you can see from **Figure 2** in Chapter 3, so we will soon need to take that into account. The front legs are the same component, but mirror images of one another; the back legs are the same components, but also mirror images of one another. We only need to modify one instance of a front or back leg. SketchUp will modify the remaining instances. Before adding the joinery let's place the components and parts that will be joined to the legs. You'll discover doing so helps to draw the joinery.

> When I am designing a new furniture piece I leave all joinery to the end of modeling, just before texturing, dimensioning and shop drawing creation (scene creation). This helps me focus on the function and form of the design, which is often an iterative process and creates numerous changes.

I assume you already have a copy of the completed BedsideTable.pdf printed out, or you can view it on your system. Before we begin modeling the aprons become familiar with their design and dimensions.

## DRAWING THE APRONS

Let's start with the back apron. It is 8¼" wide, ¾" thick and extends from the inside of one leg to the inside of the other. To draw this, choose the Rectangle tool. Click on the top left back corner of the Right Back Leg. Now drag the mouse to the back inside edge of the Left Back Leg staying on the nontapered portion of the edge. Click and read the VCB. One of the dimensions will be 15" (or 1' 3"), and it should be the first one. The other, the width of the rectangle, is meaningless and will likely begin with the tilde (~) symbol, meaning approximately. But we know that the width of the back apron is 8¼". So, before changing context (selecting another tool), type either 15,8.25, or just simply ,8.25 and *Enter*. There is not a typo in the text; ,8.25 is a shorthand way of telling the VCB that what is before the comma you wish to keep and you want to change what is after the comma to 8.25. If I wished to keep what is after the comma and change what is before it I would simply type the new value without a comma following it. The VCB is context sensitive and very helpful. Your picture should now look like that of **Figure 1**.

Now we need to set the apron face back from the leg faces by ⅛". Select the Move tool and place your

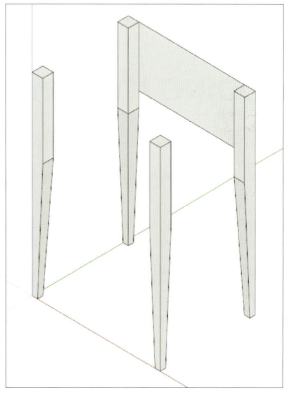

**Figure 1** | Rectangle forming the back apron

cursor over the apron face and notice that the face and edges are highlighted in blue. Click the apron face and drag it toward the middle of the front and back legs being sure the dotted green line appears indicting that you are moving the face parallel to the green axis. With the dotted green line still visible type ⅛ and *Enter*. This is a tricky move, so if it appears you got it wrong step back using the Undo tool and try again. You may want to zoom in close to be sure you didn't move the face into one of the legs. It should just touch both back legs. Now return to the home view.

We need to give the apron face thickness. Using the Push/Pull tool drag the face toward the center of the legs; type ¾ and *Enter*. Now we have a 3D shape. Following Rule 4 make this shape a component. I will describe how to do this one last time, but in the future I will assume you know how to make a component, give it a unique name, create a layer if necessary and place it there.

Click three times on the back apron with the Select tool and all faces and edges should be highlighted blue. Right click and choose Make Component. The Create Component dialog box appears; in the Name box type Back Apron, but do not hit *Enter* yet. Type a description for the component in the Description field if you desire. Make sure the "Replace selection with component" box is checked. Now press *Enter* or click Create.

In the Layers dialog box click on the Add Layer icon and a layer is added with a default name highlighted, probably Layer1. Type Aprons and *Enter*. Now, with the Back Apron component selected, in the Entity Info box with the Layer drop down choose Aprons. Also, since there is only one Back Apron in this design you can type Back Apron into the Name and *Enter*. It is not a problem that the Definition Name (component name) and Name of the instance are the same because, as we said, only one of these components is in the drawing. Also, SketchUp does not require all instance (part) names be unique, though we should always follow our self-imposed rule to make them unique.

Now I want you, on your own, to create and position the side aprons. They too will be 8¼" wide, ¾" thick and extend from the inside of one leg to the other. They will have a component name (Definition name in the Entity Info box) of Side Apron, and unique instance names of Right Side Apron and Left Side Apron. Both will exist on layer Aprons which already exists. I suggest you create one 3D shape first, make a component, place it on the appropriate layer and give it a unique instance (part) name. Then either with the Move/Copy tool, or by acquiring it from the Components dialog box, place it on the other side. Note, you are a little better off using the Move/Copy tool because when you copy a component, the copied component is on the same layer as the as the original. However, if you drag a component from the In Model library it will be on the layer it was on when created by the Create Component dialog box; in our case Layer0. If you use this latter technique you must add that instance to the Aprons layer. So go ahead and do this on your own.

OK, time's up! Did you remember to give both parts unique names? Did you remember to set both aprons in ⅛" from the leg faces? Your model should look like **Figure 2**, though without the multiple Entity Info boxes I superimposed so you can see the correct naming. If it does, you get an A+. If not, no problem – just start this chapter over.

You probably discovered a few differences in drawing the Side Apron(s) from the Back Apron. When you created the face of the apron and specified its width, you only needed to type 8.25 (or 8¼) instead of comma 8.25 (,8.25). Also, when giving the face thickness using the Push/Pull tool, you had to remain parallel to the red axis making sure to see the On Red Axis tool tip.

In this last part recall that when we drew the aprons we started with the Rectangle tool and used the legs to help us place the rectangle. The only dimension we really required was the width of the aprons and their thickness. The length of the aprons was supplied by the leg spacing. It will occur more frequently in our study that we can, and should, use available geometry to draw new geometry. This is the most efficient and usually the most error-free way to draw. Of course, if the legs are placed wrong, then everything that follows is likely to be wrong.

In this next section we will learn some new tools and techniques to help us follow these tenets.

## SKETCHUP MODELING TENETS

- Never draw unless absolutely necessary; that's why the SketchUp team created the Components library and the Move/Copy tool.

- If you must draw, use the surrounding components to aid in sizing and placement of geometry.

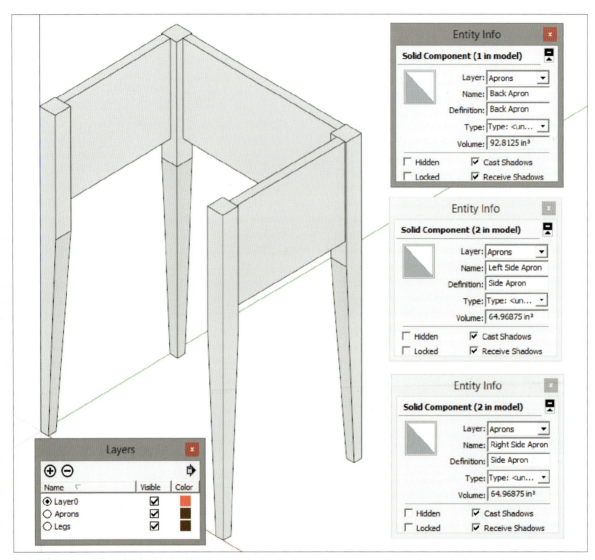

**Figure 2** | Aprons (sans tenons) added to model

## DRAWING THE TENONS

We will start with the tenon on the front surface (front end) of the Side Apron. Since the Right Side Apron and the Left Side Apron are both the same component, if we edit one, we will have edited both.

With the Select tool ↖ select the Right Side Apron and right click; choose Edit Component. Notice that the Right Side Apron is isolated with the dotted bounding box, and will remain so, until we click outside this bounding box with the Select tool. This lets us perform edits to the selected component without interference from other components, groups or primitives. However, editing this apron will be difficult with the legs obscuring it. Select menu View/Component Edit/Hide Rest Of Model. Don't confuse this tool with the context menu Edit Component, an unfortunate naming choice.

Now only the two side aprons are visible. We are going to use a new tool to help form the tenons. Our tenons will have a ¼" shoulder along the faces and a ½" shoulder on the top and bottom. Choose the Offset 🖎 tool and hover over the left front edge of the Right Side Apron. Note the blue dot highlighting, and the red square inference on the left edge. Click and move the cursor a little toward the center of the front face. Type ¼ and *Enter*. Now we have a box ¼" in from all edges. This is good for outlining the sides of the tenon, but we want the top and bottom to be ½" from the edge.

We will correct this using the Move ✤ tool. First, with the Select 🖈 tool select only the top line of the rectangle outlining the tenon. Then select the Move ✤ tool and move this line downward while making sure a blue dotted line appears (move along the blue axis) and remains while you type ¼ and *Enter*. This moves the top line down ¼" for a total of ½" from the top edge of the apron. Now choose the Select 🖈 tool and select only the bottom line of the rectangle outlining the tenon. Then select the Move ✤ tool and move this line upward while making sure a blue dotted line appears and remains while you type ¼ and *Enter*. Now the bottom edge of the tenon is ½" from the aprons edge.

In the above steps it is not necessary to use the Select tool to select the bottom and top lines; you can select them with the Move tool itself. Selecting them as we did will ensure the intended line is moved and not some other geometry. However, sometimes one forgets to select the next line or deselect the previous one and this can cause problems with subsequent operations.

The tenons need to be ⅞" long. Using the Push/Pull ✤ tool pull the tenon face to the left (toward you) and type ⅞ and *Enter*. Notice while you were doing all this editing on the Right Side Apron, the Left Side Apron was updated with the very same changes. This sure saves time and work, especially on a big model with lots of instances of the same component.

While the Right Side Apron is still in edit mode, click Back ⌂, Iso 🏵, Zoom Extents 🗙 tools to work on the back tenon. I leave it to the student to finish the edit for the back tenon. When done click outside the dotted box using the Select 🖈 tool and end component editing.

Using the same techniques place the tenons on the ends of the Back Apron. Use the Left (side) 🗄, Right (side) 🗄, Iso 🏵 and Zoom Extents 🗙 tools or Orbit ✦ and Zoom 🔎 tools to get useful views of your work area. When you have completed this task click Front ⇧, Iso 🏵 and Zoom Extents 🗙. In the Layers dialog box uncheck the Visible box for the Legs layer. Your model should now look like **Figure 3**.

As more components are added to the model, it will become harder to see what it is you are working on. You will find yourself having to zoom in and out for clarity. This means you and I may not be looking at the same picture all the time. It is important that we sync up on occasion before we get too far off track. But feel free to Zoom or Orbit in order to get a view that works for you.

## USING TENONS TO ADD MORTISES

Let's start putting the mortises in the front legs. I will describe the first one in detail and you will do the rest.

Recheck the Visible box for the Legs layer in the Layers dialog box. Using the Select 🖈 tool, select the Right Front Leg, right click and choose Edit Component. If you have View/Component Edit/Hide Rest Of Model or View/Component Edit/Hide Similar Components checked, uncheck both now so that the whole model is visible. Now we will use another new and powerful technique. Turn on the Wireframe view by clicking the Wireframe 🖲 tool. Click the Back ⌂, Iso 🏵 and Zoom Extents 🗙 icons. You should now have a view similar to **Figure 4**.

Note, in this view I used Wireframe 🖲 tool to get an image that gave me the clearest view of the tenon.

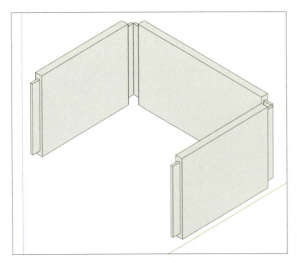

**Figure 3** | Legs layer is invisible, exposing the tenons

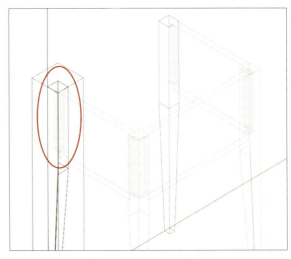

**Figure 4** | Apron and leg with X-ray and Wireframe

You can try the X-ray ⬭ tool and see if that works for you, but I find the Wireframe ⬭ tool to be the clearest approach.

> Depending on your system, monitor and template (material colors used as default) you may have to experiment with Wireframe ⬭, X-Ray ⬭, Back Edges ⬭ and Monochrome ⬭ to get a good picture. Also using the Orbit ⬭ tool to rotate the image a little can sometimes help. Experiment with these tools to see what works best for you.

Using the mouse wheel or the Zoom 🔍 tool zoom in to the area outlined in **Figure 4**. Using the Line ✏ tool we are going to trace the entire tenon. Throughout this trace, we must be sure to remain in the Edit Component mode. All lines we draw will be part of the Front Leg component. OK, let's trace the tenon where it enters the leg.

In **Figure 5** I have traced the tenon where I want you to trace it and I have selected the trace so it is highlighted in blue to make it visible. Don't worry too much if you can't see the lines you are drawing. They are difficult to see with all the features we are using

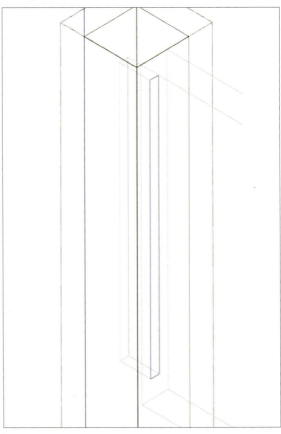

**Figure 5** | Tenon traced for mortise entry and highlighted

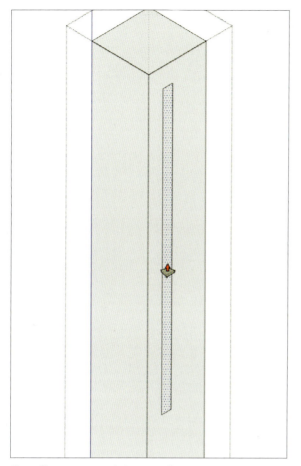

**Figure 6** | Preparing to Push the mortise face in

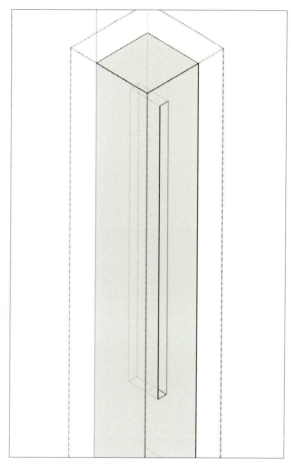

**Figure 7** | Mortise with Back Edges in Component Edit mode

turned on. When you have completed the outline check menu View/Component Edit/Hide Rest Of Model. You should now clearly see the mortise outline you just created. If not, uncheck menu View/Component Edit/Hide Rest Of Model and try again.

Click on Back Edges ⬠ and Shaded ◖. Choose the Push/Pull ✦ tool and hover over the face of the leg inside the traced rectangle. See **Figure 6**. Click and push the face into the leg. Now type ⅞ and press *Enter*.

Your model should now look like **Figure 7**. With the Select ➤ tool click outside the bounding box to exit Component Edit mode and also turn off Back Edges ⬠ view. Make the aprons invisible by

unchecking the Visible check box for the Aprons layer in the Layers dialog box. You may need to switch back to Shaded ◖ view if you switched to one of the others. Notice we have the appropriate mortise in both front legs.

I wish to digress a little here to explain what can happen if back in Chapter 3 we used several methods to place our legs, and several places to acquire them from. Suppose we drew one tapered leg and made it a component, and further suppose that we got the other tapered legs in different manners, for example: dragged one from the Components In Model library and used the Rotate ⟳ tool to mirror it; copied one with the Move/ Copy ✦ tool and mirrored it with the Rotate ⟳

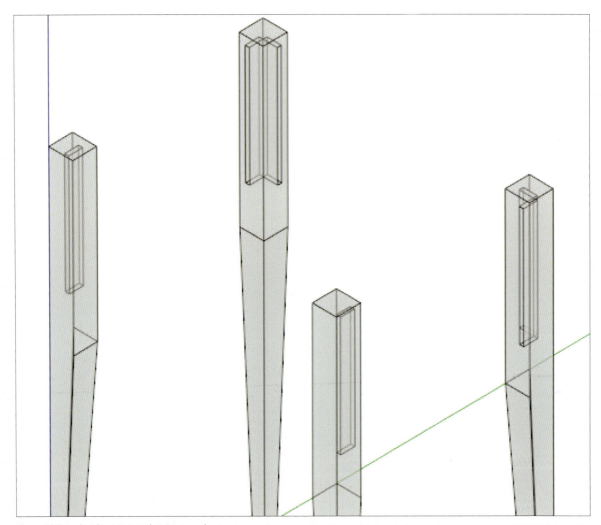

**Figure 8** | Completed mortises with X-Ray turned on

tool; copied another with the Move/Copy ✦ tool and used the Flip Along tool to mirror it.

After doing this and then editing one front leg to add the mortise perhaps the other front leg ended up with the mortise on the wrong side or position. This is a situation that cannot be fixed with a simple rotate or mirror. Don't panic. This is a result of mixing strategies for placing legs. Simply delete the bad leg. Copy a good one and place it where the deleted leg was and use Flip Along tool to mirror it. Fix the instance (part) Name and you are done.

Enough regressing; the student is now directed to complete the mortises in the back legs using this same technique. Don't forget to use the tips outlined in the shaded box on page 78. Also, make use of the View/Component Edit/Hide Rest Of Model as needed. And you might try using the Rectangle ▨ tool in place of the Line ✎ tool to trace the tenons.

OK, times up. I have mine completed. How about you? Does your model look like **Figure 8**? Note the X-ray ◈ tool is used to expose the mortises.

## DRAWING DOVETAIL SOCKETS

Let's draw the dovetail socket in the Left Front Leg's top. If you have either X-ray 📄 or Back Edges 📄 selected, deselect them at this time. Select the Shaded 📄 view. Go to the home view and zoom in to the Left Front Leg's top. We will draw the dovetail socket in the component edit mode and use the Tape Measure 🖉 tool to help outline the dovetail. Look at **Figure 9** to see what we are trying to accomplish. The dovetail is going to be hand cut in the real piece, and if you are like me I need to draw its outline on my stock; so I will give the outline dimensions I would use as we go along.

Select the Left Front Leg and enter the Edit Component mode (I assume you know how to use the Select tool by now, so I won't give you guidance or provide the icon anymore). Select the Tape Measure 🖉 tool and click on the top right front corner of the Left Front Leg. Move the Tape Measure tool up and to the right so that you are moving along the Green axis. Make sure you see the + sign in the cursor indicating you are about to add a construction line. Type ⅝ and *Enter*. (See side bar concerning construction lines.)

Start at the same corner, do the same thing and this time type 1 and *Enter*. Now you have placed two

construction lines with end points along the top right side edge of the Left Front Leg at ⅝" in and 1" in from the top right front corner.

We will now use the Protractor 📐 tool to place 14° from normal construction lines. Choose the Protractor 📐 tool and start at the closest construction point. The protractor should be blue when hovering over this point; move the cursor slightly until it is blue and click on the nearest construction point. Move the cursor to the lower left along the Green axis (in the direction of the top right front corner of the leg) and click. Rotate the protractor clockwise to nearly 90°. Type 76 and *Enter*. You should now have a construction line that is 14° from normal. Actually, you should have two construction lines, because a second line was automatically placed on the other Front Leg component.

Perform the same operation with the Protractor 📐 tool; this time click on the 1" construction point, move the cursor along the green axis toward the back corner and click, rotate the cursor counterclockwise to nearly 90°, type 76 and *Enter*. Now you will have 4 construction lines; two for the Left Front Leg and two for the Right Front Leg, which SketchUp adds to keep that instance up to date with the one being edited. Ignore those and stay focused on the Left Front Leg.

We want a construction line parallel to the edge with the construction points but ¾" in. Using the Tape Measure 🖉 tool move along the top right side edge, the edge with the construction points, until you get a tool tip that says Midpoint, click, then move the cursor to the upper left along the red axis, type ¾ and press *Enter*. Now we are going to connect the dots. Choose the Line 🖉 tool. Start at the ⅝" construction point and click. Move the cursor left where the dotted construction lines cross and a tool tip says "Intersection", click again. Move to the right to where the construction lines cross again with the tool tip indicating Intersection, and click again. Finally, move down and right to the 1" construction point where the tool tip says Guide Point, and click. Now you will see a face the shape of the dovetail, shown in **Figure 9**.

The dovetail socket is ¾" deep. Use the Push/Pull 📦 tool to move the face down ¾" creating a socket. By now you should know how to do this.

---

📁 **WHEN IS A CONSTRUCTION LINE A CONSTRUCTION LINE?**

When you can hover the Line tool over a construction line and see an On Line tool tip, the line is in fact a construction line. However, when you click once on the endpoints of an edge (or line) with the Tape Measure tool, and then extend a line and click a second time to terminate it at another point; you get a Tracer line terminated with a Construction Point. The Tracer line may look like a construction line but test it with the Line tool. You will not get an Inference Engine tool tip except at the Construction Point terminating it.

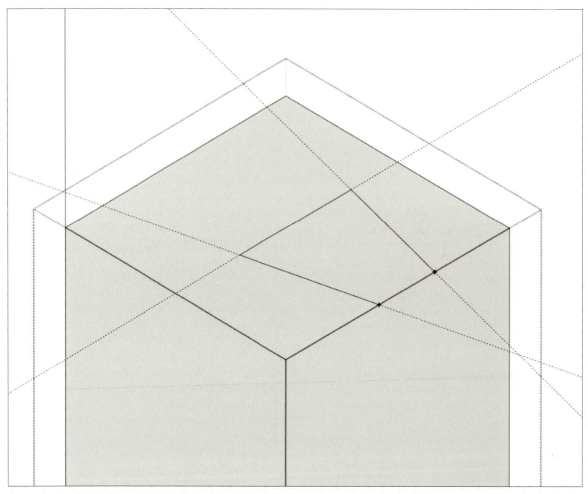

**Figure 9** | Dovetail-shaped face outlined by edge and construction lines

Click outside the dotted box with the select tool to exit the Edit Component mode. Use menu Edit/Delete Guides to delete the construction lines and points. Zoom out and have a look at what you have. Notice that SketchUp placed the dovetail correctly in the Right Front Leg. That is because we used the Move/Copy ✤ and Flip Along tools to place and mirror it. Since these legs are indeed mirror images of one another in the real world, we chose the right SketchUp tools and saved ourselves a lot of work.

There is one more mortise to place in the front legs. It starts 6½" from the top, ⅜" in from the front, ⅞" in from the back, ends 8" down from the top and is ¼" wide and ⅞" deep. Refer to **Figure 2** in Chapter 3 for help. The student can use what he/she has learned so far to complete the legs. Don't forget to enter Edit Component mode before you begin your edits. Your finished picture should look like **Figure 1** in Chapter 5. In Chapter 5 we will draw the front rails, stiles and top.

## CHAPTER REVIEW

We began this chapter with four tapered legs of two component types: Back Leg and Front Leg. Our task was to draw all the required mortises in Edit Component mode. To do this we let the spacing of the legs define the length of the aprons and also aid us in drawing rectangles using the Rectangle ▨ tool that were the aprons' face.

We then set the faces in ⅛" using the Move ✥ tool and gave the aprons thickness using the Push/Pull ✦ tool. To complete the aprons we used context menu Make Component and named them with the Create Component dialog box.

Next, in Edit Component mode we used a new tool, Offset 🔥, to create tenon outlines and modified them with the Move ✥ tool. With the Push/Pull ✦ tool we extruded the tenons.

To create the mortises in the legs we made use of the Wireframe ◈ view and the Line ✏ tool. This technique follows from a major SketchUp modeling tenet: If you must draw, use the surrounding components to aid in sizing and placement of geometry. To assist in getting the best view and rendering we introduced the Left ⬛, Right ⬛, Pan ✋, Wireframe ◈, Hidden Edges ◇ and Monochrome ◕ tools and views.

To draw dovetail sockets we first used the Tape Measure tool to place some guide (or construction) points. We learned to use a new tool, Protractor ⌀. With it we provided ourselves construction lines 14° from normal to the right top side edge of the Left Front Leg. With the Tape Measure ⌀ tool we drew a parallel construction line which completed the outline of the socket. From there it was a simple matter of drawing the socket with the Line ✏ tool and finally forming it with the Push/Pull ✦ tool.

The student was given homework to draw the last mortise on his/her own. I will grade the student's assignment in Chapter 5.

In this chapter we introduced the following new tools listed in the order they were used:
🔥 Offset
⬛ Left
⬛ Right
✋ Pan
◈ Wireframe
◈ Back Edges
◕ Monochrome
⌀ Protractor

We also used the Tape Measure ⌀ tool to form construction lines and points.

## EXERCISES FOR THE STUDENT

1. We used the Offset 🔥 tool to form the tenon's outline on the end of an apron prior to using the Push/Pull ✦ tool to extrude it. But we needed to move two lines to complete the outline of the tenon. See if you can do the same thing using only the Move/Copy ✥ tool and the Eraser ✏ tool. Also see if you can do it using only the Tape Measure ⌀ tool and the Line ✏ or Rectangle ▨ tool. There are many more ways; be creative.

2. We used the Protractor ⌀ tool to form a 14° from normal construction line. 14° is approximately the angle you get from a rise-to-run ratio of 1:4. When cutting dovetails in the shop we often use ratios to determine the angle for tails or pins. Use the Protractor ⌀ tool to form a construction line through the origin such that the angle between the Red axis and the construction line has a rise to run of 1:4. Hint: Instead of typing the number of degrees into the VCB type 1:4. Measure the angle with the Protractor ⌀.

3. What are two ways to use the Tape Measure ⌀ tool?

4. When the Protractor ⌀ tool's cursor is held over a surface it will turn red, green, blue or black. What does the color indicate?

5. Why is it easier to use Wireframe ◈ view rather than X-Ray ◈ or Back Edges ◈ when using one part to construct another?

# 05

# USING JOINERY TO DEFINE PARTS

*In this chapter you will learn to use the placement of existing components and their joinery to aid in drawing parts. This is just the opposite of what we did in Chapter 4. This chapter builds on SketchUp's second tenet: if you must draw, use the surrounding components to aid in sizing and placement of geometry. In this chapter you will learn a few more techniques to accomplish this.*

At the end of Chapter 4, you were given a homework assignment. Open your copy of Bedside Table SketchUp file and compare your model to **Figure 1**. They should be the same. If so, you get a grade of A+. If not, you have some debugging to do. Review your steps and compare them to the steps we used in Chapter 4. If you still need help I am always available via email. Check my web site for contact information.

Before going any further with drawing you need to learn about a feature called Scenes. A friend of mine, who was also a reviewer of this text during its writing, pointed out that if I taught this feature early on there would be no need to continually instruct the student "click Front ⬆, Iso ❤ and Zoom Extents ✖ in that order." I am sure the student is tired of hearing this too. In Chapter 3, I told you to equate the instruction "go home" to "click Front ⬆, Iso ❤ and Zoom Extents ✖." Now we will create a Scene called Home View and in the future when I say something like "go home" it will mean to click the Home View scene tab to resync our views.

First we need to use the old definition of "go home" one more time. Open your model to where we left off in Chapter 4. Make the Aprons and Legs layer visible. Now go home. Under the Window menu choose Scenes and the Scenes dialog box will appear. In the upper left corner click Add Scene ⊕. A warning box may appear. If so, choose the radio button Save As New Style, and click Create Scene. Right click on the new scene (which is likely called Scene 1 if no other scenes have been created) and choose Rename Scene. In the Name box type Home View and press *Enter*. Check all the boxes under Properties to save. You will learn more about Scenes later when we create shop drawings, but for now checking all the options will serve our purpose. You can close the Scenes box to unclutter your screen. You should see a Tab in the top left corner of your drawing labeled Home View. If it is not there look at menu View/Scene Tabs and be sure it is checked. Right click on the Home View scenes tab and choose Update. Your model should look similar to **Figure 1**.

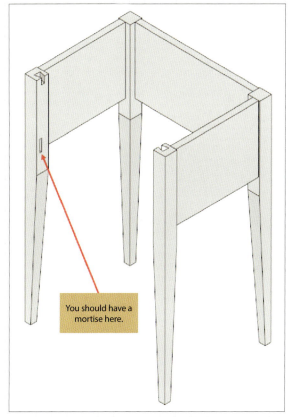

You should have a mortise here.

**Figure 1** | You should have placed a mortise in the Front Leg component

Let's see how this works. Using the Orbit ✛ and Zoom 🔍 tools rotate your view to a random position and zoom way out so the picture is small. Now click the Home View tab and see what happens. It returns you to our home view with some animation thrown in. Pretty cool!

One last comment before proceeding with drawing: The primary purpose of this book is for you to learn SketchUp. I assume you are doing that. I have been handholding you up to this point by giving you step-by-step explicit instructions and even including tool icons for easy reference. From this point forward I will drop some explicit instructions and tool icons where I feel you should have a good grasp of them. If you are confused about a tool or its icon, return to Chapter 2, "Selecting & Using Tools" to review its use.

## DRAWING A RAIL WITH A TAIL

OK, go home! Good, that was easy eh? Let's add the Upper Drawer Rail. **Figure 2** shows the Upper Drawer Rail with dimensions.

Looking at **Figure 2**, you can visually break this rail into three pieces: the middle, which is a simple right rectangular prism with dimensions 15" long by 1 ⅜" wide by 1 ¼" thick, and two dovetails. (OK, what is a right rectangular prism? That is the correct name for a 3D object with nonequal edges but all right angle corners. I am going to call it a cube even though a cube is technically six equal right faces.) Before we draw this you need one more piece of information. Recall from earlier chapters that we set the aprons in ⅛". This is to create a shadow line, which gives the table depth and character. Truth be told, it also makes it easier for the craftsman because making perfectly flush joints is not easy. Both the Upper Drawer Rail and the Lower Drawer Rail will be set in ⅛".

Now we can draw the Upper Drawer Rail. You have already learned enough to do this on your own. However, in case you need a refresher, I am going to provide detailed instructions on this first rail. Pay close attention as the Lower Drawer Rail is yours to do on your own.

We are going to do this a little different than we did in previous chapters. It's not that what we did before was wrong or inefficient, but I want to expose you to a number of methods. First, let's create a construction point for reference. Using the Tape Measure tool, click on the top right front corner of the Left Front Leg. You may have to zoom in to get a good working view. Now move the cursor along the top right front edge of the leg, making sure the green Inference Engine line remains indicating you are moving parallel to the green axis and type ⅛ and *Enter*. A construction point is added ⅛" in from the top right front corner of the Left Front Leg.

I am going to pause here again to introduce a new tool that will help when trying to move the cursor in a direction parallel to one of the axes. Let's undo what we just did by using Undo tool or menu Edit/Delete Guides. Now, using the Tape Measure tool, click on the top right front corner of the Left Front Leg. Press

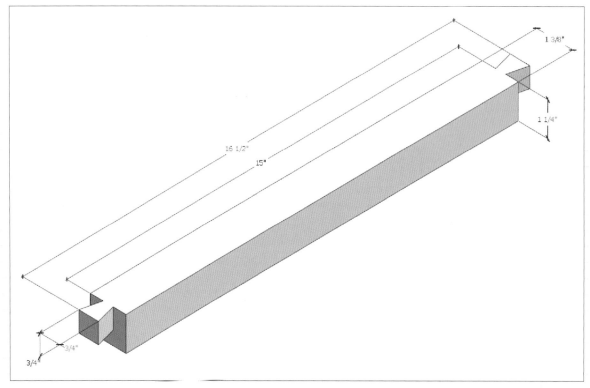

**Figure 2** | Detail of the Upper Drawing Rail

the left arrow key on the keyboard and let it go. Now move your cursor along an extended line of the edge and you will see that you are locked-on-parallel to the Green axis. Now type ⅛ and *Enter*; you again have the construction point. Press the left arrow key again to release the lock. This locking feature works with all appropriate tools – the Line tool, for example.

The arrow keys can be used to lock the cursor's movement along a line parallel to an axis. The left arrow key locks the Green axis, the up or down arrow key locks the Blue axis, and the right arrow key locks the Red axis. Press the appropriate arrow key once to lock and again to unlock. This locking feature works with all appropriate tools such as Line and Move tools.

Back to work. Go home. Using the Rectangle tool click on the origin (where the Red, Blue and Green axes cross). If the Legs layer is visible, you will see an Inference Engine tool tip that says "Endpoint in Component" instead of "Origin." Drag a rectangle any size and click. Now type 15,1⅜ and *Enter*. Using the Push/Pull tool select the face of this rectangle and pull it up and type 1¼ and *Enter*. Remember Rule 4: using the Select tool click three times on the part we just created. Context (right) click and choose Make Component. In the Create Component Name box type Upper Drawer Rail and *Enter*. Under the Window menu select Entity Info (the Entity Info dialog box may already be open). In the Entity Info Name box type Upper Drawer Rail. Recall Rule 5. We need to create a Rails layer. Under the Window menu choose Layers and the Layers dialog box opens. Click the Add Layer ⊕ icon in the Layers dialog box; type Rails in the highlighted layer name box and

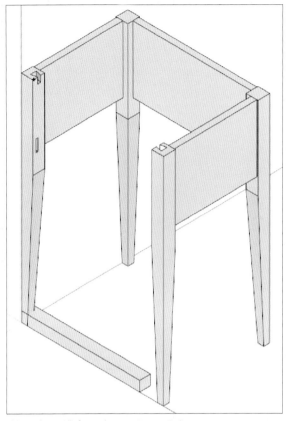

**Figure 3** | Partially formed Upper Drawer Rail

*Enter.* We now have a Rails layer. With the Upper Drawer Rail still selected, go to the Entity Info dialog box. In the Layer drop down box choose Rails.

To validate what we have done, deselect the Upper Drawer Rail component and select any leg. Notice the Entity Info dialog box now shows the Legs layer. Reselect the Upper Drawer Rail and it should show Rails for Layer, and Upper Drawer Rail for both Name and Definition. We gave this part the same Name and Definition name because there is only one instance of it in this model. If there were a right and left, or back and front instances we would have given them unique Name entries in Entity Info.

All of this naming and making components may seem like an awful lot of extra work, but believe me, if we were working on a complex model, this practice would pay off big time. So get in the habit of doing

it all the time. Develop and keep a good working practice and you will become much faster and create far fewer errors in your modeling.

OK, go home. Deselect Upper Drawer Rail and now your model should look like **Figure 3**. Let's look at this picture for a while. What we are going to do next is move the partially formed Upper Drawer Rail into position with the aid of the Move tool and the construction point we created a while back. Then we are going to complete the rail in Edit Component mode. Because we followed the Rules for 3D Modeling in SketchUp throughout this book, we had no problems with the partially formed Upper Drawer Rail sticking to the Left Front Leg while it was in primitive form, because all other parts were components and hence protected from sticking.

Select the partial Upper Drawer Rail with the Select tool. This step is not usually necessary, however, the rail is overlapping the leg and to avoid accidentally moving the leg we will first select the rail. Next, select the Move tool and click on the left top front corner of the rail. Drag it to the construction point we placed on the top of the Left Front Leg. You may find it necessary to zoom in quite a bit to see the construction point clearly. A Guide Point Inference Engine tooltip will appear; click on it. These tooltips tell you when you are precisely on a point and are very helpful.

You may have found it necessary to zoom in to accomplish this last step. In any case, you are sure to have to zoom in for the next step. With the rail still selected right click on it and choose Edit Component. You shouldn't need X-Ray view for this step. Zoom in on the area of the dovetail socket in the Left Front Leg. If you have been doing the Student Exercises at the end of each chapter, you may have already figured out that all we need to trace here is the top three socket lines on the leg. Do so using the Line tool. Notice the moment you finish the third line a face appears in the shape of a dovetail. Choose menu View/Component Edit/Hide Rest Of Model. Your model should look like **Figure 4**.

Notice the bounding box in **Figure 4** indicating you are still in Edit Component mode. You have two options at this point for completing the dovetail. If you remember that the dovetail is ¾" thick you can

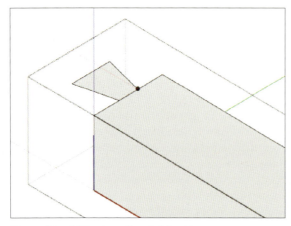

**Figure 4** | Dovetail face traced from Left Front Leg

use the Push/Pull tool to drag its face down ¾" and *Enter*. But suppose you can't remember the dimension. In that case, uncheck menu View/Component Edit/ Hide Rest Of Model. To make things easier to see choose Hidden Line ▱ and Back Edges ◈. Now with the Push/Pull tool, hover over the dovetail face and drag it down to the bottom of the socket in the Left Front Leg and click. Hint: click on an intersection point at the bottom of the dovetail socket in the leg. Deselect Back Edges ◈ and go back to Shaded ▱ view. Also choose menu View/Component Edit/Hide Rest Of Model. Now your model should looks as shown in **Figure 5**.

Notice we have an unwanted line, that is, the shortest line on the top surface of the rail forming the narrow neck of the dovetail. This line is unnecessary because the top surface of the dovetail and the partial rail are the same surface and should not be divided. Select the Eraser tool and remove it while still in Edit Component mode.

Now add the dovetail to the other end of the Upper Drawer Rail. When you are done exit Edit Component mode and click the Home View tab. Choose menu Edit/Delete Guides to delete the guide point we placed.

Notice that in the Home View that the Upper Drawer Rail shows up even though it and its layer, Rails, never existed when we defined the Home View Scene. This is a helpful feature at this point, but we will see it is a curse when we create shop drawings. It is a

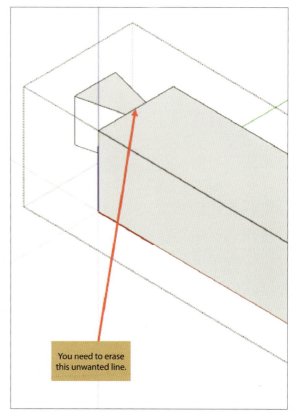

You need to erase this unwanted line.

**Figure 5** | Formed dovetail, but with an unwanted line

result of how the Add Layer ⊕ tool in the Layers dialog box works. But don't worry; we have a fix for it in the form of a Ruby script, which I will introduce later.

## DRAWING A RAIL WITH A CURVE

OK, you are on your own for the Lower Drawer Rail. **Figure 6** shows the Lower Drawer Rail with its dimensions. Follow the same strategy used for the Upper Drawer Rail; that is, break the rail down into three pieces: two tenons and a partial rail. Also, don't worry about the curved portion yet. Treat the partial rail as a cube 15" long by ¾" wide by 2" high. I am not going to give you the dimensions of the tenons because the tenants you learned for drawing in SketchUp do that for you. At this point you've done this a few times and should know this by now. However, I will tell you that the Lower Drawer Rail is

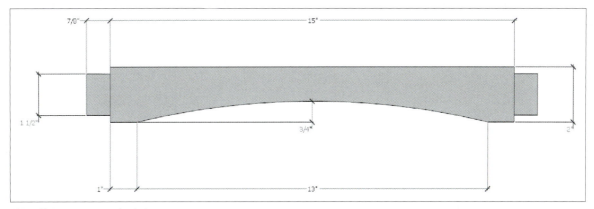

**Figure 6** | Lower Drawer Rail with dimensions

set in ⅛" just like the other rail and aprons. The top of the rail is positioned 6¼" down from the top of the Front Leg components. When you are done exit Edit Component mode and click the Home View tab. Choose menu Edit/Delete Guides to delete any guide points you may have placed. Go!

OK, I'm done. How about you? Here is what I did. First I used the Tape Measure tool to drop a construction point 6¼" down from the top right front corner of the Left Front Leg. With the Rectangle tool and starting at the construction point, I drew a rectangle 15" long and 2" wide; the rectangle stretched 15" between the inside edges of the front legs and 2" downward from my construction point. With the select tool I selected the face and perimeter of the rectangle and moved it back ⅛" with the Move tool. Then, using the Push/Pull tool, I dragged that face ¾" back to give it thickness. At this point Rule 4 kicked in and I created a component called Lower Drawer Rail. And then Rule 5: I already had a Rails layer so I just placed the partial lower rail on it.

Then I began editing the Lower Drawer Rail in Edit Component mode. I traced both mortises' rectangles at the point of entry into the legs and used the Push/Pull tool to give them a length equal to the depth of the mortises in the legs; ⅞". When finished I exited Edit Component mode, cleaned up my guide point and selected Home View tab. Along the way, while editing the Lower Drawer Rain in Edit Component mode, I made judicious use of the X-Ray, Back

Edges, Hidden Line, Shaded and View/Component Edit/Hide Rest Of Model commands and tools.

I haven't mentioned Rule 1 in quite a while, but you can bet your last doughnut that I use it all the time. This advice applies not only to SketchUp, but to any application you might use for any kind of work: Save your work frequently, don't depend on the backup file that is created automatically.

**Figure 7** shows an X-ray view of the incomplete Lower Drawer Rail. This is exactly what you did, right? You remembered all the rules and proceeded like a pro. If your model looks exactly like **Figure 7** – Great! You get an A+.

The curve in the lower rail requires the use of a new tool called the 2-Point Arc ✐ tool. The arc will start 1" in from each side of the main part of the rail (not the tenons). Refer to **Figure 6**. The arc is ¾" tall. We are going to modify, or edit, the Lower Drawer Rail. If you are using X-ray de-select it and go home. Uncheck the Visible box for the Legs and Aprons layers in the Layers dialog box. Now select the Front view and Zoom Extents. With the Pan ✇ tool pan up a little to center the lower rail. Select the Lower Drawer Rail and enter Edit Component mode.

Use the Tape Measure tool to place a construction point 1" in from the sides of the main lower rail (ignore tenons) at the bottom edge. Refer to **Figure 6**. Select the 2-Point Arc ✐ tool. Click on each of the two construction points, the order does not matter. Drag the mouse up a little and you will see an arch formed and the tooltip On Face. Type ¾ and *Enter*.

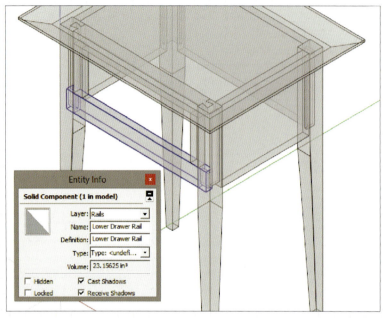

**Figure 7** | Lower Drawer Rail sans curve

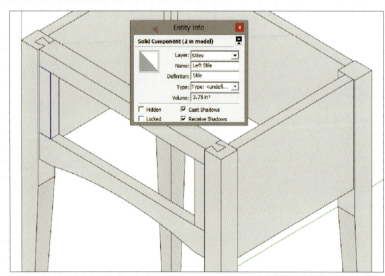

**Figure 8** | Finished Lower Drawer Rail and Stiles

Now, you may want to use the Iso view to make this next step more visible. With the Push/Pull tool move the undesired (lower) portion of the arched face back until it disappears; you should see a tool tip "Offset limited to -¾"." Now click. If it didn't disappear don't

panic; just type ¾ and type *Enter*. That will fix it. Now exit Edit Component mode. Pretty nice, huh? Use Edit/Delete Guides to clean up the model.

OK, go home. There are two stiles that go between the rails and up against the legs to finish framing the drawer opening. They are simple cubes, no joinery. In the real world these stiles are held in with glue and pocket screw joinery. Their dimensions are 5" long by 1" wide by ¾" thick. Their orientation is obvious from **Figure 8**. The student is left to create and place them in the model. Put them on a Stiles layer. Note the Definition Name and instance (part) Name shown in the Entity Info box in **Figure 8**.

## USING THE LEGS TO MODEL THE TOP

OK, let's get back together and put the top on. Then we can call it a day for this chapter. The top is ¾" thick. It overhangs the legs by 2½". It is tapered to lighten its look and the tapers begin ¼" down from the top. They extend in 2" leaving a perimeter of ¾" thick material extending out ½" all around the legs. That is a little confusing, but it will become clear as we proceed. **Figure 9** will also provide some clarity.

Using Rectangle tool, click on the top outermost corner of one leg, then drag to the diagonally opposite outside most corner and click again. A face is formed; its dimensions are that of the table footprint. Double click the center of this face; the face and its edges are selected.

A little regression here to point out something. If you want to select a primitive, for example a line or a face, click the desired primitive once. If you want to select a primitive and its connected primitives, for example a face and its edges, click the primitive twice. If you want to select all faces and edges of a 3D object that is not a component or group – for example, a cube or a tapered leg – click the object three times. If the object is a group or component, you only need to click it once – unless you are inside an Edit mode box, in which case, follow the one or two or three click rule. The speed at which you click will have an effect, but you will get the hang of it quickly.

If you want to select all faces and edges of a group or component, click three times anywhere on the object. This not only selects the faces and edges, but also places the group or component in Edit mode. OK, that's all clear – right?

Using the Offset ⟋ tool click on the selected face near an edge and drag it outward, type 2.5 and *Enter*. The inner rectangle and face should still be highlighted. Press the *Delete* key. If the inner rectangle and face are not selected click twice in the middle of the top to select them and press *Delete*.

Now using the Push/Pull tool hover over the top face; it will turn blue dots. Click and pull it upward with the Push/Pull tool, type ¼ and *Enter*. Using the Select tool, select the top face and edges by double clicking. Using the Offset ⟋ tool, click on the face near an edge, but this time drag inward. Type 2 and *Enter*.

Use the Line tool to add four lines each connecting a corner of the large top rectangle to its nearest corner of the small top rectangle. With the Select tool, select the inner most rectangle's edges and face by double clicking on its face. Your model should appear as shown in **Figure 10**.

Select the Move tool, click in the middle of the face, drag upward and notice that you can easily distort the symmetry by moving up and to the side.

**Figure 9** | Detail of the Top and its taper

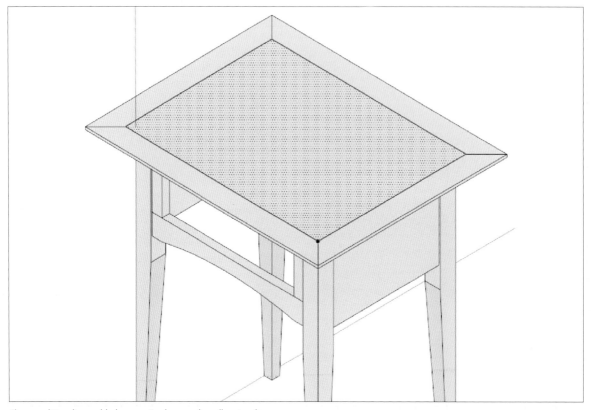

**Figure 10** | Four lines added connecting large and small rectangles

Do not click but press the *Up* (or *Down*) arrow key and now move the cursor and notice it is locked to the blue axis. Type ½ and press *Enter*. Press *Esc* (Escape) to release the blue axis lock or press the *Up* (or *Down*) arrow key again.

Great, we have a tapered top, but it is upside down. That's not exactly what we want. To turn it over, select all faces and edges of the top using the Select tool and triple click rather quickly. Right click on the top and choose Flip Along/Blue Direction. If you're paying close attention, you may have noticed that this time the Flip Along options were Red Direction, Green Direction and Blue Direction; not Component's Red, Component's Green or Components Blue. This is a subtle reminder that the entities being mirrored, or flipped, are not yet a component. You might also ask how I knew it was the Blue Direction we wanted, since we didn't perform a move to give us

a hint. Simple: Since we want to mirror the top, select the color of the axis normal to it.

While the top is still selected, right click again and choose Make Component. Name it Top. Create a Top layer. In the Entity Info box select Top layer and type Top for Name. Go Home.

The Top may now be a little out of the picture since it wasn't in the model when we defined the Scene Home View. Click Zoom Extents. Right click on the Home View Scene tab and choose Update. This will update the scene to include the entire table in the future.

Select Front view and Zoom Extents. Your model should look as shown in **Figure 11**. I have superimposed the Entity Info box for the Top. Notice the naming. We will save the drawer sliders for Chapter 6 where we will model the drawer. Oh, one last thing. Save your work now!

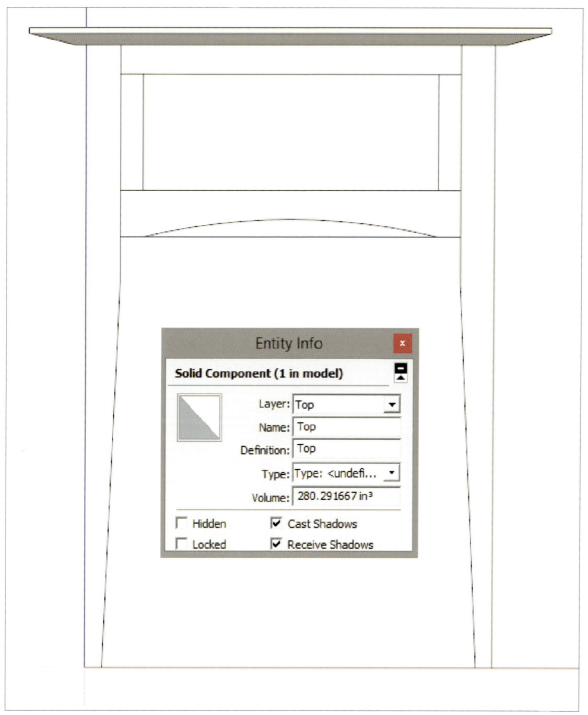

**Figure 11** | Top added to table with the aid of the legs spacing

## CHAPTER REVIEW

In this chapter you were introduced to Scenes as a way to define a home position or view. We will use Scenes much more when we get into dimensioning. The current method we use for adding layers will provide untold frustration when we generate Scenes for dimensioning. But have no fear; there is a Ruby script that will save the day. You also learned to Update a Scene.

In this chapter I took your training wheels away in the form of less step-by-step instruction and fewer tool icons. With the repetition of their use, you should be coming familiar with most of the tools we have used thus far.

You learned a number of techniques for completing parts with the aid of their mating joinery. For example, we formed a tail on a rail from a dovetail socket in a leg. This is as opposed to creating joinery from an already completed part. For example, we modeled the mortise in a leg with the aid of a completed apron's tenon.

Another tool was introduced, the 2-Point Arc ⬭ tool. This is the beginning of modeling furniture with shapes other than linear. We will do much more of that in advanced chapters in Part Three. And we will use curves far more complex than arcs and circles.

Finally, we learned that sometimes it is easier to draw a part in an inverted or mirrored fashion if the existing geometry provides us with help. Such was the case with the top. The legs spacing, the Offset tool and the Push/Pull cried out "Use me, use me, use me!" Be alert to such opportunities to save drawing. Flipping or mirroring is easy.

In this chapter we introduced the following new tools listed in the order they were used:
⬭2-Point Arc

We also used Scenes dialog box and Add Scene ⊕ to produce a Home View we could return to easily without using multiple Camera tools.

## EXERCISES FOR THE STUDENT

1. When completing the Upper Drawer Rail by tracing three lines on the dovetail socket in the Left Front Leg and using Push/Pull to form the dovetail, we were left with an unwanted line. We erased it using the Eraser tool. Try erasing it immediately prior to the Push/Pull and see what happens.

2. The 2-Point Arc ⬭ tool was used to form a curve in the Lower Drawer Rail. Is it really a curve? Look close. Read the sections labeled "Circle Tool" and "2-Point Arc Tool" in the "Tool Icons" section of Chapter 2.

3. Create two more Scenes, one called Front and one called Side. These should show the entire front view including all layers and similarly the entire side view. Experiment with these Scenes by varying the combination of checked and unchecked Visible boxes in the Layers dialog box; don't forget to use the Update function to save changes.

4. I modeled the top upside down and then used the Flip Along tool to right it. Try modeling it right side from the start and see if it is easier or harder.

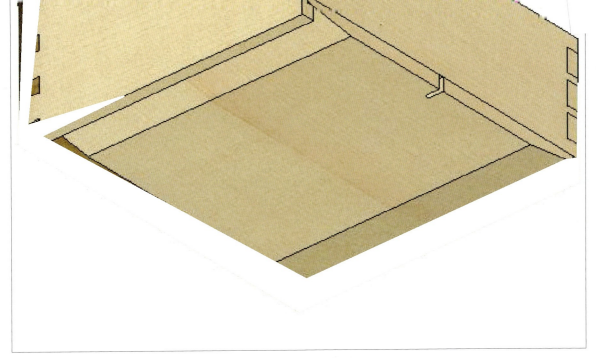

**Figure 2** | Traditional drawer bottom view

bottom edge, and is ¼" wide and ¼" deep. It will be clear later that this will provide a ¼" clearance between the bottom side of the bottom and the bottom edge of the sides.

## The Back

The back is usually ¾" narrower than the side width, allowing for the bottom to extend under it to its back side. You can see this in **Figure 2**. Note that this side has three tails in the front and three tails in the back. However these sets of tails are not the same width. The front tails are evenly and symmetrically spaced. The back tails are all the same width but biased toward the top of the side. In addition to the three tails there is a ¾" square tail on the bottom edge. The reason for this will become clear later.

The length of the back and front are determined by the opening width. I like to leave ⅟₃₂" to ⅟₁₆" on both sides for clearance. If there were no cock beading on this draw I would leave ⅟₃₂" on each side or ⅟₁₆" overall making the drawer front length the opening width minus ⅟₁₆".

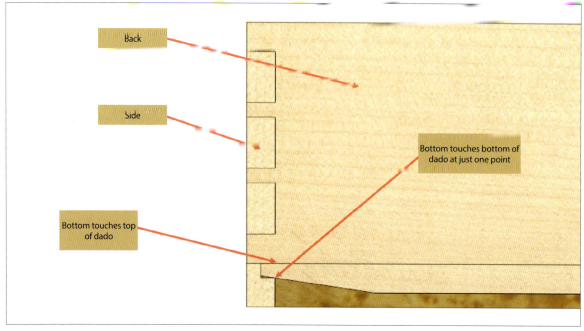

**Figure 3** | Tapered bottom fits into dado to reduce friction allowing seasonal expansion/contraction

## The Front

This particular drawer design has what is traditionally called cock beading around the perimeter of the front. The beading is approximately 3/32" in radius and hence stands proud of the front surface by 3/32". The top bead extends to the back face of the drawer front, while the bottom and side beads end at the beginning of the pins. This is done both to maintain the strength of the dovetail joints and to show them off; if you hand cut dovetails you want someone to see them when the drawer is opened!

As mentioned previously the front is usually 3/4" to 7/8" thick. It has half-blind pins on each end and a dado 1/4" wide and 1/4" deep on the inside face. The dado is positioned up from the bottom to align exactly with the groves in the sides. This distance is different on lipped fronts versus inset fronts by the dimension of the lip.

The front will also expand/contract across the width. Like the sides this needs to be compensated for. There is also the chance that because the sides and the front are different material (maple versus birch) a mismatch in expansion/contraction could cause problems.

A quick calculation reveals that they will change the same amount. Therefore the front can be cut to 47/8" as well (before trimming with the cock bead).

The length of the front is the same as the length of the back.

## The Bottom

The bottom has a taper along each edge. The taper is designed such that the top surface of the bottom just touches the top side of the dado in the sides, and the bottom of the taper touches the bottom inside corner of the dado at just one point. See **Figure 3**. This single point of contact (actually it is a line if you consider the depth of the bottom) allows the bottom to expand and contract with seasonal humidity and temperature changes without binding, which would likely happen if this were a tongue in a dado. The taper is approximately 8°.

The bottom has a tongue along its front edge as shown in **Figure 4**. This tongue seats in a dado on the inside face of the front. This joint is glued so that the bottom is anchored to the front and all expansion/contraction appears at the back as the bottom

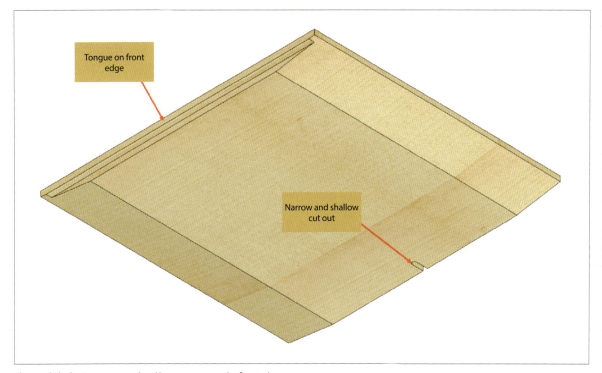

**Figure 4** | The bottom is tapered and has a tongue on the front edge

will alternately extend beyond the back or fall slightly short of the back's back surface.

It is important to know how much this total seasonal change will be and how deep the bottom should be cut at the time of assembly. Suppose for instance that you are building the drawer in May in the Northeast United States. This is just about the driest time of the year. If the stock has been in your shop for some time, it may have reached equilibrium with its surroundings and its moisture content may be low, around 7 percent. If it has not reached equilibrium it may be high, say 14 – 28 percent. You need to know the specific moisture content for your situation, and then you need to calculate how much the bottom will expand/contract around its nominal dimension. In this case it is ⅛".

I should mention at this point, for those who may not know, wood expands almost entirely in a direction across the grain. It expands negligibly in the direction of the grain. Plain-sawn lumber always expands more than quartersawn lumber of the same species, approximately by a factor of two.

There should be plenty of room behind the finished drawer to allow for the bottom to expand out the back. In this case it needs at least ⅛". Also, the drawer needs stops to keep it from sliding into the opening too far. Do not place the stop behind the drawer bottom or the position of the front, when closed, will change with the seasons.

You may have noticed in **Figure 4** that along the back edge of the bottom is a narrow and shallow cutout. This allows for a pan-head screw to provide support for the bottom. In a drawer of this dimension it may not be necessary, but in a chest of drawers it likely is. This screw should not be tightened; it is there merely for support and should allow the bottom to move freely for seasonal expansion.

## THE ROLE OF DRAWER SLIDERS

We are half way through Part 2 "The Apprentice and the Beside Table." The second half will be more interesting because you are getting a feel for

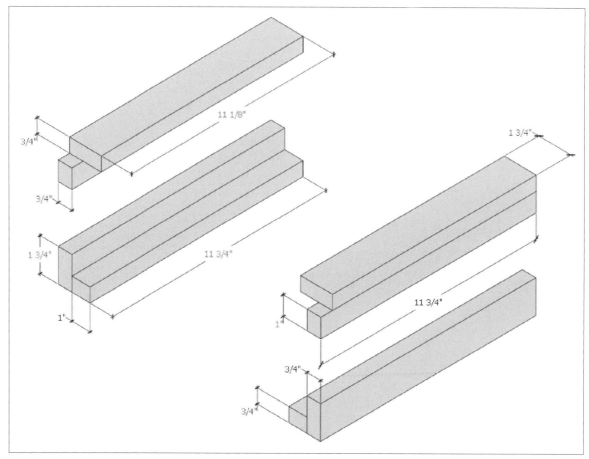

**Figure 5** | Detail of drawer sliders

SketchUp, and we can use your new skills to model more complex parts, add more detail and produce useful shop drawings, not to mention texturing for photorealistic rendering. However, let's not get ahead of ourselves; we have a drawer to model. Before we get to the more interesting parts we have simple parts to add: drawer sliders.

Drawer sliders play an important role: You can think of them as the table/drawer interface. Sliders allow the drawer to slide in and out smoothly. They house the drawer in a volume slightly larger than the drawer to keep the drawer from binding in humid conditions; but otherwise the drawer's movements are confined to in and out, not sideways or up and down. In addition, the sliders allow the drawer to be

pulled out without falling out – provided you don't pull it too far of course. Sliders don't really add to the strength of the carcass too much and are often secured with pocket-hole screw joinery but no mechanical joinery such as dovetails. And yes, pocket hole joinery is not new; pocket hole joinery existed in many antiques, dating back hundreds of years. So without further ado let's add the drawer sliders.

Open your SketchUp file to where we left off. If you didn't save your work you can open the model found at srww.com/sketchup_a_guide_for_wood-workers.html web page in the Downloads section of book Part 2, Chapter 6.

The drawer needs a framework that will allow it to slide in and out without falling to the floor or tilting

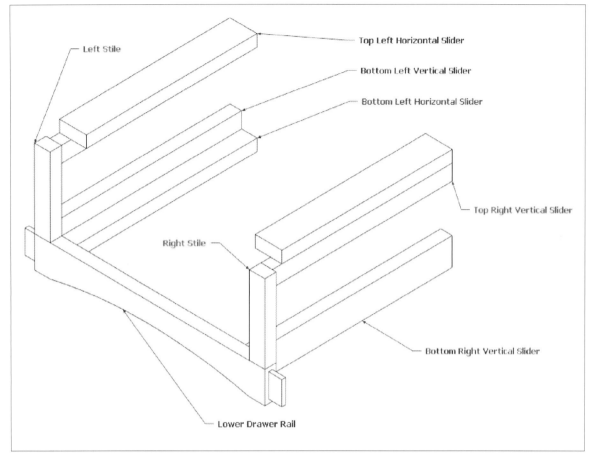

**Figure 6** | Arrangement of the sliders relative to Lower Drawer Rail and Stiles

downward. The parts required are all cubes (using the same definition of a cube that we established in Chapter 5). I will spell out the requirements here and leave you to draw the parts. Place all parts on a Sliders layer. Refer to **Figure 5** for details.

1.  Two parts ¾" T x 1¾" W x 11¾" L. They are one component called Bottom Vertical Slider. This is the Name you use in the Create Component dialog box and the Definition Name in the Entity Info dialog box. It is a little confusing, but you get the picture. By the way, you can edit and change a component's name in either box. Now give these two parts unique names in the Entity Info box Name box. Call one Bottom Right Vertical Slider and the other Bottom Left Vertical Slider.

2.  Two parts ¾" T x 1" W x 11¾" L. They are one component called Bottom Horizontal Slider. Give them unique names in the Entity Info dialog box of Bottom Left Horizontal Slider and Bottom Right Horizontal Slider.

3.  Two parts ¾" T x 1" W x 11¾" L. They are one component called Top Vertical Slider. Give them unique names of Top Left Vertical Slider and Top Right Vertical Slider.

4.  Two parts ¾" T x 1¾" W x 11⅛" L. Notice this component is ⅝" shorter than the rest. They are one component called Top Horizontal Slider. Give them unique names of Top Left Horizontal Slider and Top Right Horizontal Slider.

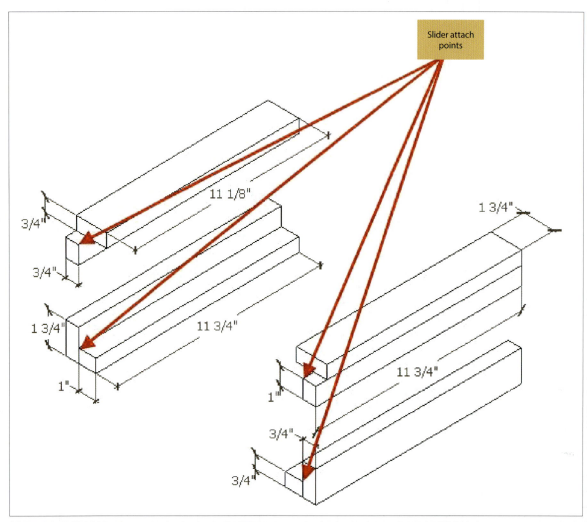

Slider attach points

11 1/8"

3/4"

3/4"

1 3/4"

11 3/4"

1"

1 3/4"

11 3/4"

1"

3/4"

3/4"

**Figure 7** | Slider attach points

## ARRANGEMENT OF SLIDERS

At this point it will be helpful to place the Upper Drawer Rail and the Lower Drawer Rail on separate layers. In the Layers dialog box double click the layer name Rails. This selects it and makes it available for editing. Change the name to Lower Rail. Also, add a new layer called Upper Rail. Select the Upper Drawer Rail (you need the Lower Rail's Visible check box checked to see it) and in the Entity Info dialog box move Upper Drawer Rail to layer Upper Rail.

**Figure 6** shows the final placement of the Sliders. To create the view shown in **Figure 6** you will either need to draw the Sliders in place or draw them elsewhere and move them into place. If you are going to draw the Sliders in place study **Figures 6, 7 and 8** very carefully before you begin. Position the sliders parts as shown in **Figure 6**. Do not change the position of the Lower Rail or the Stiles. Those are your reference for placing the Sliders parts. Within each pair, their backs and edges must align exactly. However, do not worry about the exact spacing of each pair one to the other;

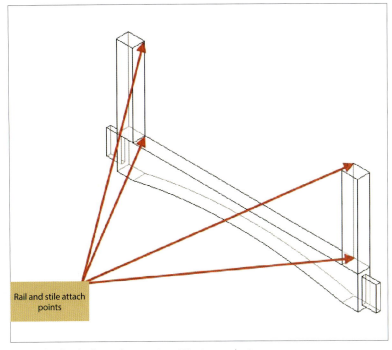

**Figure 8** | Rail and Stile attach points (note X-Ray is turned on)

just organize them visually as shown using the Inference Engine tooltips to place them exactly.

If you are going to draw them elsewhere and move them into place follow this procedure:

- Uncheck all Visible check boxes in the Layers dialog box except Layer0, Lower Rail, Sliders (you created this one, right?) and Stiles. Select the Hidden Line view.

- Now select a pair, one pair at a time, and group them. To do this use the Select tool to select one part, then, holding down the *Ctrl* (Control) key, select the other part. Now they should both appear outlined in blue. Right click on the parts and choose Make Group. Do this to each pair.

## MATING POINTS FOR SLIDERS TO ATTACH

Notice the points where the sliders meet the Lower Drawer Rail and the Left and Right Stile in **Figure 7** and **Figure 8**. The bottom slider's inside corner should meet the inside

corner of the stile and rail. The top inside corner of the top sliders should meet the top inside corner of the stiles. Using the Move tool, move the four groups into place by bringing corresponding points together. When you have them properly placed, you can select each group with the Select tool and right click, choose Explode. This will ungroup the parts.

Notice that Make Component, Make Group, and Explode all work together in a hierarchical way. That is, each time you use the Make Group or Make Component you climb the hierarchy; each time you use Explode you come down the hierarchy.

For example, suppose you have a collection of primitives (lines, faces, etc.) and call that selection A. Selection A is at level 0 in the hierarchy, meaning you can't explode a primitive. If you have another collection of primitives, called B, you have two collections, A and B, each at level 0. Now if you make selection A a component, it is now at level 1. Let's make B a component, bringing it to level 1. Now let's group A and B and the group is now at level 2. If I select the group, right click and choose Explode, the group is eliminated and the components are back to level 1. Explode one or both components and one or both will return to level 0.

You can also mix levels, for example combining a component at level 1 with a cube constructed of primitives creates a component at level 2. To back down it would take one Explode to return the combination to a component and a cube of primitives, and another Explode to return the component to its primitives.

The Edit Component also works in this hierarchical fashion. In the previous example we had a component and a group of primitives combined to make a new component at level 2. If you select, right click and Edit Component you will see that in the dotted box is a collection of primitives and a component. To edit

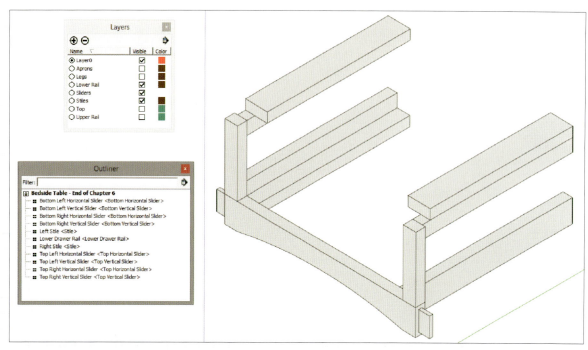

**Figure 9** | Completed sliders (note naming of components, parts (instances) and layers

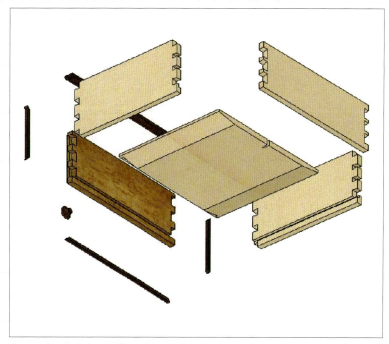

**Figure 10** | Exploded view of the traditional drawer

the component, which is still at level 1, you need to select it, right click and Edit Component. Try some combinations on your own and get a feel for it.

By the way, this levels and hierarchy explanation of how combining, exploding and editing works, is not something you will find in a SketchUp User's Guide (I don't think, anyway). It is just my interpretation of the behavior I observe. So don't blame SketchUp if I have it wrong.

OK, let's bring an end to this menial work. Your drawing should now look like that of **Figure 9**. Notice that I included the Layers dialog box and Outliner dialog box for you to compare your layers and component naming. You may also have noticed

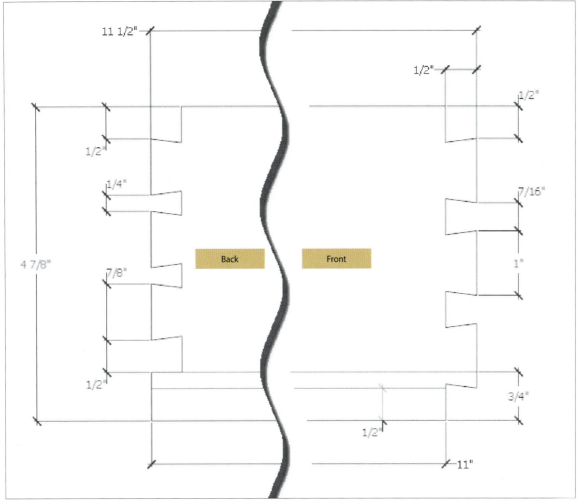

**Figure 11** | Drawer Side detail: Left tails are the back; right tails are the front

that there was no joinery involved here. In the shop these pieces will be assembled with glue and screws using pocket hole joinery.

## DRAWING THE TRADITIONAL DRAWER

Back to what this chapter is all about; actually drawing the traditional drawer. **Figure 10** shows an exploded view from the underneath rear. You can see the dado in the drawer front and the sides. No dado is needed in the drawer back because it ends at the

tapered bottom. Notice that the front and back have pins, while the sides have tails. The front and back start with a half-pin and end with a half-pin.

### Drawing the Drawer Sides

Now for the fun stuff – dovetails – I love dovetails. I use them a lot in my furniture projects, and they are always hand cut; no jigs, fixtures or templates. Now, if I were Frank Klausz (don't I wish), I wouldn't even lay out the tails or pins. I would just eyeball it and cut them freehand. But Frank Klausz is who I aspire to be, not where I am in my woodworking growth.

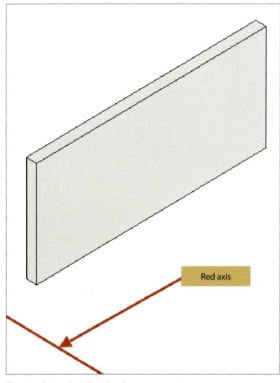

Figure 12 | Drawer Side cube alignment

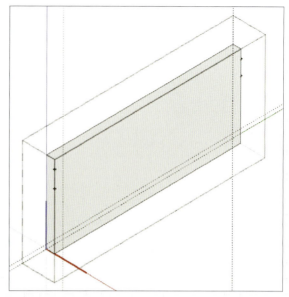

Figure 13 | Construction lines and points in Edit Component mode

So I lay them out when working in the shop, and that is what we are going to do in SketchUp.

We have some new things to learn here. Trusting that you are indeed learning as we go along, I am not going to provide detailed instructions for procedures we have covered several times. Besides, you are getting good now; it's time you use those wings. Start by studying **Figure 11**. You are looking at the outside face of the left drawer side (left as you face the front of the drawer). The dado you see is on the other side of the board, but I have X-Ray view turned on to make its placement visible.

The tails on the left are the back tails. Those on the right are the front tails. You will also notice that the back tails are not symmetrical about a horizontal center line. This is to allow for the drawer bottom to extend below the back providing expansion/contraction relief. The overall dimensions of the sides are 4⅞" wide by 11½" long by ½" thick. Go ahead and create that overall cube now. Place it such that the bottom end edge is parallel to

the red axis, and the face is in the green/blue plane. Place it anywhere along the red axis such that you have plenty of room to work unobstructed by the table. See **Figure 12**.

Make the cube a component called Drawer Side and place it on a layer called Drawer Sides. We will create the dovetails in the edit mode so select the Drawer Side component and enter Edit Component mode. We will be in this mode for some time, so try not to accidentally click outside the dotted lines with the Select tool. If you do, just re-enter edit mode.

The front tails will be ½" deep, the depth to which they penetrate the drawer front. The front tails are going to be half-blind dovetails and the back will be through dovetails. The tail angle we will use is 8° from normal. In the shop I use a marking tool that has two angles, indicated by ratios 1:7 and 1:9. The ratios are rise/run, so the higher the denominator the smaller the angle. I use the 1:7 ratio which is very close to 8°. That is what we will draw here. Chris Schwarz has a very good article on the history – and cabinetmaker's opinions – of dovetail angles on his Lost Art Press Blog if you are interested. Go to blog.lostartpress.com/2008/03/19/dogmatic-about-dovetail-angles.

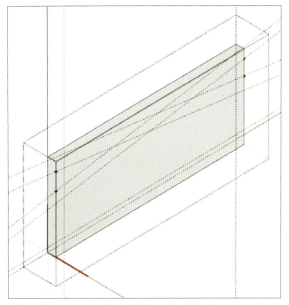

**Figure 14** | Construction lines added to outline the tails

In **Figure 12** the end closest to the Red axis is the front. (The detail on the right in **Figure 11** is also the front.) We will start by placing a number of construction lines and points in our drawing. Using the Tape Measure ⌀ tool place a construction point on the front inside edge down ½" from the top inside corner. With the Tape Measure ⌀ tool, click on the top inside corner, move down along the blue axis, type ½ and *Enter*. Repeat this procedure to place another construction point 1½" down. Make sure both measurements are referenced to the top inside corner of the front edge. See **Figure 13**.

While we have the Tape Measure tool handy, we will place similar construction points on the back inside edge. This time ½" down from the top inside corner and 1⅜" down from the top inside corner. These construction points represent the half-pin dimension of ½" that begins each dovetail joint at each end of the drawer side, and a half-pin plus tail width. In the case of the front edge that is ½" for the half-pin, plus 1" for the tail width for a total of 1½". In the case of the back edge that is ½" for the half-pin, plus ⅞" for the tail width for a total of 1⅜".

Still using the Tape Measure ⌀ tool, we will place a construction line parallel to the inside front

and back edges, ½" in from both. This is easily done with the Tape Measure ⌀ tool; place it over the inside front edge and near the center of the edge. Move the cursor around slightly until you locate the center of the edge. This will be indicated by a tooltip message of Midpoint and a light blue inference circle. Click and move the cursor to the right. Notice a construction line is formed parallel to the edge. As you move to the right the Inference Engine will encourage you to stay on a path perpendicular to the edge as indicated by a Green axis line. Type ½ and *Enter*. These construction lines mark the depth of the tails on each end.

There are two more parallel construction lines that we need to add. They are both referenced to the bottom inside edge. The first is ½" up from the bottom edge and the second is ¾" up from the bottom edge. Add those in using the same procedure used on the previous parallel construction lines. However, this time we will move the Tape Measure cursor upward along the Blue axis. These last two lines represent the dado in the Drawer Side. Your drawing should now look like **Figure 13**.

Refer back to **Figure 11** and notice that the top edge of the tails slope downward from the end toward the center. The bottom edge of the tails slope upward from the edge toward the center. As mentioned earlier the slopes are 8° from normal. We will now outline the tails.

Using the Protractor ⬦ tool, hover over the face of the inside surface of the Drawer Side. The Protractor cursor should be red. Hold the Shift key down to lock the Protractor cursor on the inside face of the Drawer Side. Move the cursor to the ½" construction point at the front edge. This is the top most construction point. As you hover over it you should see a Guide Point tooltip. Click on the guide point. Move the cursor to the right making sure to stay on the green axis and maintaining an On Face tooltip; click. Now, rotate the cursor clockwise, sloping down, type 8 and *Enter*. This procedure places a construction line that slopes 8° downward to the right and running through the ½" construction point. Repeat this procedure, but this time place the cursor over the 1½" construction point and rotate counterclockwise after the second

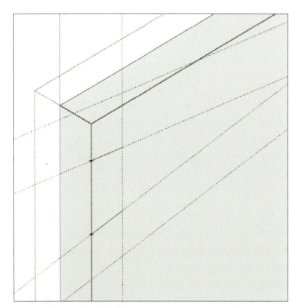

**Figure 15** | One tail outlined

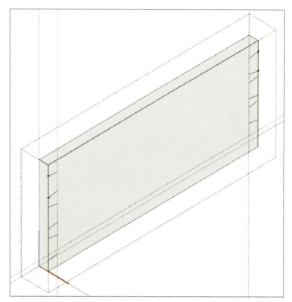

**Figure 16** | All tails outlined

click and type 8 and *Enter*. This produces an upward sloping construction line.

By now you understand the process well enough to place the construction lines on the back edge. Go ahead. When you are done your drawing should look like **Figure 14**. A little messy, but we are almost home.

With the Line tool we will outline the dovetails. Then with the Move/Copy tool and the repeat Move/Copy feature we will create the remaining tails. First outline the tails. Starting with the Line tool at the front edge and the topmost guide point, click. Move the cursor down and to the right to the intersection of the sloped construction line and the vertical construction line and click again. Press the *Esc* key to end the polyline. Next, with the Line tool at the front edge and the bottommost guide point, click. Move the cursor up and to the right to the intersection of the sloped construction line and the vertical construction line and click again. Press the *Esc* key to end the polyline.

Your drawing should look like **Figure 15**. Using the same procedure, outline the tail on the back edge. We need two more tails on each end. Working on the front edge first, use the Select tool with

the *Ctrl* key held down to select the two tail lines we just drew with the Line tool. When selected choose the Move tool and press the *Ctrl* key (you don't have to hold it down) to enter Move/Copy mode (you should see the + sign on the cursor). Click anywhere on the selected lines and move the cursor down along the blue axis; type 1⁷⁄₁₆ and press *Enter*. Type 2x and *Enter*.

The dimension 1⁷⁄₁₆" used in the last procedure is the sum of a tail width, 1", and pin width, ⁷⁄₁₆". In other words, 1⁷⁄₁₆" is the spacing from one tail to the next. You can see this if you look at **Figure 11**. While viewing **Figure 11** note that the spacing of back tails is 1⅛", the sum of ¼" and ⅞". Repeat this last procedure on the back tail to add the remaining two back tails. At this point we can use the Eraser tool to erase the four 8° construction lines, they are no longer needed. Your drawing should now look like **Figure 16**.

We need to outline the areas we are going to remove with the Push/Pull tool. Think ahead a little. We are trying to create tails, so it is the outline of where the pins will go that needs to be removed; after all we need to make room for them.

With the Line tool, and using the vertical construction lines for guidance, outline the pins to be

**Figure 17** | Tails fully formed with Push/Pull tool

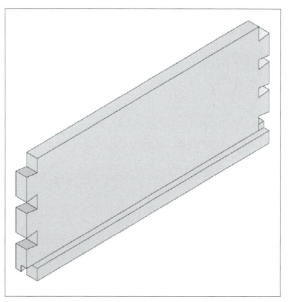

**Figure 18** | Completed Drawer Side

removed. You might also want to study **Figure 10** and **Figure 11** before drawing these lines. Look especially at the tails on the back end around the dado.

Remove those areas with the Push/Pull tool. It may be helpful to use the Iso view. With the Push/Pull tool drag the faces to the back and notice it will stop at the back edge with a tooltip message of "Offset limited to -½." Release the mouse button and the face will disappear or type ½ and *Enter*. Repeat for the remaining seven waste areas. Your drawing should look like **Figure 17**.

We have two more lines to draw and construction lines and points to delete before we use the Push/Pull tool to shape the dado and complete the Drawer Side. With the Line tool draw a line along the top construction line starting at the front edge and running all the way to the back edge. Erase the top construction line. The second line starts not at the front edge, but in ½" where the tails end and are most narrow. With the Line tool, draw a line along the bottom construction line starting ½" in from the front edge and running all the way to the back edge. Be sure both ends of this line are on the construction line. Using the Push/Pull tool, push the face of the dado in ¼". Use menu Edit/Delete Guides to delete

the remaining guide lines and points. With the Select tool, click outside the bounding box to exit Edit Component mode. The completed Drawer Side should look like **Figure 18**.

We need a right Drawer Side, which we can model with the Move/Copy and Flip Along tools. The Drawer Sides are 12⅞" apart when measured outside edge to outside edge. Choose the Move tool and press the *Ctrl* key to switch to Move/Copy tool; you should see the + sign on the cursor. Copy the left Drawer Side and move it along the Red axis, type 12⅜ and *Enter*. The dimension 12⅜" is 12⅞" minus the thickness of the side. With the Tape Measure tool check that the outside edges of the Drawer Sides are 12⅞" apart.

Recalling that we copied the Drawer Side and moved it along the Red axis, mirror the right Drawer Side using Flip Along/Component's Red. Select the left Drawer Side and in the Entity Info box give it a part name of Left Drawer Side. Now select the right Drawer Side and give it a part name of Right Drawer Side. With the hard work of modeling the traditional drawer done, we are now ready to move on to the drawer front. Like we have always done, we will use the model we have drawn so far to assist in drawing the drawer front.

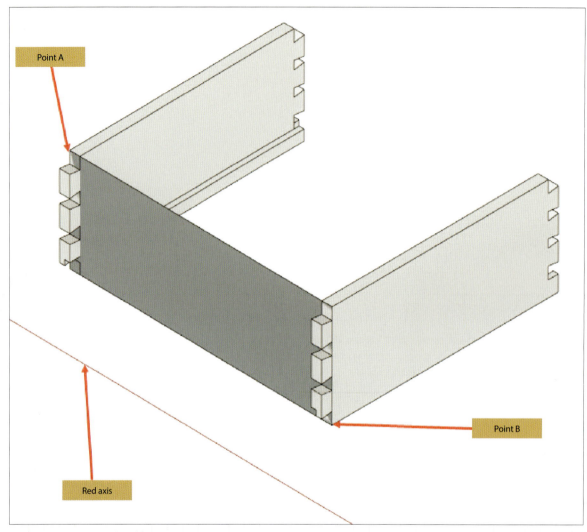

**Figure 19** | Create a rectangle and face using opposing corners

## Drawing the Drawer Front

We are going to use the sides to define the front in a number of ways. First we are going to draw a rectangle using diagonally opposing corners of the sides on the front edge surfaces where the tails terminate. Then we are going to Push/Pull that surface to create the thickness for the front. Next we will introduce a new tool, the menu Edit/Intersect Faces/With Selection tool, to create the pins in the front. If all of that works out well, and it will, the student will be given a homework assignment to draw the back.

OK, using the Rectangle tool, draw a face on the front edge of the sides using the corners farthest apart on the surface where the tails terminate. Refer to **Figure 19** for guidance. The Rectangle tool should begin at Point A and end at Point B. Check that the face is the correct size. It should be 12⅞" W x 4⅞" H. Next, with the Push/Pull tool, pull the face out ¾", the thickness of the front. Create a component of the drawer front called Drawer Front. Create a Drawer Front layer and place the Drawer Front

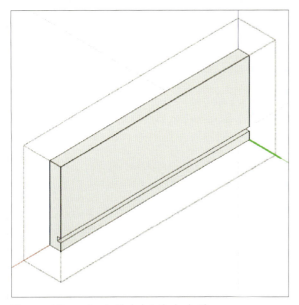

**Figure 20** | Drawer Front with dado in the back side

on it. In the Entity Info box assign a part name of Drawer Front. Not too creative, huh? Oh well, it's only a drawer.

Select the Drawer Front and enter Edit Component mode. We have a choice to make, drawer the pins first and then the dado, or the dado first and then the pins. It makes a difference in terms of the amount of work we need to do. There is really no way of knowing which way is better if you are doing this for the first time. So I will give you the benefit of my mistakes and subsequent learning.

Whenever you intend to use the Push/Pull tool where nonorthogonal planes will be involved, attempt to find a way to use the Push/Pull tool before the nonorthogonal planes are introduced.

We know the pins in the Drawer Front involve 8° planes, and it is very likely we will use the Push/Pull tool to model the dado. So our rule dictates modeling the dado first. To show that this will save a lot of work, and perhaps frustration, the student will be given the task of redrawing the Drawer Front by modeling the pins before the dado in the exercises at the end of this chapter.

Use the Back and Iso view to model the dado. Uncheck all Visible boxes except Layer0 and Drawer Front. Make all edits in Edit Component mode. The dado begins ½" up from the bottom, is ¼" wide and ¼" deep. An easy way to model this is the use the Move/Copy tool to move two copies of the line forming the bottom edge up; the first ½" up and the second ¾" up. Be sure to press *Ctrl* for each Move to switch to Move/Copy tool. The Push/Pull tool can then be used to push the dado in ¼". When completed the Drawer Front should look like **Figure 20**. In **Figure 20** I have all Visible boxes unchecked except Layer0 and Drawer Front. For the next step of modeling the pins, the Drawer Sides Visible box must be checked.

Before we can begin modeling the pins we have to do something unusual and a tiny bit counter to our rules of drawing. We are going to use a new tool; menu Edit/Intersect Faces/With Selection. This tool requires that our Drawer Front be in primitive state so that we can select all its primitives as well as both Drawer Sides. Click outside the Edit Component bounding box to exit the Edit component mode. Select the Drawer Front, right click and choose Explode on the context menu. This will return the

## THE EXPLODE TOOL

The Explode tool has a behavior that is not in line with the "Six Rules for Modeling in SketchUp." If the Explode tool is used on a component or group, all the primitives contained in that component or group are moved from Layer Zero to the layer the component or group resided on before the Explode tool was employed. You must return all primitives to Layer Zero using the Entity Info Layer drop-down box before proceeding.

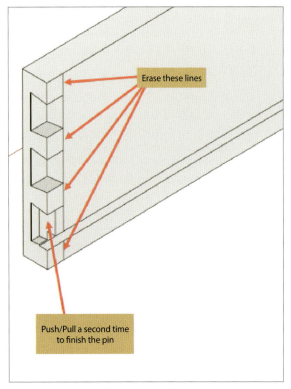

Erase these lines

Push/Pull a second time
to finish the pin

**Figure 21** | Edit/Intersect Faces/With Model requires some cleanup

Drawer Front to its primitive state and leave all faces and edges selected. Notice the Layers toolbar drop-down box and the Layer drop-down box in the Entity Info dialog box both indicate the primitives are on the Drawer Layer. This occurred as a result of using the Explode tool. Using the Entity Info Layer drop-down box return the selected primitives to Layer0.

Now for the magic; with the Select tool selected hold down the *Ctrl* key and select both Drawer Sides. Both Drawer Sides and all faces and lines of the exploded Drawer Front should now be highlighted in blue indicating they are selected. The Edit/Intersect Faces/With Selection tool has no icon; you must select menu Edit/Intersect Faces/With Selection to invoke the tool. When you do this all the blue selection highlights will disappear. Uncheck the Drawer Sides layer Visible box and examine what has happened to the Drawer Front. Lines have been added that outline where the tails of the Drawer Sides intersected with

the Drawer Front. Now our job is easy. All we need do is use the Push/Pull tool to push the tail outlines inward ½" and delete some unwanted lines with the Eraser tool.

There are some lines to clean up. This is almost always the case when using the menu Edit/Intersect Faces tool. Referring to **Figure 21** on the back we see there are vertical lines ½" in from the edge. Using the Eraser tool delete (erase) the lines indicated in **Figure 21**. The remaining vertical lines will help us determine how far to push the tails outlines in using the Push/Pull tool. Remember, we are creating pins now, so it is the tail outlines we want to push in to remove material. This allows for the Drawer Side tails to interlock with the Drawer Front pins. On the bottommost tail outline you will need to select the face a second time to finish the Push/Pull due to the Drawer Side dado outline remnant. You can see this in **Figure 21**. Orbit and inspect the dado before you Push/Pull this tail outline the first time to see why this is necessary.

When the Push/Pull and erasure have been completed on both ends, create a component of the Drawer Front called Drawer Front. Because we created this component once already, when you hit the Create button you will get a message complaining such a component already exist and asks if you want to replace it. The answer should be yes. Place the Drawer Front on the Drawer Front layer using the Entity Info box. In the Entity Info box assign a part Name of Drawer Front. Check the Visible box for layer Drawer Sides so they are back in the picture.

### Drawing the Drawer Back
The student is left to draw the Drawer Back. Use the same approach we used with the front, that is, use outside corners to draw a face, add thickness, make it a component and then edit the component. When using the menu Edit/Intersect Faces/With Selection to model the back uncheck the Drawer Front Visible box leaving only Layer0 and Drawer Sides visible. This will ensure you don't accidentally include the Drawer Front in the selection; if you do accidentally include the Drawer Front, the menu Edit/Intersect Faces/With Selection will leave a set of lines outlining the pins of the Drawer Front and tails of the Draw Side on Layer0.

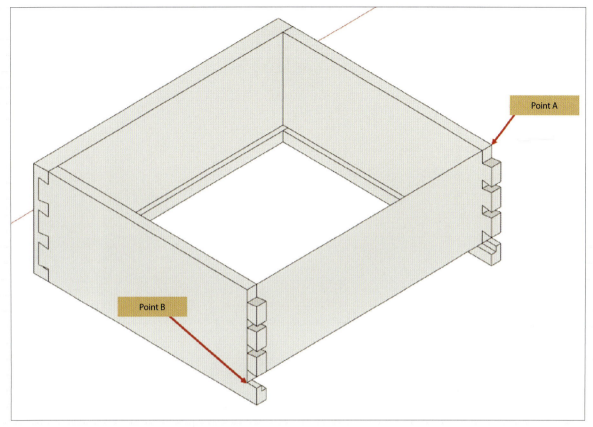

**Figure 22** | A hint about where to begin the Drawer Back

When using menu Edit/Intersect Faces in a more complex models it is easy to miss some of the lines you need to erase, and doing so can cause great problems. You will discover this in Part Three where we deal with complex curves. Be very thorough with inspections.

The Drawer Back, by the way, is only 4⅛" tall. It ends ¾" short of the Drawer Side's bottom. This is to allow the Drawer Bottom to pass under it. The back, unlike the front, is ½" thick. This is because the back dovetails are through dovetails while the front is half-blind dovetails; the front has additional material so the half-blind dovetails won't be seen from the front. Don't forget to create a component and name it Drawer Back; create a layer called Drawer Back and place the Drawer Back there; assign a part name of Drawer Back. I know, not terribly creative.

To begin modeling the Drawer Back, look at **Figure 22** for a hint as to where the initial rectangle is to be drawn. It may also be easier to suspend the "As soon as a part takes 3D shape make it a component" rule until after the pins are modeled. This is because you are going to use the menu Edit/Intersect Faces/With Selection tool and the back will need to be in primitive state anyway. This saves having to create a component, exploding it and creating it again. You will find modeling the Drawer Back to be much easier than the Drawer Front. When you have completed this task we will begin modeling the Drawer Bottom. Get to work!

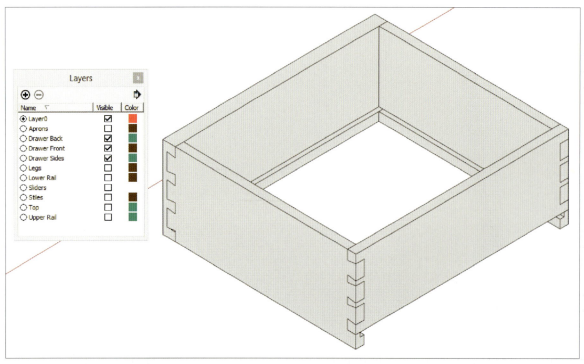

**Figure 23** | Completed Drawer Back, Sides and Front

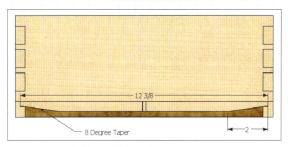

**Figure 24** | Drawer Bottom cross section details

OK, I have completed the Drawer Back, have you? If so, it should look like **Figure 23**. By the way, in your inspection for lines to clean up, did you find and erase ten lines? You should have. If your model looks like **Figure 23**, including the erasure of ten lines, you get an A+; atta boy/girl and all that warm cuddly stuff. If not you get an F-; sorry, that's the grading system here. After all, what good are shop drawings that are almost correct?

## Drawing the Drawer Bottom

Now it's time to turn our attention to the Drawer Bottom. Let's study a few figures before we begin drawing: **Figure 2**, **Figure 3**, and **Figure 4**. The bottom is beveled on both sides, has a ¼" x ¼" tongue along the front edge on the top side, is ½" thick and has a small notch on the back edge for a support screw. We are going to begin by defining the cross section of the bottom at the back edge and then we will extrude it to the Drawer Front's back, add the tongue and finally the notch.

Look at **Figure 24**. You will see that the taper is defined in one of two ways. The 8° angle is approximate if you use the 2" dimension to draw the bottom (closer to 8.1°). On the other hand, 2" is approximate if you choose to use 8° to draw the bottom. Either way will work just fine; in the shop you will likely use a combination of both followed by fine-tuning with a hand plane. We will use 2" as the defining dimension.

In **Figure 25** you see the detail of this bevel. Notice that the Drawer Bottom bevel touches the

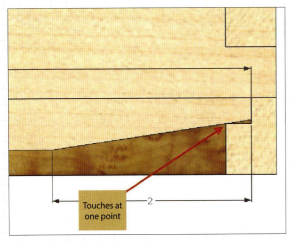

Touches at one point

2

**Figure 25** | The Drawer Bottom bevel touches at one point

sides at just one point. When we draw and dimension the width of the bottom we will show it full size, that is, touching the side walls of the dado. The cabinetmaker (craftsman) knows to run each side through the jointer (or hand plane) to take off ¹⁄₆₄" providing a total ¹⁄₃₂" clearance so the drawer bottom doesn't bind as it expands/contracts.

Uncheck all other layer Visible boxes except Layer0, Drawer Back and Drawer Sides. Choose the Back view so that you are looking at the back of the drawer. With the Tape Measure tool slide the cursor along the bottom edge of the Drawer Back and stop anywhere except the end points and click. Move down along the Blue axis, click, type ½ and *Enter*. This places a construction line parallel to and ½" below, the drawer back, defining the bottom edge of the drawer bottom.

Zoom in on the left dado. You will need to do this so that the Tape Measure tool can locate points other than the endpoints of the left vertical wall of the left dado. With the Tape Measure tool slide along the left vertical wall of the left dado and stop anywhere except the end points, click, move the cursor to the right along the red axis, type 2 and *Enter*. This places a vertical construction line 2" to the right of and parallel to the left wall of the left dado. Repeat these steps on the right dado.

Now the vertical construction lines 2" from the dado walls and the horizontal construction line ½" down from

the bottom edge of the Drawer Back form two intersection points. We will use these points to draw construction lines between them and the single point of contact for the corresponding dado shown in the detail **Figure 25**.

To do this we will use the Protractor tool. With the Protractor tool cursor appearing green, click first on the right construction intersection, where the horizontal construction line intersects the right most vertical construction line. Then move the cursor right, along the Red axis, keeping the red dotted Inference Engine line in view and click again. Now click on the single point of contact on the right dado shown in **Figure 25**. Repeat these steps on the left intersection and left dado. This forms the tapered outline.

Using the Line tool, we are going to draw an outline of the back edge of the Drawer Bottom, which will in turn create a face. The Line tool, when selected, will be in a polyline mode, meaning all you have to do is go around the loop clicking on the defining corners and it will continue drawing a line until the path is closed. This is very helpful. However, there are times in this process where you will have to use Zoom, Zoom Window and Pan tools to view and select the point you want. Use them freely, and as you do, notice that the Line tool is dimmed but still selected. This means you have paused the Line tool, but when you again click it (once) you can pick up where you left off.

OK, using the Line tool and proceeding counterclockwise, outline the Drawer Back by clicking on the following points in order: right intersection point, the intersection of the right taper construction line and the vertical wall of the right dado, upper right corner of the right dado, upper left corner of the left dado, intersection of the left taper construction line and the vertical wall of the left taper, left intersection point and finally the right intersection point to close the loop. Notice a face is created showing the back edge of the Drawer Bottom. Select this face and its perimeter to highlight it by clicking twice on the face.

It's time for another figure to make sure we are all in sync. Look at **Figure 26**. The Drawer Bottom back edge is outlined in blue (selected). Check to be sure

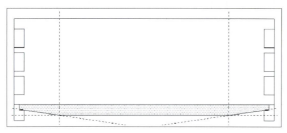

**Figure 26** | Drawer Bottom face after outlining with the Line tool

your drawing is the same. Uncheck the Visible box for layers Drawer Back and Drawer Sides. Check the Visible box for Drawer Front (Layer0 should always be visible and the active layer). Delete all construction lines using menu Edit/Delete Guides. Click Front view, Iso and Zoom extents (go home or Home View will not bring us to the position we want).

With the Push/Pull tool drag the Drawer Bottom face toward the Drawer Front and click on the back edge of the Drawer Front. Is your brain screaming "Make component, create layer, place component on layer and name part"? By now it should be. Make the Drawer Bottom a component and call it – yeah, you guessed it – Drawer Bottom. Create a Drawer Bottom layer and move the Drawer Bottom to it. In the Entity info box give the Drawer Bottom a part Name of Drawer Bottom.

You are probably wondering why we have component names that are the same as the layer names and part names. You might be thinking, this is really a waste of time and a bit anal. But what if you were modeling a chest of drawers with, say nine drawers; three on top, two one step down and four more below it; the middle drawer of the top three being smaller than the outside two; each drawer level is graduated? Now the parts of the drawers would almost all be different. For example, the top three drawers might share the same Drawer Side component, but not the unique part name. And the outside drawers might share the same Drawer Back, but not so the middle drawer. While you may want to put all the Drawer Bottoms on the same Drawer Bottom layer you would probably find that for dimensioning reasons you would want to put each level of drawer on its own layer. Remember, this table is a very simple model. You are likely to be

**Figure 27** | Image Source: dutchcrafters.com/product. aspx?intprodid=2834

drawing far more complicated models in the future. We want to establish drawing habits that work for all complexities. So, while what we do here may seem anal, sticking with it will prepare you for that high boy you are going to draw next. (See **Figure 27**.)

The front edge of the Drawer Bottom now looks exactly like the back edge. But we need a tongue to slide into the Drawer Front dado. In the shop this is done by cutting a ¼" x ¼" rabbet along the front's bottom edge. Here we will use the tape measure tool to draw a construction line ¼" down from and parallel to the top edge of the front end of the Drawer Bottom. You do this just as described when forming the Drawer Bottom's back edge cross section earlier. But first, uncheck all layer Visible boxes except Layer0 and Drawer Bottom and also select the Drawer Bottom and enter Edit Component mode.

Create the construction line parallel to the top front edge of the front end of the Drawer Bottom

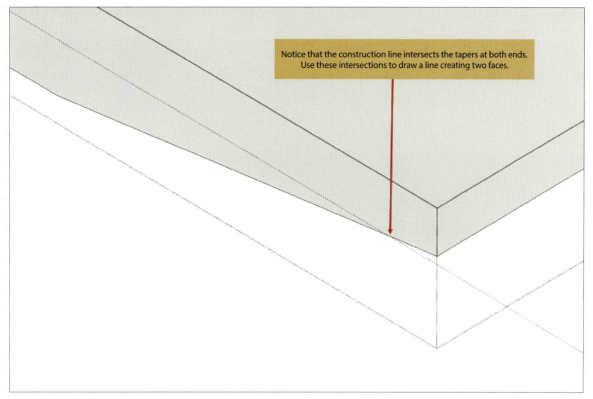

Notice that the construction line intersects the tapers at both ends. Use these intersections to draw a line creating two faces.

**Figure 28** | Detail of construction line intersection

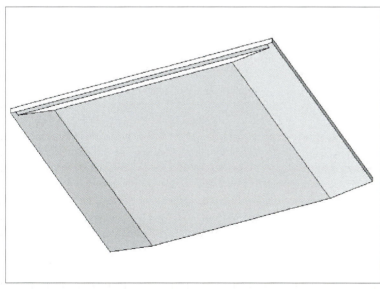

**Figure 29** | Drawer Bottom with tongue

and ¼" down. Notice in **Figure 28**, when you create the construction line, it intersects both tapers. With the line tool draw a line from the left intersection to the right intersection, dividing the front edge into two faces. Make absolutely sure it is the intersections you are snapping to. When lines cross at acute angles like this it is sometimes difficult to snap on the intersection. With the Push/Pull tool, pull the top face forward ¼". Delete the construction line with the Eraser tool or Edit/Delete Guides. Click outside the bounding box with the select tool to exit Edit Component mode.

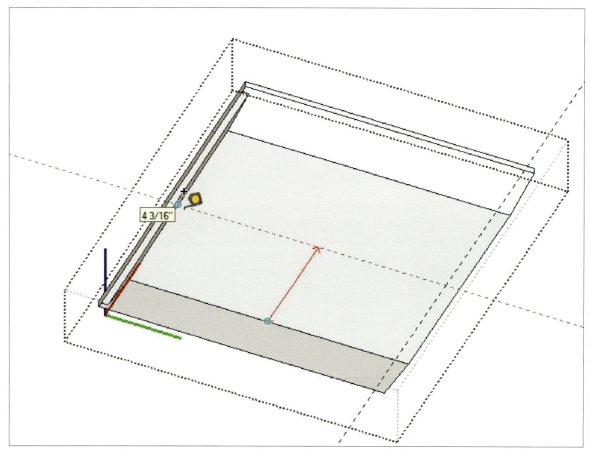

**Figure 30** | Using the midpoint to create a center line

Use the Orbit tool to view under the Drawer Bottom to ensure you created a ¼" x ¼" rabbet. Check it with the Tape Measure tool if necessary. Your model should look like that in **Figure 29**. Compare **Figure 29** with **Figure 4**. Aside from the texturing, all that remains is adding a notch in the back edge for the screw support. In the shop this notch is created with a ³⁄₁₆" diameter router bit that extends ½" into the back edge at its center. To model it in SketchUp, we will use two construction lines, the Circle tool and the Push/Pull tool. Alternatively we could also use the Arc tool in place of the Circle tool, but we have used that tool once already.

Select the Drawer Bottom and enter Edit Component mode. From the back bottom edge of the Drawer Bottom place a guide line with the Tape Measure tool ½" in. To create a center point for the Circle ⊙ tool, we need a center line. Fortunately we don't need to know any dimensions to create it. We simply hover over either taper line edge with the Tape Measure tool cursor until we find its midpoint and click. Then drag the cursor along the red axis toward the center a little and then move it to the front edge and hover around until we find its midpoint. When we find it a blue dot appears with the tool tip 4³⁄₁₆". See **Figure 30**. Click and now we have the two construction lines needed. This technique really points out the power of the Inference Engine.

Now we will use the Circle ⊙ tool to provide the arc needed. Since the router bit is ³⁄₁₆" in diameter

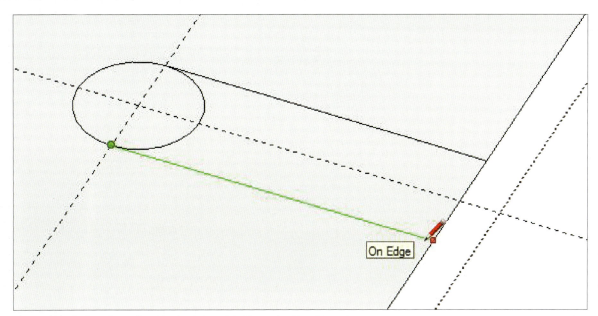

**Figure 31** | The Circle tool is used to place the circle, and the Line tool outlines the notch

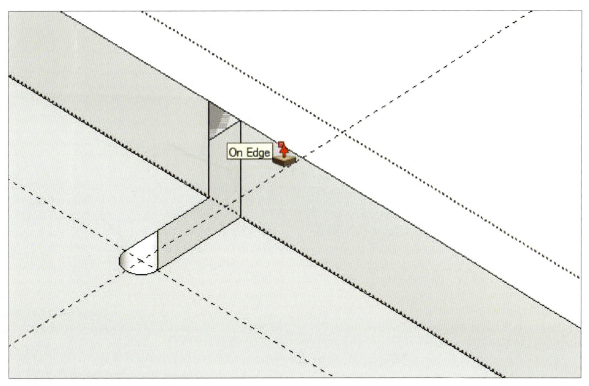

**Figure 32** | The Push/Pull tool creates the notch

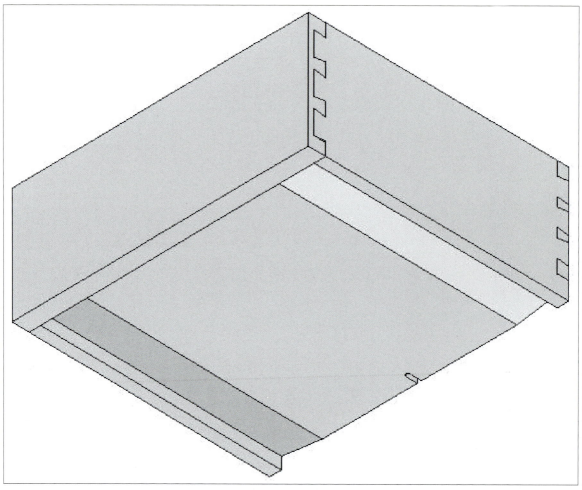

**Figure 33** | Completed drawer sans trim, pull and texturing

we need a circle with a radius of ³⁄₃₂". The Circle tool works on radii. First we select the Circle ⊙ tool, click on the intersection of the two construction lines and then move the cursor along one of those construction lines and type 3/32 and *Enter*. With the Line tool click on the intersection of the ½" construction line and the circle, and then move the cursor along the green axis until the On Edge tooltip appears and click. See **Figure 31** which illustrates these last few steps.

We need to erase the inside half of the circle with the Eraser tool and then Push/Pull the inside face to the top edge to create the notch. **Figure 32**

illustrates how this is done. Notice the On Edge tooltip on the top back edge of the Drawer Bottom is used to define the depth of the notch, which in this case is clear through. Exit Edit Component mode, delete the construction lines with menu Edit/Delete Guides and the modeling of the Drawer Bottom is complete.

At this point we make layers Drawer Back, Drawer Bottom, Drawer Front, and Drawer Sides visible (Layer0 is always visible and the active layer) and inspect our drawer with the Orbit tool. Your model should look like **Figure 33**. Compare **Figure 33** to **Figure 2**.

## CHAPTER REVIEW

We began this chapter with a short study of the design of a traditional drawer. Each of its parts was examined separately and their function and characteristics explained. A short introduction of seasonal environmental changes made us aware of its effects on wood and the resulting care that needed to be taken in the design of a piece. We learned the role and use of through and half-blind dovetails and beveled drawer bottoms.

While this background hopefully was interesting and maybe even informative to some readers, the real purpose was to get the reader to think about how to translate a conceptual design into a drawing. Through-out this book you have been fed dimensions and figures of the model we are trying to create. This is necessary because this book is not a design and architecture book, but rather a book on how to use SketchUp. But hopefully you are beginning to realize that whether you start from spoonfed dimensions, a scaled drawing or scribbling on a napkin, the mechanics of translation into a SketchUp drawing follows the form and function of the concept.

To that end, we employed many of the tools we previously learned. We created a cubic shape called a drawer side and used the Tape Measure, Protractor, Move/Copy, Line and Push/Pull tools for form tails and dado to complete the drawer side. Next, recalling a tenet of SketchUp, that we never draw unless absolutely neces-sary, we used the drawer sides to form the drawer front and drawer back. This introduced us to a very important tool which would become a mainstay in future chapters: the Edit/Intersect Faces/With Selection tool.

We again used the drawer sides and back to help us create a face to form the drawer bottom and with the Push/Pull tool we gave it 3D shape. The Tape Measure tool and inference were used in a clever way to find a center line and center for a circle formed with a new Circle tool.

A rule of thumb was introduced suggesting fore-thought before using the Push/Pull tool when nonor-thogonal planes are present or about to be drawn. This rule of thumb points out a more important concept of modeling in 3D that we haven't really emphasized in the text to this point. That concept is simple but often ignored:

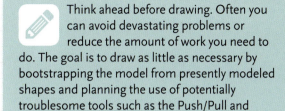

Think ahead before drawing. Often you can avoid devastating problems or reduce the amount of work you need to do. The goal is to draw as little as necessary by bootstrapping the model from presently modeled shapes and planning the use of potentially troublesome tools such as the Push/Pull and menu Edit/Intersect Faces/With Model tools.

In this chapter we introduced the following new tools listed in the order they were used:
Edit/Intersect Faces/With Selection
⊘ Circle

## EXERCISES FOR THE STUDENT

1. Recreate the Drawer Front, but this time model the pins before modeling the dado. Compare the number of steps required for each and the level of difficulty, frustration and cleanup. The results obtained by using the Push/Pull tool around nonorthogonal planes are not always predictable.

2. When modeling the Drawer Back, you were reminded that when using the menu Edit/Intersect Faces/With Selection to uncheck the Visibility box for the Drawer Front, lest an additional and unwanted set of lines be left on Layer0. For this exercise, ignore this advice and leave the Visible box for layer Drawer Front checked while modeling a Drawer Back. Include the Drawer Font in the selection prior to using Edit/Intersect Faces/With Selection and see what happens. After the menu Edit/Intersect Faces/With Selection tool is used uncheck all layer's Visibility box except Layer0. Notice the unwanted lines.

3. Recreate the notch in the Drawer Bottom, but use the Arc tool instead of the Circle tool. Is creating a center point useful or is there another approach needed? Pay attention to the tooltips produced by the Arc tool. Is the Arc tool an easier or more dif-ficult approach for this task?

# 07

# ADDING COCK BEAD & PULL

*In this chapter we will complete the drawer, thereby completing the table model itself. Cock bead trim will be added to the drawer to dress it up. We will again use the 2-Point Arc tool in addition to the Circle tool to create a profile for the drawer pull. And finally, a new and powerful tool will be introduced and used to create the drawer pull: Enter the Follow Me tool.*

This chapter is concerned with the ornamentation of the traditional drawer, specifically the trim and the drawer pull. Pulls can be metallic, glass or a combination thereof. But in the traditional drawer it is generally a wood pull turned on a lathe. The Shakers are famous for their simple yet elegant pulls. The one we will use here is a little more elaborate for purposes of adding modeling complexity and hence teaching moments.

I have no idea where the name cock beading came from. But it is a rather popular way to trim a drawer. In the old days a cock bead was formed with a beading tool that scratched a bullnose shape around the periphery of the drawer front. Then the idea of using bullnose shaped trim pieces was used. One advantage of the trim is that it can be placed either on the drawer itself, as we will model here, and as was the case with the beading tool, or around the drawer opening, as I did on the office table shown in **Figure 1**.

## ADDING COCK BEADING TRIM

In **Figure 2** you can see the finished Bedside Table with cock beading around the drawer. A closeup is shown in **Figure 3**. Notice how the cock beading, in this case walnut, set the drawer apart from the cherry stiles and rails and draws your attention to the blistered maple drawer front and cherry pull.

We will now model the cock beading. Make only Layer0 and the Drawer Front layers Visible. We are going to cut ¼" off the top of the Drawer Front, and cut a ¼" x ¼" rabbet around the other three sides. Put the Drawer Front in the Edit Component mode. Start with the Front, Iso, Zoom Extents view and using the Tape Measure tool, place a construction line ¼" down from and parallel to the top on the front face. The construction line and the edges of the Drawer Front will form a long narrow rectangle. To completely outline the rectangle draw a line from edge to edge along the construction line. See **Figure 4**. Then push

**Figure 1** | Office table with cock bead trim and lathe turned drawer pull

**Figure 2** | Finished Bedside Table with cock beading

**Figure 3** | Close up of drawer with cock beading

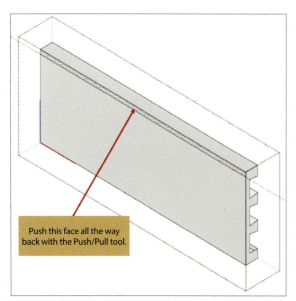

**Figure 4** | Long thin rectangle outlines the face to be pushed all the way back

Push this face all the way back with the Push/Pull tool.

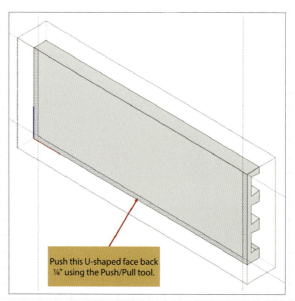

**Figure 5** | Use construction lines and Line tool to outline the U shape ¼" wide face

Push this U-shaped face back ¼" using the Push/Pull tool.

this face all the way back removing ¼" from the top of the Drawer Front.

Use this same technique on the ends and bottom, forming a U-shaped face (see **Figure 5**).

Instead of pushing all the way back, push the U-shaped face back ¼". You will be left with three faces on each end that need to be eliminated (see **Figure 6**). Do this by erasing their outermost edge with the Eraser tool. Exit Edit Component mode and with the Edit/ Delete Guides get rid of the construction lines.

We butchered this Drawer Front pretty well, so let's dress it up. To do this we are going to use the Rectangle tool to create a path for the Follow Me tool, which we will use to create the trim from a 2D cross section. We will create the path first, then the 2D cross section.

We would normally want to create the path in the place where it will do the most good, but without adding a few more figures to this chapter, that will be hard for me to describe. Therefore, we will create a rectangle on the Drawer Front face outlining its edges.

Using the Rectangle tool, we drag it from one corner to the opposite. Make sure you are creating the rectangle on the plane of the front most face of the

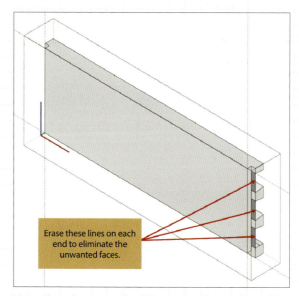

Erase these lines on each end to eliminate the unwanted faces.

**Figure 6** | Use the Eraser tool to delete unwanted lines and hence faces

Drawer Front. The rectangle should measure 12⅜" x 4⅜". Hide the Drawer Front layer by unchecking its Visible box. This will leave only the face we just created. It is visible on the active Layer0.

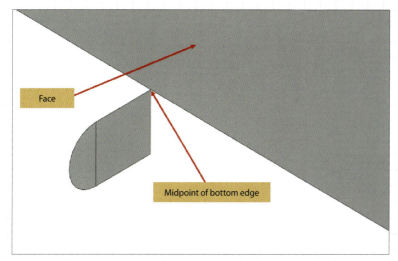

Face

Midpoint of bottom edge

**Figure 7** | Cock bead profile formed with Line and 2-Point Arc tools

Double click the face of the rectangle to select its face and all edges. With the Move tool move this rectangle back (toward the inside of the drawer) along the Green axis ¼". While it is still highlighted you can make the Drawer Front visible just to see where it ended up. Make the Drawer Front invisible again and deselect the rectangle by clicking in open space with the Select tool.

Study **Figure 7** to see what we want to accomplish in the next few steps. In **Figure 7** you are looking at the bottom edge of the rectangle at its midpoint, and a cock bead cross section has been created. To draw the cock bead cross section draw a ¼" x ¼" square with one corner at the midpoint of the bottom line. We will use the Line tool for this rectangle because it will make it easier to place it in the correct plane. Start at the midpoint and draw down ¼" along the Blue axis, out (away from the face) along the Green axis ¼", up along the Blue axis ¼" and close the square by click-ing on the starting point.

Now we are going to use the 2-Point Arc tool to complete the cross section. Select the 2-Point Arc tool. Click on each of the outermost (furthest away from the face) two corners of the small square we just completed. Slide the cursor out along the green axis and type 1/8r and press *Enter*. The r tells the 2-Point Arc tool to make the arc a semicircle of ⅛" radius or ¼" diameter. See **Figure 7**.

With the Erase tool, delete the diameter line so that there are no lines inside the periphery of the cock bead outline. Be patient, we are almost there. With the Select tool, select the face of the large rectangle (not the cock bead). Finally, select the Follow Me tool and with its cursor hover over the cock bead face and click. Select the face in the middle of the trim and delete it. Your picture should look like **Figure 8**. If your trim has the incorrect face coloring, don't panic. Simply triple click on the trim to select all primitives. Then right click on the trim to bring up the Context menu and choose Reverse Faces.

I bet you thought we were done because I said so. Well, I lied. We have a little more to do. We are going to delay making this trim a component for a few minutes. Using the Orbit tool rotate the trim until you can see its back and notice the back face is one surface. We need to draw little diagonal lines to create joints at the mitered corners. Do this with the line tool. See **Figure 9**.

## FOLLOW ME TOOL

When using the Follow Me tool always use one of two methods:
1. Choose a face whose perimeter will serve as the path.
2. Choose a path itself.

Then use the Follow Me tool's cursor to select the profile you wish to extrude. Many books, including SketchUp's own manuals, teach a method of tracing the path with the cursor. Avoid this method. It is frustrating and error prone.

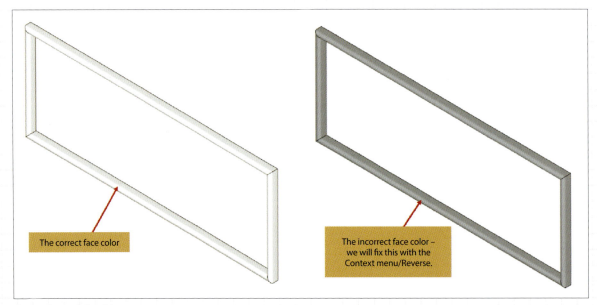

**Figure 8** | Extruded cock beat trim

The correct face color

The incorrect face color – we will fix this with the Context menu/Reverse.

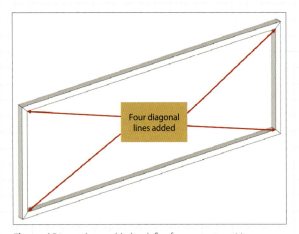

Four diagonal lines added

**Figure 9** | Diagonals are added to define four separate entities

three copies to create three different components. **Figure 10** shows the result of this copy operation.

In the original copy we are going to erase the vertical trim sections and the bottom section, leaving only the top section. In the second copy we are going to erase the vertical trim sections and the top section, leaving only the bottom section. In the third copy we want to leave only one vertical section and

Either with the select tool, or by triple clicking the trim, select all edges and faces. Using the Move/Copy tool make two additional copies of the cock bead trim and place them along the Red axis. Be sure to provide total separation between each copy because all copies are still in primitive form and will stick together if they touch. Use the Undo tool if you make a mistake. Do not move the original. What we want to end up with is three separate pieces of trim. We will use these

## SELECT TOOL

The Select ▶ tool is a powerful and multifaceted tool.

If you create a selection box by dragging left to right every object that is completely within the rectangle will be selected.

If you create a selection box by dragging right to left every object that is partially within the rectangle will be selected.

We will use these two techniques often to judiciously select only the desired objects.

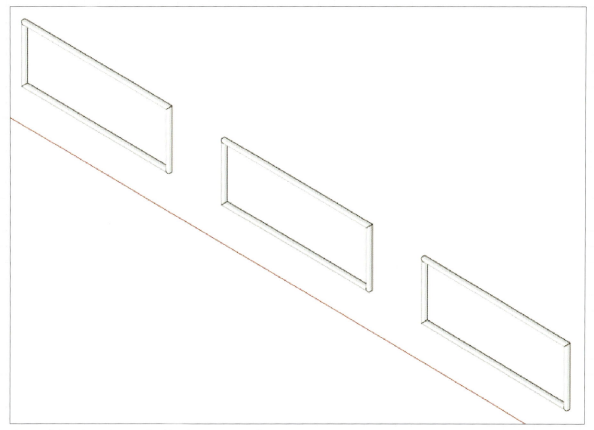

**Figure 10** | Three identical copies of cock bead trim in primitive form

erase the rest; arbitrarily we choose to leave the left vertical section.

There are several ways to do this erasure operation. First I will describe a method I don't recommend in this case. We could use the Erase tool as a paint brush; instead of clicking on an object to erase it we will hold down the left mouse button and wipe across the object, near its center, and then release the mouse. Repeat this until there are no unwanted primitives left. We do not want to erase anything close to the corners since that is where the curvature outline defines the miters of the pieces we want remaining. However, near the unwanted corners there will be small curvature lines that are difficult to see and may be missed. In addition you may find that you have to wipe across unwanted geometry many times. So in this instance I don't recommend this technique.

A better way to accomplish this erasure is to use the Select tool to create a selection box in the right to left manner. This way anything that is partially in the selection box will be selected. Using this approach we can capture the unwanted corners completely by surrounding them with the selection box while also capturing the unwanted edges partially. Viewing Front, Iso and Zoom Extents your picture should look like **Figure 11** (no other layers beside Layer0 should be visible at this point).

With the Select tool, create a selection box in a right to left motion that at least partially captures the vertical sides and the bottom of the original trim. Don't get close to the top miter joints. Release the mouse to make the selection and then press the *Delete* key leaving only the top primitives, see **Figure 12**.

**Figure 11** | Front view of three copies of the trim

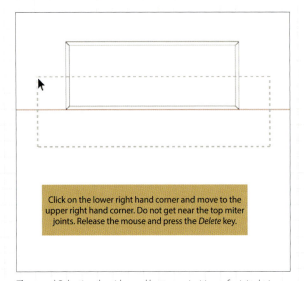

Click on the lower right hand corner and move to the upper right hand corner. Do not get near the top miter joints. Release the mouse and press the *Delete* key.

**Figure 12** | Selecting the sides and bottom primitives of original trim

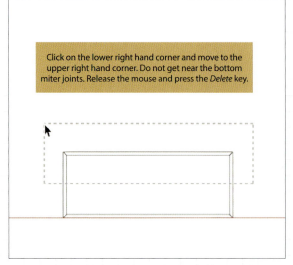

Click on the lower right hand corner and move to the upper right hand corner. Do not get near the bottom miter joints. Release the mouse and press the *Delete* key.

**Figure 13** | Selecting the sides and top primitives of the second trim

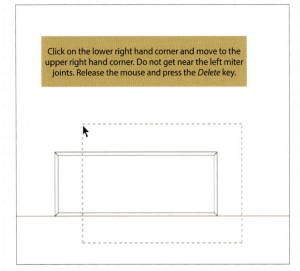

Click on the lower right hand corner and move to the upper right hand corner. Do not get near the left miter joints. Release the mouse and press the *Delete* key.

**Figure 14** | Selecting the top, bottom and right side primitives of the third rim

With the Select tool, create a selection box in a right to left motion that at least partially captures the vertical sides and the top of the original trim. Don't get close to the bottom miter joints. Release the mouse to make the selection and then press the *Delete* key leaving only the bottom primitives (see **Figure 13**).

With the Select tool create a selection box in a right to left motion that at least partially captures the right vertical side, top and bottom of the original trim. Don't get close to the left miter joints. Release the mouse to make the selection and then press the *Delete* key leaving only the left side primitives (see **Figure 14**).

Select the left vertical trim piece and make it a component called Side Cock Bead. Create a new Trim layer and place it there. The Trim layer must be visible for this next step. Select the Side Cock Bead and in the Entity Info box Name field name the instance

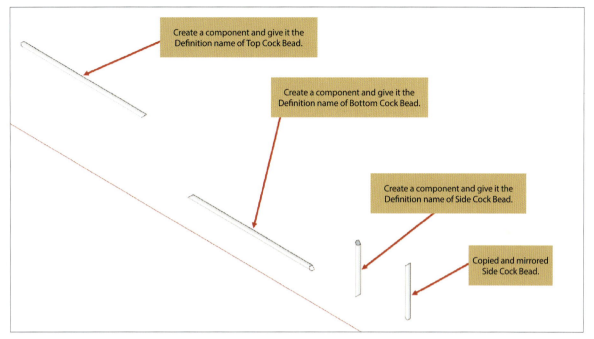

**Figure 15** | Three different components make up the cock bead trim

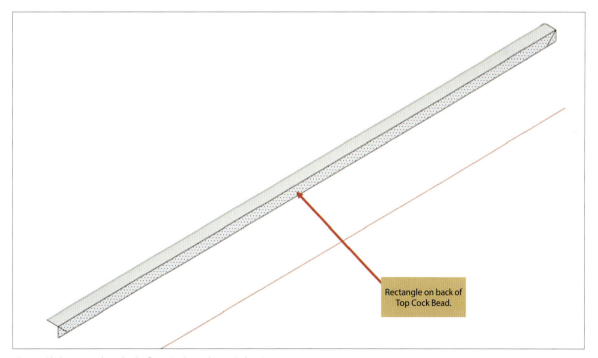

**Figure 16** | The rectangle on back of Top Cock Bead is 12 ⅞" by ¼"

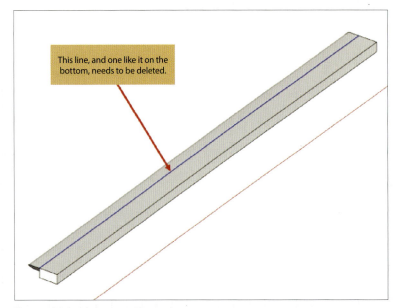

This line, and one like it on the bottom, needs to be deleted.

**Figure 17** | Delete the unwanted line as shown

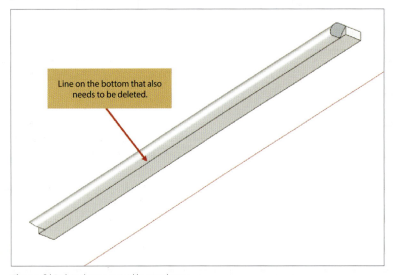

Line on the bottom that also needs to be deleted.

**Figure 18** | Delete the unwanted line as shown

Left Side Cock Bead. Leave Trim layer visible. Use the Move/Copy tool to copy this piece and move it along the Red axis. With Context menu Flip Along/Components Red, mirror it and change its instance name (Name in the Entity Info dialog box) to Right Side Cock Bead. Make components of the bottom and top

trim pieces; name them as shown in **Figure 15**. Their instance name (Name in Entity Info dialog box) can be the same as their component name.

OK we are almost done. Really! But we need to add some stock to the upper trim piece. Check to make sure you put all four parts on the Trim layer. Make only Layer0 and Trim layer visible. Choose view Back, Iso and Zoom in on the back of the Top Cock Bead. The top edge of the back face of Top Cock Bead is 12⅞" long. Use the Tape Measure tool to verify it. We want to create a cube (remember our definition) 12⅞" long by ½" wide (into the drawer along the Green axis) by ¼" thick. Do not put the Top Cock Bead in Edit Component mode. Leave it a component for now.

With the Rectangle tool create a rectangle 12⅞" x ¼" with the upper left corner of the rectangle coincident with the upper left corner of the Top Cock Bead's back face, and the ¼" dimension running down the Blue axis. See **Figure 16**. With the Push/Pull tool, pull this face toward you (toward the inside of the draw); type 1/2 and press *Enter*.

Select the Top Cock Bead, right click on it and choose Explode. Before doing anything else and while the Top Cock Bead's primitives are still selected look at the Entity Info dialog box and notice that these primitives have been placed on the Trim layer. This is a consequence of the Explode command. When you explode a component with the Explode command, all its primitives are placed on the layer

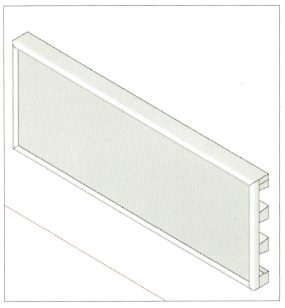

**Figure 19** | Cock bead trim pieces positioned on the Drawer Front

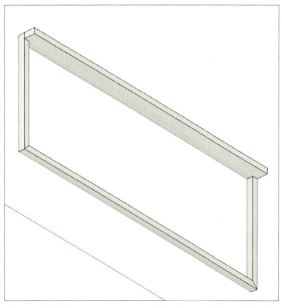

**Figure 20** | Back view looking up at cock bead trim, sans Drawer Front

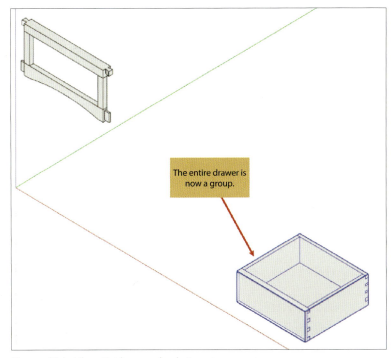

The entire drawer is now a group.

**Figure 21** | Select the entire drawer and make it a group

that the component resided on prior to the Explode command being used. You must return them to Layer0. Using the Entity Info Layer drop-down select Layer0.

The exploded primitives that once belonged to the Top Cock Bead instance are now attached to the primitives of the added cube. The line separating the cube and the exploded primitives now needs to be deleted as well as a similar line on the bottom. See **Figures 17** and **18**.

You may notice that some surfaces of the cock bead trim pieces are different colors than others. Those that seem to be the wrong color can be changed by placing that component in Edit Component mode, right clicking on the offending face and choose Reverse Faces. Make layer Drawer Front visible, and with the Move tool,

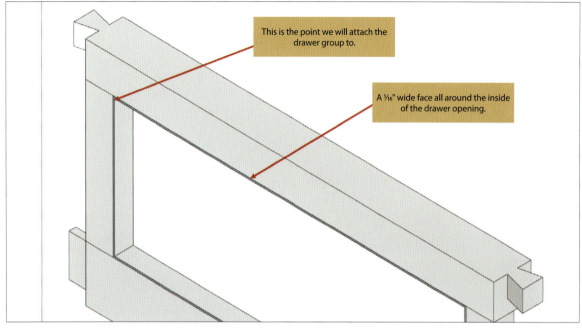

Figure 22 | The 1/16" wide face all around the drawer opening provides assistance placing the drawer group

move all cock bead trim pieces into position. Their positions should be obvious. The Front, Iso, Zoom Extents view should look like **Figure 19**.

Choose the Back and Iso view. With the Orbit tool look at the cock bead trim from underneath. Uncheck the Drawer Front Visibility. The back view should now look like **Figure 20**.

Before we go any further, let's place the drawer in the table where it belongs. Make visible the active Layer0, Drawer Back, Drawer Bottom, Drawer Front, Drawer Sides, Stiles, Upper Rail, Lower Rail and Trim. Select only the entire drawer, no part of the table carcass, using the Select tool. Right click on the selection and choose Make Group. This may be the only time we used Make Group in the whole text so far. The Component structure is much more powerful and efficient than the Group structure, but a Group is sometimes useful on a temporary basis for moving things around. Your model should look like **Figure 21**.

Use Front view and Zoom Extents. If you measure the overall dimension of the assembled drawer and the drawer opening in the table, you will see that the assembled drawer is 1/8" smaller in each direction.

This is to allow a 1/16" space all around the drawer for expansion/contraction and to keep the sides from binding. We will use the Rectangle tool to make an outline for positioning in the table opening by clicking on opposite corners of the opening, i.e. where the stiles and rails meet.

Next, use the Offset tool to create a smaller rectangle (and face) by dragging inward 1/16". Select the inside face and delete it. **Figure 22** shows the remaining 1/16" wide face. Notice the point in the upper left hand inside corner that we want to use as an attach point for the drawer group. Now, with the drawer group selected, use the Move tool to place the drawer group in the smaller opening. Hint: the cock beading should be proud of the stile and rail faces by 1/8". Use an endpoint of a corner curve (miter) to pick the group up and place it. See **Figure 23**. Select the drawer group, right click and Explode to eliminate the temporary group.

Uncheck all layer Visible boxes except the active Layer0 and then delete the primitives we used to center the draw. Make all layers visible. Choose Front, Iso and Zoom Extents and your model should look

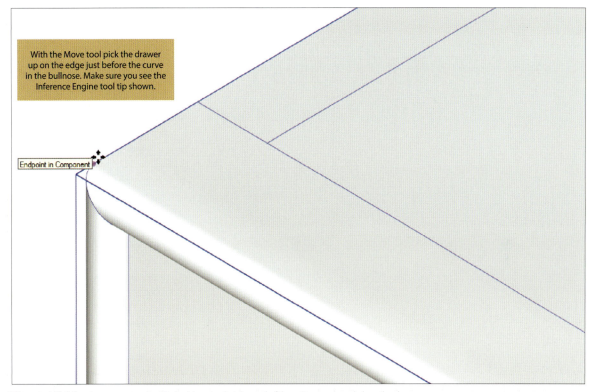

With the Move tool pick the drawer up on the edge just before the curve in the bullnose. Make sure you see the Inference Engine tool tip shown.

Endpoint in Component

**Figure 23** | Pick the drawer group up with the Move tool at the end of the miter curve and place the drawer

**Figure 24** | Completed Traditional Drawer with cock bead centered in drawer opening sans drawer pull

like **Figure 24**. The drawer should be centered in the drawer opening with the drawer's front face, stile's front faces and rail's front faces all on the same plane. The cock bead trim should stand proud of this plane by ⅛".

## ADDING A DRAWER PULL

Our table is almost complete. Did I promise that once before? Sorry! All we need to complete it is a drawer pull, which we will add now.

Make all layers invisible except active Layer0 and the Drawer Front layer. We will start by finding the center of the drawer front's face, the surface where the pull will be attached. This is done with the Tape Measure tool using opposite corners to create two diagonal construction lines. Be sure to place these lines on the front surface of the Drawer Front. Select the Tape Measure tool and be sure the cursor shows a + sign. If it does not display a + sign press the *Ctrl*

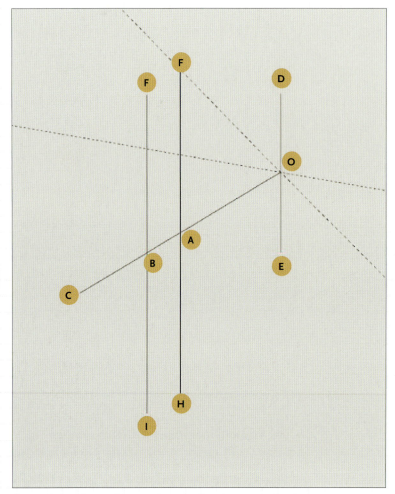

**Figure 25** | Layout lines and annotated points to form the Drawer Pull outline

With the Line tool, draw the following line segments: OA normal to the Drawer Front face and ⅜" long, line AB extended from OA ⅛" and line BC extended from AB ¼". The total line OC should be ¾" and normal to the Drawer Face. Assuming we are all on the same axis this normal line will be parallel to the Green axis.

Now we are going to draw six lines perpendicular to the normal line we just drew and parallel to the Blue axis. There will be three line pairs with lines in opposite directions, sort of like equal but opposite vectors (scared you with that physics stuff, huh?). The first pair is OD and OE, each ¼" long and on the face of the Drawer Front. The second pair, AF and AH, start at point A which is ⅜" out from the face and are each ½" long. The last pair, BG and BI, starts at point B which is ½" out from the face (⅛" + ⅜"), and are each ½" long.

Providing we did everything right so far, we can draw a line DF and EH, which will create two coplanar faces. Also draw lines FG and HI to create two more coplanar faces. These faces are temporary and are there to assist us in drawing arcs coplanar to these planes.

With the 2-Point Arc tool click first on F and then G. Raise your cursor a little bit along the Blue axis until you see the Blue axis guide line. Use the Up arrow key if you need assistance obtaining the Blue axis. Type 1/16 and press *Enter*. This places an arc between F and G that has a bulge height of ¹⁄₁₆", but because F and G are ⅛" apart, chord FG is also the diameter of a circle ¹⁄₁₆" in radius. Repeat these steps with points H and I, this time pulling the arc down along the blue axis guide line and typing 1/16 and pressing *Enter*.

key to get it. Using the Tape Measure cursor click on one corner of the Drawer Front face and then click on the diagonally opposite corner. Do the same thing with the remaining two corners. This will create two construction lines that cross at the Drawer Front's center and are the construction lines that appear in **Figure 25**.

Review **Figure 25**. Shown are the essential layout lines that will define the pull. I hope to avoid nightmares of high school geometry class, but we will refer to these lines by addressing them as line segments, e.g. OA is a line drawn from the origin (point O in this drawing) to point A.

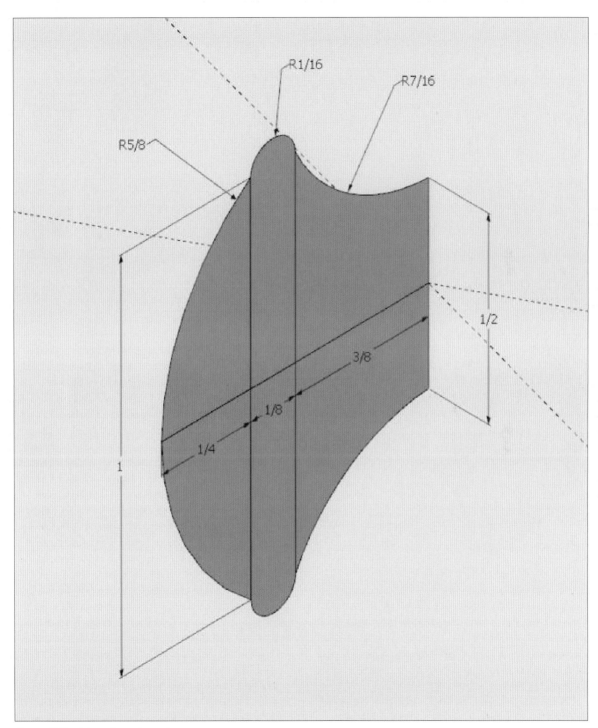

**Figure 26** | Check these dimensions to be sure yours are correct

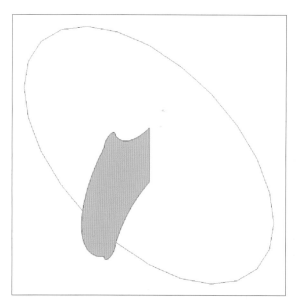

**Figure 27** | Drawer Pull outline and path for the Follow Me tool

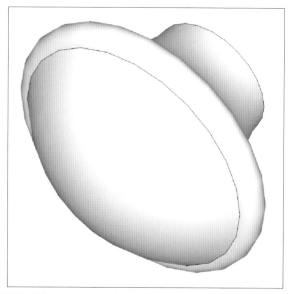

**Figure 28** | Completed Drawer Pull but with sharp circular transitions

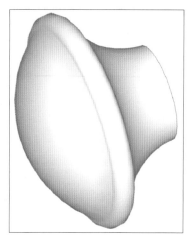

**Figure 29** | Completed Drawer Pull with smoothed circles

DF and EH. Your drawing should now look like **Figure 26**, minus the dimensions, which I added so that you can check to see you have drawn things correctly.

Delete the construction lines and all internal straight lines leaving only one straight line (DE) forming the edge along the Drawer Front face. Select the Circle tool and hover over the Drawer Front face away from the pull outline until you get a green Circle tool cursor. Hold the *Shift* key down and click on Point O. Release the *Shift* key and move the cursor up along the Blue axis and type 1 and press *Enter*. This places a 1" radius circle on the face of the Drawer Front centered at Point O. Select its face and delete it; we only need the circumference of the circle as a path for the Follow Me tool.

Make the Drawer Front layer invisible. Only Layer0 and the Drawer Pull outlines should be visible as shown in **Figure 27**. Select the circle which will be used as the path for the Follow Me tool. Select the Follow Me ✿ tool, and with it, click on the face of the Drawer Pull outline. You now have a Drawer Pull in primitive form. You may have a situation similar to **Figure 8** where the Drawer Pull is the wrong color. If you do simply triple click on the Drawer Pull, right click and choose Reverse Faces.

Using the 2-Point Arc tool, click first on D and then F. Drag your cursor downward. This time you will not get a Blue axis guide line, but you should get a tool tip saying On Face. Be sure you do, then type 1/16 and press *Enter*. Do the same with points E and H, but drag the cursor upward.

With the 2-Point Arc tool, click first on point G, then I and finally C. This will place an arc GCI. Now you can erase straight lines FG, HI,

**Figure 30** | Completed Bedside Table model in Perspective view

Triple click the Drawer Pull and Make Component. Give it both a Definition name and instance Name of Drawer Pull and place it on a Drawer Pull layer. Delete the circle path, it has done its job and is no longer needed. Your drawing should now look like **Figure 28**.

When the Follow Me tool is used in this fashion it is a simple tool to master. However, if you try to use it the way it is taught in most Trimble SketchUp documentation and many books, you will find it very frustrating. If ever you see a method that involves tracing a path with the Follow Me cursor, ignore that approach. It will surely get you in trouble and frustrate you. Use one of the methods outline in the shaded box called Follow Me Tool.

Our Drawer Pull looks OK at this point, but let's make it look a little better. The Erase tool operates in a couple of modes; used with only the *Ctrl* key it softens and smooth's lines. We have two circles we want to soften and smooth. These are the circles that were formed by Points F, G, I and H in **Figure 25**. In Edit Component mode use the Eraser tool with the *Ctrl* key held down to accomplish this. Use the Eraser tool's cursor like a paint brush to drag over the lines and soften them. The Front and Back views can be used to access the circles easily. Exit Edit Component mode when done.

The Drawer Pull in **Figure 29** looks more natural than the one in **Figure 28**, and when textured it will look great. We could have used the Circle and 2-Point Arc tools with more line segments to better approximate circles and arcs, but it would take more computer resources and bloat the model's file size. It is a judgment call as to whether that is worth it.

Make all layers visible. Click the Home View Scene tab. Go to menu Camera/Perspective and click. Click Zoom Extents. Right click the Home View Scene tab and choose Update. Select "Save as new style" and Update. Our model is now complete as far as modeling it goes. We still need shop drawings, and we want to texture the entire model. But for all intents and purposes this is our completed model and it should look like **Figure 30**. Note that **Figure 30** is a Perspective view. The only occasions I use Perspective views are when I want to present a model in a visually

realistic or photorealistic manner. Open the Scenes dialog box by going to Window/Scenes. There should be one scene called Home View; select it to highlight it. In the Name field change the name to Perspective and press *Enter*.

We are finally done with modeling the traditional drawer. See, I promised! In Chapter 8 we will learn how to add attachments to our SketchUp tool called plugins, specifically the Layers Management tool. Then, in Chapter 9 we will dimension the entire piece (or at least the student will). Don't forget to save your model.

## CHAPTER REVIEW

We began this chapter with a short description of cock beading and the various ways it can be implemented. The cock bead is essentially a bullnose trim. It can be formed directly on the drawer front with a scratch tool. Mitered cock bead pieces can be added in a rabbet around the drawer front or alternatively around the drawer opening.

In this text we chose to add cock bead trim in a rabbet around the drawer front. To accomplish this we used the Tape Measure tool to add construction lines and then the line tool to form two types of faces: a long narrow face and a U-shaped face. We used the Push/Pull tool to push the long narrow face back the entire depth of the Drawer Front removing ¼" of material. The U-shaped face was pushed back ¼" completing the rabbet.

With the now smaller face, smaller by ¼" on all sides, we used the Rectangle tool to form a face and edges, which eventually served as our path for the Follow Me tool to follow. To put the path in the appropriate place we moved it back ¼" with the Move tool.

Next we created the cock bead outline using the Line and 2-Point Arc tools. And then we introduced a new tool: the Follow Me 🖘 tool. With it we placed bullnose trim all around the Drawer Front. This left us with a one piece cock bead trim, something we would find difficult to build in the shop. We cut this trim into three distinct pieces using the Line, Eraser and Push/Pull tools, and made each a component. The side piece was used twice, one of them a mirror of the other which we accomplished with the Flip Along tool. All pieces were then arranged in the rabbet with the Move tool.

To create the Drawer Pull we used the Tape Measure, Line and 2-Point Arc tools. The path for the Follow Me tool was provided by the Circle tool. We again used the Follow Me ✆ tool to extrude the Drawer Pull. Note that we used the Follow Me ✆ tool to form two components: the cock bead trim and the Drawer Pull. In the first case we chose a face whose perimeter would provide the path and then used the Follow Me ✆ tool. In the second case we chose the path directly: a circle. Then we again used the Follow Me ✆ tool. Both these methods are automatic and easy. I cautioned you against using a popularly taught technique of tracing the path with the Follow Me ✆ tool.

Finally we dressed up the Drawer Pull with the Eraser tool and the *Ctrl* key to soften some hard edges. We grouped the assembled drawer with the Make Group tool, something we had not done before. To provide assistance in placing the assembled drawer in the drawer opening we used the Rectangle tool and the Offset tool. When the assembled was in place we Exploded the Group and erased the assisting face.

Throughout this chapter we used an impressive array of tools as I just outlined. Some of these tools are very powerful, though sometimes difficult to use if you don't understand their subtleties. I intentionally gave you less handholding in the form of step-by-step instructions, but hopefully provided enough pictures for you to follow and understand what those steps should be.

In this chapter we introduced the following new tools listed in the order they were used:
✆ Follow Me

We again used the 2-Point Arc, Circle and Offset tools, which we have used sparingly in this text, but discovered they have numerous uses.

## EXERCISES FOR THE STUDENT

1. We formed the rabbet around the Drawer Front with the Tape Measure and Line tools. You should be able to do it in fewer steps with the Offset tool. Try it.

2. Try forming the cock bead trim and the drawer pull using the Follow Me tool and tracing the path. Compare the level of difficulty to the way we did it in this text.

3. Remake the Drawer Pull. This time, when drawing the path circle, change the default segments of 24 to something larger, like 48 or 60. Notice how much more appealing the Drawer Pull is.

# 08

# RUBY SCRIPT EXTENSIONS

*Ruby scripts are like jigs and fixtures. They are often written by the hobbyist code hackers for use in their own copy of an application, SketchUp, in this case. Like woodworkers who build jigs and fixtures and share them with fellow woodworkers, hackers also share their Ruby scripts with fellow applications users.*

*The large majority of Ruby script extensions are free, though some cost a few bucks. They are found on the Internet and are easily downloaded and installed. Most also come with a license to modify, copy or otherwise use except commercially.*

*SketchUp Ruby script extensions, when installed, increase the functionality of SketchUp, much like a jig or fixture enhances a tools capabilities. In this chapter we discuss how and where to find Ruby script extensions and how to install them. In fact, we will install one of my own called Layers Management tool.*

SketchUp Make 2015 and SketchUp Pro 2015 was a transition year for SketchUp. For example, SketchUp became a 64-bit application with the 2015 release. A change we are interested in, and a point I need to clarify, is the use of Ruby scripts, plugins and extensions nomenclature.

## RUBY SCRIPTS

Ruby scripts are rather small software programs written in the Ruby language. (Script is a term used by software engineers to indicate short lengths of code written in a runtime interpreted language to control or debug a process or application.) When you add a

Ruby script to your SketchUp application you are adding functionality in the form of new tools or behavior. In a sense you are customizing your application. Because there are so many SketchUp Ruby scripts available, you can choose only those most useful to you and in so doing create an application unlike any other; somewhat like custom furniture.

Most Ruby scripts can be viewed in a text editor such as Microsoft's Notepad. When viewed this way they appear as a cryptic English language code. In fact they are. Ruby scripts are essentially source code, they are not compiled until called on by an application (software engineers refer to this as runtime inter-preted). In order for an application to call on a Ruby script it must have the ability to interpret the source code while it is running. SketchUp has this ability. Built into SketchUp is a Ruby applications programming interface (API), meaning SketchUp has the hooks necessary to interpret Ruby code. The SketchUp Ruby API not only understands Ruby code but it has extensions to the basic code set that understands how to access SketchUp specific properties such as line lengths, circle radii, component names and most importantly how to activate SketchUp tools. Both Ruby and Sketch-Up's Ruby API are well documented on the Internet and both are easy to learn. However, it is not necessary to learn either of these languages to locate install and use Ruby scripts. Everything you need to know will be presented in this chapter.

## PLUGINS VERSUS EXTENSIONS

Ruby scripts written specifically for SketchUp prior to release 2015 appeared on the Plugins menu when installed. Most SketchUp users refer to SketchUp Ruby scripts simply as plugins. In fact, the actual Ruby script code files are placed in a folder called Plugins. I'll provide more on that later. With the release of version 2015 the Plugins menu has been changed to Extensions to be consistent with the Preferences page used to activate them and the Preference button used to install them. However, the folder in which the Ruby script code files reside is still called Plugins. One should think of Plugins and Extensions as the same. I will use them interchangeably except when referring to the Plugins folder, which I will always call Plugins.

I am going to show you how to install an extension (plugin) using the Preferences Extensions page's Install Extensions button, which requires a RBZ Ruby script file extension. This procedure will work with any Ruby script extension file with a RBZ file extension, or even a Ruby script extension with a ZIP file extensions by first changing the ZIP extension to RBZ. Do not confuse the use of the word extension in "Ruby script extension file" with "RBZ Ruby script file extension" or simply "file extension." The first refers to the plugin and the second and third to the last three letters of a file name.

To demonstrate this installation process I am going to use one of my own extensions called Layers Management tool. Layers Management tool is a tool you will need to create shop drawings which is the subject of Chapter 9. But first let me outline the general SketchUp Ruby script extension installation procedure.

## RUBY SCRIPT EXTENSION INSTALLATION PROCEDURE

The procedure that follows can be used to install any Ruby script extension file with an RBZ or ZIP file extension.

1. Download the Ruby script extension you wish to install. Save it in your Downloads folder or on your desktop. Be sure to remember where you saved it.
2. If the Ruby script extension you are trying to install has a ZIP file extension change it to .rbz.
3. Log into your computer as an administrator before installing any Ruby scripts. This will make the installation go more smoothly and ensure that files get installed in the proper places. If yours is the only user name on the system you are likely already logged in as administrator.
4. In SketchUp select Window > Preferences (Microsoft Windows) or SketchUp > Preferences (Mac OS X). The Preferences dialog box is displayed.
5. Click on Extensions. The Extensions page is displayed.
6. Click on the Install Extension button. The Open dialog box is displayed.
7. Locate and select the Ruby script extension file to install (.rbz). You likely saved it in your Downloads folder or on your desktop.
8. Click on the Open button. The Ruby plugin appears in the list of extensions.
9. You may see a message asking if you trust the author of this Ruby script. If you do click the Yes button. (Hint: I am trustable.)
10. You may get a message announcing successful installation. Click OK.
11. In the Extensions panel you may see the extension you just installed; not all extensions register in

the Extensions panel. If it is there make sure to check it.

12. Close SketchUp. On the Mac make sure all model windows are closed and indeed the SketchUp application itself is closed. Now reopen SketchUp.

## THE LAYERS MANAGEMENT TOOL

SketchUp is a great tool and one that seems ideally suited for woodworking or more correctly the woodworker. However, like many shop tools we use, there is often missing capability and we woodworkers build jigs and fixtures to overcome those shortcomings. SketchUp is no different. Fortunately, the designers of SketchUp provided a wonderful method for filling the voids in its functionality: The SketchUp Ruby API provides a means for anyone to write Ruby programming language scripts to extend SketchUp's functionality. Because layers are such an important tool to the woodworker, one he/she needs to design and document custom furniture, and because SketchUp has missing functionality to effectively manage layers, I wrote this script (tool).

There are two personalities to the Layers Management tool: Layer0 Warning, which attempts to keep one out of trouble by warning the user when he/she changes the active layer to other than Layer0; and Layer Tools which are a tool set used to create layers and make them all visible or invisible.

## LAYER ZERO WARNING

I have taught SketchUp to a large number of students; through live courses, DVDs and online videos. Based on their feedback and conversations I have had with other instructors, it is clear there are two dominant areas students struggle with.

1. The stickiness of SketchUp is stumbling block number one. Anytime two primitives touch they become connected. This is useful if those primitives are meant to touch, such as when they are pieces of the same part. But if they are pieces of different parts, this stickiness creates huge

**Figure 1** | The View menu showing Layer Zero Warning enabled

**Figure 2** | Layer Zero Warning message box

made active, a warning message will appear as shown in **Figure 2**.

Notice that the message tells you which layer will become the active layer and also how to disable the warning. If a layer other than Layer0 is currently active and then Layer0 made active, no warning is given because Layer0 is the desired layer for modeling. Note that this is just a warning; Layer0 Warning will not prohibit the layer change. The user must decide if this change was intentional or accidental. If the latter, the user must manually change back to Layer0. Click OK to close the warning message box.

I should point out that I am an experienced SketchUp user and I never disable Layer0 warning. It is too easy to accidentally change the active layer and get into serious modeling trouble.

## LAYER TOOLS

Depending on how you use SketchUp you may find these tools helpful. I tend to use a lot of layers and scenes in my models, especially when it comes to dimensioning them. For example, I typically use one scene per dimensioning view and add those dimensions and components to a matching layer. If you add layers via the ⊕ icon in the Window/Layers dialog box a new layer is added but visible to all existing and new scenes. This requires going back to all current scenes as well as future scenes and making the new layer invisible if not desired. If the number of current scenes is large this is a time consuming task.

Many moons ago I discovered add_hidden_layer.rb coded by Jim Foltz. It allowed me to add a layer hidden to all current and future scenes. It was a life saver but still had a few minor problems; there was no tool icon, and I really wanted to add a layer visible to the current scene but hidden in all others.

Another little annoyance is that SketchUp provided no tool to make all layers visible or all invisible, both of which I found I could use frequently. That was when I

problems. The solution is for students to follow the "Six Rules for 3D Modeling in SketchUp" found at the beginning of Chapter 3. I have found that students who follow these rules, particularly Rule 4, "As soon as a part takes 3D shape make it a component," escape this problem entirely.

2. The second largest stumbling block is the accidental or intentional violation of Rule 2: "Layer0 (Layer Zero) should always be active when modeling." To help students avoid this problem I have added functionality to the Layers Management tool that will warn of a Rule 2 violation.

The intent of Layer0 Warning is to let a beginner know when he/she is about to change from active Layer0 (Layer Zero) to another layer. By default Layer0 Warning is enabled the first time the Layers Management tool is installed as shown in **Figure 1**. From then on the last state of Layer0 Warning will be stored upon closing SketchUp and recalled upon subsequently opening SketchUp.

If you wish to disable the warning, go to menu View/Layer0 Warning and uncheck it.

If you wish to re-enable Layer0 Warning, go to menu View/Layer0 Warning and check it.

When enabled Layer0 Warning will monitor the active layer (the layer with the radio button selected to the left of its name). If a layer other than Layer0 is

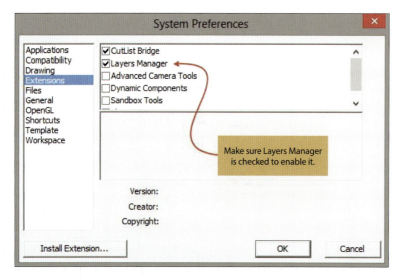

Figure 4 | Extensions Page with Layers Manager checked

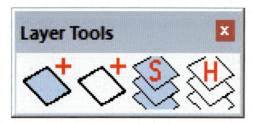

**Figure 3** | The Layer Tools toolbar

The Layer Tools toolbar is available under View/Toolbars; make this toolbar visible by choosing View/Toolbars and checking Layer Tools. The toolbar is shown in **Figure 3**.

Add Visible Layer ◇ adds a visible layer to the currently active scene, but invisible to all existing and new scenes. Add Visible Layer always adds a layer to the Layers list but its Visible check box is unchecked in all scenes *except* the scene that is currently active (scene tab is blue), or if only one scene exists it is the active scene. If there are no scenes a layer is added and its Visible check box is checked.

Add Invisible Layer ◇ adds an invisible layer to all existing and new scenes. Add Invisible Layer always adds a layer to the Layers list but its Visible check box is unchecked in all current and future scenes. If there are no scenes, a layer is added and its Visible check box is *checked*.

Show All Layers ◈ makes all layers visible.

Hide All Layers ◈ makes all layers invisible.

> ✏️ Once you have created a scene in your model, I suggest you no longer use the Add Layer tool found in the Layers dialog box. Use either Add Invisible Layer or Add Visible Layer instead. This will save you untold cleanup work. If you don't know which one to use, the Add Invisble Layer is the most harmless.

discovered layers_show_hide_all.rb coded by Madcello. It was perfect except it also had no tool icons.

To make my life easier, I combined these tools into one Ruby script adding the tool icons and the visible layer for the current scene functionality. I called this new extension Layers Management tool, which embeds both the Layer Tools and Layer0 Warning functionality.

The Layer Tools can be found in the View menu as shown in **Figure 1** and has its own Layer Tools toolbar with the following icons:

- Add Visible Layer ◇
- Add Invisible Layer ◇
- Show All Layers ◈
- Hide All Layers ◈

## INSTALLING THE LAYERS MANAGEMENT TOOL

Download the Layers Management tool found at srww.com/sketchup_a_guide_for_woodworkers.html web page in the Downloads section of the book (Part 2, Chapter 8) to a folder

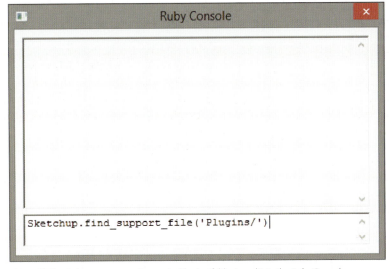

**Figure 5** | Toolbars dialog box with Layer Tools checked

where you can easily find it. Either your Downloads folder or your desktop would be a good place to choose. Use the installation procedure outlined in the section of this chapter titled Ruby Script Extension Installation Procedure.

When SketchUp is reopened go to the View menu and be sure Layer0 Warning is checked as shown in **Figure 1**. In the Window/Preferences dialog box choose the Extensions page and be sure Layers Manager is checked. See **Figure 4**.

Lastly, go to menu View/Toolbars and check (select) Layer Tools as shown in **Figure 5**. This will place the Layer Tools toolbar somewhere on the SketchUp window (or possibly even on your desktop area outside the SketchUp window). You can drag and drop it anywhere you want.

## REPORTING PROBLEMS WITH LAYERS MANAGEMENT TOOL

I hope this script improves your efficiency a little. Please report all bugs and strange behavior to: jpz@srww.com.

## LOCATING YOUR PLUGINS FOLDER

You don't need to know where your Plugins folder is to install Layers Management tool, or any other tool for that matter, but you might want to know where it is to verify you installed an extension correctly

**Figure 6** | The Ruby statement to locate the Plugins folder typed into the Ruby Console

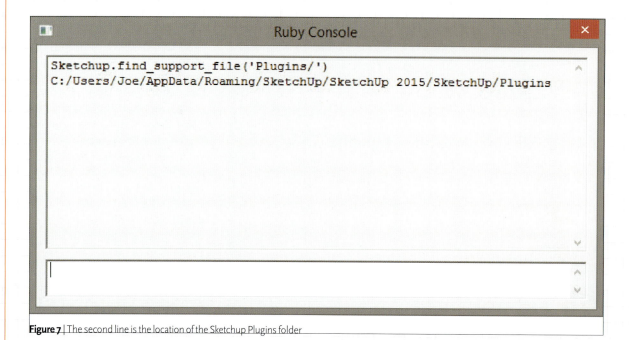

```
Sketchup.find_support_file('Plugins/')
C:/Users/Joe/AppData/Roaming/SketchUp/SketchUp 2015/SketchUp/Plugins
```

**Figure 7** | The second line is the location of the Sketchup Plugins folder

**Figure 8** | The Warehouse toolbar

or to remove an extension. If you don't know where it is you can find it using the Ruby Console. To open the Ruby Console go to the Window menu and click on Ruby Console. The Ruby Console will appear. In the white area at the bottom type the following line of text exactly:

SketchUp.find_support_file('Plugins/')

It should look like **Figure 6**. Press the *Enter* key and you will see the results shown in **Figure 7**. Note that I had to drag the right side of the window to enlarge it so the folder location would appear all on one line. The Plugins folder location is shown on the

second line. Copy and paste the folder location and save it for future reference.

## THE EXTENSION WAREHOUSE

There are a number of places on the internet where you can go to get Ruby script extensions. Built into SketchUp is the Extension Warehouse, which is a repository of extensions that are distributed by Trimble and the SketchUp team. To access the Extension Warehouse you must first access the toolbar. Under menu View choose Toolbars and bring up the Toolbars dialog box. Under the Toolbars tab look for and check Warehouse. This will place the Warehouse toolbar shown in **Figure 8** on your desktop. Click on the Extension Warehouse 🛞 icon to bring up the Extension Warehouse window.

The Extension Warehouse window, shown in **Figure 9** is really a web page. On the right is a scroll bar and if you scroll down you will see extension types and quantity listed by catagories and industries. Along the right hand side you will see the top extensions

**Figure 9** | The Extension Warehouse window

**Figure 10** | The SketchUpcation toolbar

(popularity) and top developers. At the top is a search field. Type Bezier into that field; there is no need to press *Enter*. A dropdown appears with further choices. Choose Bezier Curve Tool. A new page appears with still another list. At the time of this writing the second extension on the list is the Bezier Curve Tool by the SketchUp Team. If you select this line item a page appears where you can install the tool by selecting the Install button. We will need this extension for Part Three, so install it now.

At the time of this writing there were 320 extensions in the Extension Warehouse and growing almost daily. The good news about Extension Warehouse is that installion is as simple as clicking on an Install button.

## SKETCHUCATION PLUGIN STORE

Another place to find Ruby script extensions is the SketchUcation Plugin Store. You will first want to install the SketchUcation Plugin Store extension. In your web browser go to:

sketchucation.com/plugin-store-free-download

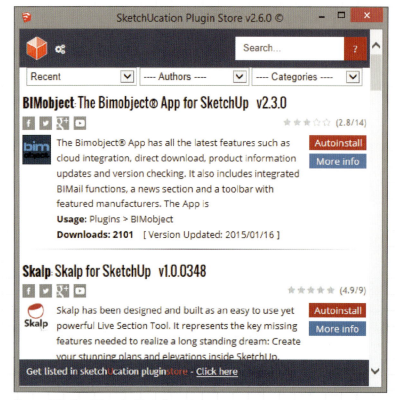

**Figure 11** | The SketchUpcation Plugin Store window

Store window shown in **Figure 11**. Along the top of the SketchUcation Plugin Store window you will see a Search box. If you know the name of the extension you are looking for, you can type it into the box and search for it. For example, type Bezier into the box and press *Enter*. At the time of this writing, the first extension returned is Fredo6: Bezier Spline v1.7a. Fredo6 is the author's handle, as the CB radio users used to say. Bezier Spline is the name of the extension and v1.7a is the revision number. We will come back to this one later on because we will need it in Part Three.

If you don't know the name of the extension, along the top you have drop-down boxes to help you locate the one you are looking for. In one drop-down you can choose Full List, Recent or Popular. In a second dropdown you can choose the author's name, and in a third, the category. These three drop-downs combine as a filter for the extension list.

Notice in **Figure 11** that installing a SketchUcation distributed extension is a simple matter of clicking on the Autoinstall button. I am not sure how many extensions are in the SketchUcation Plugin Store, but I suspect the number is more than are in the Extension Warehouse at the moment.

You will be asked to join or sign in. You can use a Google account username and password if you have one. Once you join or sign in you will arrive at a page where you can download the SketchUcationTools.rbz file. When asked, save the file to your Downloads folder or desktop. Then use the general installation procedure outlined earlier in this chapter to install the SketchUcation tools.

After completing the installation procedure under the Window menu choose Preferences and select the Extensions page. Make sure SketchUcation is checked. Next go to View/Toolbars to bring up the Toolbars dialog box. Under the Toolbars tab locate and check SketchUcation Plugin Store. The SketchUcation toolbar will appear as shown in **Figure 10**.

When you want to go to the SketchUcation Plugin Store simply select the SketchUcation Plugin Store icon. This will bring up the SketchUcation Plugin

## EXTENSIONS YOU WILL NEED OR WANT GOING FORWARD

Here is a list of extensions you will need as you go forward in this book or might want to make your work easier. Tools that are authored by me can be found at the companion web page srww.com/sketchup_a_guide_for_woodworkers.html in the Downloads section for Chapter 8.

## The Layers Management Tool

This tool is needed in future chapters. The Layers Management tool is authored by me. You should have installed it "The Layers Management Tool" section of this chapter.

## Bezier Curve Tool

This tool is needed in future chapters. The Bezier Curve tool is authored by the SketchUp Team. It is distributed in the Extension Warehouse where you can find it by searching for Bezier Curve tool.

## Weld

This tool is needed in future chapters. The Weld tool is authored by the Smustard team. It is distributed in the Extension Warehouse where you can find it by searching for Weld.

## Construction Plus

This tool is actually a set of tools. It is not needed, but certain of its tools may prove helpful when drawing Bézier curves, particularly the Construction Line and Construction Point tools. Construction Plus is authored by me.

## CutList Bridge

CutList Bridge is not needed for this text. But once you have completed this text, I am quite sure you will design your own furniture projects to build in your shop. This tool will help you create cut lists automatically and assign attributes to parts such as material type and name, subassembly name, oversize dimensions, etc. CutList Bridge is authored by me and has an extensive user's guide.

## OTHER SOURCES OF SKETCHUP RUBY SCRIPT EXTENSIONS

There are numerous places on the Internet where you can find SketchUp Ruby script extensions. Here are a couple I keep my eye on.

## Smustard.com

Smustard.com is a web page that contains a large number of extensions. Many of the extensions listed on Smustard.com cost a few bucks, but not all. Smustard.com also has a forum where you can get help. The home page is smustard.com.

## Ruby Library Depot

The Ruby Library Depot is another good repository for extensions. It is a French site but you can get it in English at rhin.crai.archi.fr/rld/index.php. This site also has many links to other sources of extensions and forums where you can get help.

## Chiefwoodworker's Blog

My own blog is where you will find my extensions targeted at woodworkers. You can get to it at srww.com/blog.

# 09

# CREATING SHOP DRAWINGS

*Our Bedside Table is complete as far as modeling is concerned. Many modelers end their 3D models at this point or perhaps go on to texture them to produce photorealistic images. But we are woodworkers; we need shop drawings from which to craft our pieces. Shop drawings are the focus of this chapter.*

*Creating shop drawings involves two primary operations: creating scenes of the components we wish to dimension, and adding dimensions to those scenes. These two important operations are what we will learn in this chapter, but to do so we need a little help from a Ruby script. Ruby scripts were discussed in Chapter 8 where you should have installed the Layers Management tool extension. When this chapter is completed we will be able to adjourn to the shop and begin crafting.*

In this chapter we are going to create shop drawings by creating Scenes, each with a different view and content, and nearly all with dimensions for that content. To keep things readable we are going to put all dimensions on their own dimension layer. For example, we will dimension the Top and place its dimensions on a Z-Top layer. I have the habit of prefixing all dimension layers with Z so that they appear at the end of the alphabetical layer list. This helps when you want to look at the model only, without dimensions. This is not necessary, but it's my convention. You may develop your own convention later, but for now we will follow this one.

I have one other convention: I prefix all cross sections and exploded views with X. A cross section of the Drawer might appear on layer X-Draw AA meaning it is a cross section of the Drawer with view AA. This model doesn't need a cross section drawing because of its simplicity, but we will do one anyway just to see how it works.

We will add numerous layers and scenes as we go along (actually I will show you how to do a few and you will do the rest), and the order in which we add them may be rather random. SketchUp has what I consider an annoying oversight in features relative to adding layers. Let's say you have a number of scenes

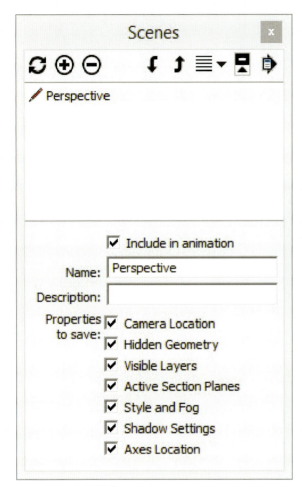

Figure 1 | The Scenes dialog box

Figure 2 | The Styles In Model dialog box showing one style

defined (there are 21 in the Bedside Table model), and each scene has a different combination of layers that you specify because they make sense to you. Later you decide to add another scene with another combination of layers including one or more layers not yet created. When you add a layer in the way we have been doing so far in this text – using the Add Layer ⊕ icon in the Layers dialog box – SketchUp is going to add that layer(s) to the definition of *all* currently existing scenes. This is not likely what you intended. Unfortunately, it can only be remedied by manually going back to each scene and redefining it. I know of no way to prevent this short of adding functionality via a Ruby script.

Good news! Such a script exists. It is written by yours truly and is the Layers Management tool and you should have installed it in Chapter 8. If not, go back to Chapter 8 and do so now.

## WHAT ARE SCENES?

Let's get the tough stuff out of the way first. A scene is a SketchUp object with attributes. The scene's object is stored in the model's file (.skp) so that it follows the model's file from machine to machine. The object, when created by SketchUp, has a unique identifier (ID), which the user never sees. The user can give the scene's object a name, but there is no requirement that the name be unique. The scene's object name is seen by the user, so it is possible to have two scenes with the same name that look totally different to the user.

OK, that description is very close to technically correct; at least as technically speaking as we want to get in this text. But now let's simplify it so that you can understand and use the terminology. We will refer to the object as simply a scene. The scene's name will be the object's name given by the user and we would

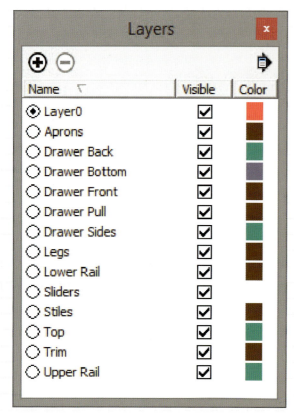

**Figure 3** | The Layers dialog box with all layers visable

Our model already has one scene called Perspective; let's look at it in more detail. **Figure 1** shows the Scenes dialog box with our only scene called Perspective. Notice that all the check boxes are checked indicating some of the properties we want saved with a scene. Most important here are Camera location, Visible Layers, and Style and Fog. In our shop drawings we will not use Shadows so we might uncheck that one, but I generally leave all the check boxes checked.

**Figure 2** shows the Styles dialog box with one style. This is the Woodworking Style we set up in Chapter 1, "Configuring the Workspace." One of the properties of this style is the Shaded With Textures View/Face Style. That is appropriate for the Perspective scene because once we texture this model, the Perspective scene will be our photorealistic scene intended to give a prospective client a photo like image to evaluate. However, for our shop drawing we will want to use Monochrome View/Face Style so we will soon create another style for our model.

In **Figure 3** we see the Layers dialog box for the Perspective scene. Note that all the layers we have made so far are visible because we want a completed model for the photorealistic Perspective scene. Something we could do here is uncheck the Visible boxes for Drawer Back, Drawer Bottom, Drawer Sides and Sliders since these components are internal and don't show in the Perspective view anyway. In a large model this may be worth doing to improve model performance if you are going to employ animation. But for our purposes we leave them checked.

Compare the Layers dialog box for the Perspective view from the finished Bedside Table model shown in **Figure 4** to ours at this point shown in **Figure 3**. Notice that none of the Z layers are visible because they don't apply to a photo of the finished table. It's time to create some more scenes and dimension this model.

## CREATING A SCENE

A Scene is an individual view of a model that can be printed to scale as a shop drawing. Most models will have many scenes and hence many shop drawings to make up a shop drawing set.

hope the user doesn't assign the same name to two different scenes. I will call the object's attributes properties. A short, and not complete list, of properties a scene can have are: Style defined by the Styles' In Model dialog box; visible layers defined by the Visible check boxes checked in the Layers dialog box; Face Style as defined by menu View/Face Style; other properties defined by the View menu such as Hidden Geometry, Axes, Guides, Section Cuts, etc.; and Camera position, which may be defined by the menu Camera/Standard Views or by any of the Camera tools.

There is a very strong partnership between Scenes, Camera, Styles, Face Styles and Layers. Scenes are largely defined by Camera position, the Style used, the Face Style chosen and the Layers made visible. As mentioned, there are other properties that may be included such as Perspective or Parallel Projection, but the former are the primary properties.

## Layers

| Name | Visible | Color |
|------|---------|-------|
| ⦿ Layer0 | ☑ | |
| ◯ Back | ☑ | |
| ◯ Drawer Back | ☑ | |
| ◯ Drawer Bottom | ☑ | |
| ◯ Drawer Front | ☑ | |
| ◯ Drawer Pull | ☑ | |
| ◯ Drawer Sides | ☑ | |
| ◯ Drawer Trim | ☑ | |
| ◯ Legs | ☑ | |
| ◯ Lower Rail | ☑ | |
| ◯ Sides | ☑ | |
| ◯ Sliders | ☑ | |
| ◯ Stiles | ☑ | |
| ◯ Top | ☑ | |
| ◯ Upper Rail | ☑ | |
| ◯ Z-Back | ☐ | |
| ◯ Z-Drawer Back | ☐ | |
| ◯ Z-Drawer Bottom Back View | ☐ | |
| ◯ Z-Drawer Bottom Side View | ☐ | |
| ◯ Z-Drawer Bottom Top View | ☐ | |
| ◯ Z-Drawer Front | ☐ | |
| ◯ Z-Drawer Pull | ☐ | |
| ◯ Z-Drawer Sides | ☐ | |
| ◯ Z-Drawer Sides Detail | ☐ | |
| ◯ Z-Drawer Trim | ☐ | |
| ◯ Z-Leg | ☐ | |
| ◯ Z-Lower Rail | ☐ | |
| ◯ Z-Overall Front | ☐ | |
| ◯ Z-Overall Side | ☐ | |
| ◯ Z-Sides | ☐ | |
| ◯ Z-Slider Arrangement | ☐ | |
| ◯ Z-Sliders | ☐ | |
| ◯ Z-Stiles | ☐ | |
| ◯ Z-Top | ☐ | |
| ◯ Z-Upper Rail | ☐ | |

**Figure 4** | The Layers dialog box for the finished model with only applicable layers visable

Open SketchUp with the Bedside Table model we completed in Chapter 7. Select the Add Invisible Layer ◇ tool. An input box will appear titled Add Invisible Layer. In the Name box type Z-Overall Front and click OK. Notice the new Z-Overall Front layer in the Layers dialog box and that its Visible box is not checked; it has been added as a hidden layer. Just to be sure, click the Perspective scene tab and notice it is still not checked.

Let's give our new tools a test drive. Select Hide All Layers ⬚ and notice that there are no Visible boxes checked except Layer0. Now select the Show All Layers ⬚ tool and notice all layer Visible boxes are checked including Z-Overall Front's Visible box.

Let's create a scene called Front View. In the Scenes dialog box click the Add Scene ⊕ icon. In the

## ALWAYS USE PARALLEL PROJECTION FOR DIMENSIONED SCENES

While it is possible to dimension scenes displayed in Perspective view, and indeed many SketchUp books and tutorials do just that, it is not only technically incorrect, but a big mistake. The whole purpose of dimensioning is to create shop drawings that can be used to craft a piece. To that end we want to print these scenes out and bring them to the shop.

Shop drawings are most helpful when they are scaled. It often matters not what the scale is. You can use a 6" or 12" scale in the shop to compare and measure dimensions from scaled drawings. This is impossible to do with perspective drawings because perspective drawings cannot be printed to scale.

Further, if you wish to make a 1:1 drawing to use as a shop template, it must be a parallel projection.

See "Configuring the Workspace" on page 25 for further detail.

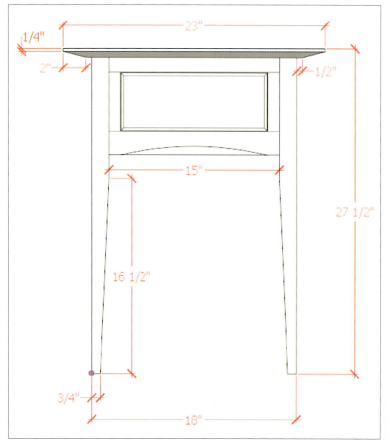

**Figure 5** | Front View dimensions (notice the outside labeling)

scene was a future scene. Now check the Visible box for layer Z-Overall Front. Right click on the Front View tab and choose Update.

Alternately select between the scene tabs to observe their behavior and the animated transitions. Observe the Visible box for layer Z-Overall Front in each scene. Notice it is only checked for the Front View scene. Choose the Front View scene.

## DIMENSIONING THE MODEL

With the Front View tab selected and the Z-Overall Front layer Visible box checked, we are ready to add some dimensions. You will have to zoom in and out a lot to assist dimensioning; we need space around the model for the dimensions and we need to look very closely at the points we choose with the tool. A mouse with a scroll wheel is very helpful for this.

Name field type Front View. Check the "Include in animation" box and all boxes under "Properties to save" if they are not already checked. Choose the Front view. Also choose Camera/Parallel Projection and Zoom Extents. Right click on the Front View tab and choose Update.

Notice that the Visible check boxes are the same as they were in the Perspective scene. There are two reasons for this: First, we didn't reconfigure the Visible check boxes prior to updating the Front View scene; second, the Z-Overall Front layer was added using the Add Invisible Layer ◇ tool which makes it invisible to all future scenes unless explicitly configured otherwise. Since Z-Overall Front layer was added before we created the Front View scene, Front View

Start with the top. Select the Dimension ✴ tool and click on the top left front corner of the top, then the top right front corner. Now move the cursor up to a height that looks right for the dimension placement and click again. The Dimension tool is very simple, intuitive and predictable. However, it also has some intelligence as we will see in a moment, and we need to manage that intelligence.

The top dimension in the Front View is 23". Check your dimension. If your model is reading in feet and inches you may want to choose menu Window/Model Info and on the Units page select Fractional in the Format drop down box.

Now, using the Dimension ✴ tool, click on the lower right front corner of the right leg, and then click on the top right front corner of the top. Pull the

**Figure 6** | A warning that you have changed a style; you need to make a selection

cursor to the side and up slightly. Notice that even though the points we chose are not vertically aligned, the Dimension � tool has figured out that we want an overall height measurement. Click when the placement looks right. If we had not "pulled up slightly" in the latter step the Dimension � tool would have assumed we wanted the straight line dimension between the points we picked, and sometimes that is just what we do want. Experiment with the Dimension ✗ tool and dimension the rest of the Front View.

On a few dimensions you will notice there is no room for the labels to fit inside the dimension arrows. Simply right click (context click) on the troublesome dimension and choose Text Position and then either Outside End or Outside Start. This will reposition the text so it is clearly readable.

Sometimes you have to orbit the model in the middle of using the Dimension ✗ tool to click on a point you want. Either before selecting the Dimension ✗ tool or between dimension endpoints choose a Camera tool such as Orbit to reposition your scene and then click the Dimension tool again to resume with the dimension. Often you can accomplish the same thing by using Wireframe view.

When you are done and your model looks like **Figure 5** click Front view and Zoom Extents to be sure all dimensions are included. Also choose Monochrome view because unlike the Perspective view, this will be

a shop drawing and does not need to be textured. Texturing would just make the drawing more difficult to read in the shop. Right click on the Front View scene and choose *Update*. This is necessary because you have added dimensions, and when you used Zoom Extents your model got smaller in the window to allow for the dimensions. Also we made a change to our style with the Monochrome rendering view.

A Warning – Scenes and Styles dialog box will appear as shown in **Figure 6**. Select the "Save as a new style" radio button.

## MOVING DIMENSIONS TO THE APPROPRIATE LAYER

The dimensions we added are on Layer0. We need to put them on layer Z-Overall Front. The following sequence will do that:

1. Select menu Window/Entity Info to open the Entity Info dialog box.
2. Select the Hide All Layers ✖ tool to make all layers except Layer0 invisible.
3. Use the Select tool to create a selection box to select all dimensions and highlight them. You can also use menu Edit/Select All.
4. In the Entity Info dialog box select layer Z-Overall Front in the Layer drop down box. (At the time of this writing there is a software bug that sometimes results in errors when using the Layer drop down box in the toolbar. It is best to use the Entity Info box for this purpose.)
5. Click the Front View scene tab and make visible layer Z-Overall Front.
6. Click Zoom Extents.
7. Right click the Front View tab and choose Update.

Alternately choose the Perspective scene and the Front View scene tabs. Observe the rendering Style Face alternate between Monochrome for Front View scene and Shaded With Textures for Perspective scene. Also look at the Camera menu after each scene selection and notice how Parallel Projection and Perspective alternate. Lastly, look in the Styles' In Model dialog box and notice a new style called Woodworking Style 1. SketchUp added the 1 on the new style. You can

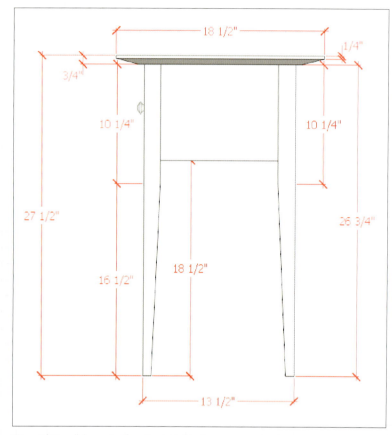

18 1/2"

1/4"

3/4"

10 1/4"

10 1/4"

27 1/2"

26 3/4"

16 1/2"

18 1/2"

13 1/2"

**Figure 7** | Overall dimension from the right side view

change it if you like, but for the purposes of being consistent with the text leave it as is.

## ADDING MORE SCENES

We are now going to add another scene called Side View. But before we do make sure the Front View scene tab is selected. Notice that the Z-Overall Front layer is visible. Now in the Scenes dialog box click the Add Scene ⊕ icon. Notice that even before we give the scene a name a scene tab has been added (likely) called Scene 3 and for Scene 3 all layers are visible except Z-Overall Front. Recall how Add Invisible Layer ♦ works; when used, the added layer is invisible in the current and all future scenes. In the Scenes dialog box Name field type Side View and make sure all the check boxes are

checked. Click Right view and Zoom Extents.

Add another layer called Z-Overall Side, but this time use the Add Visible Layer ♦ tool. Notice that layer Z-Overall Side is checked but Z-Overall Front is not. Right click the Side View scene tab and choose Update; we will update scenes whenever we make changes to them. Now go to the Perspective scene and notice that neither Z layer is checked. Go to the Front View scene and notice Z-Overall Front layer is checked but not Z-Over-all Side. Lastly, go to the Side View scene and notice that Z-Overall Side is checked but not Z-Overall Front. By now you are probably getting the hang of how the Layer tools work.

Since both sides are identical we only need to dimension one side. Click the Right view icon so that we are looking at a 2D drawing of the right side. From this point on you must manage the layers you want in the scene. The Layers Management tool can help, but you must choose the layers you want. At this time we want all layers except Z-Overall Front visible, which should be the case.

Dimension the Side View as shown in **Figure 7**. You will find that if you switch to Wireframe Face Style during dimensioning you can access the endpoints for your dimensions much easier. Once you have done that make sure to switch back to Mono-chrome Face Style and click Zoom Extents to be sure all dimensions are included. Right click on the Side View scene tab and choose Update.

Now use the procedure under heading "Moving Dimensions to the Appropriate Layer" with the appro-priate views and layers to put these dimensions on the Z-Overall Side layer. Now click the Side View tab and check your results which should appear as **Figure 7**.

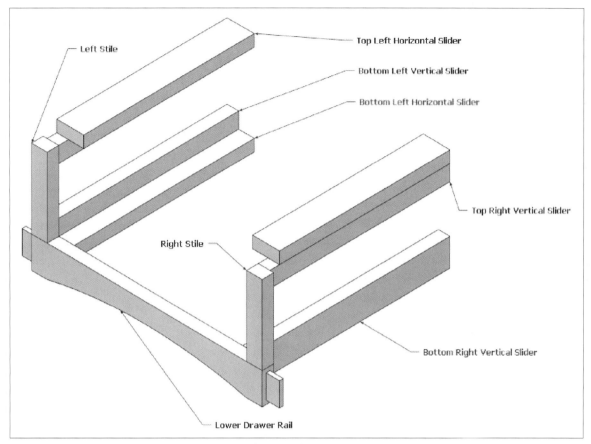

Left Stile

Top Left Horizontal Slider

Bottom Left Vertical Slider

Bottom Left Horizontal Slider

Top Right Vertical Slider

Right Stile

Bottom Right Vertical Slider

Lower Drawer Rail

**Figure 8** | Slider Arrangement scene from the Bedside Table reference model

Continue this process to create all scenes, layers and dimensioned views. Use the completed Bedside Table reference model to check your progress and correctness. It is located at srww.com/sketchup_a_ guide_for_woodworkers.html – you will find it under Downloads, Part Two, Chapter 3.

Sometimes it is more beneficial to use an Isometric view (Iso view icon) for dimensioning. In the Bedside Table reference model look at scene Legs where this approach was employed. This allows you to dimension in 3D and is quite helpful in situations like this. There are times when dimensioning a scene can be aided by turning on the X-Ray tool. This would allow dimensioning facets of a component that would otherwise be difficult to dimension, for example dados that are not visible otherwise. However, when you do this you may want to make a note that X-Ray is turned

on to expose detail otherwise hidden to avoid confusion. I haven't done this in the reference drawing. However, if you download the Shaker Tall Clock model via the Free Plans page of my srww.com web site, you will see a scene called X-Ray Base Bottom. In this case, the X-Ray tool gives the woodworker a good idea of the various millings required to form the base bottom components.

## ADDING LEADER TEXT AND NOTES

Leader text and notes can easily be added to a scene. I have never used the 3D Text ✎ tool for any useful purpose and will not discuss it here, though I am sure it has its place. The Text 🄰 tool, however, is an essential part of dimensioning. It is used much like the Dimension tool.

## ADDING LEADER TEXT

To place leader text simply click on a point with the Text tool cursor, then click a second time to position the text box where you want it, enter the desired text and finally click on white space in the SketchUp workspace; you are now ready for the next Leader Text.

When you click the second time with the Text tool to position the text box a suggested label will appear. That suggested label will be highlighted and ready for editing. If the component you first clicked on has an instance name (part name found in the Entity Info box Name field), it will be the suggested label. If the component has no instance (part) name, then the component name (found in the Entity Info box Definition field) will be the suggested label. However, you don't need to use the suggested label. While it is selected and highlighted in blue, type your desired label into the text box. **Figure 8** is the Slider Arrangement scene from the Bedside Table reference model and an example of accepting the suggested labels.

Select a leader text object and look at the Entity Info box. Note that in the Arrow field you can choose Closed arrow, Open arrow, Dot or None. I like closed arrows, but this is a personal choice. Note also that you can hide the entire leader by choosing Hidden in the Leader drop-down field. Instead of selecting a leader text and making these changes in the Entity Info dialog box you can also right click on a leader text to bring up the Context menu and make the same selections there. You can select multiple leader text objects and use either the Entity Info dialog box or the Context menu to make changes to more than one object. If you want to change a default for your model or update the default to your template, use menu Window/Model Info's Text page and make selections in the Leader Lines section.

## ADDING NOTES

Creating notes is similar to creating leader text. In fact, you can create a note just like creating a leader text by making the following two changes: First, override the suggested label with your note; second, hide the leader. The leader and its arrow can be hidden via the Entity Info dialog box or Context menu as explained earlier.

A simpler method is to click with the Text tool icon on white space in the workspace roughly where you want the note. A text box is opened with the words "Enter text" highlighted. Type your note and when you are done click in white space. Now you can use the Move tool position your note.

Look in the Bedside Table reference model at scenes Back and Drawer Bottom Back View. In the Back scene you will see an example of a note with no leader. In the Drawer Bottom Back View scene you will see an example of a note with a leader. Use notes liberally; wherever you need to explain something or point out a build process.

## CREATING AN EXPLODED VIEW

Exploded view scenes can easily be created by copying an entire model or subassembly, and placing it on an exploded layer. I use a convention of beginning the name of the layer with a capital X and hyphen, for example X-Layer Name. This is similar to the Z convention for the dimension layers.

I am going to create a Drawer Exploded scene using these general steps:

1. Add a new scene called Drawer Exploded using the Add Scene ⊕ icon in the Scenes dialog box.
2. Add a new layer called X-Drawer using the Add Invisible Layer ◇ tool icon.
3. Make all layers except Layer0 invisible using the Hide All Layers 🦑 tool icon.
4. If you haven't already, rename the Trim layer to Drawer Trim (this is not necessary but just to be consistent with the Bedside Table reference model).
5. Make Drawer Back, Drawer Bottom, Drawer Front, Drawer Pull, Drawer Sides and Drawer Trim visible. This displays just the entire drawer and no carcass parts.
6. Select the entire drawer and with the Move/Copy tool. Make a copy and move it to the right along the Red axis (be sure the copy is well clear of the original). Before doing anything else type 2x and press *Enter* to make two copies. See **Figure 9**. In this step be sure you do not move the original drawer.
7. Select the two drawer copies on the right and with the Entity Info box place them on layer X-Drawer.

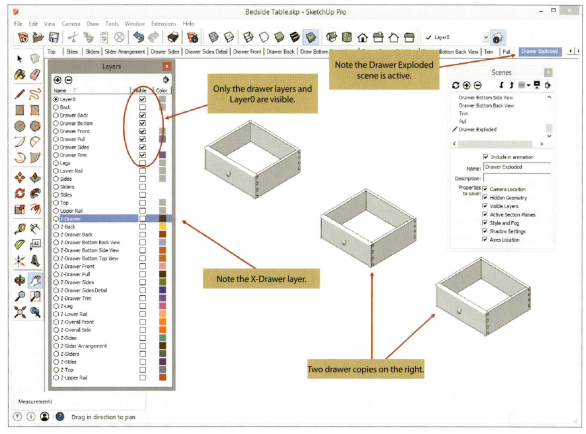

**Figure 9** | Original drawer on the left and two copies on the right

8. Using the the Hide All Layers ⬚ tool icon, make all layers invisible, except Layer0.
9. Make layer X-Drawer visible. You should now have two complete drawers in the workspace and no other parts.
10. Using the Move tool, pull the individual parts apart and arrange them as you would like and label them with leader text. This is an iterative process and you may have to move the entire right most box further to the right along the Red axis to make room.
11. Label the pulled apart parts with the Text ⬚ tool.
12. Make sure that only the X-Drawer and Layer0 layers are the only layers visible at this point. Use menu Edit/Select All and place the drawer copies and the leader text on the X-Drawer layer.

13. Zoom Extents and right click on the Drawer Exploded view and choose Update.

Your model should now look like **Figure 10**. This is a fairly simple exploded view, but you can see how powerful it can be in a more complex design.

## CREATING SECTION VIEWS

Although not needed for the Bedside Table, let's add a section view just for fun. Add a scene called Section AA just as we did for all other scenes. With the Section AA scene tab selected, choose menu Camera/Parallel Projection, Front, Iso and Zoom Extents. If the Section tools are not visible in your workspace, check Section in the Toolbars dialog box. Choose the Section Plane ⬚ tool and move the cursor over the

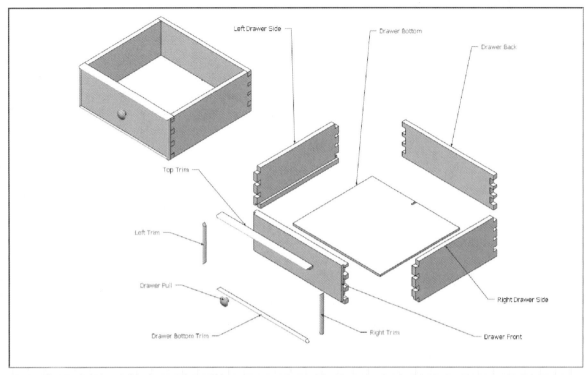

**Figure 10** | An Exploded view of the drawer subassembly

**Figure 11** | A section cut created with the Section Plane tool

model. As you move it, the tool selects a plane parallel to the one you are over. Move your cursor over the drawer front and click. An orange section plane appears. With the Select tool, select the section plane by clicking on one of the corners, and then choose the Move tool to move it back and forth. Position it about in the middle of the model and click. Deselect Display Section Planes ✏, found near the Section Plane ✦ tool. Right click the ISO Section scene tab and choose Update.

Now switch between the Section AA scene and any other scene and back to Section AA scene. It may take a little time for the section to draw when returning to the Section AA scene, so be patient. Your picture should look like **Figure 11**.

Note that the cross section exposes inside faces of solid material. This is because, unlike traditional 3D drawing packages such as AutoCAD and TurboCAD, SketchUp is not a solids modeler. You can download a Ruby script called SectionCutFace.rb written by TIG ©, which places a command on the context menu. This command restores the faces on the exposed ends. A little cleanup is required, but the results produce a much more readable and pleasing picture.

You can add dimensions to section planes, which can be tremendously helpful in complex drawings. We are not going to go any further with sectioning, but I suggest you experiment with it to get a feel for its capabilities. You should complete dimensioning of the bedside table and reproduce all 21 scenes of the reference model.

In the next chapter, we will texture the entire table with several wood textures and see if we can make it look photorealistic.

## CHAPTER REVIEW

This chapter began with a completed model of the Beside Table. Our task was to create shop drawings. Shop drawings created in SketchUp Make are a series of scenes, each scene with a different arrangement of layers, including layers that contain only dimensions. Since we were careful during the modeling phase to place components judiciously on appropriate layers, this task was relatively easy.

To make things easier, we introduced a Ruby script extension called Layers Management tool. This tool allowed us to add layers without upsetting our current scene definitions and to display all or hide all layers. From this day forward we swore to never use the dastardly Add Layer ⊕ tool again.

We created a Perspective scene with Perspective rendering instead of Parallel Projection. This is because in the next chapter we will use the Perspective scene, once textured, as our photorealistic image. We can then show this photorealistic image to prospective clients should we have the need.

The remaining scenes we created generally included one layer with only dimensions. When we created these dimension layers we used a convention of naming them with a prefix of Z-. This placed them at the bottom of an alphabetical list of layers.

We judiciously created scenes by figuring out what components we wished to include for dimensioning.

That defined the layers that needed to be visible. We chose a viewing angle using the standard views in parallel projection so that our shop drawings would be to scale. Then we dimensioned the components and placed all dimensions on a companion Z layer. The layer choices, viewing angle and dimensions became our scene definition. We repeated this process until all components were dimensioned.

We also learned how to create notes and annotated exploded views and even experimented with a cross section view.

In this chapter we introduced the following new tools listed in the order they were used:

◇ Add Invisible Layer
◆ Add Visible Layer
◈ Hide All Layers
◈ Show All Layers
✸ Dimension
▣ Text
✧ Section Plane
◉ Display Section Planes

We again used the Add Layer, Remove Layer, Add Scene and Remove Scene tools.

## EXERCISES FOR THE STUDENT

1. Make a layer other than Layer0 active and observe the behavior of the Layer0 Warning tool. Experiment with enabling and disabling Layer0 Warning to further observe its behavior. When done, make Layer0 active.

2. At the very beginning of this chapter, we added a Z-Overall Front layer with the Add Invisible Layer tool and showed that this new layer was not visible in the Perspective scene. That was rather simple proof of the benefit of these Layer Management tools. To see even more striking proof use the Add Layer ⊕ tool in the Layers dialog box to add a layer called Test. Select the Hide All Layers ◈ tool so that only Layer0 is active and visible. Draw a 9" x 9" x 9" cube at the origin. Make it a Group and place it on the Test layer. Now click on each scene tab and see what has happened. When you

are done use the Delete Layer ⊖ tool to delete the Test layer and its contents.

3. What is Perspective view and what purpose does it serve?

4. What is Parallel Projection used for and why?

5. When dimensioning, what layer are the dimensions initially placed on (assuming you are following the "Six Rules for 3D Modeling in SketchUp")?

6. Why do I prefix my dimension layers with Z and place all applicable dimensions on that layer?

# 10

# TEXTURING THE BEDSIDE TABLE

*We have dimensioned prints that will allow us to begin crafting. But what if we designed this Bedside Table on commission? We would need the client's approval to begin crafting. To present our design to the client in its best light we might want to create a photorealistic image.*

*This is where texturing enters the picture as a woodworkers tool. SketchUp makes texturing easy and the results are quite good. They can be improved upon with rendering engine add-ons, which I will introduce you to in this chapter, but our focus will be texturing using the basic SketchUp tools.*

In this chapter we will texture the Bedside Table with wood grain of the species the finished piece will have. To obtain the wood grain textures I used photos I took of previous furniture pieces I had built and applied finish.

With the help of Adobe Photoshop I was able to create JPG files of representative grain for each species used in the Bedside Table. I am not going to describe the steps I performed in Photoshop since that is beyond the scope of this text, but you can use any JPG file (or many other file formats) as a texture. The quality of the JPG will determine whether your model looks realistic or not. The tradeoff is that higher quality requires larger files and bloated models. The choice is yours. For this text I have opted for a reasonably high quality to demonstrate the capabilities of SketchUp. However, rest assured, I am not an expert SketchUp modeler; an expert can do far better than I have here, but I think the objectives of this chapter will be achieved, as demonstrated by **Figure 1**. Compare **Figure 1** with **Figure 30** in Chapter 7. Which one would you prefer to present a prospective client?

## WHAT LEVEL OF PHOTOREALISM CAN ONE ACHIEVE?

**Figure 1** is a good example of what can be achieved with the basic SketchUp tools available in SketchUp Make and Pro versions. But there are many add-ons on the market for very reasonable prices that can do much better. Before we begin texturing our Bedside Table with SketchUp's basic tools, I want to introduce you to a few.

**Figure 1** | When this chapter is completed, your picture should look like this one

**Figure 2** | Stand-up desk rendering

## WARREN SNOW'S TEXTURING & SU PODIUM EXPERIENCE

I first heard from Warren when he left feedback on my blog February 20, 2011. While looking for tutorials on SketchUp he ran across my web site. Five days later he had completed the beginner's tutorials (Warren had previous experience with other CAD tools) and was asking my opinion of add-on renderers for SketchUp.

On March 1 he wrote me to say he had chosen SU Podium. In his note he outlined the criteria that led to this choice.

On March 10 he sent me his first rendering; a dining table on a stone-tiled floor against pale green walls. It was quite good but not a finished product. On March 15 he sent a first rendering of a Stand-up desk at around 10 a.m. This was followed by the final

**Figure 3** | Modeled by Joe Zeh; rendered by William Manning

rendering at 6 p.m. that evening. You can see the results in **Figure 2**.

The point of this detailed chronology is that Warren went from beginning SketchUp tutorials on one day and less than a month later had learned SketchUp enough to create an original design, texture it, learned to use SU Podium, a rendering add-on, and produce a professional looking photorealistic image. Granted he had experience with other CAD tools, but often that gets in the way of learning a new tool, especially one so different from other tools as SketchUp is.

Notice how real the shadows look in **Figure 2**. The books were a nice touch and done with texturing. The carpet actually appears to have a 3D texture.

Su Podium V2 Plus is a SketchUp photorealistic rendering add-on, though SU Podium calls it a plugin. Essentially it replaces the rendering engine in SketchUp. SU Podium sells for $198 and is available for both the PC and Mac. For more information see suplugins.com.

## IDX RENDITIONER'S RENDERING OF MY CHERRY CHEST OF DRAWERS

William Manning is former Senior Director, IDX Division, IMSI/Design, makers of the IDX Renditioner photorealistic add-on for SketchUp. William contacted me one day and asked if he might download my Cherry Chest of Drawers model from my web site and render it for inclusion in their website. I said, "Sure, why not?" He sent me several rendered images. Two are shown in the Overview of SketchUp section of About "SketchUp: A Guide for Woodworkers." Another is shown here in **Figure 3**.

**Figure 4** | Textured traditional drawer

Notice the dovetails have end grain treatment. The wood grain in the top shows two cherry boards glued together. On the back you see lower quality cherry grain with gum spots and the wrought iron nails used to attach the ship lap boards are visible.

Look closely at the shadows and you will see they are from two light sources. One thing not modeled in these renditions is the drawer pulls. My model does not include them, hence they do not show up in the rendition. But they would be easy to add. You might compare these renditions to my actual photos on my srww.com gallery page.

IDX Renditioner is available for both the PC and Mac. It comes in two versions: Renditioner v3 and Renditioner Pro v3. The prices are free, $100 and $200 respectively. For more information see: imsidesign.com/Products/Renditioner/tabid/1756/Default.aspx

Be sure to check out their Gallery page at: http://www.imsidesign.com/Products/Renditioner/Showcase

## USING JPEG IMAGES AS TEXTURES

The Bedside Table reference model is a completely textured model using jpeg files you will need for this chapter. Those files are available at srww.com/sketchup_a_guide_for_woodworkers.html web page in the Downloads section under book Part 2, Chapter

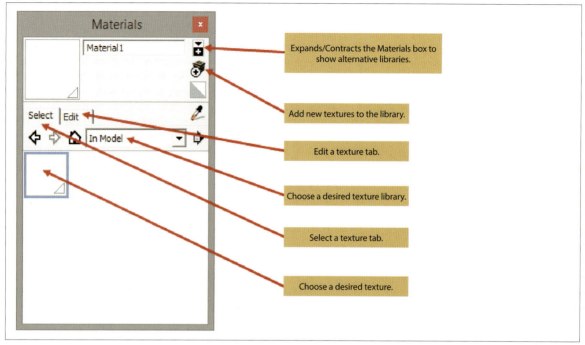

Figure 5 | Elements of the Materials dialog box

10 and are listed below:
- blistered_maple_h.jpg
- cherry_h.jpg
- cherry_v.jpg
- maple_v.jpg
- walnut_h.jpg
- walnut_v.jpg

You may notice that some of the above files are marked with an h or v for horizontal and vertical. For example, cherry_h.jpg and cherry_v.jpg; these files are identical except one is rotated 90 from the other. I did this for any texture that will be used on curved surfaces. The reason will become clear later in this chapter, but put simply, curved surfaces can be textured, but once applied textures cannot be easily edited in some aspects such as orientation. Therefore, separate horizontal and vertical textures are useful. If there is a curved piece in a model of your design, you may want to create a separate texture for that situation. Rotating an image is a basic function any image editor can perform.

In the Bedside Table there are few places where end grain is exposed. The table's top is one, but the leg ends are hidden in all normal views. Nearly all other situations are hidden by joinery. Consequently, I opted not to use separate textures for end grain. This would only serve to further bloat the model and add very little to the photorealism. However, there are situations where this would be useful. For example, **Figure 4** is a picture of the Traditional Drawer. The drawer dovetails would benefit from end grain textures to highlight the difference in color and texture of end grain and straight grain. This is most needed in the back side dovetails in the drawer. The front dovetails are accentuated simply because of the difference of the species used, whereas the back dovetails are entirely maple. Contrast my lazy treatment of end grain to that of William Manning's in **Figure 3**.

Before we actually begin to texture the Bedside Table, let me describe generally the steps we will use. The textures are only visible in the Shaded With Textures ⬢ view so make sure it is selected at this point and remains selected. The first time a jpeg

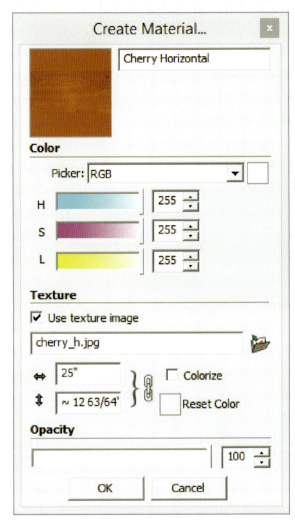

**Figure 6** | Create Material dialog box

step back, choose the alternative horizontal or vertical texture and retexture. If the surface is planar we can either choose the alternative texture or we can context click (right click) and use the Texture/Position tools to change orientation. We will also use the Texture/Position context tool to choose the best portion of the texture for the surface we are working on. I will guide you through several surfaces, textures and techniques, and you will do the remainder on your own.

Before moving on to applying textures I want to discuss the sizing of textures. Ideally if you are going to texture a component with a digital image texture you should take a quality picture of a finished piece with very similar dimensions. For example; the Bedside table is 23½" wide. It is best if I have a digital image JPG of a piece of cherry wood 25" long and with a finish similar to the one I intend to use on the new piece. When you shoot the image take at least two shots; one without a scale in the picture and one with. The scale will help you to measure the size of the JPG image. For example, the Cherry Horizontal image we will use in this chapter is a digital image 2616 pixels wide by 1359 pixels high. I know that the image is of a 25" long cherry piece. Therefore, knowing that the aspect ratio calculated in pixels has to be same as the aspect ratio calculated in inches, I can calculate the width as 12⁶³⁄₆₄". Later on in this chapter you will need to type horizontal and vertical dimensions into a dimension box in the Create Material dialog box; see **Figure 6**. These are the numbers you will use for the Cherry Horizontal texture and the reverse will be used in the Cherry Vertical piece. You should calculate similar numbers for the remaining texture. You can assume that the long dimension is 25". Now let's get started applying textures.

## APPLYING A TEXTURE

Open your model to where we left off in the previous chapter. We will texture the top first. Check that Layer0 is active and the Visible boxes for all other layers except layer Top are unchecked. Select the top, right click and choose Edit Component. Click the Paint Bucket ⊛ tool icon to select it. The Materials dialog box will open. Select

texture is used it must be brought into the In Model ⌂ Materials dialog box library. Horizontal and vertical files are different textures and therefore both versions must be placed in the library. Once a texture is in the In Model library it can be used on any surface.

Textures will be applied to each surface of a component, using the Paint Bucket ⊛ tool, while the component is in Edit Component mode. If a texture is applied to a surface and the grain is in the wrong direction we have two choices for fixing it. If the surface is a curved surface we will use the Undo tool to

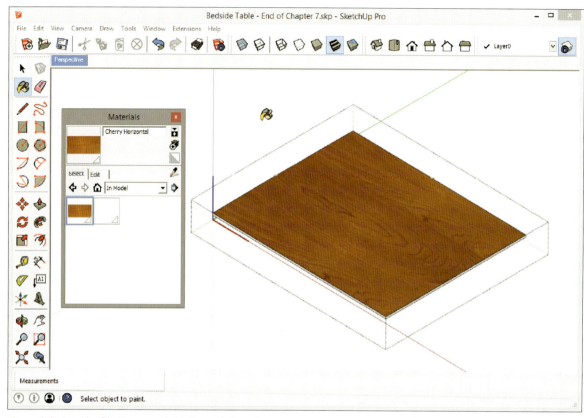

**Figure 7** | The top side of the Top textured with Cherry Horizontal texture

the In Model 🏠 icon and the Materials dialog box will appear as shown in **Figure 5**. Your In Model Materials library may have other materials, but don't worry about that.

## THE MATERIALS DIALOG BOX

Referring to **Figure 5** let's examine what functions the Materials dialog box provides. At the top right just below the Close icon (red box with white X) is an icon that will expand/contract the Materials box to show alternative libraries. For now we are only interested in the In Model library (i.e. the library of all textures used in the model). Click this icon until it shows a + sign and down arrow.

Next is an icon that allows the user to add a new texture to whatever library is chosen. This Create

Material icon is the one we will use to add textures to the In Model library.

There are two tabs. The left most tab is a Select tab, which displays the materials (or textures) that are available to be chosen. The only material in the model at the moment is Material1. The tab on the right is the Edit tab, which can be used to modify a texture's size, color, etc.

## THE CREATE MATERIAL DIALOG BOX

The drop-down box allows selection of the library the user wishes to use, or add textures to. For this tutorial we will focus entirely on the In Model library, so make sure it is selected at this point.

Click the Create Material 🎨 icon to open the Create Material box. In the third section check "Use texture image," which opens a Choose Image box. In

**Figure 8** | Mismatched top and end grain

the Choose Image box locate the file cherry_h.jpg and highlight it; click Open. The Choose Image box closes and the cherry texture is displayed in the Create Material box. Next to the texture sample in the first section type Cherry Horizontal to name the texture. In the third section there are two boxes chained together (if the chain is broken click it and it will be connected). Note: You may need to move your cursor away from the icon to see the change. The Top is 23½" wide so we will type 25 into the top box. This will make the texture image large enough to ensure we don't have to tile textures in the grain direction anywhere we use this texture. The Create Material box will now look like **Figure 6**. Click OK.

Now there is a new texture in the Materials box and if you hold your cursor over it, a Cherry Horizontal tooltip appears. Choose it, move the cursor with

the Paint Bucket pointer over the top side of the Top and click. It is now textured with cherry grain with the grain running from left to right (long direction) across the top as shown in **Figure 7**.

I will not describe how to add a texture again because it will always be done this way. So you may have to refer back to these directions occasionally until you get the procedure down. Of course, the texture name and dimension will change with each texture.

There are two places on the Top where we need to think about how we will texture and what texture we will use. That is the end grain and the bevels on the ends adjacent to the end grain. Since we chose not to use a specific end grain texture we will use either the horizontal or vertical cherry texture file. It is a matter of personal taste or judgment, however I

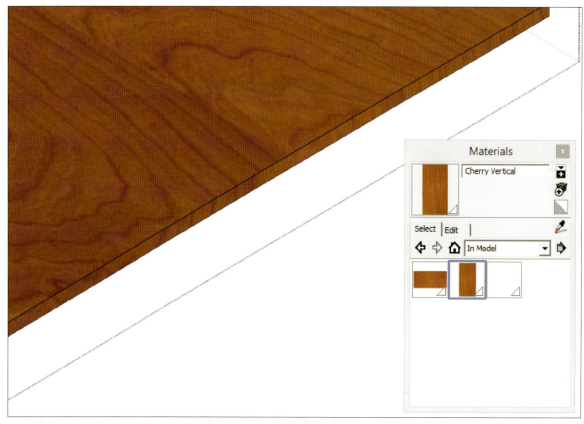

**Figure 9** | Improved matching of grain

feel the vertical texture appears more realistic. Using the method above add the cherry_v.jpg to the In Model library. Be sure to name it Cherry Vertical and this time change the lower (vertical) dimension to 25. The upper dimension should now be 12⁶³⁄₆₄". If it is not, click the chain icon until it is broken and type 12⁶³⁄₆₄" in the upper (horizontal) dimension. Texture the end grain with the Cherry Vertical material. Notice that the grain in the end grain and top surfaces may not match up well. See **Figure 8**. We can improve realism by choosing the position of the texture on the end grain such that it lines up better. We may not get it to line up perfectly, but we can make it better.

With the Select tool, select the end grain surface, right click (context click) and choose Texture/Position. The texture image will appear in the same plane

as the end grain surface and the cursor will change to the Pan cursor. Pan the texture until its grain and color line up with the top surface's grain and texture. Right click and choose Done and inspect the match. Repeat the process until you are satisfied with the look. See **Figure 9** to see how close I matched the grain. It is not perfect but it's pretty good. Note the colors tend to match as well.

Use the Orbit and Pan tools to move to the opposite end and texture it. Make sure you are still in the Edit Component mode. Now position the model to either bevel adjacent to the end grain surface. Texture it with the Cherry Horizontal texture. Notice that the grain is going in the wrong direction. You have two choices for fixing this. One is to use the Undo tool to back up, choose the Cherry Vertical texture and re-texture the bevel. But let's try another way. Select the

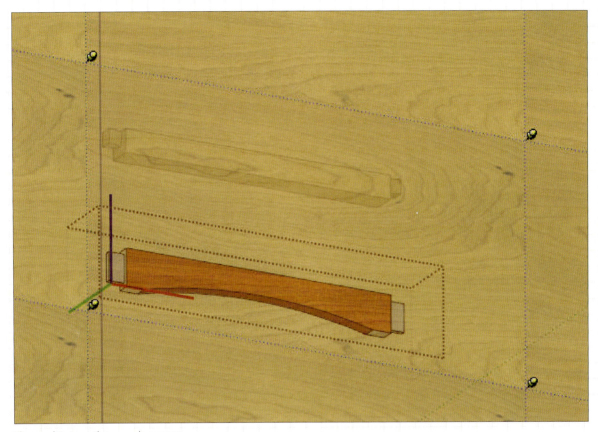

**Figure 10** | Textures tile to cover large areas

bevel surface, right click and choose Texture/Position. Again the texture image appears in the same plane as the bevel surface. This time, with the Pan cursor over the texture image, right click and choose Rotate/90. The texture will rotate 90 and the Pan cursor will now be available to position the texture to align grain to the end grain. Use this same approach to texture the remainder of the Top.

Change the visible layers to Layer0 and Drawer Trim with Layer0 as the active layer. Use the Front view, Iso view and Zoom Extents to bring the trim into view. Place the Top Cock Bead in Edit Component mode. Choose the Paint Bucket tool and bring the walnut_h.jpg into the In Model library. Don't forget to name the texture Walnut Horizontal and make the long dimension 25. Now texture the curved surface. Orbit around to the back and texture the back. Also texture the ends. On this piece I wouldn't fuss with the end grain of the ends because they are too small and too dark to notice. Also, there is an end grain surface that is a 45° surface that forms the joinery. You may choose to skip them all together. These surfaces are judgment calls. Remember what you are trying to accomplish, and if additional work doesn't add to the goal you may choose to save the time and work. Don't make texturing the end game, creating a model that looks photo realistic is the goal. Now place a side piece in Edit Component mode, bring in the walnut_v.jpg texture and texture it. You may want to use the wrong texture and try to use Texture/Position to fix it. You will discover you can't. This is why we need both horizontal and vertical texture files. This will be necessary for the bottom curve of the lower drawer rail as well.

One last point I want to discuss. Look at **Figure 10**. Notice how images are tiled. This is to provide sufficient material to cover a large piece. We choose to make the long dimension (grain direction) of all images 25" long so that they will be long enough to cover any piece in the model without having to tile in the grain direction. However, you must check to be sure the painting of the texture is such that the piece lies completely within a single image in the grain direction. You cannot always make this happen in the cross grain direction, but that is fine. Tiling in that direction appears as a glue-up and looks quite natural. In the grain direction this would look very wrong.

Making a texture large enough to cover the largest piece in a model, in the grain direction, requires a JPG image of a board large enough to provide natural looking grain. Notice the blue dotted lines that outline a single image in **Figure 10**. This helps position the grain correctly. Notice also the push pins. These can be used to stretch and distort a texture. This is beyond the scope of this text. SketchUp provides a number of tools and functionality which is very powerful when used to texture buildings and other models such as stone walls and landscapes with textures and pictures. I recommend viewing the video tutorials provided by Trimble to extend your knowledge of texturing. I have touched on only the basics.

## CHAPTER REVIEW

In this chapter I introduced you to SketchUp's capabilities for producing photorealistic images. Photorealistic images, by definition, can be used by woodworkers to present a virtual view of a new design that is very close to a picture of the finished piece. This is a very powerful tool for a range of woodworkers from weekend hobbyists to professional cabinetmakers.

I showed you how native SketchUp can produce images like **Figure 1**. For more polished photorealism, one can purchase a commercial SketchUp extension and produce results similar to **Figure 2** and **Figure 3**. With photorealism as a goal, the remainder of chapter was spent on learning the basics of texturing.

The first step in texturing is to obtain a wood grain texture. Textures are available on the internet, but the approach used in this chapter was to use a digital image of a furniture piece with the same wood species, wood finish and size. I described an approach for taking a picture of wood grain that included a scale in the image to estimate the physical size the image represented. From that physical size and the pixel aspect ratio of the image we can calculate both horizontal and vertical dimensions. These numbers were later used to fit the texture to our model.

Next we learned to apply a texture by first adding a texture to the In Model library using the Materials dialog box's Create Material 🎨 icon. We then used the Create Material dialog box to import, name and size the texture. You should have done this for each texture used, making sure the horizontal and vertical dimensions were of the same aspect ratio of the textures pixel aspect ratio.

Lastly we learned to apply a texture using the Paint Bucket 🖌 tool and to position it using the Context menu Texture/Position tool. We paid particular attention to how each face's texture aligned with the bordering faces and we were careful to keep texture seams from appearing in the grain direction. While I described this process for the Bedside Table's Top, you were asked to texture the remainder of the table.

In this chapter we introduced the following new tools listed in the order they were used:
🖌 Paint Bucket
🎨 Create Material

We also introduced the Materials and Create Material dialog boxes.

Well folks, we have come to the end of Part Two "The Apprentice & the Bedside Table." It was a long and detailed journey. Speaking of journey, if you have read each chapter, completed the Bedside Table correctly and done the exercises at the end of each chapter, you are no longer an apprentice. Congratulations; you are now a journeyman and are ready for Part Three to begin your training with master sketchman as your goal.

## EXERCISES FOR THE STUDENT

1. What file type can you use to capture wood grain for texturing?
2. When bringing a JPG image into the Materials library what JPG file parameters can you use to set the dimensions of the texture?
3. If a texture seam is distracting or unsightly, how do you change the size of the texture to eliminate it?
4. Do you need horizontal and vertical textures or can you use just one texture? What must you do if you only have one texture and the grain direction is wrong?
5. What Context menu tool do you use to line up grain on adjoining faces?

# PART THREE:
# THE JOURNEYMAN & NONRECTILINEAR PIECES & COMPLEX CURVES

In Part Three you begin your journeyman training and the apprentice training wheels come off. With your new understanding of SketchUp and modeling skills you should find it relatively easy to venture into new areas. To that end, and in the interest of covering a lot of advanced material, I will not provide detailed procedures in the remaining chapters. You will be expected to fill in the detailed steps between strategic or high-level steps. More than any section in this book I encourage you to read each chapter through without attempting to model anything. Study the figures and try to picture in your head the detailed steps you would use to get from one figure to the next. Then go back and do the modeling. Don't hesitate to start a chapter over; that is part of the learning process. Realize that your goal in Part Three is to become a master sketchman.

In the interest of covering as much material as I can in the remaining pages, in addition to suspending detailed modeling steps, I am going to suspend the Chapter Review section. You will notice that most of the chapters in this section deal with one or two components, not a furniture piece. These components can often be used in many different furniture designs. We want to focus on advanced modeling techniques applicable to furniture design in general.

# 11

# SPLAYED PIECES: THE DOUGH BOX

*In this first chapter of Part Three we begin our study of nonrectilinear component modeling using the Dough Box as a learning vehicle. If you are not familiar with Dough Boxes and their use, see this excellent description on Home Things Past (homethingspast.com/dough-box-kneading-trough). The Dough Box, as you might have guessed, was used to hold dough while it was rising.*

*The Dough Box components we will model include splayed legs and sides; the splayed sides include through dovetails. You will draw the remaining components of the Dough Box (aprons, bottom, lid and trim) on your own. After all you are now a journeyman and should have no problems with these rectilinear pieces.*

A while back a student wrote me and asked how I might go about drawing a Dough Box in SketchUp. He sent me a hyperlink to a miniature that he wanted to scale up and build. I copied the image, brought it into SketchUp and scaled the length and height to the dimensions he wanted. Then I took dimensions of other parts from the scaled picture and created the model in **Figure 1**. The student wanted to build his with dovetail joinery and so I added them.

## MODELING THE TAPERED & SPLAYED LEGS

We begin by focusing on the legs. One issue you should be aware of when modeling pieces such as this Dough Box: you will encounter a number of odd dimensions due to the complex angles. It is extremely important that you zoom in close and be sure to use the Inference Engine tooltips to enable you to connect precisely to end points. The Window/Model Info Units page must be set to the highest resolution available. In my shop I measure to $\frac{1}{64}$", and so my dimensions are labeled and accurate to the nearest 64th of an inch. Since the Dimension tool rounds dimensions to the resolution specified in the Model Info Units page you will not see the tilde (~) symbol when dimensioning. But as you are modeling and using the Tape Measure tool, it is not uncommon in a nonrectilinear model to see the tilde symbol indicating an approximate dimension.

**Figure 1** | The completed Dough Box model

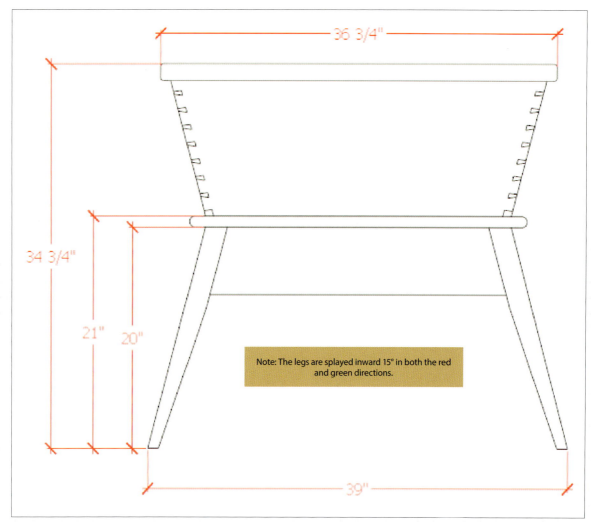

Note: The legs are splayed inward 15° in both the red and green directions.

**Figure 2** | The Dough Box front dimensions

Look at the front view Dough Box dimensions show in **Figure 2**. Notice the lid length of 36¾". This dimension is more a consequence of the complex angle than actual design parameters. You will see this as we go along. Notice also that the legs are splayed inward in both the red and green direction 15°. Because they are splayed in two directions they produce multiple compound angle cuts you must perform in the shop.

In the end view Dough Box dimensions shown in **Figure 3** you will see a similar dimension for the lid of 18¼". The actual leg dimensions are also going to

be determined by splaying and not easily specifiable as a design goal. But we will start off with the legs being 20" tall, 2" square at top, beginning to taper 7" down from the top, and tapering to 1" square at the bottom. The leg splay is 15° from vertical. These dimensions and angle are for drawing the leg profiles before we splay them. Again, when we are done you will see that the actual dimensions and angles are quite different.

Begin modeling the leg by drawing the outline shown in **Figure 4**. This outline is drawn in the Red/Blue plane. The leg has not yet been splayed. A very

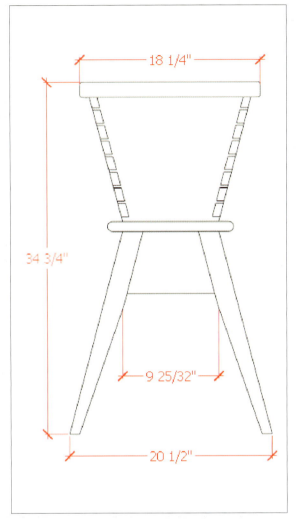

**Figure 3** | The Dough Box end dimensions

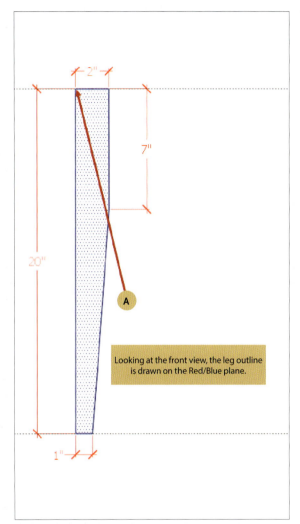

A

Looking at the front view, the leg outline is drawn on the Red/Blue plane.

**Figure 4** | Leg outline drawn in the Red/Blue plane

important part of this step is the construction lines drawn parallel to and coincident with the leg's top and bottom edges. I have shown the leg outline and face selected because in the next step we are going to splay the leg by rotating the selected primitives clockwise 15° around point A in **Figure 4**. We are not going to rotate the construction lines. The construction lines represent the floor and top of the legs and must remain parallel to the red axis.

With the Rotate tool we will splay the leg in the Red/Blue plane (Green cursor) around the point of

rotation, point A in **Figure 4**. In **Figure 5** notice we are rotating the leg 15° clockwise. Also notice that the bottom part of the leg is lifted off the floor, represented by the bottom construction line. In addition, the top right corner falls below the top construction line. We will correct that next.

The left side of **Figure 6** shows how construction lines are added to complete the outline of the leg. Five lines are added and two lines deleted to correct the outline from the effects of splaying. The right side of **Figure 6** shows the completed out-

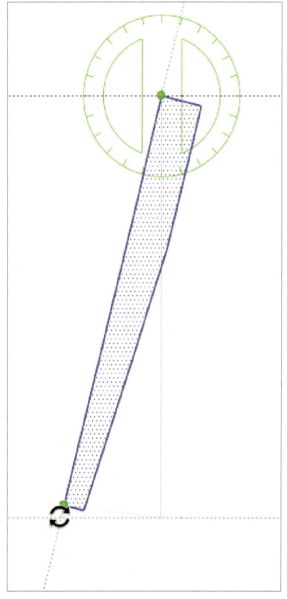

**Figure 5** | Splaying the leg 15° in the Red/Blue plane

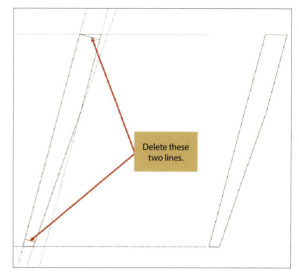

**Figure 6** | Corrected leg outline after splaying (some cleanup needed)

line. This outline now needs to be extruded to give the leg outline three dimensions. We are going to extrude it toward the positive Green axis and again toward the negative Green axis. The amount of extrusion is somewhat arbitrary, though it has to be enough to extend beyond the Red axis dimension

of the resulting bounding box. This will be clear in the next two steps.

**Figure 7** shows the leg extruded in both the positive and negative Green axis direction and temporarily made a group. The dimension $7^{24}/_{64}"$ defines the minimum extrusion dimension. Note that both arbitrary extrusion dimensions are larger than this dimension. Also notice that the construction lines are still present in the model. We will next copy this leg and rotate it 90°.

The direction of rotation is important because we want the tapers of a leg to face its complementary leg. **Figure 8** shows the direction to be counterclockwise 90°. Though it is not shown in **Figure 8** because the axes are not shown, the point of rotation is where the blue axis intersects the top left edge of the leg. Our next step is to explode both groups, select all primitives and use Edit/Intersect Faces/With Selection. When the Intersect Faces operation is complete, the Selection tool can be used to remove unwanted primitives. The remaining leg is then made a component.

In **Figure 9** the Leg component is shown with a bounding box that is too large, i.e. it is not the bounding box we need to produce correct cut list information. If we don't correct this, our cut list will reflect a requirement for stock $7^{24}/_{64}"$ x $7^{24}/_{64}"$ x 20".

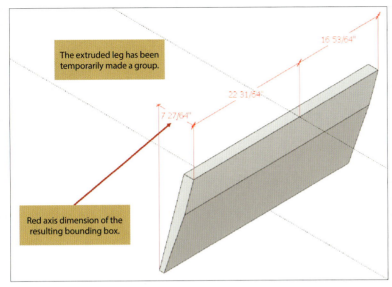

The extruded leg has been temporarily made a group.

Red axis dimension of the resulting bounding box.

16 53/64"

22 31/64"

7 27/64"

**Figure 7** | The leg extruded in both the positive and negative green axis direction

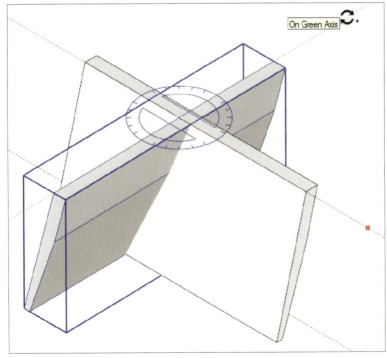

On Green Axis

**Figure 8** | Copying and rotating the leg

Further, if we were to cut the leg from this inflated stock it would result in grain running at an angle on its faces. Logic and visual geometry would tell us that the stock requirement should be closer to 2" x 2" x 20". The actual stock requirement is 2" x 2⁹/₆₄" x 22²⁷/₆₄" as we will see when we correct the bounding box.

To correct the bounding box we right click on the selected Leg and choose Change Axes. With the cursor click on the lowest, left front point of the leg and then click on the other end of the long edge connected to that point. Finally move the cursor out along the Green axis until we see the Inference Engine tooltip "On Green Axis" and click. **Figure 10** shows visually how this operation is performed.

With the bounding box corrected, we have a Leg shown in **Figure 11**. We need to understand a subtlety here. When we corrected the bounding box we made a long edge the Red axis and then used SketchUp's Green axis as the component's Green axis. This changed the axis of the component definition for the Leg that exists in the Component library. We will see exactly what that means in a moment.

First, recall how we used a rectangle in the section titled "Adding Similar Components to the Model" of Chapter 3 to create three more leg instances from the left front leg. We are going to do a similar thing here. Only this time, because we changed the bounding box of our Leg, we are not going

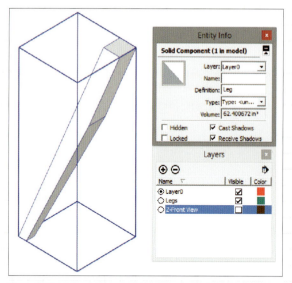

**Figure 9** | The Leg component with too large bounding box

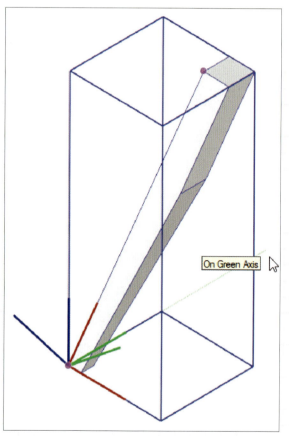

**Figure 10** | Using the Change Axes Context tool to correct the bounding box

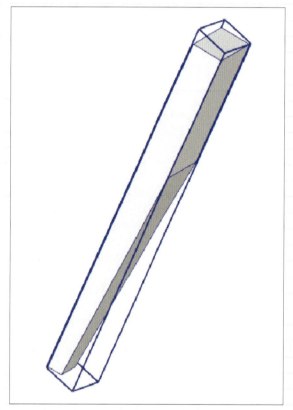

**Figure 11** | The completed Leg with a corrected bounding box

to use Flip Along after a Move/Copy to correct for orientation. Instead we are going to use the Rotate tool after Move/Copy to rotate the copied legs around the Blue axis (Blue cursor). Look at **Figure 12** to see the final placement. The rectangle has done its job and can be deleted at this point.

Notice in **Figure 12** the additional Leg; the one whose long side is lying horizontally. Recall when using Change Axes we made the long edge the Red axis and used SketchUp's green axis as the Legs new Green axis. That changed the component definition for the Leg. Now when you pull a Leg out of the Component library, its axes are aligned with SketchUp's axes. This is also why we couldn't use Flip Along to correct the Leg orientation after a Move/Copy.

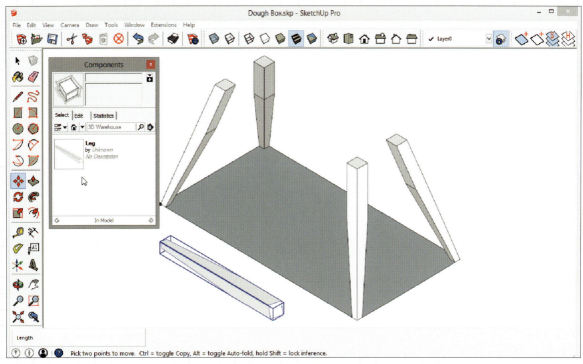

**Figure 12** | Three additional Legs placed at the corners of the rectangle and another Leg from the Component library

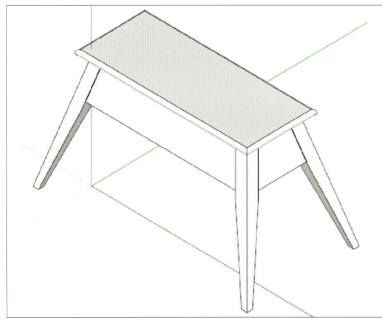

**Figure 13** | You should have completed the Dough Box model to this point

## DRAWING THE LONG SIDES

You should be able to model the aprons and bottom. The splayed aprons may present a challenge, particularly modeling the mortise and tenons, but you have the knowledge and skills to do it. Accept the challenge and bring your model to the level shown in **Figure 13**. We are now going to focus on the long sides, which are made of ¾" thick stock and splayed outward 15°. Typical of our approach to let the model help define the next part we will use the Rectangle tool to outline the inside edges of the bottom trim and then use the Offset tool to

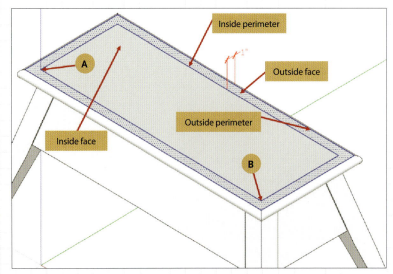

Figure 14 | Outline of where the side's outside edges intersect the bottom

shrink that rectangle by 1" all around. That will provide an outline of where the long and short sides touch the bottom at their outside edges.

Looking at **Figure 14** you can see the result of the last few steps. We can delete the inside face, outside face and outside perimeter, leaving only the inside perimeter and make the inside perimeter a group. The inside perimeter marks where the outside edges of the long and short sides intersect the bottom, i.e. 1" in from where the trim is attached to the bottom.

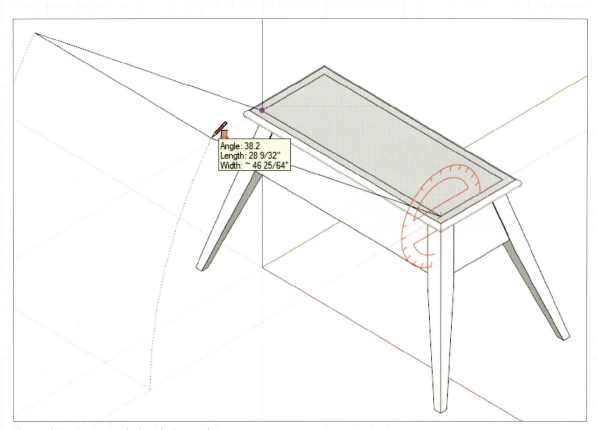

Figure 15 | Creating a rectangle slanted 15° outward

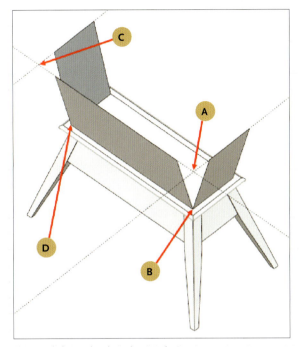

**Figure 16** | Three sides slanted outward 15°

**Figure 17** | Slicing plane we will use to trim each side group

I now want to introduce you to a new tool, the Rotated Rectangle ▣ tool. This tool is not only new to you, but is new to SketchUp as it was introduced in SketchUp 2015. I am going to give instructions on how to use the Rotate Rectangle ▣ tool, but I also encourage you to pay attention to the Status Bar and to use the Instructor dialog box found in the Window menu.

Select the Rotated Rectangle ▣ tool and click on point A in **Figure 14** followed by clicking on point B. Move the cursor up along the Blue axis and out along the negative Green axis as shown in **Figure 15**. Now type 75,15 and press *Enter*. This places a rectangle on the front long edge of the outline group, slanted 15° forward (90° - 75°) and 15" wide. I chose 15" because it is substantially larger than 13", which is the height we want the sides to extend above the bottom. Make this rectangle a group. Repeat this process using each end edge of the outline group. Be sure to make each rectangle a group as soon as it is created so that the primitives of the rectangles do not touch and stick. Now place a construction line parallel to and coinci-

dent with the top edge of each of the slanted sides. This produces a model shown in **Figure 16**.

Picture the slanted sides in **Figure 16** extended until they completely intersect. We can create that shape for all three sides by using points A, B, C and D in **Figure 16**. Place the long front side in Edit Group mode. With the Line tool, draw lines AB, CD and AC. Erase the old end lines inside the new face. Exit Edit Group mode. With the Move/Copy and Rotate tools make a copy of the long front side and place where the long back side should be. Next edit each end slanted side to look like **Figure 17**.

Recall when we used the Rotated Rectangle tool we typed 75,15 into the VCB. I mentioned that the second parameter was 15" chosen to be substantially larger than 13", which is the height we wish the sides to rise above the bottom. **Figure 17** shows a slicing plane, which we will use to trim each side group in Edit Component mode to terminate 13" above the bottom. Next we will create a layer called Temp and place the two short side groups, the back long side group and the original outline group on the Temp

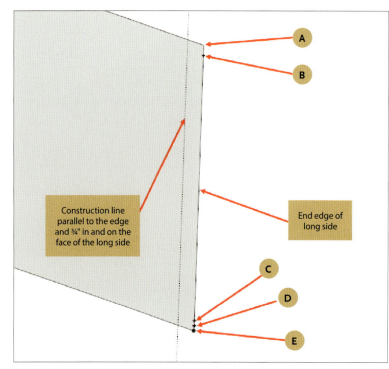

**Figure 18** | Setup required to create the tails

Construction line parallel to the edge and ¾" in and on the face of the long side

End edge of long side

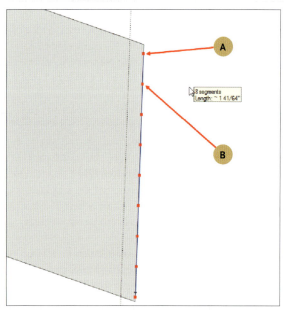

**Figure 19** | Dividing a line into equal segments with the Context Divide command

8 segments
Length: ~ 1 41/64"

layer. This will leave only the front long side on Layer0. Lastly we will create a Sides layer, place the front long side on the Sides layer, and make all layers invisible except the Sides layer. We will now outline the dovetail tails.

## CREATING THE DOVETAIL TAILS

We want eight tails. The half pins at top and bottom will be ½" each. Pins between the tails will be ¼". If the number of tails is eight then the number of pins between them is seven. We can use the Tape Measure tool to measure the length of the long side end edge, which is ~13²⁹⁄₃₂". What we don't know is how wide the tails are. A simple algebraic equation can be solved to calculate the tail width. But the approximate dimension of the long side end edge will make this calculation messy at best, and who wants to do messy arithmetic? Fortunately, SketchUp has the functionality we need to avoid messy arithmetic and to draw precisely. Before using that functionality we need to do some setup.

What we would like are markers along the end edge of the long side. We can place a construction point ½" down and along the edge from the top corner and a similar construction point ½" up from the bottom corner. Between those two construction points we need markers for eight tails and seven pins. Without knowing the dimension of the tails, those markers are going to be difficult to create. However, the Line tool has a feature that can help. Here is how it works. If you use the Line tool to draw a line by clicking on two points and then immediately context click (right click) while the cursor is hovering over the line and choose Divide, you can type an integer into the VCB, which will then divide the line into

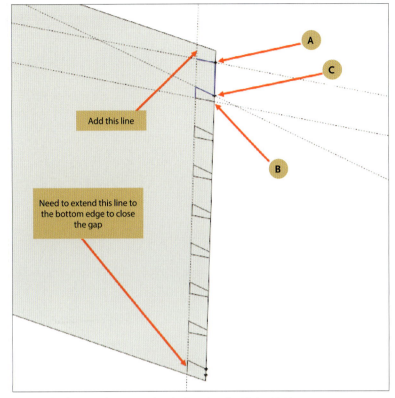

Add this line

Need to extend this line to the bottom edge to close the gap

A

C

B

**Figure 20** | Tail/pin combination outlined, selected and highlighted in blue

a construction point has been added at point D; the distance CD being ¼", the dimension of a pin. Now between point B and point D is sufficient length for eight tails and eight pins. We don't have to actually draw the pin at the bottom but we can now use the Line tool to draw a line from point B to point D and divide it into eight segments.

With the long front still a group, draw line BD with the Line tool and hit *Esc* to exit the polyline. Because you have drawn this line over a group you will have to select line BD with the Select tool, right click, and choose Divide. When you choose Divide you will get an image similar to **Figure 19**. The red squares represent where the line will be divided and you can move the cursor to choose other integers of division, but at this point type 8 and press *Enter*. While line BD in **Figure 18** is on the edge of the long side it cannot stick to it because the long side is protected by virtue of being a group.

In **Figure 19**, as mentioned, the red squares represent where line BD in **Figure 18** will be divided. That will leave Endpoint markers on the line. Referring to **Figure 19,** point A is where the first tail will start. Point B is where the first pin will end. Since we know the dimension of a pin we can add a construction point ¼" up from Point B. That permits us to create a tail/pin combination as shown in **Figure 20**.

**Figure 20** shows a tail/pin combination outlined with the Line tool and consisting of four lines. Those four lines are shown selected and highlighted in blue. Points A and B in **Figure 20** are the same points A and B shown in **Figure 19**. Referring to **Figure 20,** points A and B represent the total dimension of a tail

equal length segments specified by the integer typed into the VCB.

We now have to decide what an equal segment is. We are going to use the segment length to equal the width of a tail plus pin. But we don't have an equal number of tails and pins. No problem, we will make an equal number of tails and pins.

**Figure 18** shows the setup we need to create the tails. The construction line, which is parallel to the end edge of the long side and ¾" in and on the face of the long side, represents the depth of the tails. The depth of the tails is equal to the thickness of the sides, particularly the end sides. Point A is the corner and the distance AB is ½", the half pin dimension. Point E is the bottom corner and length CE is ½", the bottom half pin dimension. Between point B and point C we need eight tails and seven pins. To make an even number of tails and pins,

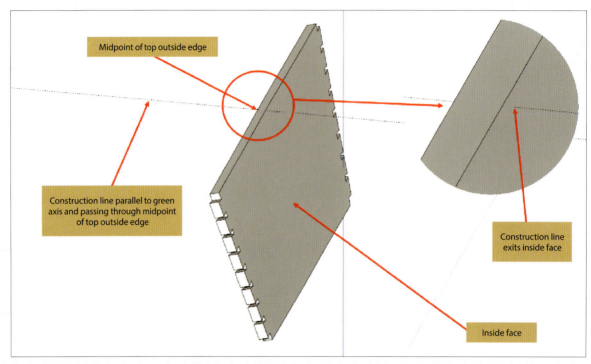

**Figure 21** | New long side with construction line parallel to green axis and passing through midpoint of top outside edge

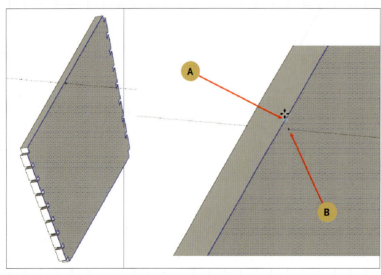

**Figure 22** | Inside face and its perimeter selected

and pin. The distance between point B and point C is ¼", the distance of a pin width. Therefore distance AC is the width of a tail according to simple arithmetic. Now we can place construction lines with the Protractor tool 8° from horizontal (Red axis) at points A, B and C and outline the tail/pin combination with the line tool. Next, with the Move/Copy tool we can pick up the selected tail/pin combination at point A and place it at point B and immediately type 7x and press *Enter* to reproduce the combination seven more times. Lastly, we have some minor cleanup as shown in **Figure 20**. We need to extend a line at the bottom to connect the last tail to the bottom edge. We also have

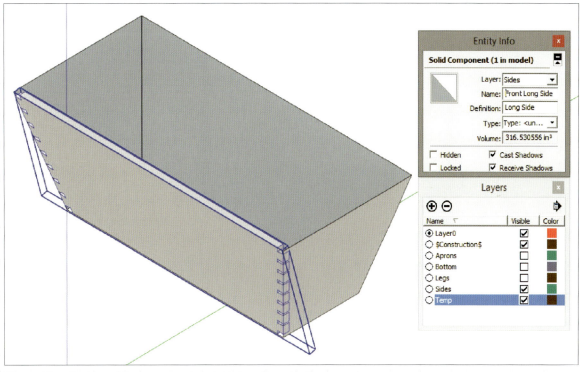

**Figure 23** | Completed Long Side component selected with three side and outline groups shown

to add a line to connect the first tail to the top edge. These two lines complete the outline of the half pins.

At this point, with only Layer0 and Sides visible, we have the long side group and the outline of the eight tails and seven pins showing. Using the Move/Copy tool we can copy the outline of the tails and pins, Flip Along/Red Direction and place at the appropriate place on the left end edge of the long side group. Next, we can delete the long side group, connect the tails and pins outlines together along the top and bottom and delete some unwanted lines. Using the Push/Pull tool we give the new long side ¾" thickness. We now have the model shown in **Figure 21**. In **Figure 21** a construction line parallel to Green axis and passing through midpoint of top outside edge has been added.

**Figure 22** shows the inside face and its perimeter selected on the left side, and a blowup of the construction line entering the top outside edge at the midpoint and exiting on the other side at point

B. Also shown is the midpoint of the top inside edge labeled point A. With the Move tool, whose cursor is shown, we will move point A to point B. This will slide the inside face down, keeping it on the same plane, and correcting for the effects of the Push/Pull tool when giving the side ¾" thickness. Recall how Push/Pull works; it extrudes a face along the face's normal (a normal is a unit vector perpendicular to the face). This is great for giving a part the correct thickness, and works well for all parts whose faces are parallel to the red/green, green/blue or blue/red planes. But when a plane is slanted, as this long side front face is, we need to correct for the inside edge being higher (along the blue axis) than the outside edge as a result of the Push/Pull operation.

**Figure 23** shows the completed Long Side component selected. Notice we have corrected for the bounding box. Looking at the Entity Info dialog box you can see that it has a component name Long Side, a part name Front Long Side and it is on the Sides layer.

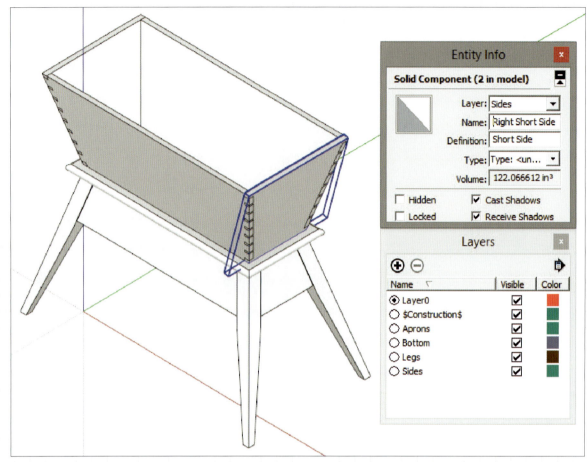

**Figure 24** | Completed Dough Box model to the point of Long and Short Sides modeled

In the Layers dialog box notice that the Temp layer is visible. On the Temp layer are four groups: two end side groups, one back side group, and our original outline group. You should now be able to use the Move/Copy and Rotate tools to create and place the Back Long Side. Once both Long Sides are in place it is easy to create both Short Sides.

**Figure 24** shows the completed sides and the rest of the model to this point. The Temp layer and its contents have been deleted. You should have no trouble modeling the lid and dimensioning the Dough Box. The Dough Box has been a good exercise in complex or compound angles. The Dough Box falls into a category of design one might call linear but not rectilinear. In chapter 12 we are going to up the ante

and model turned and splayed legs and rungs that attach in a mortise and tenon fashion.

## EXERCISES FOR THE STUDENT

1. Check the bounding box dimension for the leg length and compare it to the 20" design goal. Check the bounding box dimensions for the width and thickness. Notice one says 2" and the other says ~2 ⁶⁄₆₄. If you build these legs and measure the finished width and thickness with a caliper you will measure 2" each. Explain the difference.

2. When we created three more instances of the Leg using Move/Copy you were instructed to use the Rotate tool to correct for orientation. Redraw the

four legs using the Flip Along command instead of the Rotate tool and see what happens.

3. Try creating and placing the Back Long Side with the Move/Copy tool and Flip Along command. Do not use the Rotate tool. Again observe the problem it creates.

# 12

# SPLAYED PIECES:
# THE SHAKER SHOP STOOL

*"The Book of Shaker Furniture" by John Kassay is a treasure trove for SketchUp generation woodworkers. John Kassay has done a first-class job of drawing 2D sketches of original Shaker furniture that we can translate into 3D models and produce shop drawings. What better way to build reproduction Shaker furniture?*

*The Shaker Shop Stool found on page 222 of that book and shown in **Figure 1** is the subject of this chapter. This piece provides the student some significant challenges. The legs are lathe turned and splayed inward on all sides. More challenging still are the rungs, whose ends are tenons that are mortised into the legs. The seat and cushion are relatively easy to model so we won't model those in this chapter; rather they are an exercise left to the student.*

**B**efore we begin modeling the Shaker Shop Stool we need to introduce a new tool that we will use throughout the remainder of this book. It is called the Bezier Curve tool and is an extension developed by the SketchUp development team. In The Extension Warehouse section of Chapter 8 you were instructed to install this extension. If you didn't do so at that time please do so now.

## THE BEZIER CURVE TOOL

Chapter 12 continues our study of nonrectilinear designs and also begins our study of noncircular curves. The Circle and Arc tools found in SketchUp are based on the parametric equation for the unit circle. Bézier curves are parametric curves that can produce irregular but smooth curves using control points. While not developed by him, Pierre Bézier, a French engineer first used them in the design of Renault automobiles in 1962. Anyone who has taken a high school or college drafting class is familiar with the French curves drawing tool used to produce smooth shapes shown in **Figure 2**. Usually a draftsperson would have a set of these tools, each one a collection of different curve shapes. You can think of Bézier curves as the computer graphics equivalent of the French curve drawing tool.

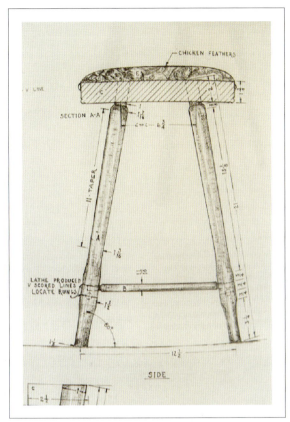

**Figure 1** | The Shaker Shop Stool, Source: "The Book of Shaker Furniture" by John Kassay

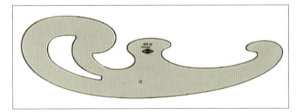

**Figure 2** | A typical French curve drafting tool

The Bezier Curves tool that we installed in Chapter 8 is quite simple to use and produces surprisingly good results. However, if you are modeling a curve that has a number of inflection points you will want to break the curve up at those points and use the Bezier Curves tool on each section. For example, to reproduce the curve shown in **Figure 3,** I would break the curve into three sections and apply the Bezier Curves tool three times: section AB, section BC and section CD.

This works well with the Bezier Curves tool because we only have four control points to work with. I will describe how to use the Bezier Curves tool to recreate section AB of **Figure 3**. Select the Bezier Curves tool in menu Draw/Bezier Curves (the tool does not have a tool icon). Click on point A; this is the first control point and the beginning of the curve AB. Next click on point B; this is the second control point and the end of curve AB. This is where you have to pay close attention. Choose a place to click for the third point such that the line from point A to the third click point forms a line tangent to curve AB at point A. Lastly, choose a place to click for the fourth and final point such that the line from point B to the fourth click point forms a line tangent to curve AB at point B. I should point out that there are times, which we will see in the Shaker Shop Stool, when you want a discontinuity at the end of a curve and therefore do not want to choose a point that creates a tangent line.

**Figure 4** is a screenshot demonstrating the use of the tool. Point A is the first point, point B is the second point, point a is the third point and point b is the fourth and final point. The On Line in Group Inference Engine tooltip refers to the grid group that point b is on. Line Aa is tangent to curve AB at point A while line Bb is tangent to curve AB at point B. Once I click on point b the curve is set. However, if I select the curve with the Select tool, I can context click on it and choose Edit Bezier Curve. Then I can reposition points a and b or move lines Aa, ab or Bb to fine-tune my fit. Moving lines Aa or Bb, however, also moves points A and B which are the end points, so that is likely something that is not desirable.

**Figure 5** shows the original curve and the new curve superimposed on one another. The fit is not perfect, but it's very close. In the shop I would use a full scale printout of the curve and trace it onto my wood stock, cut and sand it to shape. The small difference would never be noticed. You can spend a lot of curve editing time to match these curves almost exactly but it is not worth it. When they are sandpaper close, call it quits.

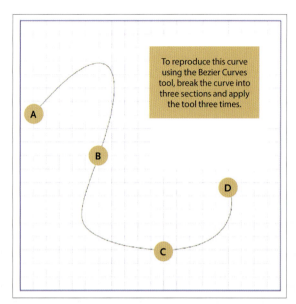

To reproduce this curve using the Bezier Curves tool, break the curve into three sections and apply the tool three times.

**Figure 3** | A curve divided into three noninflection segments

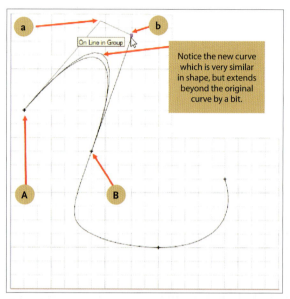

On Line in Group

Notice the new curve which is very similar in shape, but extends beyond the original curve by a bit.

**Figure 4** | New Bezier curve produced by clicking on points A, B, a and b respectively

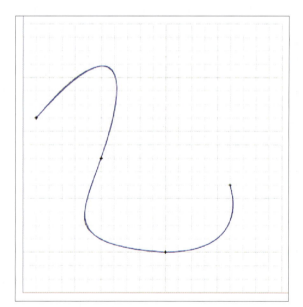

**Figure 5** | The completed new Bezier curve superimposed on the original

## THE COMPLEXITIES OF SPLAYED & TURNED DESIGNS

**Figure 6** shows the completed SketchUp model of the Shaker Shop Stool shown in **Figure 1**. The 2D drawings found in the John Kassay book can be confusing and misleading if you do not have extensive experience reading 2D drawings. The first thing you have to remember is that the pictures are an artist's rendition of a 3D object projected on to a 2D plane. Almost all the dimensions are accurate and can be taken at face value so long as you understand what the dimensions are referring to. For example, the dimensions depicting the layout of the leg turning are dimensions along the axis of the leg, which is splayed with a complex angle. They are not dimensions of the projected 2D image on the Blue/Green plane.

One dimension in particular cannot be taken at face value; that is the dimension for the splay of the legs shown as 80° in **Figure 1**. Actually, 80° is the splay angle of the projected leg on a 2D plane. The actual splay angle of the leg is approximately 76°. This can trip you up big time if you are not aware. You can accurately use 80° to create the splay if you know how to do so, and that is the first thing I will explain in modeling the Shaker Shop Stool.

**Figure 6** | The completed SketchUp model of the Shaker Shop Stool

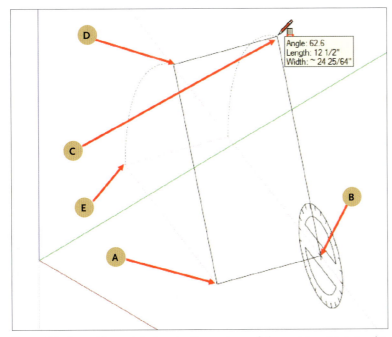

Angle: 62.6
Length: 12 1/2"
Width: ~ 24 25/64"

**Figure 7** | The Rotated Rectangle tool requires the user to specify three points: points A, B and C

Compound miter cuts, spayed and tapered legs and tapered boxes fall into a category that should be called complex angles instead of compound angles, because they are complex to describe mathematically and their complexity makes them difficult to understand and visualize. But fear not; SketchUp provides the tools to handle them with relative ease. In Chapter 11 I introduced you to the Rotated Rectangle tool. It and the Follow Me tools are going to be the stars of Chapter 12. At this point I want to look at the Rotated Rectangle tool a little closer.

The Rotated Rectangle tool requires the user to supply three points. When you choose the Rotated Rectangle tool and look in the Status Bar it says "Select first corner." You can choose a point for the first corner by randomly clicking anywhere in 3D space with the cursor or use the Inference Engine to help select a point. Oddly enough you cannot numerically specify a point by supplying the X,Y,Z coordinates in the VCB. Once you select the first corner the Status Bar changes to "Select second corner or enter value. Alt = lock protractor plane." In **Figure 7** I specified a second corner by entering 12.5 in the VCB. Let's study **Figure 7**, which is a screen capture of the SketchUp window immediately after the second of three clicks while using the Rotated Rectangle tool. Point A is the first corner and point B is the second corner. Point C is where I happen to be hovering with the cursor at the time of the screen

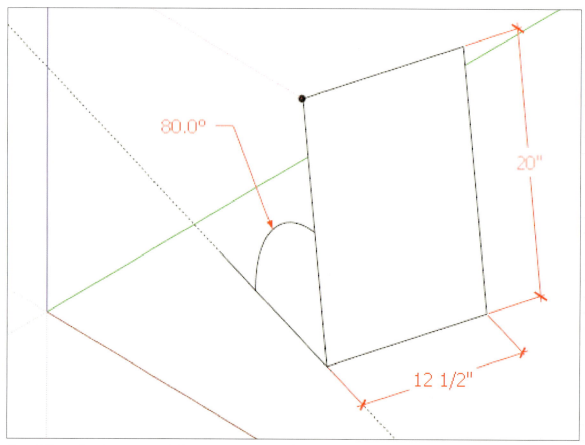

**Figure 8** | The resulting Rotating Rectangle from parameters 12 ½", 80° & 20"

capture. Notice the yellow filled box. The first line says Angle: 62.6 (degrees), which is angle DAE. The second line says Length: 12 ½", which is the distance between A and B, which I specified with my second corner input. At this point the Status Bar says "Select third corner or enter values(s). Alt = set protractor baseline." The key word here is the word "value(s)." What the VCB is looking for is an angle followed by a width. After I enter 80,20 I get **Figure 8**, which I have annotated to show the results.

In **Figure 8** you see a plane 12 ½" by 20". The first dimension was specified by the second corner input and the second dimension by the second parameter of the third corner input. The 80° angle was specified by the first parameter of the third corner input. Notice that the orientation of the 12

½" line is randomly placed on the Red/Green plane. It could have been randomly oriented in R,G,B or X,Y,Z space. The Rotated Rectangle tool is very powerful and useful. In terms of what makes SketchUp the powerful tool it is, the Rotated Rectangle is right up there with the Push/Pull tool (but is a little more difficult to understand and visualize). With this more in-depth understanding of the Rotated Rectangle tool, let's move on to modeling the spayed and turned legs.

Referring to **Figure 9** notice the spacing of the legs is 12½" between the intersection of the axis of the legs and the floor plane. The legs are splayed inward 10° (90° – 80°) in both the red and green direction. That would suggest that the splay of the leg is 80°. However, we will see that if you measure

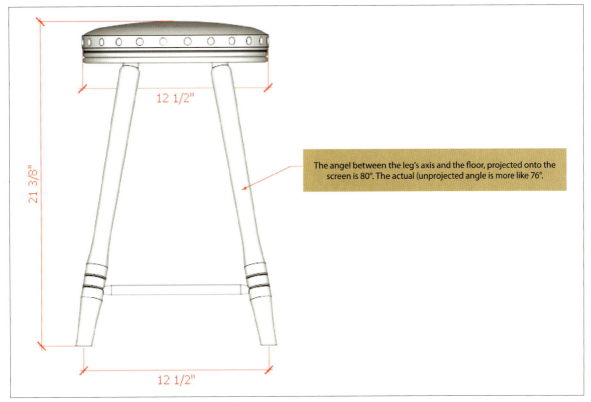

12 1/2"

21 3/8"

The angel between the leg's axis and the floor, projected onto the screen is 80°. The actual (unprojected angle is more like 76°.

12 1/2"

**Figure 9** | Front view of SketchUp model with overall front dimensions

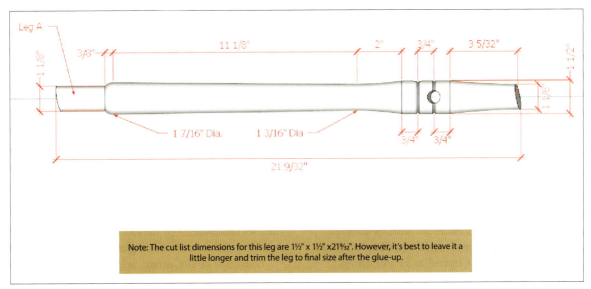

Leg A

1 1/8"

3/8"

11 1/8"

2"

3/4"

3 5/32"

1 1/2"

1 7/16" Dia.

1 3/16" Dia

3/4"

3/4"

21 9/32"

Note: The cut list dimensions for this leg are 1½" x 1½" x21⁹/₃₂". However, it's best to leave it a little longer and trim the leg to final size after the glue-up.

**Figure 10** | A dimensioned drawing of the leg intended for lathe-turning use

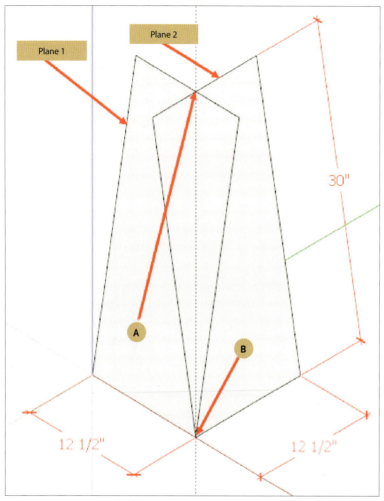

Plane 1

Plane 2

30"

A

B

12 1/2"

12 1/2"

**Figure 11** | Two rotated rectangles whose intersection forms a leg axis

in **Figure 10** that the rung mortise is drilled into the legs at an angle because the legs are splayed. In **Figure 10** I have labeled curves with diameters because in the shop that is what you want to set calipers to. In SketchUp you are more likely to want radii, so you might calculate those and write them down. Notice the overall leg length, including the compound cuts at each end, is 21⁹/₃₂". Let me make two comments about this dimension: first, if you measure this distance with the Tape Measure tool you will get ~21¹³/₆₄" because the Dimension tool rounds dimensions; second, when dealing with nonrectilinear components, such as splayed legs, you will almost certainly end up with uncommon dimensions.

There are a number of ways to model this leg. For instance, we could model it with its axis parallel to the blue axis and when we are completed align its axis with a splayed construction line. In this text, since we need to create a splayed construction line anyway, I am going to show you how to model it in situ.

the angle between the axis of the leg and the Red/Green plane it is closer to 76° due to the compound splaying. Notice also in **Figure 9** that by inspection the leg length along its axis is north of 20" but certainly less than 30". We will use 30" when we use the Rotated Rectangle tool later.

Figure 10 is the detailed dimensions for the leg. **Figure 10** can be used at the lathe to turn the leg. Study the dimension lengths and diameters and notice in particular the turned nicks and drilled mortise. The Shakers would nick their turned legs to mark where the rungs would enter them. You can see

## ESTABLISHING A SPLAYED SURFACE TO DRAW ON

We are going to use the Rotated Rectangle tool to establish two planes that intersect. The intersection of those planes will establish the splayed axis of the leg. Each plane will be tilted 80° to the Red/Green plane. Each will measure 12½" by 30". Here are the corner inputs for each rotated rectangle:

- Plane 1 – First Corner: origin; Second Corner: 12 ½" along the Red axis; Third Corner: 80° and 30".

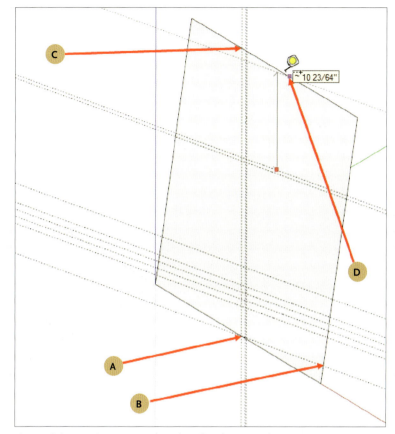

**Figure 12** | Plane 1 with construction lines that reflect dimensions from Figure 10

1. Since the construction line is the axis of the leg and is on Plane 1, Plane 1 must bisect the leg. Hence, I can use Plane 1 to draw the outline of the leg on and then use the Follow Me tool to extrude the leg around the construction line or leg axis.

Using the model shown in **Figure 11,** create a layer called Planes and place Plane 2 on it. Make the Planes layer invisible. In Edit Group mode, extend the 12½" dimension of Plane 1 to arbitrarily 24" by extending it to the right and leave Plane 1 on Layer0 for now. In **Figure 12** all construction lines are drawn on Plane 1. Start by drawing construction line AB 90° to construction line AC, the leg's axis. Use the Protractor tool and hold the protractor tool's cursor over Plane 1 until the cursor turns black and then hold the *Shift* key down. This locks the protractor to Plane 1. Click first on point A. Second click on point C. Then type 90 into the VCB to produce construction line AB. Next create the remaining construction lines parallel to AB using the dimensions in **Figure 10**. To make sure that all construction lines are on Plane 1 create them using the Tape Measure tool by first clicking on a construction line you want to be parallel to, then hold your cursor over point D (a point on the top edge) and then type the distance into the VCB. This last step is critical because you may visually think you are drawing construction lines on Plane 1, but in reality you may not be. The procedure outlined will ensure that you are.

Now we need to create an outline of the leg. We will use the Line tool and the Bezier Curve tool extension. In **Figure 13** a construction line has been added below line AB of **Figure 12**. This is to extend the leg below the floor line. Once the leg has been turned with the Follow Me tool we will slice it off even with

- Plane 2 - First Corner: Second Corner of Plane 1; Second Corner: 12 ½" along the green axis; Third Corner: 80° and 30".

In **Figure 11** I created two rotated rectangle per the specifications of Plane 1 and Plane 2. Immediately upon creating each rectangle I made it a group so that the two rectangles wouldn't stick to one another. Then using the Tape Measure tool, I created the construction line that passes through points A and B, which is also the intersection of Plane 1 and Planes 2. This construction line is the axis of the leg. The lower and upper edges of Planes 1 and 2 are at 90° one to the other because Plane 1's lower edge was drawn along the red axis and the lower edge of Plane 2 drawn parallel to the Green axis. Think about Plane 1 and the construction line. The construction line is on Plane

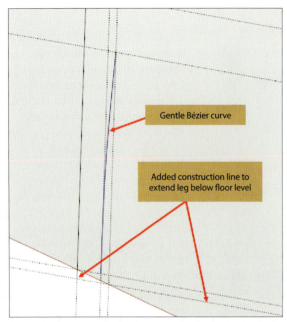

Gentle Bézier curve

Added construction line to extend leg below floor level

**Figure 13** | Added construction line at bottom of leg and gentle Bezier curve

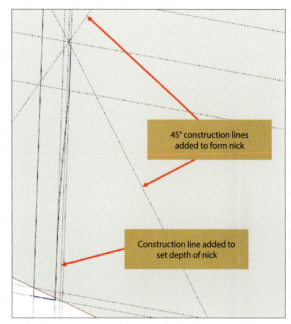

45° construction lines added to form nick

Construction line added to set depth of nick

**Figure 14** | Construction lines added for nicks

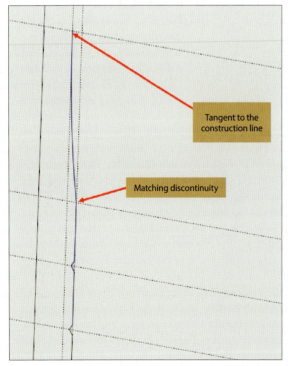

Tangent to the construction line

Matching discontinuity

**Figure 15** | Nick copied, connecting lines and matching gentle curve added

the floor. Also in **Figure 13** a gentle curve has been drawn, shown in blue, with the Bezier Curves command found in the Draw menu. Notice it is tangent to the construction line at the bottom but not tangent to a construction line at the top. In this case we wanted a discontinuity or sharp junction. As we continue to draw the leg you should refer back to **Figures 10** and **12**

**Figure 14** shows three construction lines added to create the nicks shown in **Figure 10**. Nicks are scores made on the lathe and were commonly used by Shakers for chair, stool and table legs to mark where rungs enter the legs. I exaggerated them with two 45° lines for a 90° nick that is ¹⁄₁₆" deep. In actuality in the shop the lathe score lines would be much finer. Notice in **Figure 14** that five lines have been added with the Line tool and shown selected in blue. We don't need to add construction lines for the next nick. Rather we use the Select tool to select the first nick and then use the Move/Copy tool to place it.

**Figure 15** shows the nick copied and placed. Two connecting lines have been added with the Line tool and a matching gentle curve is added with the Bezier Curves command. Notice in **Figure 15** that the curve

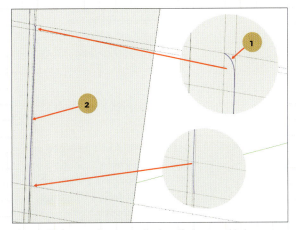

**Figure 16** | A long gentle curve and a sharp final curve added

starts with a matching discontinuity and ends with the curve tangent to the construction line. The next curve will start out tangent to this same construction line providing a continuous smooth curve.

**Figure 16** shows a long gentle curve connecting the previous short curve and the final short and sharp curve. Shown in **Figure 16** are two circular blowups to provide a better view of the transitions. When drawing this part of the leg the short sharp curve was drawn first and the long gentle curve second. The long gentle curve is tangent to the construction lines at both ends. The short sharp curve is tangent to the construction line at the lower end but tangent to an imaginary 45° line at the top end. The leg outline can now be completed with the Line tool.

**Figure 17** shows the completed leg outline. Actually it is one half of the outline whose left edge is the leg's axis splayed inward from the Red/Blue and Green/Blue planes. Notice in **Figure 17** that the top of the outline is formed by two parallel lines and a third line perpendicular to the first two. From **Figure 10** we see that the distance between the parallel lines is ⁹⁄₁₆"; half of 1⅛" as shown on the left end of **Figure 10**. We will use the Follow Me tool to extrude the outline in a circular manor around its axis. To do that we need a circular path whose plane is normal to the outline's axis. There are a number of ways to do this. The way we are going to use makes use of the Rotated Rectangle tool. Before we can do that we need to temporarily make a group of the leg's outline face and

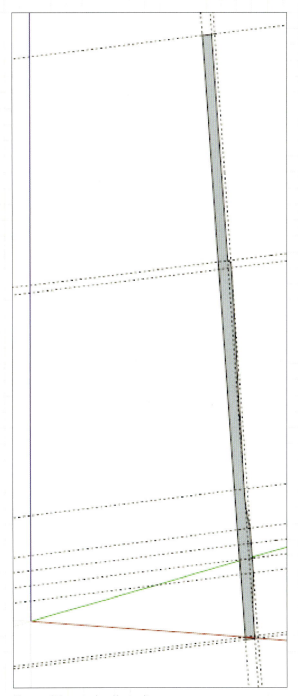

**Figure 17** | The completed leg outline

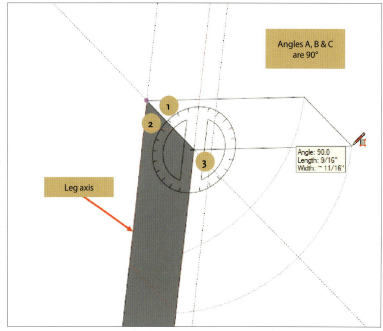

Figure 18 | The Rotated Rectangle tool screen capture just prior to the third input click

perimeter. Clicking twice on the leg's outline to select all primitives, we then Context click and choose Make Group.

## TURNING A SPLAYED LEG

Look carefully at **Figure 18** and notice that angles 1, 2 and 3 are all 90°. **Figure 18** is a screen capture just prior to the third input click for the Rotated Rectangle tool. In the Inference Engine tooltip you can see that the distance between the leg's axis and outside edge is 9/16" as discussed in the previous paragraph. You can also see that the rectangle that will result is at right angles to the leg's outline

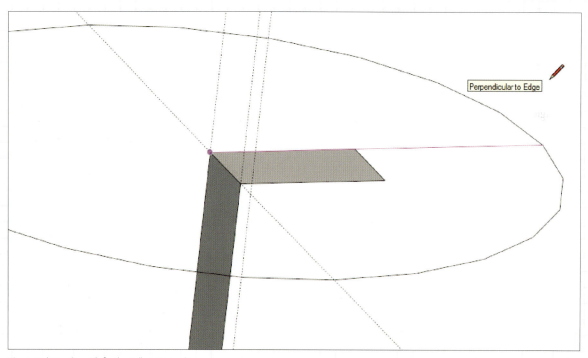

Figure 19 | Circular path for the Follow Me tool

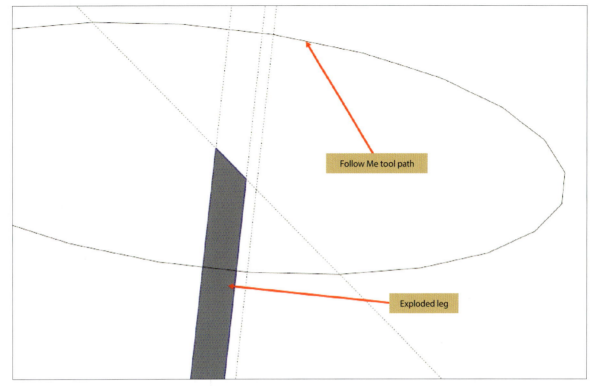

**Figure 20** | The circle's face is deleted and the leg outline group is exploded

surface. This is going to allow us to use the plane of the rotated rectangle to set the protractor's plane for the Circle tool. The width of the rotated rectangle, shown as ~¹¹⁄₁₆" in the Inference Engine tooltip, is arbitrary. What is important is that the Angle be 90°.

**Figure 19** shows the circular path we will use for the Follow Me tool. We start by selecting the Circle tool, holding its cursor over the rotated rectangle and depress and hold the *Shift* key. This locks the Circle tool's protractor to the rotated rectangle's plane. Doing so ensures the circle face we will draw is normal to the leg's axis. With the *Shift* key held down we move the cursor to the corner of the rotated rectangle that lies on the leg's axis and click. Next we move the cursor out along the edge of the rotated rectangle guided by the magenta Inference Engine line. The circle's radius is arbitrary, but should be larger than the width of the rotated rectangle, as shown in **Figure 18**.

When the circle is completed, we select its face and delete it. We only need the circumference (perimeter) for the Follow Me tool's path. We must also select the leg outline group and explode it into its primitives as shown in **Figure 20**. Now we are ready to use the Follow Me tool. With the Select tool, select only the circular path. Next choose the Follow Me tool; hover over the leg's outline face and click. The leg will be extruded as though it were turned on a lathe.

The extruded leg shown in **Figure 21** may have an incorrect surface color. We can easily correct this by triple clicking on the leg, context click and choose Reverse Faces. There are a few other cleanup details we need to address in **Figure 21**. First, we want to extend the bottom of the leg further below the floor (Red/Green plane) arbitrarily 6". We use the Push/Pull tool to pull the bottom surface down 6". Next, there are three lines we need to Smooth/

Soften shown in **Figure 21**. We do this using the Eraser tool with the *Ctrl* key held down and use the cursor in a paint brush fashion. These lines are lines at the connection of tangential curves and hence should not be displayed. In general only lines that provide borders between discontinuities should be displayed. All but one of the construction lines have served their purpose and we will get rid of them. But first create a layer called Axes and place the leg's axis construction line on it. Use the Eraser tool, not Edit/Delete Guides, to delete the remaining construction lines. Temporarily make the leg a Group.

   **Figure 22** shows the cleaned up leg with two encompassing rectangles: one rectangle on the red/green plane; the second rectangle is a copy of the first and positioned upward along the Blue axis at a height of 20⅜". This is the height of the top surface of the wooden seat on which the cushion will be attached. The leg mortises through the wooden seat and ends flush with its top. Though you can't see it in **Figure 22**, the leg extends 6" below the bottom rectangle. We can now explode the leg into its primitives and triple click on one of the planes. This should select all primitives of the two planes and the leg. We use Edit/Intersect Faces/With Selection to create rings around the leg where the rectangles intersect them. Now we delete the perimeters of the rectangles, which in turn will also eliminate their faces. Looking at the leg using the Front view, we use the Select tool in a right to left bounding box fashion to cut the top and the bottom of the leg off above and below the circles created by the Intersect Faces tool. Lastly, we triple click on the leg, context click and choose Make Component.

   I call the rectangles we used in the previous paragraph – to cut off the legs using the Intersect Faces tool – slicing planes, and I call the process I described slicing. We will use slicing planes much more in Part Three. **Figure 23** shows the completed leg with its axis plane visible. At this point we should create a layer called legs and place the leg on it with a definition name of Leg. This will turn out to be the Right Front Leg, but we can worry about that in a moment.

   Recall that the spacing of the legs are 12½" at the floor where each leg's axis intersects it. To find the

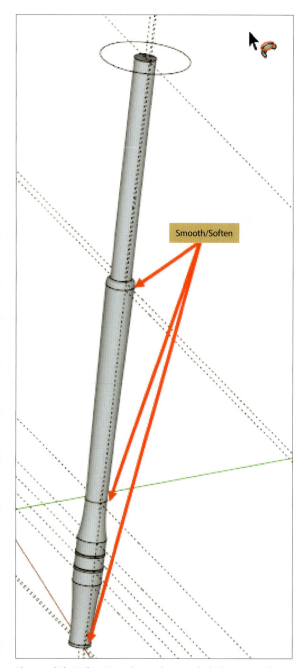

Smooth/Soften

**Figure 21** | The Follow Me tool is used to extrude the leg in a circular manner

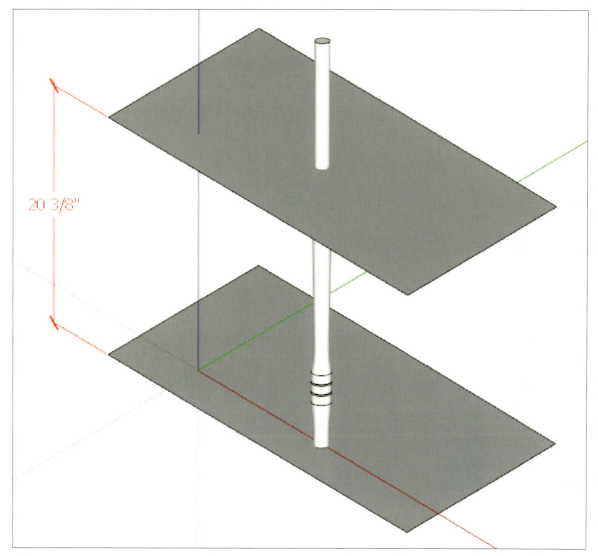

**Figure 22** | The cleaned up leg with slicing planes

center point of all four legs we create a construction line on the Red/Green plane parallel to the red axis and 6¼" back in the positive green direction. Next we create a construction line on the Red/Green plane parallel to the green axis and 6¼" right in the positive red direction. Where these construction lines cross is the center. Next we select the Leg along with its axis then select the Rotate/Copy tool (don't forget to press the *Ctrl* key). Place the cursor of the Rotate/

Copy tool at the center point and click. Move the cursor out along a construction line and click again. Move the cursor counterclockwise and type 90 into the VCB to copy and rotate a Leg 90°. Immediately type 3x into the VCB to make 3 copies of the leg. We now have four Legs and their axes as shown in **Figure 24**. Notice the construction lines used to find the center of the legs and used as the axis of rotation for the Rotate/Copy tool.

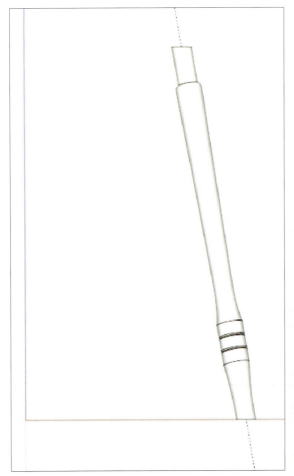

**Figure 23** | The completed leg with its axis

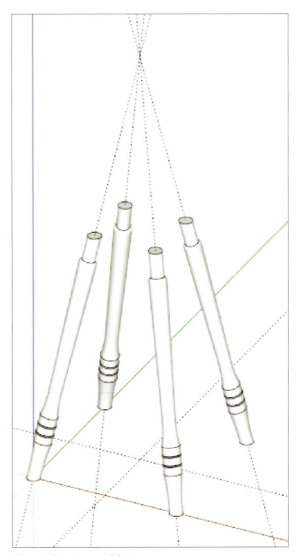

**Figure 24** | Four Legs and their axes

## DETERMINING THE RUNG LENGTH

I have mentioned a couple of times that the nicks in the leg serve a purpose and that is to locate the rungs. In **Figure 24** we have four Legs with their axes. We also have two construction lines we used to find the center of the Legs on the floor or Red/Green plane. We will move the center construction lines to a layer called Center Lines and make it invisible. **Figure 25** shows the four Legs, their axes and Planes 1 and 2. Plane 2 is not a player in this next step but simply there because it is on the Planes layer. Plane 1 bisects both Legs and also passes through their axes. Studying **Figure 25** reveals a very important point that is more obvious in the blowup sections. That is the point where the intersection of Plane 1 and a Leg forms a V in the upper nick of each Leg. The V in the Right Front Leg is not visible until you rotate the Leg to see its inside intersection with Plane 1 as shown in its blowup. The vertex of the V in each Leg is a point we will click on with the Tape Measure tool to

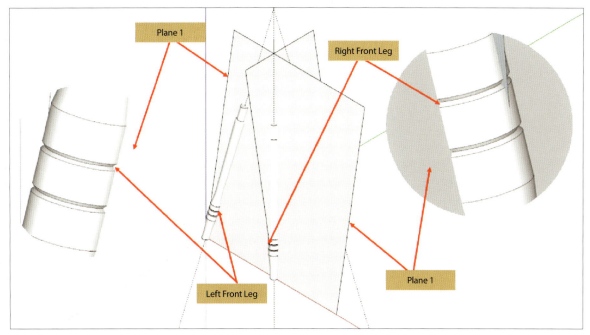

**Figure 25** | Plane 1 bisects each front Leg and passes through their respective axis

create a construction line. This construction line, as we will see in a moment, stretches to infinity in each direction, passes through the axes of the two front Legs and by construction passes through the vertex of each V. To successfully complete this step it is necessary to zoom in very close to the vertex of the V on each leg and use the Inference Engine for confirmation before clicking. The mouse scroll wheel is the preferred method of zooming.

Referring to **Figure 26,** the rung construction line created in the previous steps is shown passing through the Leg's axes. These two intersections mark the ends of the rung at the center of their end faces. If the distance between these two intersections is measured with the Tape Measure tool the result is ~10 $^{61}/_{64}$". As mentioned a number of times, when dealing with non-rectilinear and Bézier curve pieces you are likely to be dealing with odd dimensions too. However, we want to draw precisely, so we will now connect these two intersections with a line using the Line tool. This line will become the axis of the front rung and

also the axis of rotation for the Follow Me tool when we extrude the rung.

You should be able to model the rung at this point without instructions from me. Refer to **Figure 26** for dimensions. The rungs on the left and right are the front and back rungs. Notice they are slightly shorter than the left and right rung shown on the top and bottom. This difference is due to the fact that the Legs are splayed and the front and back rungs enter at the top nicks while the left and right rungs enter at the bottom nicks, which are further apart. However, the tenons (the tapered ends) are all identical. The important things to notice about the tenons is that they taper from $^9/_{16}$" at the end to $^{11}/_{16}$" at 1 ¼". However, there is no curve for the first ½" and then there is a gentle curve from ½" to 1 ¼" in. Here is a hint for constructing the rung: looking at the front view and using the line that connects the two intersecting points create a rectangle with one edge the rung line and the rectangle parallel to the red/blue plane. Use this rectangle to draw one half of the rung outline just as we did the splayed Legs. Use the Follow Me tool to extrude the rungs in a circular fashion.

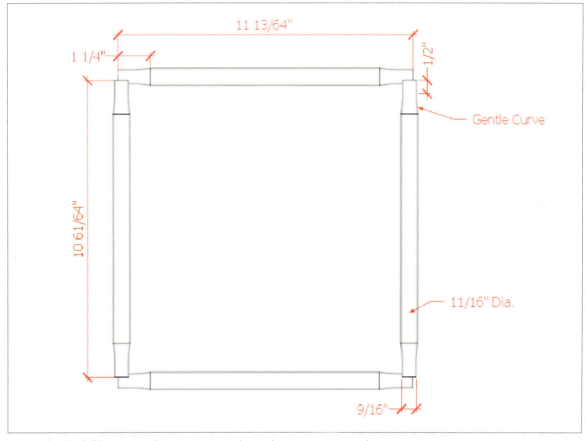

**Figure 26** | With aid of the X-Ray view the rung construction line can be seen intersecting each Leg's axis

## CREATING THE RUNG MORTISES

**Figure 27** shows an X-Ray view of the Legs and completed Rungs. The Legs are not completed because they are missing the mortises for the Rungs. We are going to use the Intersect Faces tool to help create the mortises in the Legs, but I need to point out some limitations and provide you with some tricks to overcome them. Here are some things we need to be aware of:

1. When we create the mortises we will end up erasing and deleting Rung instances. The good news is that we have two of each length in the model so we must be careful to destroy only one at a time. That way we can use the Rotate/Copy tool and the Center Lines to restore a destroyed instance of a Rung.

2. When we use the Context menus Explode command the instances primitives are placed on the layer the instance resided on prior to exploding. We must immediately return them to Layer0.

3. When using Intersect Faces to create lines of intersecting faces the tool does just that; it only creates lines where faces intersect. In the case of intersecting a Rung with a Leg, only a hole will be outlined on the surface of the Leg, but no lines or faces will be created inside the Leg. We need to use part of the Rung's edges and faces to fill in.

4. When using Rung tenon part to create Leg mortise parts, inside faces become outside faces and we need to use Context menu Reverse Faces to correct for this.

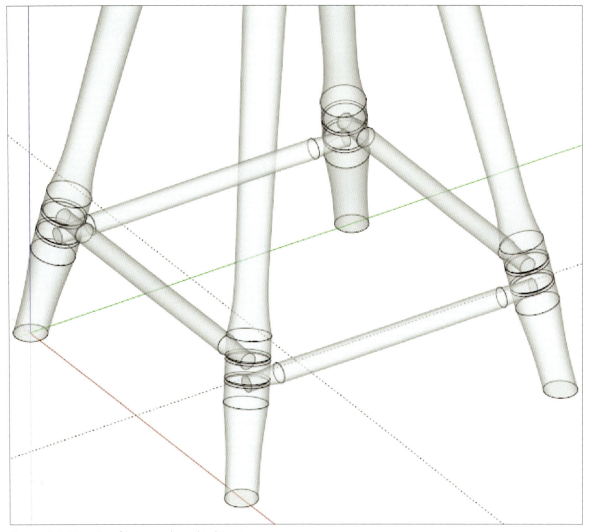

**Figure 27** | The X-Ray view of the Legs and completed Rungs

5. The Intersect Faces tool may produce results with missing faces. This happens because faces below a certain size, having to do with computing resolution limits used in SketchUp, are not drawn and small faces are often created when using nonrectilinear constructions. To minimize this we will use the Scale tool to scale things up by a factor of ten before using the Intersect Faces tool. When done we will scale them back down.

We start by selecting the Left Front Leg and the Front Rung. Notice in **Figure 28** that both the Left Front Leg and the Front Rung are selected. The top, right and back grip is the one we will use and we will Uniform Scale about Opposite Point a factor of 10. We need to remember which grip point we used, because we will need to scale down the result a factor of $\frac{1}{10}$th using the same grip point if we wish to maintain the Legs position in the model. When the Leg and Rung are scaled up, and while they are both still selected,

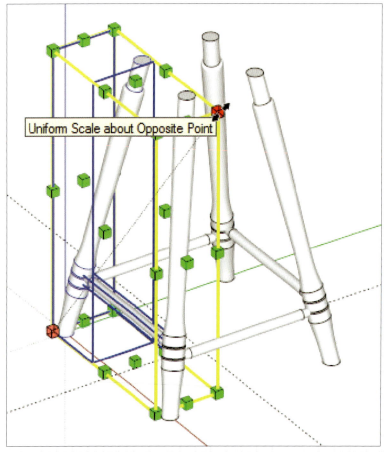

Uniform Scale about Opposite Point

**Figure 28** | Scaling the Left Front Leg and Front Rung up a factor of 10

selected. This will select the Rung entities that are outside the Leg leaving only those entities that are inside or on its surface. See the selection on the left side of **Figure 29**. Using the *Delete* key, we delete the selected entities.

Next we need to delete the surface where the Rung enters the Leg. Notice in **Figure 30**, on the right side, the outline of where the Rung enters the Leg. Using the Select tool, we very carefully delete the surfaces and the unwanted lines as shown on the left side of **Figure 30**. Be very careful not to delete any of the faces behind the surface. These are the surfaces that appear a darker color in **Figure 30**; they appear a darker color because they are the Rung's inside faces of its tenon and are now the outside faces of the Leg's mortise. We need to use Context menu Reverse Faces to correct this. Lastly, we use the Scale tool to scale the leg primitives back down to $\frac{1}{10}$th its size.

We don't make the leg a component at this time because we have one more mortise to model in it. With the Select tool, we select all the primitives of the leg with the mortise and include in the selection the remaining rung that is entering the leg's back side. With the Scale tool, we scale them both up a factor of 10. The Rung must be exploded and its primitives placed on Layer0. We repeat the process of creating the remaining mortise and scale the leg back down by a factor of $\frac{1}{10}$th. **Figure 31** shows the scaled down leg with both mortises and still in primitive form. We need to make the leg a component, but what should we call it. If you study the finished model shown in **Figure 32** you will notice that the two front legs are not the same component. Rather diagonal sets are the same. This is because of the sequence in which the Rungs

right click on them with the Select tool and choose Explode. Immediately upon exploding use the Entity Info box to place all primitives on Layer0. While the primitives are still selected use command Edit/Intersect Faces/With Selection.

Now we are going to delete unwanted portions of the Rung leaving only the portion that is inside the leg and on its surface. We do this with the Select tool. On the right side of **Figure 29** notice that we used the Select tool in a right to left fashion. We start to the lower right of the Rung and drag to the upper left. Our goal is to get very close to, but not include any portion of the Leg. When using the Select tool in a right to left fashion any component, group or entity that is partially included in the selection box is

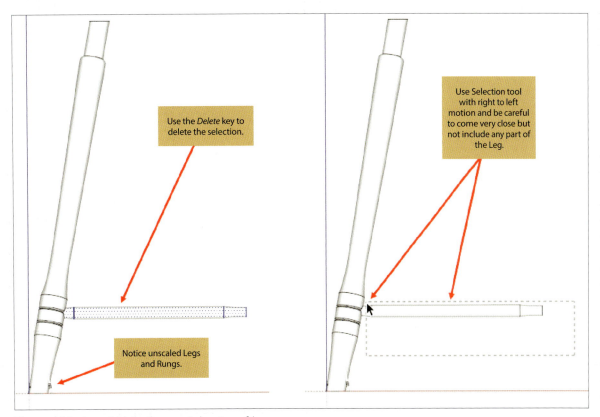

**Figure 29** | Selecting and deleting the unwanted portions of the rung

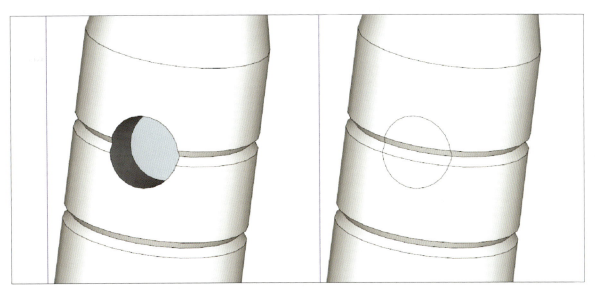

**Figure 30** | The surface of the leg where the tenon enters needs to be deleted

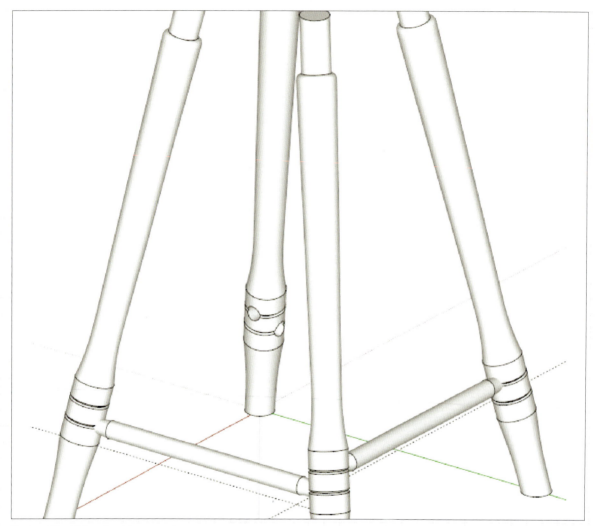

**Figure 31** | The left front leg with two mortises

enter each leg. So we will make this leg a component with a Definition name of Leg A. An instance of Leg A can be used for the Left Front Leg and the Right Back Leg.

I will leave it to you to create Leg B and use instances of it for the Right Front Leg and the Left Back Leg. You will need to restore the left and front Rungs using the Rotate/Copy tool and the Center Lines. Do this before starting work on Leg B. Also model the Seat and Seat Cover with tacks. Hint: Draw one tack and use the Rotate/Copy tool to place

copies of it. When you are done you should have the model shown in **Figure 32**.

In Chapter 13 we are going to return to circular curves for a while. We will learn to create parts that curve in two dimensions. In addition, we will learn to use slicing planes to model nonstandard miter joints and calculate the angles. Lastly we will learn some of the problems associated with curves that are represented by line segments and how to work around such problems. In Chapter 14, we will return to Bézier curves.

**Figure 32** | The completed Shaker Shop Stool

## EXERCISES FOR THE STUDENT

1. We located the legs axis with the intersection of two rectangles: one on the Red axis and tilted in the positive Green direction 20°; the other on the green axis and tilted in the positive Red direction 20°. Create a construction line that is parallel to the Blue axis and intersects with the leg's axis. Measure the angle between the legs axis and this construction line at the point of intersection. What does it measure and why is it not 20°?

2. Look at the bounding box of the Right Front Leg. How do you correct for its excessive size? Hint: Use the axis of the leg.

3. Try creating the leg mortises without scaling the leg and rung up. Look closely at the mortise and see what problems exist.

4. When you have completed the Shaker Shop Stool model, create shop drawings complete with angles for drilling mortises in the legs and seat.

# 13

# MODELING A CLOCK HOOD WITH TWO-DIMENSIONAL CIRCULAR CURVES

*In this chapter the Shaker-Style Chain Driven Wall Clock shown in **Figure 1** will serve as our learning vehicle. This clock is a wall-hanging clock inspired by Shaker clocks I have seen. It was a variation in a series of models I presented to my daughter. She was to select the one she liked the most and I would build it as a gift for graduating from law school. Typical of my daughter she chose one that had no curves and was most faithful to the Shaker style.*

*Still, this model has some use as a learning vehicle, as we will see. Only the arched bonnet is of interest to us. I am using the term bonnet loosely because it is normally used to refer to the removable top of a grandfather or tall clock. The pieces we are going to model are the door's arched rail and the cove and bullnose trim piece. The arched door rail is a good example of concentric circles and the problems they can pose. The trim pieces present a different set of problems: They curve in two dimensions and require nonstandard miters.*

**F**igure 2 shows the front view of the door and bonnet trim with arched features. The door is typical frame and panel construction, the panel being glass, the side vertical pieces are the stiles and the horizontal pieces are the rails. In this case the top rail is an arch.

The trim is comprised of two traditional pieces: a bullnose and a cove. The bullnose and cove run horizontally along the sides and part of the front, but also run in an arched fashion through the middle of the front. The horizontal pieces are joined to the arched pieces at an angle, which is *not* the typical 45°. We will learn in the next part how to construct the arched trim and determine the angle joining the trim pieces. We will start simple and learn how to draw the arch – though the arch is not as simple as it looks in this front view.

## THE ARCHED DOOR RAIL

Take a moment to study the dimension details of the arched door rail in **Figure 3**. Notice there are tenons on either end of the arch. On the back you can see and arched inset with horizontal inset extensions. This inset is to receive the glass panel for the door. The tenons join the stile's mortises to form a bridle joint.

There are three arched radii we are concerned with. The largest and smallest radii form the outer edges of the Arched Door Rail. An in-between radius defines the inset width. Notice that the center point for all radii is offset from the bottom by 7/64". This is an important point to remember.

The tenons are ¼" thick and centered front to back, leaving a ¼" shoulder on both sides of the ¾" stock. The front face of the tenons extends 1½" in from each end. However, the back face of the tenons extends 1⅛" in from each end. The ⅜" difference allows for continuation of the glass inset down the length of the stiles. Note that the inset depth is ½". Also note the three radii: 2½", 2⅞" and 4", all centered on the 7/64" offset and a vertical center line of the stock. Lastly note the overall dimensions of the stock, 12" long by ¾" thick by 4 7/64" tall.

Before leaving this drawing visualize the construction lines that would be helpful in drawing this component. On the front view, four horizontal construction lines would help to define the offset, bottom edge of the tenons, top edge of the tenons and the 2½" radius. The 4" radius is defined by the top edge of the stock and the overall reference for horizontal construction lines is the bottom edge of the stock. Also on the front, three vertical construction lines would be useful; one for the center line and one for each tenon inset. I leave it for you to figure out how many construction lines would be useful to draw the back side.

Now let's draw the arched door rail. We begin by drawing a block that represents the overall stock dimension of 12" x ¾" x 4 7/64". Draw this in the parallel projection Front and ISO views. On the front side we use the Tape Measure tool to add the construction lines discussed above as shown in **Figure 4**. Notice all construction lines are relative to a stock edge except the topmost construction line, which

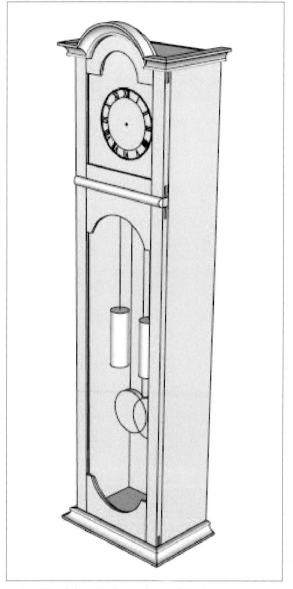

**Figure 1** | The Shaker-Style Chain-Driven Wall Clock

defines the 2½" radius. It is relative to the 7/64" offset. The Tape Measure tool lets you drag construction lines from lines or other construction lines, which is helpful in this case.

Before we place any circles on the drawing, let's review a few things about SketchUp circles. Circles in SketchUp are actually formed by a many-sided

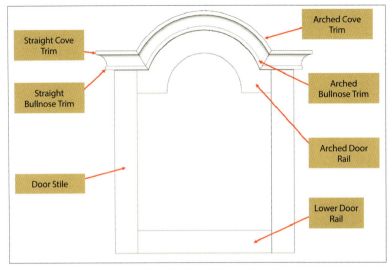

Figure 2 | The Shaker Style Chain Driven Wall Clock door and trim pieces

polygon. The default is 24 sides. I have found that for furniture drawings this looks rather clumsy. I prefer a circle of at least 60 sides. One downside of this is that it increases the model's file size rather substantially. But I still prefer it because of the looks. The second thing to remember about circles is that because they are formed by a many-sided polygon, there are many line segments, each with endpoints. Whenever drawing circles make sure these defining endpoints fall in a strategically useful place. In most furniture drawing that means

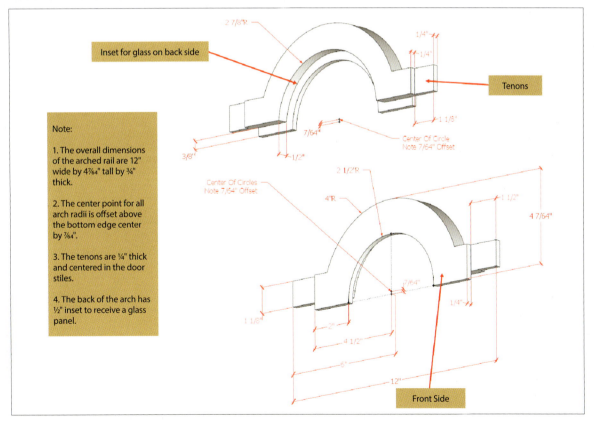

Note:

1. The overall dimensions of the arched rail are 12" wide by 4⁷⁄₆₄" tall by ¾" thick.

2. The center point for all arch radii is offset above the bottom edge center by ⁷⁄₆₄".

3. The tenons are ¼" thick and centered in the door stiles.

4. The back of the arch has ½" inset to receive a glass panel.

Figure 3 | Dimensions for the arched door rail

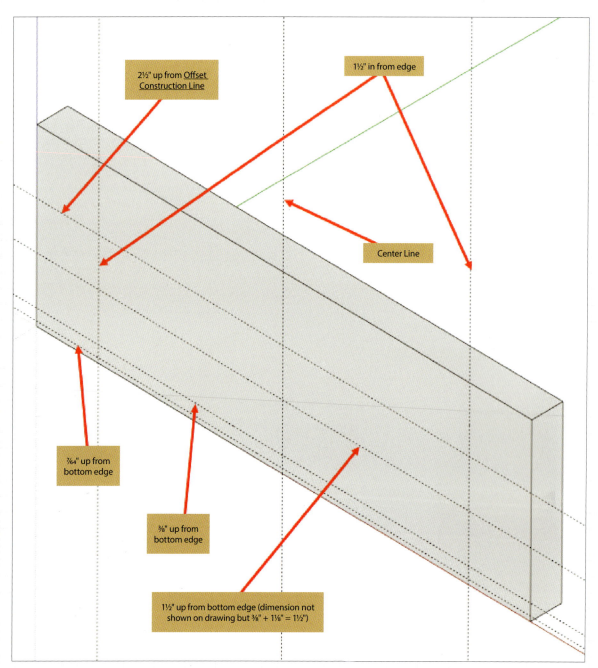

**2½" up from Offset Construction Line**

**1½" in from edge**

**Center Line**

**⁷⁄₆₄" up from bottom edge**

**⅜" up from bottom edge**

**1½" up from bottom edge (dimension not shown on drawing but ⅜" + 1⅛" = 1½")**

**Figure 4** | Block with annotated construction line

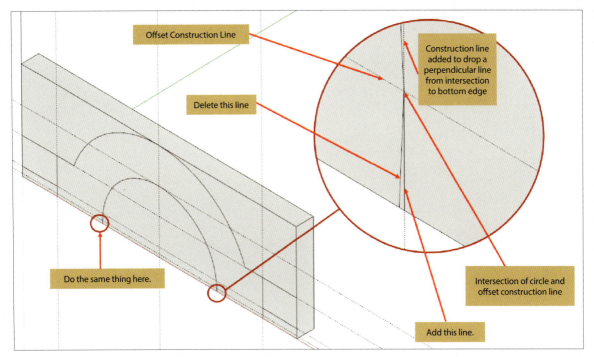

**Offset Construction Line**

**Construction line added to drop a perpendicular line from intersection to bottom edge**

**Delete this line**

**Do the same thing here.**

**Intersection of circle and offset construction line**

**Add this line.**

**Figure 5** | Correcting for inside circle extending beyond a semicircle

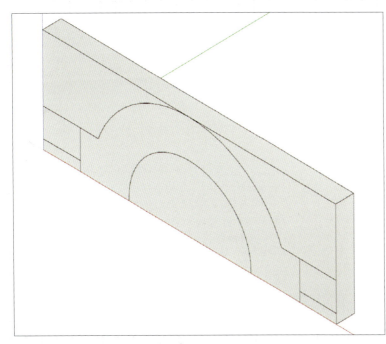

**Figure 6** | Arched door rail outline on front face

endpoints should be on an axis. Otherwise you may end up with clumsy-looking concentric arches as might happen in this model. Especially the gap between the top of the door's arch and the bottom of the bullnose trim.

Using the Circle tool and starting at the intersection of the offset line and the center line, draw two circles. You don't have to enter the radius if you use the intersections of the center line and the top most construction line and the top edge to define them. That is why we use construction lines. Don't forget to use circles with 60 sides. Notice that the arches are not actually semicircles as drawn due to the ⁷⁄₆₄" offset. That is, they extend beyond a semicircle below the offset line and intersect

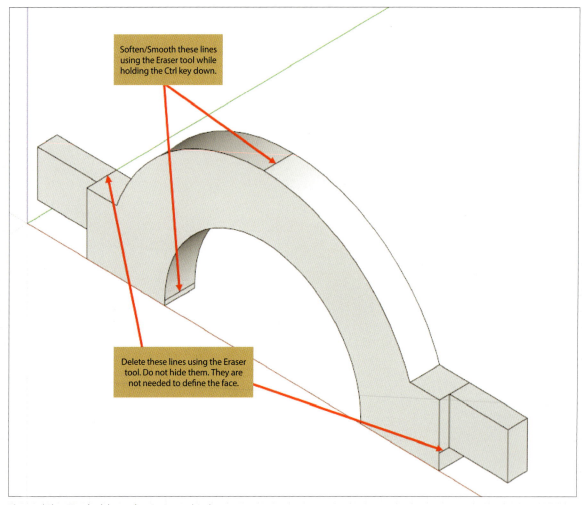

Soften/Smooth these lines using the Eraser tool while holding the Ctrl key down.

Delete these lines using the Eraser tool. Do not hide them. They are not needed to define the face.

**Figure 7** | The 3D arched door rail, not yet completed

with the bottom edge in an extension of the circle. We should correct this at this point by adding very short tangent lines from the intersection of the offset construction line and the circle and perpendicular to the bottom edge. It is best to do this at this point and not after the circles have been operated on by the Push/Pull tool. Otherwise we have a lot of cleanup to do. Refer to **Figure 5** for details.

Next, using the Line tool add the lines needed to outline the tenons and remaining rail. After erasing some unwanted lines using the Eraser tool and removing the construction lines (Edit/

Delete Guides), your drawing should now look like **Figure 6**.

With the Push/Pull tool push the lowest and left/right-most rectangles all the way through to eliminate those surfaces. Push each tenon face in ¼". Push the lower and center arch all the way through eliminating that surface. Also eliminate the top most and left/right-most surfaces by pushing them all the way through. Your drawing should now look like **Figure 7**. Follow the cleanup instructions outlined in **Figure 7**. Rotate the model and be sure to clean up the lines you can't see from this view. Notice that some lines we

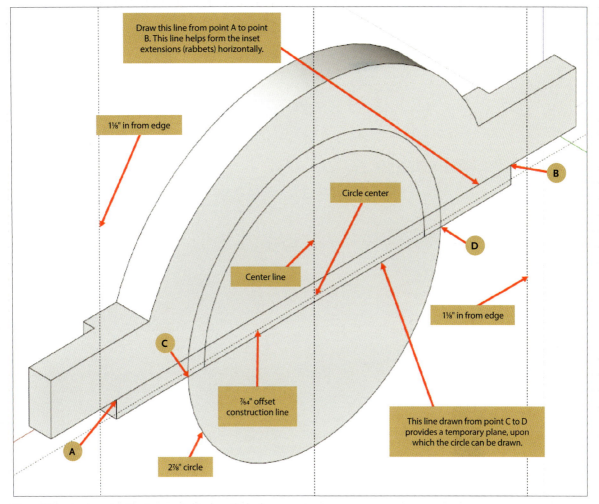

**Figure 8** | Lines and construction lines needed to shape the back

The following labels appear in Figure 8:

- Draw this line from point A to point B. This line helps form the inset extensions (rabbets) horizontally.
- 1⅛" in from edge
- Circle center
- Center line
- 1⅛" in from edge
- ⁷⁄₆₄" offset construction line
- This line drawn from point C to D provides a temporary plane, upon which the circle can be drawn.
- 2⅞" circle
- A
- B
- C
- D

chose to Soften/Smooth and others we chose to delete. The general rules are: If a line is separating two planes that are coplanar it should be deleted; if a line is separating two surfaces and at least one of those surfaces is a curved surface it should be smoothed/softened. There are also times we want to hide lines, which we shall see later.

Now we are ready to model the back side. Choose Parallel Projection, Back and ISO. Remember you were to figure out the number, direction and dimension of construction lines needed to draw the back view. To aid you in your homework I have provided a view with the answer in **Figure 8**. Notice this time we draw a line using the Line tool from point A to point B. This line forms the horizontal projection of the ⅜" inset or rabbet. We also draw a line from point C to D to provide a temporary plane on which to draw the 2⅞" circle.

When your drawing looks like **Figure 8,** you can add two vertical lines to form the tenon insets, erase unwanted lines, remove the construction lines and push the inset in ½". Also push the tenons in ¼". Rotate around and underneath and look for any lines that need cleanup. Erase lines that are not

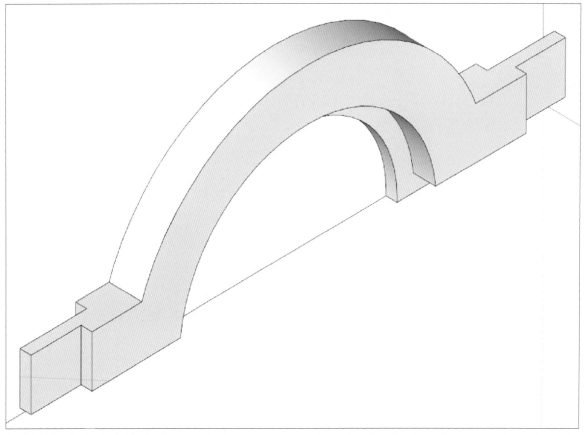

**Figure 9** | Completed Arch Door Rail

needed to define a face. Every redundant line defines a triangle or rectangle that adds to the file size and looks amateurish. After cleanup, your model should look like **Figure 9**. At this point you can triple click on any surface to select all primitives, then right click and choose Make Component. Now you can put it on the appropriate layer. This completes the Arched Door Rail. We will now model the Arched Cove Trim.

## THE ARCHED COVE TRIM

We now turn our attention to drawing the cove and bullnose trim that make up the bonnet of the Shaker-Style Chain-Driven Wall Clock. The front view dimensions and trim detail dimensions are shown in **Figure 10**. Study the dimensions.

The circle center highlighted with an arrow in the picture is an important reference point. It is the same circle center used in **Figures 3** and **8**. If you recall it was ⁷⁄₆₄" above the bottom front edge of the stock. In this drawing it lies on the frontmost plane; that is the same plane as the ¼" flat surface of the cove trim. This will be obvious soon.

Notice that the circle radii are ¹⁄₃₂" greater than either a whole inch or inch and a half. This is to allow a ¹⁄₃₂" gap (clearance) between the top of the door's arch and the bonnet.

The bonnet trim is made of two pieces: a cove trim made from stock that is 1" by 1¼" in cross section and bullnose trim made from stock that is ¼" by ⅝" in cross section. Refer to **Figure 11** for dimension details. **Figure 12** shows the side view of the bonnet

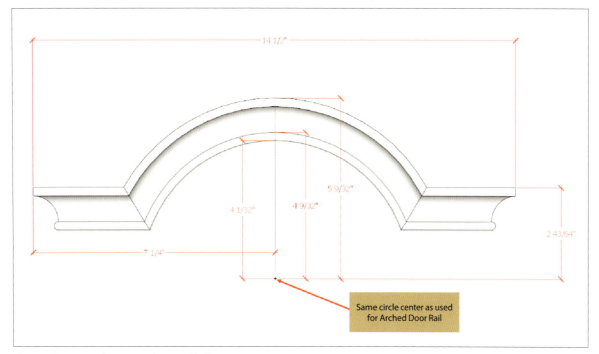

**Figure 10** | Front view dimensions of cove and bullnose trim

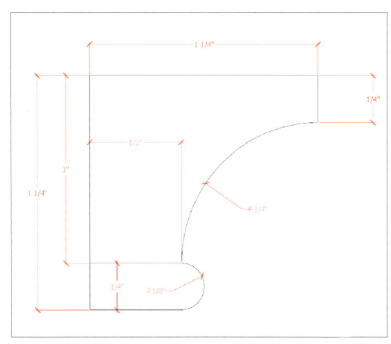

**Figure 11** | Cross section dimensions of the cove and bullnose trim

trim. Note it extends from the frontmost face back 9⅜".

There is symmetry to this bonnet on either side of the vertical center line, and we are going to make use of that symmetry to reduce the amount of work we need to do to create these components. Let's start by making the side cove. The star of this show is the Follow Me tool. First, using the Line and 2-Point Arc tools we make an outline of the cove and a path to follow with the Follow Me tool. See **Figure 13** for details. We first use the Rectangle tool to make a 1¼" square in the Red/Blue plane. Next we add three construction lines: ¼" down from the top; ¼" up from the bottom; and ½" in from the right side. The bottom construction line leaves

Figure 12 | Side view dimension of cove and bullnose trim

room for the bullnose trim later on. The intersection of the left edge and the topmost construction line is point A (the first point to click on with the 2-Point Arc tool). The intersection of the bottommost construction line and the vertical construction line is point B (the second point to click on with the 2-Point Arc tool). Lastly we type 3/4r into the VCB to create an arc with a radius of ¾" as shown in **Figure 13**. We now need to delete all the lines not needed to outline the cove cross section

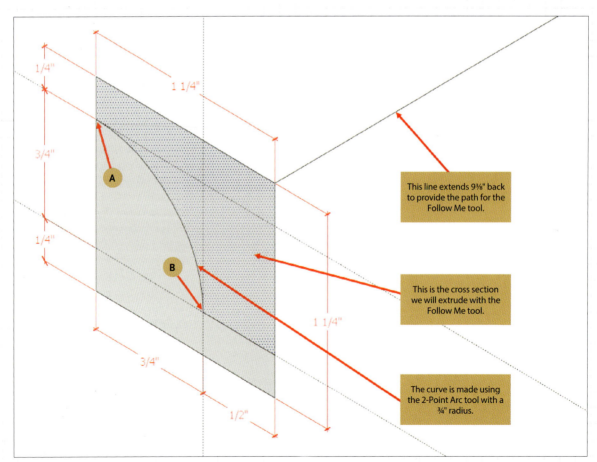

This line extends 9⅜" back to provide the path for the Follow Me tool.

This is the cross section we will extrude with the Follow Me tool.

The curve is made using the 2-Point Arc tool with a ¾" radius.

Figure 13 | Drawing the cross section of the cove molding

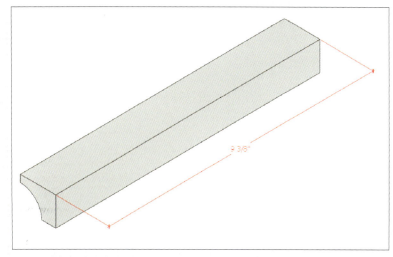

**Figure 14** | The extruded side cove trim, 9³⁄₈" long

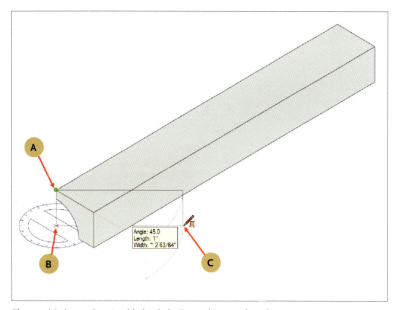

**Figure 15** | A slicing plane is added with the Rotated Rectangle tool

reside on an edge, preferably one that aligns with an axis. It is especially true in the modeling of trim like this where curves constructed with circles will end up coming together. This technique does not always produce a perfect seam, as we will see shortly, but it does create a much better seam than a nonperfect circle otherwise would (remember these circles are actually polygons). In this case we used the 2-Point Arc tool, but the same principle holds.

We now have the partially completed side cove trim shown in **Figure 14**. We need to miter this trim piece with a 45° miter cut (virtual of course). What better tool to do this than the Rotated Rectangle tool, with which we create a slicing plane.

Referring to **Figure 15** we click first on point A with the Rotated Rectangle tool's cursor. We then move the cursor down along the Blue axis and type 1 into the VCB and *Enter*; the cove trim is 1" thick. This creates point B. We drag the cursor out approximately 45° and beyond the opposite side of the cove trim and type 45,2 into the VCB and *Enter*. The first parameter of 45 specifies a 45° degree angle. The 2 is arbitrary but it must be large enough to extend the rectangle beyond the cove trim.

Referring to **Figure 16,** we add a line as shown in step 1. We can erase the rectangle beyond the cove trim but it's not necessary. In step 2, we select all the primitives and use the Edit/Intersect Faces/With Selection tool to create the curved lines needed to form the miter. In step 3, we delete all the unwanted lines with the Eraser tool and, if necessary, use the

and, with the Eraser tool, delete the three construction lines. Next, we select the 9³⁄₈" path line with the Select tool followed by selecting the Follow Me tool. Hover over the cross section face with the Follow Me tool cursor and click.

Remember, when using the Circle tool always strive to have the second point (the noncenter point)

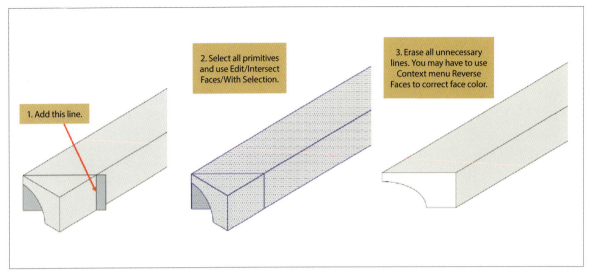

**Figure 16** | Using the slicing plane and Intersect Faces to miter the cove trim

Within the figure:

1. Add this line.

2. Select all primitives and use Edit/Intersect Faces/With Selection.

3. Erase all unnecessary lines. You may have to use Context menu Reverse Faces to correct face color.

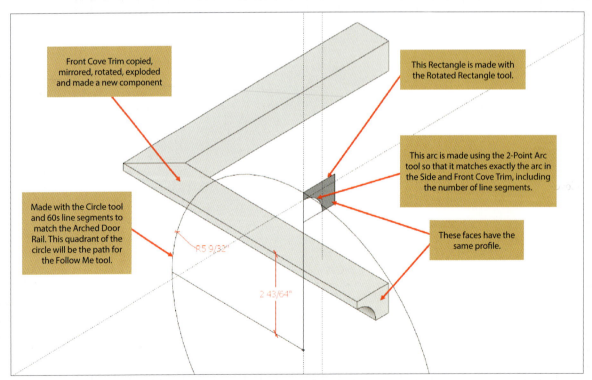

**Figure 17** | Front Cove Trim, the Follow Me path and the Arched Cove Trim profile

Within the figure:

Front Cove Trim copied, mirrored, rotated, exploded and made a new component

This Rectangle is made with the Rotated Rectangle tool.

This arc is made using the 2-Point Arc tool so that it matches exactly the arc in the Side and Front Cove Trim, including the number of line segments.

Made with the Circle tool and 60s line segments to match the Arched Door Rail. This quadrant of the circle will be the path for the Follow Me tool.

These faces have the same profile.

R5 9/32"

2 43/64"

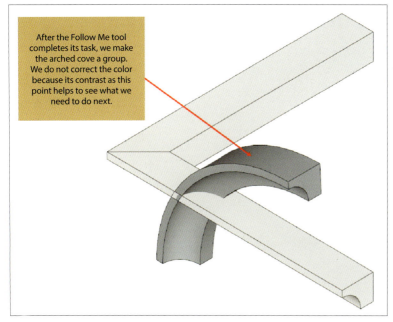

After the Follow Me tool completes its task, we make the arched cove a group. We do not correct the color because its contrast as this point helps to see what we need to do next.

**Figure 18** | The arched cove extruded with the Follow Me tool

Context menu Reverse Faces to correct for incorrect coloring. Lastly we select all the primitives and use the Context menu to Make Component and give it a Definition name Side Cove Trim.

This Side Cove Trim in **Figure 17** is longer than half the front width of 14½" (see top dimension in **Figure 10**). So a copy can be used to form the Front Cove Trim. Using the Move/Copy, Flip Along/Component's Green and Rotate tools we place the Front Cove Trim. We need to use Context menu Explode to return the copied instance of Side Cove Trim to its primitives. Whenever we explode a component or group we need to return its primitives to Layer0, so we do that. Now we can make these primitives a component called Front Cove Trim.

With the Side and Front Cove Trim pieces in place, we can use the Tape Measure, Line, Rotated Rectangle, 2-Point Arc and Circle tools to create the construction lines, cove outline and a path for the cove arch. Refer to **Figure 17** and note that the large circle is constructed using the Circle tool with 60s as the segments parameter. This is done to match the circular curves in the Arched Door Rail. Also notice that

the arc in the arched cove profile is made with the 2-Point Arc tool with the default segment parameter to precisely match the Side and Front Cove Trim. You can see that the arched cove profile is the same as the Side and Front Cove Trim's profile. The 1¼" x 1" rectangle that outlines the arched cove profile is created with the handy Rotated Rectangle tool, which you should be familiar with by now. Lastly, note that the center of the large circle is the same Circle Center used for all concentric circles including the Arched Door Rail. Only the left upper quadrant of the large circle is going to be used as the Follow Me path for the arched cove profile.

At this point we delete all the unnecessary lines and construction lines and, with the Follow Me tool, produce an arched cove that is one quadrant of a circle. It is important that we use the full quadrant so that the arched cove goes completely through the Front Cove Trim. This will be obvious in a moment. **Figure 18** shows the single quadrant of arched cove. Do not correct the surface color at this point. The difference in color can be corrected easily later. For now it provides a contrast that is actually helpful. Temporarily we will make the arched cove a group.

At this point we want to create a slicing plane just as we did for the side cove miter joint. But this miter joint will not be 45° (when the drawing is completed you can measure it and find it to be 58.4°). To create the slicing plane with the correct miter angle we need to use two very critical points. See points 1 and 2 in **Figure 19**. Use the Orbit tool to get this view of the backside. Zoom in very close with the Rotated Rectangle tool and click on point 1 first and point 2 next. It is necessary to zoom in close because the circles are made of polygons and the Inference Engine could confuse a nearby endpoint for an Intersection. Points 1 and 2 are intersections, not endpoints. Complete

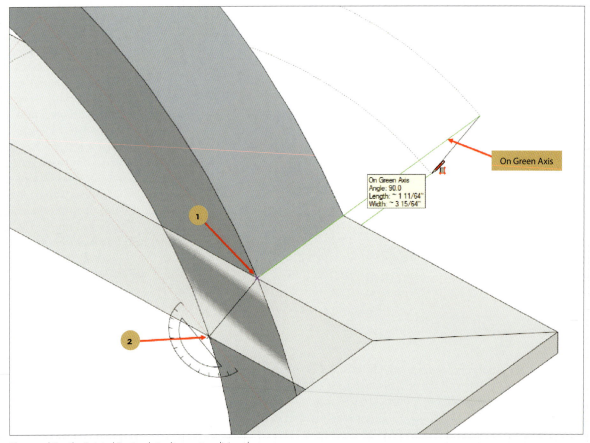

On Green Axis

On Green Axis
Angle: 90.0
Length: ~ 1 11/64"
Width: ~ 3 15/64"

**Figure 19** | Use the Rotated Rectangle tool to create a slicing plane

the plane as a rectangle so that it will encompass the intersecting coves. An easy way to do this is to move the Rotated Rectangle cursor along the green axis significantly further than 1¼" and click, or alternatively type 90,3 into the VCB and *Enter*. This will create the slicing plane we are looking for. We should immediately make the slicing plane a group and place it on a Slicing Plane layer so that we can make it visible and invisible. We are going to need it for two Intersect Faces operations.

We will be using this slicing plane twice; once for the arched cove and once for the front cove. We are going to miter the arched cove first, so let's move the Front Cove Trim back along the green axis 12" to get it out of the way. With the Select tool, we click on the arched cove and use Context menu Explode to return

the arched cove to its primitives. Remember, when we explode things we have to return the primitives to Layer0. With layer Slicing Plane visible we have the model as shown in **Figure 20**. We can now select all the arched cove primitives and the slicing plane Group and use Edit/Intersect Faces/With Selection to miter the arched cove. Next, we make layer Slicing Plane invisible and delete the unwanted lines to complete the miter.

**Figure 22** shows the partially completed Front Arched Trim. We will eventually make the arched cove a component with the Definition name Front Arched Trim, but for now let's just leave it as primitives. We have a problem to correct.

Using the Parallel Projection and Front View look closely at the right end of the arched cove. Zoom in

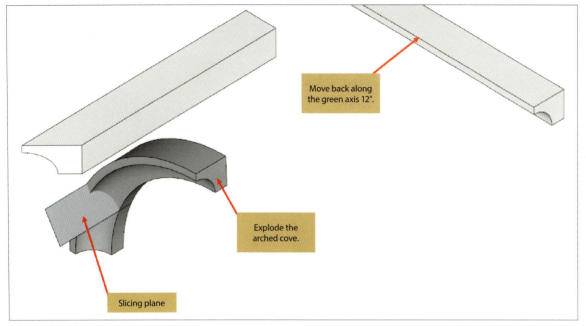

Move back along the green axis 12".

Explode the arched cove.

Slicing plane

**Figure 20** | The slicing plane intersecting the arched cove

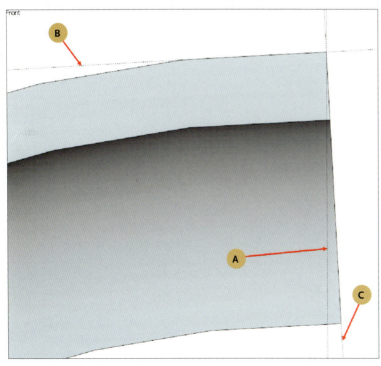

Front

B

A

C

**Figure 21** | Notice the right end of the arched cove is not mitered to a vertical plane

until you get an image like **Figure 21**. In **Figure 21** three construction lines have been added to demonstrate the problem we have to fix. Notice construction line A is the center line; it is 7¼" from the left edge of the Side Cove Trim. Construction line A is parallel to the Blue axis and should be on the plane of the right end face of the arched cove, but it is not. What happened is a side effect of using the Follow Me tool. Remember the path we used for the Follow Me tool in **Figure 17**. That path is not a circle but rather a 60-sided polygon representing a circle. Construction line B in **Figure 21** is coincident with the end segment of that path. The way the Follow Me tool works is similar to the way the Push/Pull tool works. It takes the face or cross section you

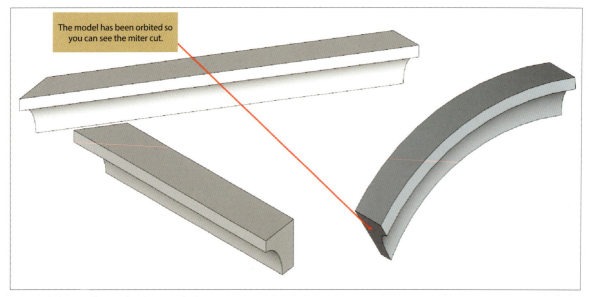

The model has been orbited so you can see the miter cut.

**Figure 22** | The partially completed Front Arched Trim

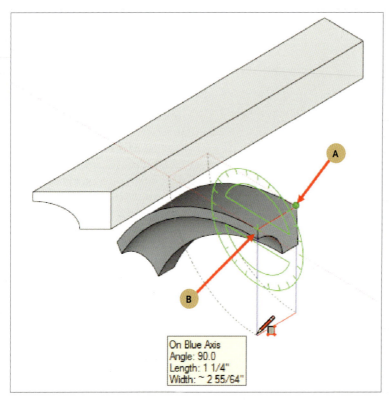

A

B

On Blue Axis
Angle: 90.0
Length: 1 1/4"
Width: ~ 2 55/64"

**Figure 23** | Use the Rotated Rectangle tool to create a slicing plane

choose and projects it on a plane normal to the first line segment and then Push/Pulls it to the next End-point of the path. At that Endpoint it again projects the face on a plane normal to the second segment of the path and Push/Pulls it to the next set of endpoints. It keeps doing this for all line segments of the path. At each set of Endpoints it has some cleanup to do to bring each extruded section together cleanly. But you can see that when it projected the face on a plane normal to the first path segment it essentially kicked the starting face out at an angle. Construction line C is at 90° to construction line B, which is essentially the first path segment. The angle of "kick out" or displacement of the face, is the angle between construction lines A and C. We need to slice the extra material off to return the right end to a vertical miter.

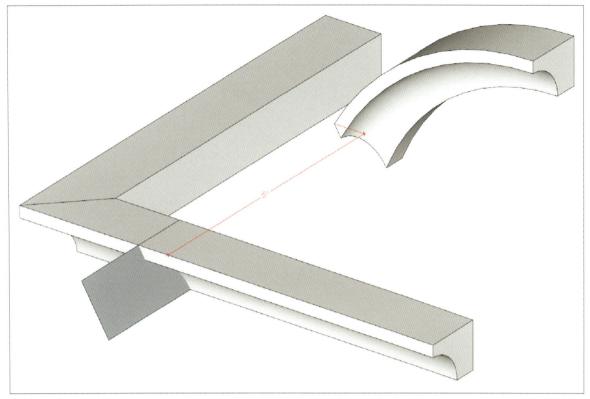

**Figure 24** | Use the slicing plane to miter the Front Cove Trim

Again we will use the Rotated Rectangle tool to create a slicing plane as shown in **Figure 23**. You should be expert with this tool by now. Click first on point A; click second on point B. Then move the cursor down along the Blue axis or alternatively type 90,3 into the VCB and *Enter*. This will create the necessary slicing plane. Triple click on the arched cove to select its primitives and the slicing plane's primitives. Use Edit/Intersect Faces/With Selection to create the correct end curves and then delete the unwanted lines and faces. Use Context menu Reverse Faces to correct the arched cove face color. Make the arched cove a component with the Definition name of Front Arched Trim.

Now we can move the Front Cove Trim back in its place; using the Move tool we move it forward 12". We can also move the Front Arched Trim back 6" to get it out of our way temporarily. Now we make the Slicing Plane layer visible to bring back our slicing plane. See **Figure 24**. We want to miter the Front

Cove Trim using the slicing plane so we need to explode it using Context menu Explode. Don't forget to return all primitives to Layer0 any time we use the Explode command. In this case the component itself was on Layer0 so the Explode command placed all its primitives on Layer0. But this is a special case. It is best you get in the habit of returning primitives to Layer0 any time you use the Explode command. I won't mention this again, so be forewarned.

Next we select all of the front cove primitives and add the slicing plane to the selection. Now we can use our old friend Edit/Intersect Faces/With Selection to create the appropriate miter lines. Using the Select tool in a right to left fashion we delete the unwanted geometry. Next, we select all the remaining primitives of the front cove, Context click and choose Make Component. We give the component the same name it had prior to being exploded, Front Cove Trim. A message appears asking if we want to replace a

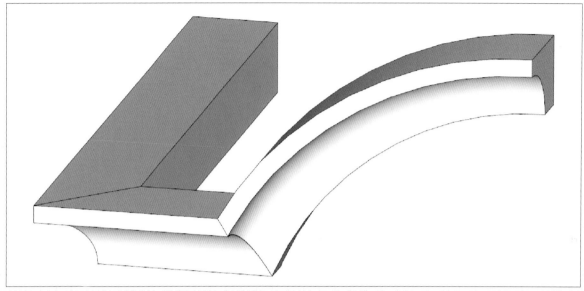

**Figure 25** | Completed Side and Front Cove Trim and half the Front Arched Trim

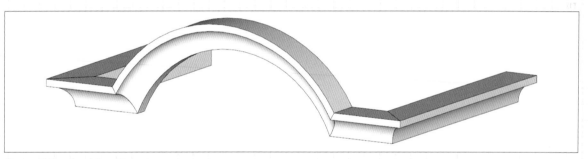

**Figure 26** | Completed Cove Trim

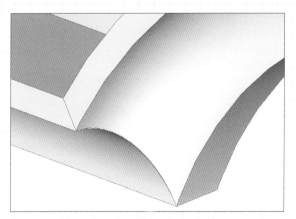

**Figure 27** | Problem with the slicing plane technique with curves

component with the same name with the selected one and we answer *Yes*. Lastly we move the Front Arched Trim forward 6" and we have **Figure 25**.

Now we have all three pieces of the cove trim completed. We need to make a flipped copy of the Arched Cove Trim and add it to the original to form a two-quadrant arched cove. This simply requires that we explode both pieces and clean up the seam where they come together. Then we can make a component of this part and give it the same name of Arched Cove Trim. Lastly, we use the Move/Copy and Flip Along/Component's Red tools to create the companion Side and Front Cove Trim pieces. We now have **Figure 26**.

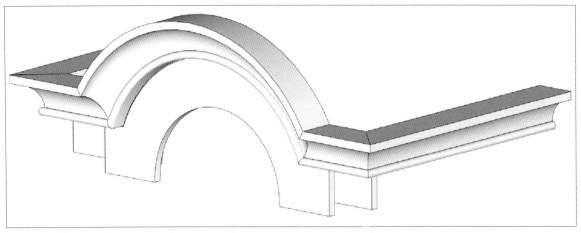

**Figure 28** | Completed Cove and Bull Nose trim and Arched Door Rail

Referring to **Figure 27** you can see an obvious problem using slicing planes with curves that are represented by polygons. In the shop, when coves that are made with perfectly radiused router bits are cut with miter or table saws, we get perfect joints. However, the coves in SketchUp are made with approximations to circles. The curve that made this joint was a product of the 2-Point Arc tool with its default 12-segment arc. If we use a higher segment arc, say 48s, we would have a much better joint.

**Figure 28** shows the completed cove and bullnose trim and the Arched Door Rail. The student is left to model the bullnose trim using the same technique used to model the cove trim. Be sure to use 60s as the segments parameter for the Circle tool and the default 12s for the 2-Point Arc tool.

In Chapter 14 we are going to mix circular and Bézier curves to model and edgeless office tabletop.

## EXERCISES FOR THE STUDENT

1. Redo the quarter segment of the cove trim with 24s and 48s as the segment parameter for the 2-Point Arc tool. Look at the miter joint and see if it is better or worse. Your slicing plane will be different with each of these exercises.
2. Repeat Exercise 1 with 120s as the parameter for the Circle tool.
3. In Exercises 1 and 2 what happened to the "kick out" at the right end of the quarter Arched Cove Trim?
4. Make yourself a list of issues to be concerned with when modeling with non-perfect circles (or curves).

# 14

# TABLETOP EDGES WITH NONCIRCULAR CURVES

*In this chapter we will focus on drawing the table top pictured in **Figure 1**. Looking closely at **Figure 1** the title of this chapter might better be called "Modeling an Edgeless Tabletop" because this top has no definable discontinuous edge. The purpose of course is to avoid arm or wrist pain while working at it for hours each day.*

*In addition to modeling an edgeless tabletop we are going to learn how to model the cut of a router bit and apply it to a furniture part. The particular bit used in this model is one that is normally used on stair rails to provide a smooth edgeless grip. So let's continue our study of Bézier or noncircular curves begun in Chapter 12.*

Look at the corners and edges shown in **Figure 1**. Notice how smooth the corner and edges are and how they are void of ugly delineating lines. This is the effect we want to achieve in our SketchUp model of the Office Table top.

## THE OFFICE TABLE TOP EDGELESS PROFILE

**Figure 2** is the profile for the edge including the upper and lower edge curves. It is formed along the bottom with a standard ¼" round over router bit. We will model it with one quadrant of a ¼" radius circle.

The top edge is formed by a special router bit that is used to cut gradually sloping edges on table tops and stair handrails. We will model this profile with the aid of the Bézier tool.

There are a number of ways to place points that outline this profile for the Bézier tool to follow. You can go to the particular router bit manufacturer's catalog and scan the profile in, such as shown in **Figure 3**. Then, using the dimensions provided in the catalog, adjust the JPG image in SketchUp to correct size; place points at strategic places on a separate layer. Or you can do as I did, which was to make a few measurements on the actual bit and estimate the

**Figure 1** | The Office Table with its edgeless tabletop

profile by eye. That is what we will do here.

## MODELING THE OFFICE TABLE TOP

The overall dimensions of the top are 1" thick by 30" wide by 72" long. The thumbnail curve extends back from the edge 1" and down from the edge ½". The bottom curve is cut with a ¼" round over bit. Doing the math this leaves a ¼" flat on the edge for the router bit bearings to follow. Since the thumbnail curve extends into the

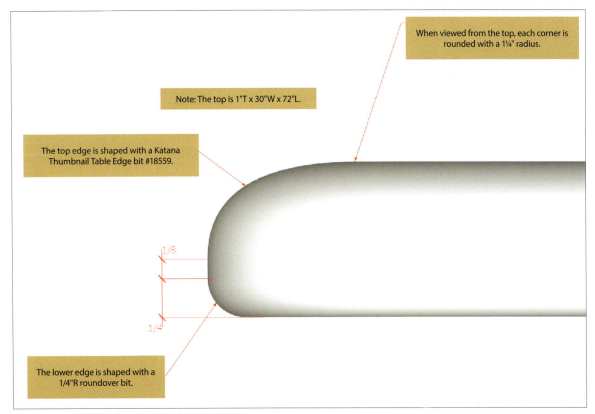

When viewed from the top, each corner is rounded with a 1¼" radius.

Note: The top is 1"T x 30"W x 72"L.

The top edge is shaped with a Katana Thumbnail Table Edge bit #18559.

1/8

1/4

The lower edge is shaped with a 1/4"R roundover bit.

**Figure 2** | Details of the upper and lower edge

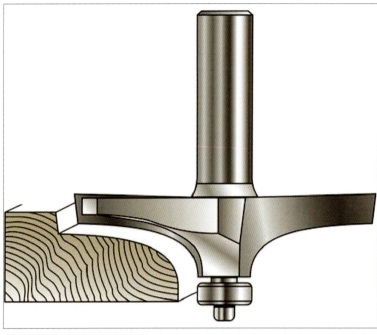

**Figure 3** | Profile of the Katana Thumbnail Table Edge router bit

top 1" we must subtract 1" from each side or subtract 2" from the length and width and draw a rectangle that size. Next, using the Push/Pull tool, we give the top 1" thickness. Using the Rotated Rectangle tool, we place a 1" square on one edge at its midpoint. This aids in drawing the edge profile by providing a surface on which to draw. Now we have to put a radius on all four corners. The radius, looking from the Top View, is 1¼". However, since we brought each edge in 1" to account for the profile we are going to add, the actual radius we need to draw is ¼" at each corner. Note that for drawing purposes it is convenient that the corner radius is larger than the profile

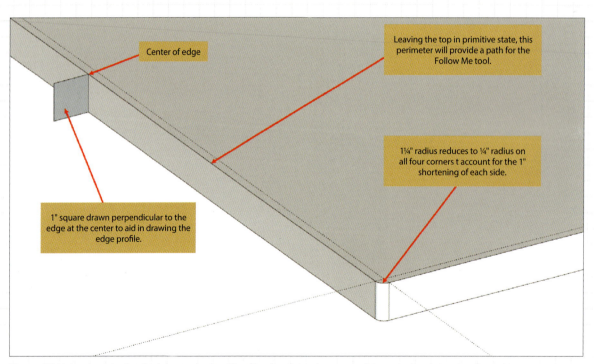

Center of edge

Leaving the top in primitive state, this perimeter will provide a path for the Follow Me tool.

1¼" radius reduces to ¼" radius on all four corners t account for the 1" shortening of each side.

1" square drawn perpendicular to the edge at the center to aid in drawing the edge profile.

**Figure 4** | Table top drawn to 1" undersize on each edge, ¼" radius placed at each corner and 1" square placed at center of one edge

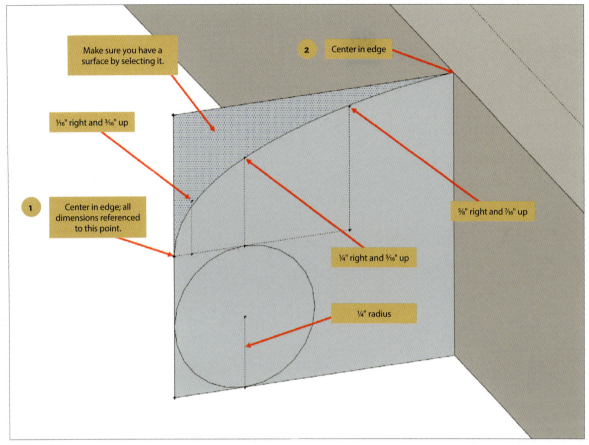

Make sure you have a surface by selecting it.

2 Center in edge

1/16" right and 3/16" up

1 Center in edge; all dimensions referenced to this point.

5/8" right and 7/16" up

1/4" right and 5/16" up

1/4" radius

**Figure 5** | The edge profile drawn with the Bézier tool and the Circle tool

depth. After drawing the radius, we use the Push/Pull tool to round all four corner corners. Check closely to be sure that all four corners are rounded appropriately or the Follow Me operation will not work. Our model now looks like **Figure 4**.

Now we can draw the edge profile. Refer to **Figure 5**. First we draw the ¼" radius on the bottom/outside edge using the Circle tool. The default 12s segment parameter is sufficient. Next we need to plot some construction points with the Tape Measure tool. This is as much artistry and trial-and-error as it is drawing. Coming up with construction points that exactly match the profile you want is almost impossible. But you can come very close if you spend enough time. For this exercise I chose the following

points referenced from the center point of the outside edge of the square box. If you think of this point as the origin (0,0) in an X-Y plane, plot the points (1/16",3/16"), (¼",5/16") and (5/8",7/16"). There are now five points to use with the Bézier tool. The origin, or center of the outside edge of the square, the three points we just plotted and the center or the table top stock. Select the Draw/Bézier Curves tool and click on point 1 in **Figure 5**. Next click on point 2, the center in edge. Pick a point along the left edge that comes close to fitting the points we plotted and click. Now click on a point near the top edge, but not on it, that further enhances the curve fit and click. We can now select this curve with the Select tool, Context click and choose Edit Bezier Curve if you need to fine-tune

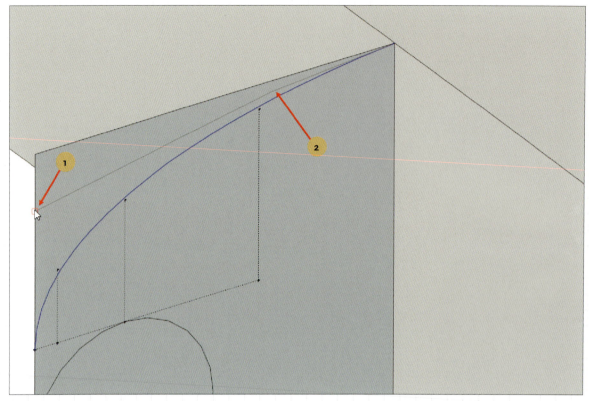

**Figure 6** | The Bézier curve in Edit Bezier Curves mode with control point shown

the curve. Notice that the curve is not perfect, but then neither were the points we plotted. Curves don't have to be perfect unless you are designing an airplane where a poorly plotted curve can substantially change the lift of a wing. This is not a problem when designing furniture.

I need to point out a flaw in the Bezier Curves tool at the time of this writing. **Figure 6** shows the curve we drew in Edit Bezier Curves mode. You can see the control points 1 and 2. If control point 2 is placed on the upper edge and close to the path it will produce unpredictable results when the Follow Me tool is used to extrude the edge. I haven't yet figured out why, but when I do I will submit a bug report. For now we can avoid the problem by placing control point 2 slightly below the edge.

When finished with the Bézier tool, select the surface you will delete, shown in **Figure 5**, to be sure

there is a surface; it becomes highlighted with blue dots, which is what we want. Now we can clean up the profile by deleting lines, faces and construction lines and points we don't need. With the Select tool we select the top surface of the tabletop; its perimeter will provide the path for the Follow Me tool. Next we select the Follow Me tool and click on the face of the edge profile. After softening and smoothing the unwanted lines and making the table top a component we have the model shown in **Figure 7**.

## WHO NEEDS A BÉZIER CURVE ANYWAY?

Don't get too carried away with Bézier curves. Bézier curves are a very helpful tool, but they are not the only way to draw noncircular curves. **Figure 8** shows

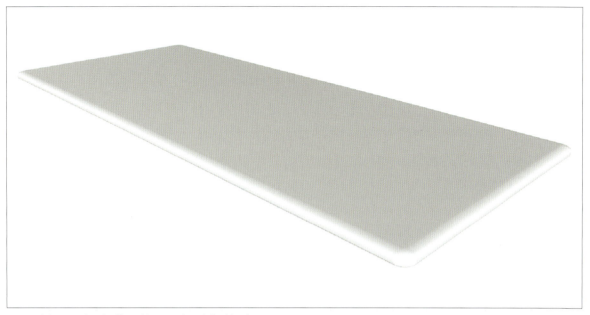

**Figure 7** | The completed Office Tabletop with no definable edges

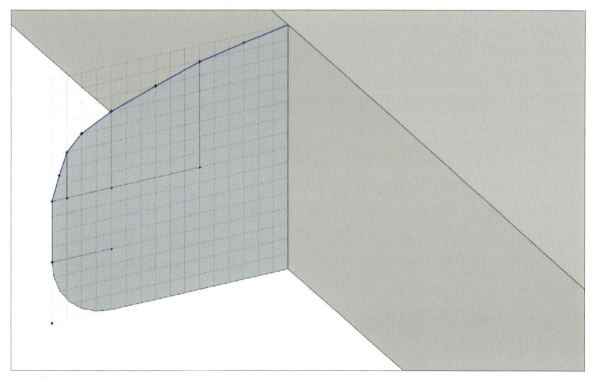

**Figure 8** | A Bézier curve approximated with Line tool line segments

how to use a grid tool to plot ¹⁄₁₆" spaced construction lines in the Red and Blue direction. On that grid you can estimate the shape of a curve by plotting construction points. Then you can connect the points with the Line tool and when done select all the line segments and weld them into a polyline using the Weld tool (available as an extension). How many line segments you need depends on the complexity of the curve. When the resulting edge profile is extruded and the edges are softened and smoothed, you cannot tell the difference from **Figure** 7.

This has been a relatively short chapter, but one that points out some useful modeling techniques, especially for tabletops. Not all tabletops are rectangular, but the techniques used here are just as applicable on a kidney shaped top as a rectangular top. In Chapter 15 we are going to model bracket feet, which have noncircular or Bézier curves in two dimensions.

## EXERCISES FOR THE STUDENT

1. Redo the edge profile with control point 2 in **Figure 6** on the upper edge of the square and close to the path's edge. Use the Follow Me tool to extrude it and examine the results. Look particularly at the corner curves and zoom in close. What do you see?
2. Redo the edge profile using the Line tool to approximate a Bézier curve.

# 15

# BRACKET FEET WITH BÉZIER CURVES

*In this chapter we are going to learn how to model ogee bracket feet. The technique required for this is new and slightly more complex than the techniques we have used so far.* **Figure 1** *shows the base of a Six-Pane Oak Hutch. I designed this piece in SketchUp and crafted it for my sister-in-law. I have left the cupboard top out of the picture so that you can get a better look at the feet we will be sketching.*

*Though there are six feet required to complete the set, there is really only one model required. The two front feet are made by mitering and gluing together two sets of two feet. The back feet are not mitered.* **Figure 2** *is a close-up of three mitered feet. These feet are constructed from quartersawn white oak. They are not glued, merely positioned to look like they are. But in this picture you can see how they were cut from the same stock in a sequence that allowed for grain matching at the miter. Bracket feet are fun to craft, but that is a book for someone else to write. We need to turn our attention back to SketchUp modeling.*

**F**igure 3 shows the SketchUp rendered version of the Ogee Bracket Feet. This is the goal of Chapter 15. However, we will concern ourselves less with how accurately we reproduce these feet than learning the technique or procedure. So if your feet look slightly different than these, but you end up with well sketched feet, we have succeeded. Using the Bezier Curves tool to draw these curves takes a good deal of experience, which you can get with practice, once you know the procedure. So let's get started.

## THE TWO SHAPES OF A BRACKET FOOT

We begin by downloading two JPG images we will need for this chapter. They are called Feet End View.jpg and Feet Front View.jpg. You will find them at srww. com/sketchup_a_guide_for_woodworkers.html web page in the Downloads section under book Part 3, Chapter 15. Please download them now and place them on your desktop or in a folder you will easily recall.

**Figure 1** | The Six-Pane Oak Hutch base

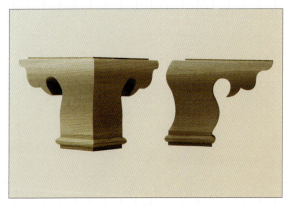

**Figure 2** | Three mitered Ogee Bracket Feet

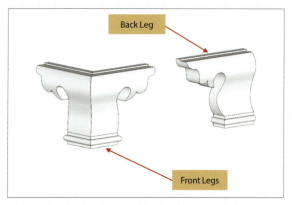

Back Leg

Front Legs

**Figure 3** | The SketchUp version of the Ogee Bracket Feet shown in Figure 2

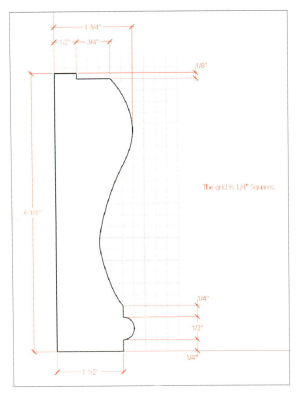

**1 3/4"**
**1/2" 3/4"**
**1/8"**
**The grid is 1/4" Squares.**
**6 1/8"**
**1/4"**
**1/2"**
**1/4"**
**1 1/2"**

**Figure 4** | The feet end view

**Figure 4** shows the Feet End View.jpg. This is the view we will draw first. I have included a grid of ¼" squares for your reference. Notice the origin of the grid is at the SketchUp origin. The overall dimensions are 1¾" thick by 6⅛" tall. Notice the ledge in the upper right hand corner. It is ⅛" deep and ¾" wide. The ledge starts at ½" horizontally to the right from the upper left corner and ends at 1¼". That is where the reverse S-curve begins. The S-curve ends at a point 1½" horizontally to the right from the origin and 1" up. All of this outline, except the reverse S, can be drawn with the Line and Circle tools. I will not spend time instructing you how to do that; after all you are a journeyman at this point. So when we begin drawing I will start with all but the reverse S drawn.

The second view we will draw is shown in **Figure 5** which is the Feet Front View.jpg image. The overall dimensions are 6⅛" tall and 7½" wide. Like before I have included a grid for reference. The origin of

the grid this time is the lower left hand corner. The curve is more complex in this view, so when we draw it we may choose to break it into pieces. It starts at ⅛" down front the outline's upper right hand corner and ends at a point 3¼" horizontally right from the lower left hand corner and 1" up. When we draw this view we will start with the Line and Circle tool geometry already drawn and concern ourselves only with the curves.

## MODELING AND EXTRUDING THE FEET END VIEW

Referring to **Figure 4** and **Figure 6**, which shows the simple geometry and the backward S-curve construction points, open a new SketchUp file and construct this geometry. Notice that though this is the Feet End View, it is to be drawn on the SketchUp Front view (red/blue plane) and at the origin. In addition, be sure you have Camera/Parallel Projection selected. When you draw your layout, there is no need to include the dimensions. They are simply for your reference.

I determined the construction point placements by looking at **Figure 4**, which has the grid. It appeared to me (actually I know this) that the reverse S-curve is not symmetrical, so I looked for points that would allow me to plot the maximum, minimum, center and end points. This will give me a smooth curve.

The most helpful point in terms of locating the construction points is point 1, the upper endpoint in the drawn geometry. The construction points are placed using the Tape Measure tool. Point 2 is ½" to the right along the red axis and 1⅛" down along the Blue axis from Point 1. Point 3 is 2½" down along the Blue axis from Point 1. Point 4 is 3¾" down along the Blue axis and ¼" to the left along the red axis from point 1. And finally Point 5 is the lower endpoint in the drawn geometry.

At this point we want to import the Feet End View.jpg into SketchUp. Be sure you have Front view and Camera/Parallel Projection selected before importing. Using menu File/Import and selecting "JPEG Image (*.jpg)" as the "Files of type" to locate your Feet End View.jpg file and click on Open. The

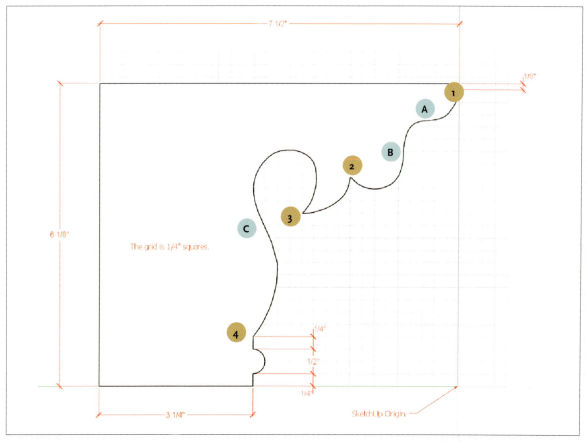

**Figure 5** | The feet front view

image will now be attached to your cursor and you will have to click twice: once to place at a desired point and next to choose its orientation and size. Get the orientation right, but don't worry too much about the size at this point. **Figure 7** shows my results after importing. Yours will look different. Notice that I positioned the image to the right of my drawn geometry and the image appears smaller than my drawn geometry.

We need to scale the imported image to the correct size. In **Figure 7**, points 1 and 2 indicate the corners of the outline in the image. We know from **Figure 4** this distance is 6⅛". Using the Tape Measure tool we are going to measure the actual distance between points 1 and 2. Be sure to zoom in very close to each point before clicking on it; we want an accurate measurement. Record the results of the measure-

ment shown in the VCB. My results are ~2 ¹⁷⁄₆₄" but yours, of course, will be different. Whatever the result we want to use the Scale tool to scale the image such that this distance is 6⅛". In my case I need a scale up factor, which is a number greater than 1; you may need a scale down factor, which is a number less than 1. Simple arithmetic with a calculator gives me a scale up factor of 2.70344827586207. I am going to use all these digits when I type the scale factor into the VCB.

We now need to select the image with the Select tool followed by selecting the Scale tool. With the Scale tool cursor, we hover over the upper right corner of the image until we see the tool tip Uniform Scale about Opposite Point as shown in **Figure 8**. When you have the tool tip shown step away from your mouse and type the long scale factor into the

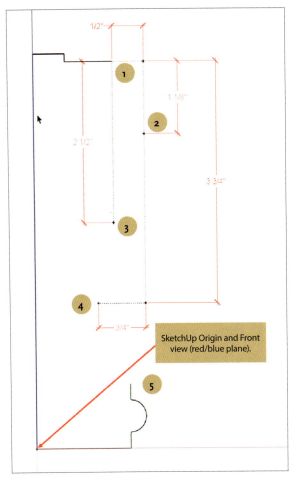

**Figure 6** | Feet end view simple geometry and S-curve construction points

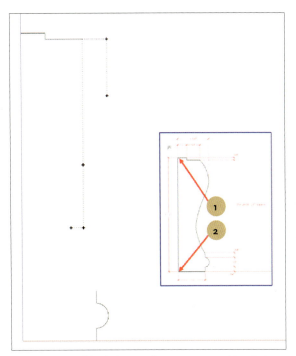

**Figure 7** | The model with drawn end view geometry and Feet End View.jpg imported

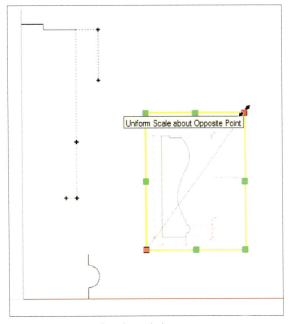

**Figure 8** | Using the Scale tool to scale the image to correct size

VCB and Enter. The image will scale up or down to its correct size.

Next we select the image with the Select tool and then use the Move tool to place it over the drawn geometry. To do this I clicked on point 2 of **Figure 7** with the Move cursor, dragged it to the origin and clicked again. **Figure 9** shows the result. You can see at the top of **Figure 9** that the fit is not perfect, but it is close enough.

Let's go back and study **Figure 6** with attention to the construction points. We are going to use the Bezier Curves tool to draw the backward S-curve. But we are going to do it in four sections: the first section

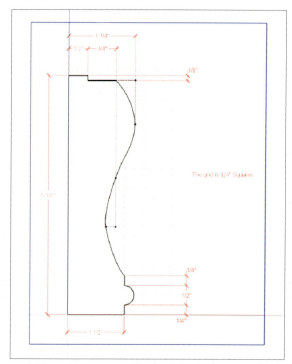

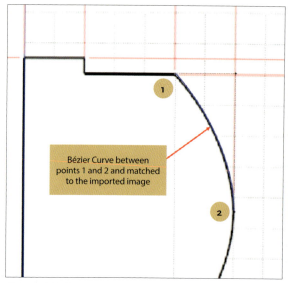

**Figure 10** | The first Bezier Curves tool section from point 1 to point 2

**Figure 9** | The imported Feet End View.jpg image scaled and positioned over the simple geometry

is the curve from point 1 to point 2, then 2 to 3, followed by 3 to 4 and finally 4 to 5. We will use the image to shape the curves. **Figure 10** shows the result of the first section. When you do this be sure to first click on point 1, the endpoint of the geometry, then point 2, the first guide point. We have to be sure that all four curve segments are connected and that the ends of the backward S-curve are connected to the geometry. Else we will not produce a face to extrude.

**Figure 11** shows the second section of the curve drawn and highlighted in blue; but in this figure the curve is in Edit Bezier Curve mode so you can see the control points and lines. If you look closely at the curve between points 2 and 3 you will see an inflection point nearer point 3. Note that the control lines for points 2 and 3 are tangent to the curve at those points, but they are on opposite sides of the curve. This indicates an inflection point in between somewhere. The curve in **Figure 11** is fit quite well, but if

fine-tuning is needed the control points can be moved to change its shape.

**Figure 12** shows all four segments of the curve drawn and highlighted in blue. Hopefully yours looks similar. You can see the fit is reasonably close, though not perfect. We could spend a lot of time trying to make these curves perfect; but why spend the time? Think of what is going to happen in the shop. The shaping of this foot is done with a combination of running stock through the table saw at an angle to the blade, a handplane and lots of sandpaper. It is the final shop part where you want to spend time approaching perfection, not in SketchUp.

Before we can extrude the end view we need to do a few more steps. First we will create a layer called End View Template and place the imported image on it. We can get rid of the construction line and points with Edit/Delete Guides. This will leave the simple geometry and the four curve segments on Layer0 by themselves. If we were to extrude the end view now we would have unsightly lines at each point the curves are connected. It's not a big problem because we could soften and smooth them later, but what I suggest is selecting all the curve segments and then use the Weld tool to make them a polyline. Now we can extrude the

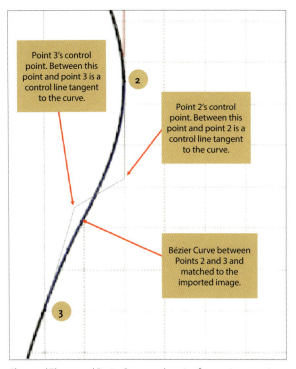

**Figure 11** | The second Bezier Curves tool section from point 2 to point 3

Point 3's control point. Between this point and point 3 is a control line tangent to the curve.

Point 2's control point. Between this point and point 2 is a control line tangent to the curve.

Bézier Curve between Points 2 and 3 and matched to the imported image.

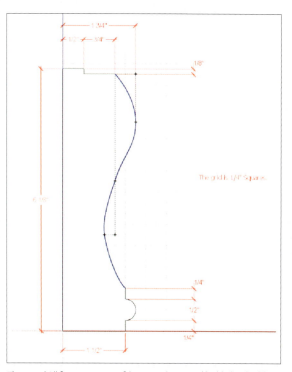

**Figure 12** | All four segments of the curve drawn and highlighted in blue

**Figure 13** | The extruded end view

end view about 10" in both the positive and negative Green axis directions using the Push/Pull tool. You should now have the model shown in **Figure 13**. Triple click on the extruded end view and make it a group temporarily. Name it Group 1. Create a layer called Group 1 and place Group 1 on that layer. We will come back to it later.

## MODELING AND EXTRUDING THE FEET FRONT VIEW

Modeling and extruding the Feet Front View will be a little more challenging because of the more complex curve involved. But we will use essentially the same techniques. First click the Left view icon and choose Camera/Parallel Projection. If layer Group 1 is visible you will be looking at the back of the extruded end view, Group 1. Make layer Group 1 invisible and add a layer called Front View Template.

Using menu File/Import and selecting "JPEG Image (*.jpg)" as the "Files of type" to locate your

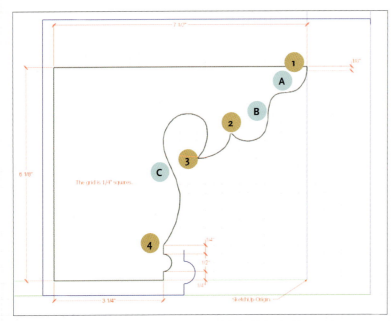

**Figure 14** | The imported Feet Front View.jpg image and the highlighted in blue simple geometry

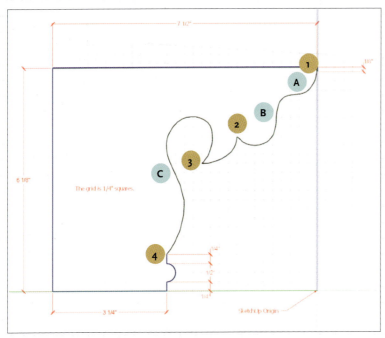

**Figure 15** | The imported Feet Front View image adjusted for size and positioned

Feet Front View.jpg file and click on Open. The image will now be attached to your cursor and you will have to click twice: once to place at a desired point and next to choose its orientation and size. Get the orientation right but don't worry too much about the size at this point. Place it on the Front View Template layer and make this layer visible.

I have done all of this and also drew the simple geometry using the dimensions shown on the imported image for reference. The results are shown in **Figure 14** with the simple geometry highlighted in blue. The Feet Front View.jpg file we imported to help us draw the curves is on the Front View Template layer where it will be visible for tracing but will not get in the way of our drawing.

Before we can begin tracing the curve we need to adjust the size of the image just as we did for the Feet End View.jpg image. We use the Tape Measure tool to measure the actual length of the 6⅛" side and record it. We could also use the 7½" side, but for consistency I chose to use the 6⅛" side. Your choice which side you use. My measurement is ~4¾", which means I need a scale up factor, a number greater than 1. So I will divide 6⅛" (6.125) by 4¾" (4.75) using a calculator and record the results; 1.28947368421053. Just like before, I will use the Scale tool to scale the image up by this factor and then use the Move tool to place it. You need to do the same with your model. The end results

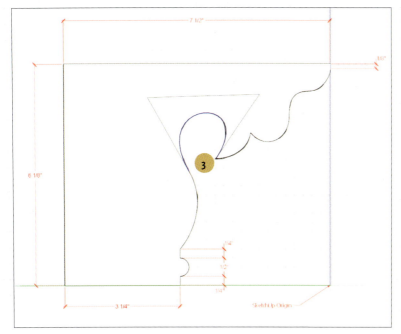

Figure 16 | The completed curve with segment point 3 to point C in Edit Bezier Curve mode

Figure 17 | The extruded Feet Front View

(i.e. points where a curve changes its direction of curvature). I recommend using the Bezier Curves tool to create at least six connected curves: point 1 to point A; point A to point B; point B to point 2; point 2 to point 3; point 3 to point C; and point C to point 4. You may also choose to break the curve between points 3 and C into two curves. Go ahead and create your segments while I do the same and let's compare results.

OK, I'm done and I am pretty pleased with my results. How about you? My results are shown in **Figure 16**. Notice I chose not to break the curve between points 3 and C into two curves, but rather handle it as one curve. In **Figure 16** I selected that curve and it is shown highlighted in blue and in Edit Bezier Curve mode so you can see the control lines and points. When using the Bezier Curves tool always plan how you are going to attack a curve. Look for the discontinuities. Discontinuities always have to be an endpoint in a curve segment. Inflection points are often a good place for a segment endpoint, though the Bezier Curves tool can handle one inflection point between endpoints of a segment, but definitely not more than one. Segments like the one highlighted in **Figure 16** are good candidates for breakup, but I wanted to point out how it is possible to handle these as one segment. Normally I would have broken it up.

We are not done with this curve yet. We need to choose the curve segments between each set of discontinuities and use the Weld tool to create polylines, else we would have a lot of cleanup to do post extru-

of both our efforts should be the same and look like **Figure 15**.

Now we are ready to begin tracing, but we will do it in sections, just as we did for the Feet End View. In **Figure 15** you see points 1 through 4; these are points of discontinuity (i.e. abrupt changes in direction of the curve). Points A, B and C are points of inflection

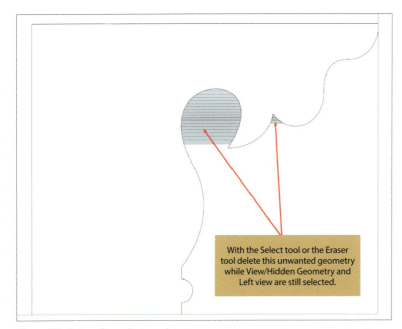

With the Select tool or the Eraser tool delete this unwanted geometry while View/Hidden Geometry and Left view are still selected.

**Figure 18** | Left view after preliminary cleanup

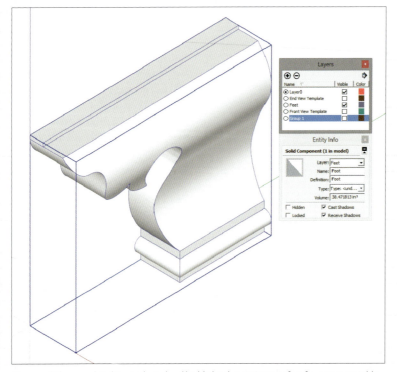

**Figure 19** | The completed Foot selected and highlighted so its Entity Info information is visible

sion. Select the curve segment between points 1 and 2 with the Select tool and then use the Weld tool to create a polyline. Do the same for curves between points 3 and 4. If there is only one curve segment between points 2 and 3 you don't have to further weld them. We now make the Front View Template layer invisible and extrude the front view face 10" in both the positive and negative red axis directions. We now have the model shown in **Figure 17**.

## OBTAINING THE INTERSECTION OF END AND FRONT EXTRUSIONS

Now we have a Feet Front View extrusion and a Feet End View extrusion. What we want is a part that is the intersection of both. You have probably guessed that this is going to involve the Edit/Intersect Faces/With Selection tool, and you would be right.

Make layer Group 1 visible. Select the Group 1 group and explode it. I hope what I hear in the background is you placing all exploded primitives on Layer0, because you should know to do that after any use of the Explode tool. Now we triple click on the primitives to select them all and choose Edit/Intersect Faces/With Selection. Next we select View/Hidden Geometry; this is a very important step because failing to do so will result in the loss of needed faces and lines. With the Front and then Left views and the Select tool, in a right to left

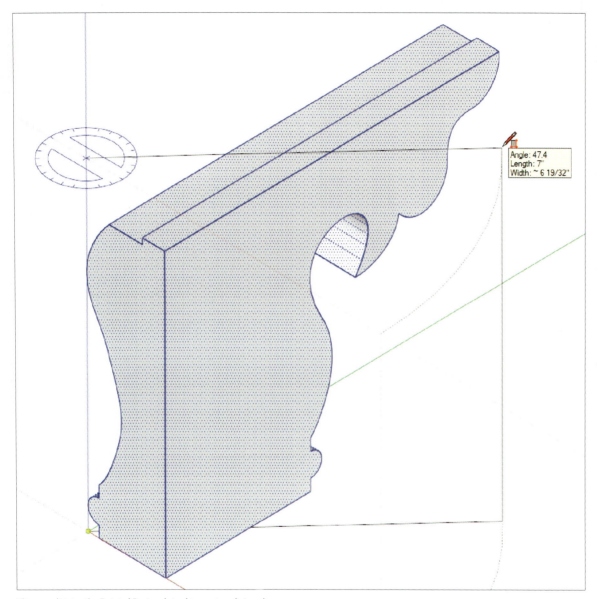

**Figure 20** | Using the Rotated Rectangle tool to create a slicing plane

fashion, we delete the unwanted geometry. While viewing the Left view and with View/Hidden Geometry still selected, use the Select tool in a right to left fashion, or the Eraser tool in a paint brush fashion, to delete any remaining unwanted geometry. **Figure 18** shows what I had to cleanup for my model. Yours may be somewhat different because our specific curves are slightly different. Use the Orbit tool to closely inspect for voids in the face or missing lines. You may need to create a few lines and faces, but hopefully not. The Intersect Faces tool, while quite powerful, is not perfect.

At this point we can deselect View/Hidden Geometry. We triple click on the primitives, be sure they are

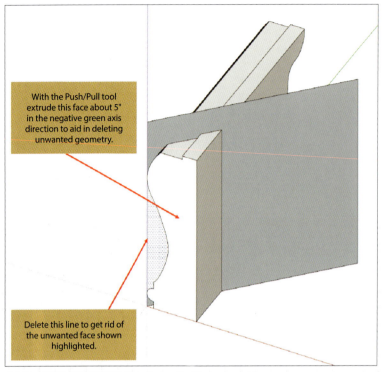

With the Push/Pull tool extrude this face about 5" in the negative green axis direction to aid in deleting unwanted geometry.

Delete this line to get rid of the unwanted face shown highlighted.

**Figure 21** | The Rotated Rectangle tool introduced an unwanted face

Enter. Next we drag the cursor out as shown in **Figure 20** and type 45,7 into the VCB and *Enter*. These last few steps create a slicing plane to miter the foot primitives with. Our miter is the standard 45° variety. Now we triple click on the primitives to select all foot primitive and slicing plane primitives. With this selection we use the Intersect Faces/With Selection tool to create the miter outline.

The Rotated Rectangle created the slicing plane we wanted but is also introduced a face we don't want; see **Figure 21**. Delete the line shown in **Figure 21** to delete the unwanted face. Next we extrude the end face in the negative green axis direction with the Push/Pull tool to make it easier to delete the remaining unwanted geometry.

Now we can easily use the Select tool to delete the unwanted geometry. It may be necessary to correct the face color of the end face using the Context menu Reverse Faces tool. With all that done we triple click on the primitives and create a component shown in **Figure 22** with its Entity Info. In **Figure 22** I have copied the Mitered Foot, used Flip Along/Component's Red to mirror it and the Rotate tool to rotate it 90°. Then it is simply a matter of using the Move tool to place the Mitered Foot next to its companion.

all on Layer0, and Context click to Make Component. Give the foot the Definition name Foot, the instance or Name name Foot and place it on a new layer called Feet. See the completed Foot in **Figure 19** along with its Entity Info. We will later rename the feet when we create the whole set.

## MITERING A FOOT

We now have a Foot, but in order to make the front feet we need a foot with a miter cut. Since our Foot is safely in the Component In House library we can modify the Foot on Layer0. We first select this Foot and Context click and choose Flip Along/Component's Red. We repeat this step, but this time we choose Flip Along/Component's Green. While the Foot is still selected Context click and choose Explode and place all primitives on Layer0. With the Rotated Rectangle tool selected, we click on the origin and then move the cursor along the positive blue axis and type 7 into the VCB and

## ASSEMBLING THE FEET

I leave it to you the journeyman to assemble the Mitered Foot and Foot into a set of Bracket Feet as shown in **Figure 23**. This chapter showed us how to use two different profile cross sections to produce a part that has curves in two planes. Though we have used the Bezier Curves tool before, this chapter pointed out its real power in creating rather complex curves. In Chapter 16 we are going to extend our already large repertoire of modeling skills. We will again use the intersection of two

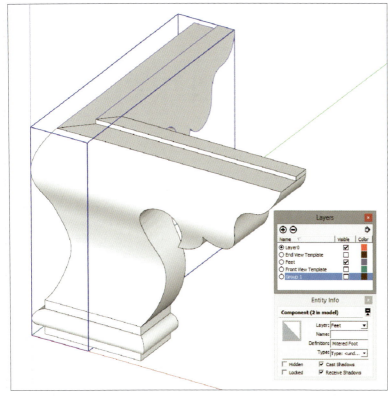

**Figure 22** | The completed Mitered Foot paired with a mirrored and rotated companion Mitered Foot

profiles, only this time the same profile, and we will learn to sculpt two rather different shapes together to model a Cabriole leg.

## EXERCISES FOR THE STUDENT

1. After we used the Intersect Face/With Selection and before we started to delete unwanted geometry in the Obtaining the Intersection of End and Front Extrusions section, we made sure to select View/Hidden Geometry. Try redoing this step without using View/Hidden Geometry and look at the problems it causes. Why is this?

2. Referring to **Figure 21** try mitering the foot without extruding the face with the Push/Pull tool. See how difficult it is to delete unwanted geometry.

**Figure 23** | The completed set of bracket feet

# 16

# CABRIOLE LEGS WITH BÉZIER CURVES

*In this chapter we are going to learn how to model the cabriole leg with a slipper like foot shown in **Figure 1**. Cabriole legs go back as far as the ancient Greeks and Chinese but are more commonly associated with Queen Anne, Chippendale and Louis XV period furniture. They are characterized by the S-shape where the top of the leg bows outward and the bottom bows inward. The foot can be anything from a slipper like shape to a ball and claw. The cabriole leg is generally completed with a knee brace for dressing. The finished set of cabriole legs in **Figure 1** are textured with a cherry grain.*

*When crafted in the shop, this leg is shaped both on the lathe and the band saw. So too in SketchUp this leg is modeled in two shapes that have to be sculpted together. The techniques required are both new and borrowed. The techniques involved in sculpting are new, and more art than science or method. The techniques required to shape the curved portions of the leg we borrow from Chapter 15, with a slight twist.*

As an example of a table that uses the cabriole leg, I made a quick and dirty modification to an office table with results shown in **Figure 2**. Notice the table also uses the top we drew in Chapter 14. The knee in this example extends entirely between the legs. Often it is just a brace that finishes the look of the leg. I am not proposing this design as an example of period furniture; as I said it is a mock-up to show what cabriole legs might look like in a finished piece.

## THE SLIPPER FOOT CABRIOLE LEG AND ITS PARTS

We begin by downloading a SketchUp file we will need for this chapter. It is called Tall Cabriole Leg Completed Drawing.skp. You will find them at srww. com/sketchup_a_guide_for_woodworkers.html web page in the Downloads section under book Part 3, Chapter 16. Please download it now to your desktop and open the file. Our work will be performed in this

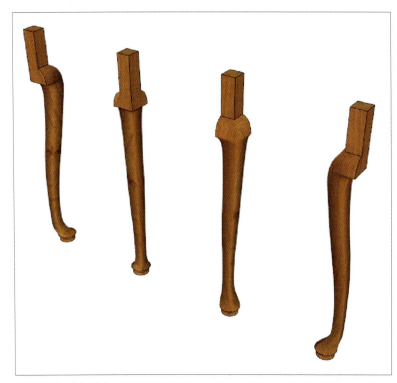

**Figure 1** | The Cabriole leg

**Figure 2** | The Office Table with tapered legs replaced with cabriole legs

file. The file has two scenes: the Perspective scene shows a set of finished legs that were used to create **Figure 1** and the Template and Dimensions scene is the one we will refer to for drawing the simple outline geometry and tracing the leg's curves.

This chapter will be a bit more complex than any so far. Kind of like your final exam. As you proceed through your work, and at points where you are sure you have a correct model at that stage, save your model explicitly by using File/Save. Do not depend on AutoSave; that is a backup emergency plan. By saving your work at points where you know your model is correct you have a place to step back to should you make a serious mistake you can't correct with the *Esc* key or Undo tool. If you make unrecoverable mistake that can't be fixed with your saved copy, you can always download the model again, so don't hesitate to experiment. That is an important part of the learning process.

With the Tall Cabriole Leg Completed Drawing file open, select scene Template and Dimensions. It will look like **Figure 3**. The JPG used as our template is already on the Template layer and registered to the grid. However, the grid is superfluous in this chapter and can actually be made invisible, so I have provided the actual dimensions for reference. Referring to **Figures 1** and **3** and starting from the top the first 4" of the leg is square and 1½" thick. This section of the leg serves to

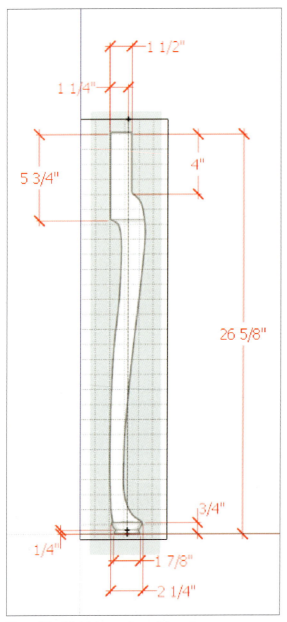

**Figure 3** | The Cabriole leg template and dimensions

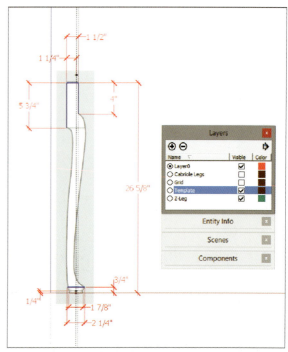

**Figure 4** | Simple straight line geometry required for the Cabriole leg

join the aprons with mortises in this part of the leg and the tenons on the apron. Starting at the bottom of the leg and going up ¾" is the section called the pad; it is the pad of the slipper foot and since it is shaped on the lathe, it is round. Between the first 4"

and the pad is the cabriole shape; formed in the shop by the band saw and then shaped with hand tools. This section is the work of the Bezier Curves tool in SketchUp. Both parts above the pad we will refer to as the upper leg. Our strategy for modeling the cabriole leg will be as follows: model the upper leg first, model the pad second, sculpt the upper leg and pad together third, and smooth the entire leg fourth.

## MODELING THE UPPER LEG

We start by drawing all the straight lines first. In **Figure 4** notice that the construction points lay on a construction line that is the center axis of the cut list stock that will be used to create the cabriole leg. It is also the axis of rotation when the stock is on the lathe to form the pad. Using this construction line, the construction points and the dimensions shown, create the straight lines highlighted in blue in **Figure 4**. Notice in **Figure 4** only layers Layer0, Template and Z-Leg is visible. No other layer is

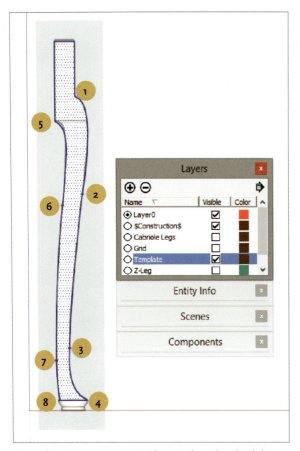

**Figure 5** | Six Bézier cure segments drawn to shape the cabriole leg

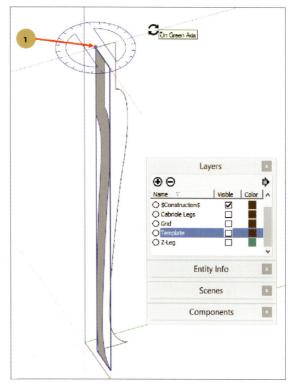

**Figure 6** | Upper leg face group copied and rotated at point of rotation 1 with the Rotate/Copy tool

visible. Also, I have selected Front and X-Ray views and of course Camera/Parallel Projection is always selected when we are modeling. The straight lines are all drawn on Layer0.

We are now ready to use the Bezier Curves tool to draw the curves on the left and right. I am not going to lead you step by step. You are nearly a graduated master sketchman. But in **Figure 5** I have shared with you my strategy for drawing the curves. Notice I have drawn the two curves in three segments each. Look closely at point 5 and you will see my fit isn't perfect, but it is primarily because I didn't scale and register the template as accurately as I could have. Also look closely at point 8 and notice that I ended the curve slightly in from the endpoint of the line, though on

the line. Before extruding the face I will have to delete the little line segment on the left.

How does your results compare to **Figure 5**? It will likely be a little different, but that is OK. We are learning the process of modeling a leg such as the cabriole leg. Once we have the process down we can work on perfecting our sketchmanship. We now need to create polylines of the three curve segments on each side and clip the dangling line segment off. Don't be in a hurry to extrude this face quite yet. Instead make the upper leg a group. We have a little twist in the procedure we used in Chapter 15 coming.

We need two identical faces to extrude and form an intersection part. The easiest way to do that is to use the Rotate/Copy tool as shown in **Figure 6**. Remember, the upper leg is a group so we are now creating a second group, 90° to the first, by using the blue cursor of the Rotate tool at the point

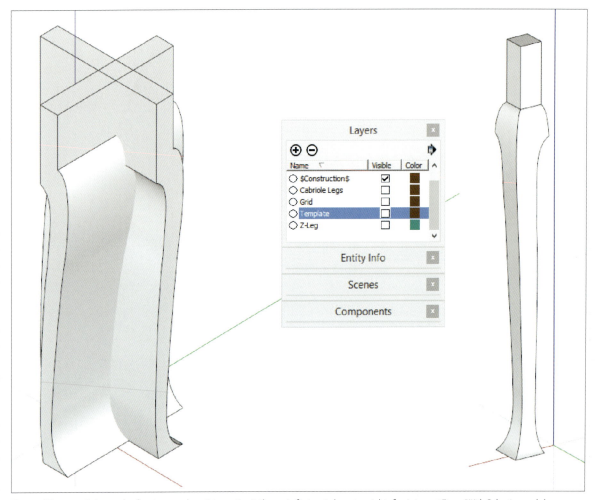

**Figure 7** | Two extruded upper leg face groups whose intersection is the part of interest shown on right after Intersect Faces/With Selection and cleanup

of rotation 1 shown in **Figure 6**. Our task now is to extrude each group 5" in both directions in Edit Group mode.

When both groups have been extruded they can be exploded using the Context menu Explode. You should know the procedure from here; select all primitives, use Intersect Faces/With Selection, select View/Hidden Geometry, delete all unwanted geometry, fix any problems created by the Intersect Faces tool and make the resulting primitives temporarily a group. **Figure 7** shows the intersecting extruded groups on the left and the resultant upper leg group

on the right. Notice the camera is positioned differently in the two parts of the image. The leg looks pretty good and is beginning to look like a cabriole leg. We must now create the pad group.

## MODELING THE SLIPPER FOOT PAD

Before we can begin modeling the pad, we need to put the group on a new layer called Upper Leg. Make the Cabriole Legs and Upper Leg layers invisible and all other layers visible. Referring to

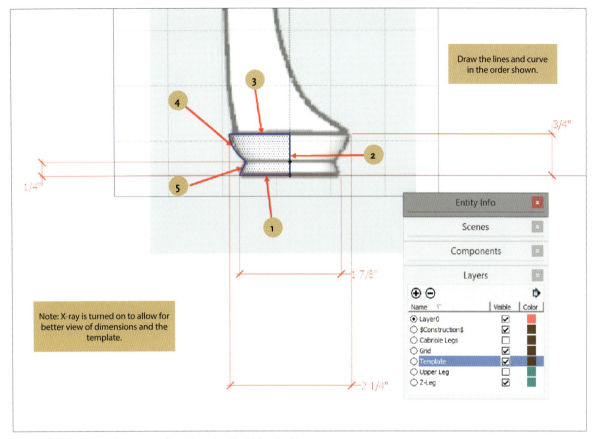

Draw the lines and curve in the order shown.

Note: X-ray is turned on to allow for better view of dimensions and the template.

3/4"

1/4"

1 7/8"

2 1/4"

Entity Info

Scenes

Components

Layers

| Name | Visible | Color |
|---|---|---|
| ⊙ Layer0 | ☑ | |
| ○ $Construction$ | ☑ | |
| ○ Cabriole Legs | ☐ | |
| ○ Grid | ☑ | |
| ○ Template | ☑ | |
| ○ Upper Leg | ☐ | |
| ○ Z-Leg | ☑ | |

**Figure 8** | One half the pad outline and face selected and highlighted in blue

**Figure 8** draw half of the pad outline; draw lines 1, 2 and 3 first with the Line tool, then the curve with the Bézier Curves tool, and lastly connect the Bézier curve endpoint to line 1's endpoint with the Line tool. This will produce a face as shown selected in **Figure 8**.

We will now extrude the pad outline using the Follow Me tool. You know the procedure. We first create a path with the Circle tool. **Figure 9** shows how we do this. Whenever we use the Circle or Arc tools, we want a line segment endpoint to be on one of the axes. In this case the Red axis. After the circle is created we delete its face. We don't need it, and it only serves to block our view of the pad outline. We next select the circle as our path, and then select the Follow Me tool and with its

cursor click on the pad outline's face. This will produce the extruded pad.

We will need center lines on the top of the pad so we add them as shown in **Figure 10**. We now select all primitives and make the pad a group. To complete the pad work, we create a new layer called Pad and place the group on the Pad layer.

**Figure 11** shows our completed Upper Leg and Pad together. We can begin to see the cabriole leg with slipper foot shaping up. Notice I have placed the axis of lathe rotation in the drawing, just where it appeared in **Figure 3**. It is clear from **Figure 11** that we need to align the Pad to this axis. Once we do this our task will be to sculpt the Upper Leg to provide a transition to the Pad. This is not as difficult as one may think, but it requires a few tricks.

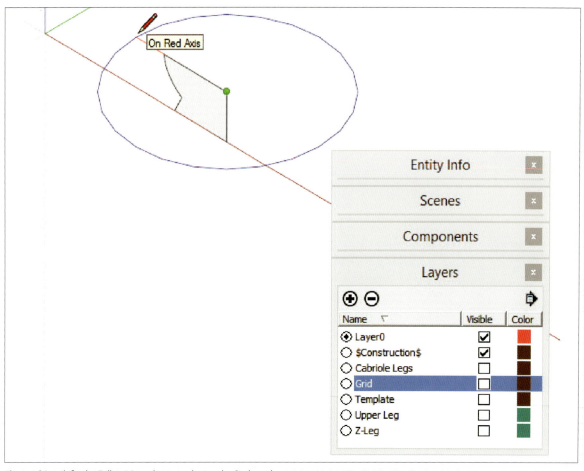

On Red Axis

**Figure 9** | A path for the Follow Me tool is created using the Circle tool

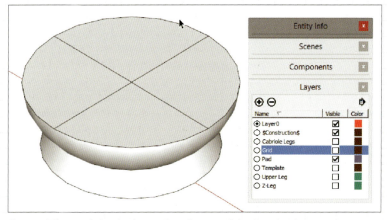

**Figure 10** | The extruded pad with center lines drawn parallel to the red and green axes

## REGISTERING THE UPPER LEG AND THE FOOT

The basic problem we have to solve is to transition the square termination of the Upper Leg to the round termination of the Pad; sort of like fitting a square peg into a round hole. There are simple techniques for doing this that look quite nice when viewed from above (looking down at an angle at the leg). But those techniques

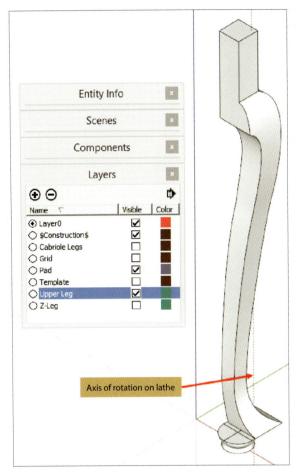

Figure 11 | The completed Upper Leg and Pad in current position

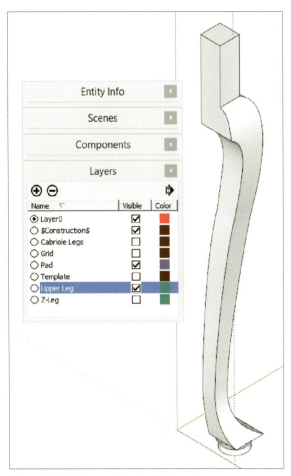

Figure 12 | The Pad center aligned to the Upper Leg

don't look good when viewed from the bottom of the Pad looking up. With these simple techniques, the foot appears square at the bottom. You can also go to the other extreme and shape each rectangle or triangle, one by one, until you have meticulously carved and shaped the leg. The latter technique is very time consuming and adds little to the quality of the drawing. We are going to take a middle-of-the-road approach, which is relatively quick and attractive. First we need to align the Pad to the Upper Leg by moving it along the positive green axis 1¼" as shown in **Figure 12**.

It is important that you look at, and study each of the pictures presented from here on out, paying

particular attention to rectangles, triangles and lines I have included or erased. As you sculpt this leg it is easy to get to a place that is overwhelming to repair; when that happens, frustration will destroy the learning process. Getting through this chapter with a successfully completed and attractive leg will prove to you just how doable it is. Later you can make lots of mistakes with the knowledge that the task can indeed be accomplished. So pay careful attention to each figure.

In **Figure 13** I have used the Orbit tool to view the heel of the upper leg. When the Pad is positioned correctly the Pad will extend beyond the edges of the Upper Leg as shown. Note also in **Figure 13**

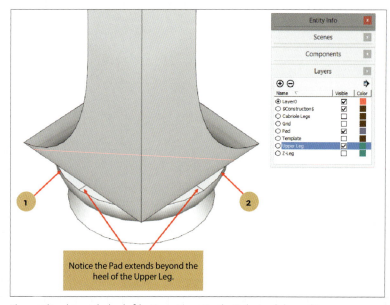

Figure 13 | Looking at the heel of the Upper Leg notice the Pad extends beyond it

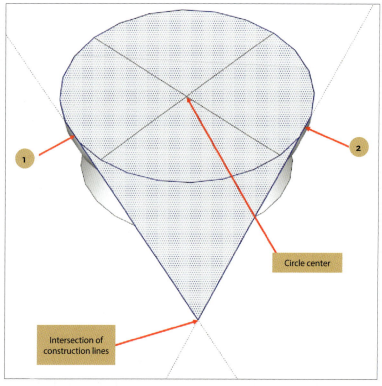

Figure 14 | Tangent lines and a circle form the tear shape that will become a mask

line segments 1 and 2. These are segments of the Pad's top surface; a polygon that approximates a circle. This is where more artistry than SketchUp knowledge comes in. The toe of the Upper Leg sticks over the front of the Pad. We are going to trim this overhang so that the toe conforms to the shape of the Pad by creating a mask.

## CREATING A MASK TO SHAPE THE UPPER LEG

With the Tape Measure tool we create two construction lines; one coincident with line segment 1 and the other coincident with line segment 2. Next we recreate the Pad's surface circle using its circle center and the endpoint of one of its diameter lines. Lastly we use the Line tool to connect the endpoint of line segment 1 to the intersection of the construction lines and we repeat this to create a line from the endpoint of line segment 2 to the intersection of the construction lines. This will give us the teardrop-shaped outline shown in **Figure 14**. In **Figure 14** I have selected the teardrop outline. We can delete the circle segment on the inside of the tear drop. It is not needed for the mask.

You might be wondering why I chose line segments 1 and 2 to form the construction lines. The answer is by trial-and-error, but I was looking for a specific result. You will see when we complete this mask, that it rounds the sides

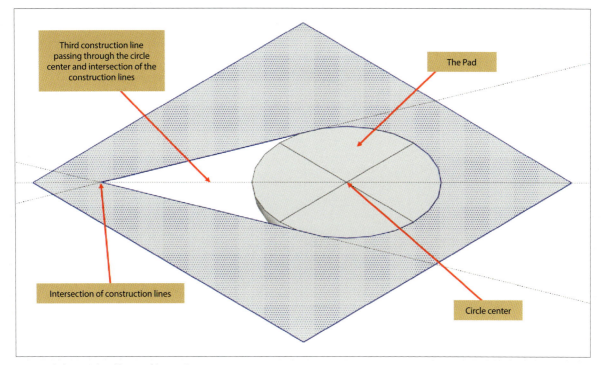

Third construction line passing through the circle center and intersection of the construction lines

The Pad

Intersection of construction lines

Circle center

**Figure 15** | The completed layout of the mask

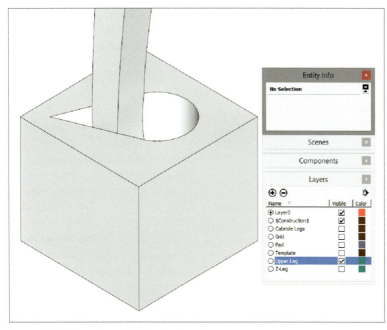

**Figure 16** | The Upper Leg masked by a tear drop shape

and toe as we want, it doesn't misshape the leg much and it clears the leg at a reasonable point as it extends upward. This will be obvious soon.

We next add a bounding rectangle to complete the layout of the mask. Add a third construction line that passes through the circle center and the intersection of the construction lines. This construction line is used with the Rectangle tool to place a bounding rectangle that clears the inner teardrop shape by a reasonable amount (at least an inch for comfort). Delete the face of the teardrop leaving only the face of the mask shown selected and highlighted in blue in **Figure 15**.

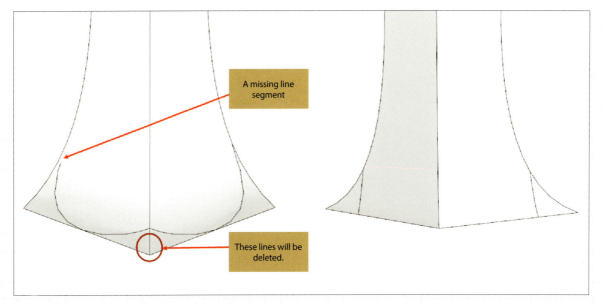

Figure 17 | Inspecting the toe and heel after an Intersect Faces operation

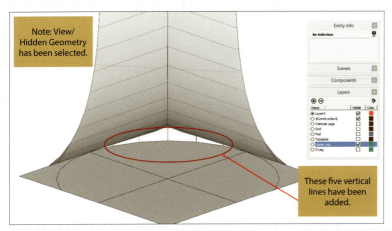

Note: View/
Hidden Geometry
has been selected.

These five vertical
lines have been
added.

Figure 18 | Vertical lines have been added as shown

## STITCHING THE UPPER LEG TO THE FOOT

With the Select tool triple click on the mask, Context click and Make Group. Select the Upper Leg, right click and choose Explode. You did remember to place all primitives on Layer0 after an Explode, right? Select all primitives of the Upper Leg and the mask group and Edit/ Intersect Face/With Selection. Wait patiently for the blue outlines to disappear; there are a lot of calculations your computer needs to make. Now delete the mask group. Zoom in closely to inspect the toe and heel. **Figure 17** shows my results with the toe and heel superimposed on the same image. Notice that I have one missing line segment that I need to add with the Line tool. You may get entirely different results. The Intersect Faces tool almost always leaves the user a little repair work to do.

We will start shaping at the toe, then the sides and finally the heel. The toe is relatively clean and easy, so

We now want the Pad layer invisible and the Upper Leg layer visible. With the Push/Pull tool extend the mask's face downward about an inch. Now, again with the Push/Pull tool extend the top side of the mask's face up another 2". The resulting mask should be at least 3" tall, extending below the Upper Leg by 1" and extending up the leg about 2". Choose Front and ISO views. Your model should look like that of **Figure 16**.

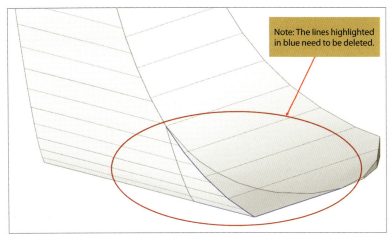

Note: The lines highlighted in blue need to be deleted.

**Figure 19** | The blue highlighted edges need to be deleted to begin the shaping of the side

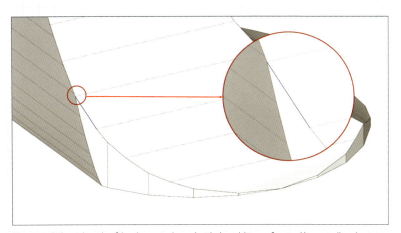

**Figure 20** | The right side of the slipper is shaped with the addition of vertical lines at all endpoints

your model. **Figure 19** shows the starting point. The edges highlighted in blue need to be deleted. When selecting these edges use the Select tool with the *Ctrl* key. If you add something to the selection that you don't want momentarily press the *Shift* key to remove it from the selection. Do not use the Select tool with a selection box; you will surely include something in the back you can't see and end up deleting wanted geometry. You can also use the Eraser tool like a paint brush, but I find it less accurate.

With the line selection made I delete them. This again opens a hole in the upper leg, which I must shape with vertical lines. But where to place them is the question. Like before, I place vertical lines at each endpoint in the circle that forms the bottom face of the upper leg. Recall the missing line in **Figure 17**. **Figure 20** shows that same line; take note of where I connected it, because if you don't place it at the correct point it becomes very hard to create faces. You can see in the enlarged circle where it has been connected. At this point you can refer to **Figures 19** and **20** and catch your model up with mine. You can also bring the left side of the slipper to the same point.

All we have left to sculpt is the heel and soften edges. Take a look at **Figure 21**. On the part of the heel closest to the toe we need to add material. On the back of the heel we need to remove material. In order to make the transition from the Upper Leg, defined by two line segments, to the Pad, defined by a number of segments in an arc, we will start up a ways on the leg. Where to start is quite arbitrary and based solely on the modeler's mental image of what the final result will look like. **Figure 21** shows where I wish to start.

I will clean up my toe first and show you the result so you can refer to it for yours. I first select View/Hidden Geometry. While I won't need it for the toe, it may come in handy later. Then I delete the lines shown in **Figure 17**. I use the Orbit tool freely to get an idea of what I want to do. Inspecting the bottom of the leg and the top of the toe it becomes obvious I need to add five vertical lines (i.e. parallel with the Blue axis), at each endpoint in the circle that forms the bottom face of the leg in the toe area. **Figure 18** shows my results. Check this against your results. They should be the same.

Now I will work on the sides of the slipper. When I am done you can view my results and follow suit in

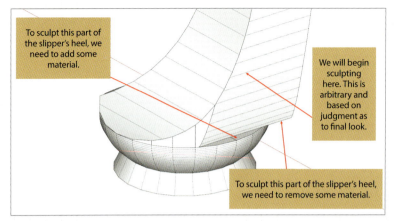

To sculpt this part of the slipper's heel, we need to add some material.

We will begin sculpting here. This is arbitrary and based on judgment as to final look.

To sculpt this part of the slipper's heel, we need to remove some material.

**Figure 21** | With the Pad made visible we get our first look at sculpting the heel and we form a strategy

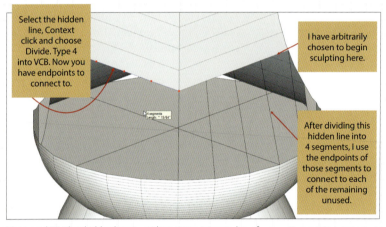

Select the hidden line, Context click and choose Divide. Type 4 into VCB. Now you have endpoints to connect to.

I have arbitrarily chosen to begin sculpting here.

4 segments
Length ~ 19'44

After dividing this hidden line into 4 segments, I use the endpoints of those segments to connect to each of the remaining unused.

**Figure 22** | Dividing hidden lines provides appropriate number of connection points

Again, I will model the heel and you can catch up once you see my results.

Look at **Figure 22**. We are looking directly at the back of the heel. I selected, arbitrarily, a point above where the curve in the slipper side ends to begin sculpting the heel. I have erased all the unwanted lines up to that point. I then counted the number of unused vertices' on the upper defining circle of the Pad; there are 9. I connected the middle one to the back edge of the heel leaving 4 unused vertices' on each side. Next I divided the bottom line on each side of the Upper Leg into 4 segments to give me mating connect points between the Pad and the Upper Leg.

I make all those connections for a total of 9 lines. Remember that the Pad is a group, and although I am connecting to its vertices', those circle segments will have to be added because they aren't shared by the group.

Now it is just a matter of adding the circle segments and completing the triangles. See **Figure 23**. Note that I also filled in the area near the curvy line that ended the slipper side. On each side I added three lines from that circle vertex shown in **Figure 23** to all the endpoints between the side curve's endpoint and the endpoint of the divided hidden line. You need to bring your model to the same state as mine. Compare the results closely. Our results should be nearly identical.

## SMOOTHING THE LEG

When you are satisfied that your model is the same as mine choose the Pad, explode it and return its primitives to Layer0. Select all pad and upper leg primitives and make a component called New Cabriole Leg. Place it on a new layer called New Cabriole Leg. At this point I can get rid of all layers except New Cabriole Leg – Cabriole Legs, Grid, Template and Z-leg. Pad and Upper Leg have no meaning or content anymore. All editing now will be done in Edit Component mode. After softening/smoothing all lines and edges that we don't want to show with the Eraser tool and *Ctrl* key, we have the final model shown in **Figure 24**. You can compare this New Cabriole Leg to those shown in **Figure 1** by making layer Cabriole Legs visible. In fact if you modeled your leg at the same point I modeled mine the two legs should overlap and you can see how close you came to the original.

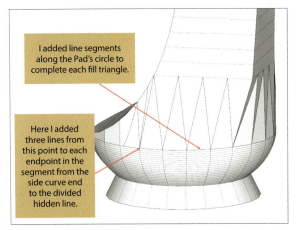

I added line segments along the Pad's circle to complete each fill triangle.

Here I added three lines from this point to each endpoint in the segment from the side curve end to the divided hidden line.

**Figure 23** | The sculpting of the heel is completed with the addition of circle segments and diagonals

This completes your journeyman training. If you have successfully completed all chapters in this book you are now a master sketchman. Congratulations! Seriously though, I hope you have accomplished what you set out to do when you picked this book up. I hope I have fulfilled my promise to provide you with valuable and useful training. Don't let your skills wither away. Use SketchUp in all your shop projects whether it is designing furniture, an outdoors deck, a shed or an addition. Only through constant use do you become comfortable with SketchUp – but then it becomes the most useful tool in your shop.

## EXERCISES FOR THE STUDENT

If you have completed this entire text you deserve a break. Go out and celebrate, you deserve it. Besides, you are no longer a student but a master sketchman. Congratulations!

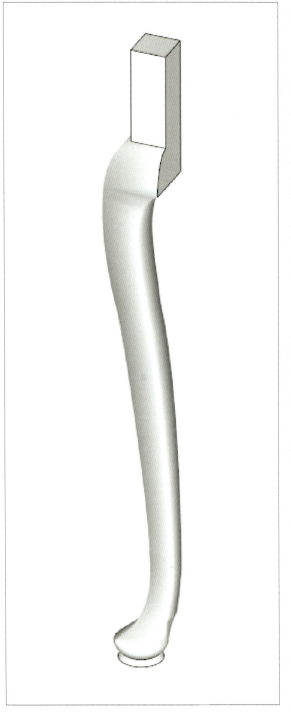

**Figure 24** | The completed New Cabriole Leg

# MAC OS X USER HELP

## MAJOR KEYBOARD DIFFERENCES

There are two significant differences in keyboard keys between Windows and Mac OS X that you need to be aware of. The *Ctrl* key in Windows is the *Command* key in Mac OS X. The *Alt* key in Windows is the *Option* key in Mac OS X.

You can get a SketchUp Quick Reference card for most commands by going to the following web page (at the time of this writing): help.sketchup.com/en/article/116693

Choose either Microsoft Windows or the Mac OS X download link.

On the Quick Reference Card you will find handy keyboard shortcut keys and use instructions. Mac users might want to download both the Microsoft Windows and Mac OS X versions to get a comparison of key commands – on the PC a Move/Copy requires the *Ctrl* key with the Move tool. On the Mac you use the *Option* key instead. Study this card, it is very useful.

## WHERE IS PREFERENCES ON THE MAC?

To locate Preferences on the Mac go to the SketchUp menu and choose Preferences.

## HOW TO CUSTOMIZE A MAC SKETCHUP TOOLBAR

To customize your toolbar on a Mac do the following:
1. Go to menu View and choose Customize Toolbar or right click on the toolbar and choose Customize Toolbar. A window will open with all the available tool icons on it, including any plug-in tool icons. You may need to use the scroll bar to see them all.
2. Drag and drop any icon or tool sets such as Standard Views, from this window onto the SketchUp toolbar. You can also drag and drop tools from the SketchUp toolbar to this window to get rid of them.
3. When you are finished customizing the toolbar click the Done button.

You will find the Measurements tool in about the middle of the page. But it is probably already in your SketchUp work area. Look at the lower right corner or the lower left corner.

Versions of Mac SketchUp prior to SketchUp 2015 had one little idiosyncrasy you should be aware of: The Mac permits multiple model files to be open at the same time. This causes some problems. When SketchUp is first opened (the first model is opened) the toolbar is set up before the plugins folder is evaluated and plugins recognized. That means the first copy of SketchUp will not have the plugin icons in the toolbar. So a good practice is to open SketchUp to a blank model first, then open the model you wish to work on. In this second model, the toolbar will be set up to your customized settings. This problem was fixed in SketchUp 2015.

Unfortunately, on a Mac you cannot remove icons from a predefined toolbar.

The icons and toolbars I recommended in Part One are not available in equivalent toolbars on the Mac. Go to View/Tool Palettes and use the Large Tool Set as the base. Then use the other toolbars in Tool Palettes, and/or customize your toolbar as described above to access the rest of the tools.

## INSTALLING RUBY SCRIPT PLUGINS ON MAC OS X

To install a plugin select SketchUp then Preferences.

A window opens that has a list on the left. Select Extensions. The area on the right shows plugins you currently have. Ensure you have a check mark in the box next to the ones you need.

To add another extension, click the button on the lower right labeled Install Extension.

A Finder window opens for you to navigate to your desired installation file, which must have a .rbz file extension. If you are trying to install an extension with a .zip file extension, simply change the .zip file extension to .rbz and follow the above procedure.

## CAN'T SEE THE ENTIRE ENTITY INFO DIALOG BOX

You may find that you can't expand the Entity Info dialog box; even though there may be a slider, it doesn't work. This has been a bug on Mac versions of SketchUp for a while. To fix the situation go to SketchUp Preferences, choose the Workspace page and under the Workspace tile click the Reset Workspace button.

## LAYERS DROP-DOWN BOX CHANGES ACTIVE LAYER

When attempting to change the layer an entity or entities are on with the Layers drop-down box it changes the active layer. It seems that any layer chosen with the Select tool in the Layers drop-down box will change the Active Layer to that selection. This is a bug in Mac OS X versions of SketchUp. Ironically, I discovered this very same bug on the PC using SketchUp 8 back in March of 2011. I reported the bug and it got fixed on the PC, but apparently it still remains in the Mac versions.

The solution is to use the Entity Info box to choose a destination layer and not the Layers drop-down box. Unfortunately, this bug renders the Layers drop-down box useless for Mac users.

## ADDING A NEW MATERIAL TO THE MATERIALS DIALOG BOX

To add a JPG texture image to the In Model Materials dialog box library use menu Window/Materials. Click on the In Model icon. In the Materials window right click in the open field and choose New Texture. Locate and highlight the desired JPG file and click Open. Follow the instructions given.

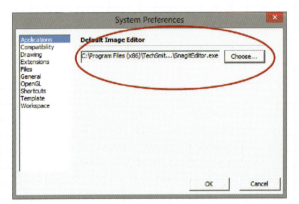

**Figure 1** | You can specify a default image editor of your choice or leave it blank

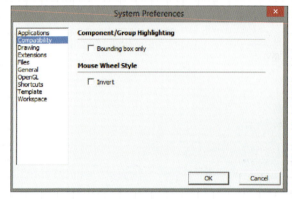

**Figure 2** | You can leave both check boxes blank

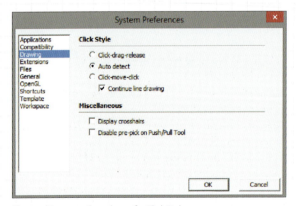

**Figure 3** | I suggest Auto detect for Click Style

The Preferences dialog box provides for application-wide settings. Use the menu Window/Preferences to access the Preferences dialog box. On the left side of the Preferences dialog box is a list of pages contained in it. Each page is shown in this Appendix B section, and you will find my recommendation for each Preferences page. Once you have finished this book, experiment with these settings

to learn other options. You may find you have a drawing style that is substantially different than mine.

Remember, any settings or changes you make in Preferences are application-wide. If you wish to make Model specific changes use the Model Info dialog box.

## APPLICATIONS

**Figure 1** hows the Applications page of System Preferences. The only option on this page is to specify a default image editor you want to use to edit images while still in SketchUp. My favorite is TechSmith's Snagit Editor as shown.

## COMPATIBILITY

**Figure 2** shows the Compatibility page of System Preferences. I suggest leaving the Component/Group Highlighting check box unchecked. The Mouse Wheel Style check box should be set for personal style.

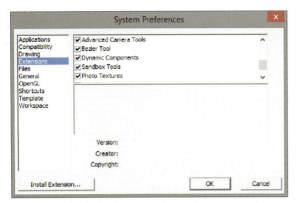

**Figure 4** | Be sure to check the box next to any installed extension you wish to use

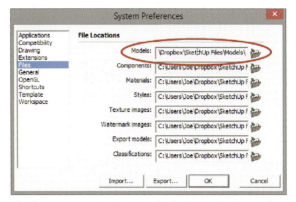

**Figure 5** | You can specify a default folder for SketchUp to place files of various types

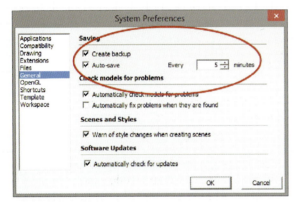

**Figure 6** | Be sure to set the Saving section just as you see in the red ellipse

## DRAWING

**Figure 3** shows the Drawing page of System Preferences. I suggest leaving the Auto-detect radio button selected. The "Continue line drawing" check box should be set as a personal style. Checking this box means that the Line tool will continue drawing lines from point to point versus one line at a time when unchecked. I have sometimes cursed the continuous line drawing, but in most cases I find it helpful.

## EXTENSIONS

**Figure 4** shows the Extensions page of System Preferences. This page shows all the registered

extensions you currently have installed. It doesn't necessarily show all the extensions you have installed because many older extensions didn't use the registering feature; in fact this feature didn't exist until recent versions. Be sure to check any installed and registered extensions you wish to use. If you highlight an extension in the right window you will see its version, creator and copyright in the panel below. This page is also used to install new extensions by clicking the Install Extensions button.

## FILES

**Figure 5** shows the Files page of System Preferences. This page shows all various types of files that SketchUp might save. You can specify a default folder for each one. For example, I like to place all my model files in a Dropbox folder located at C:\Users\Joe\Dropbox\SketchUp Files\Models. That way I can access them from any of my computers, tablets or smart phones.

## GENERAL

**Figure 6** shows the General page of System Preferences. This page shows the application's general settings. Be sure to set the Saving section exactly as shown in the red ellipse. The remaining settings are personal preferences and style.

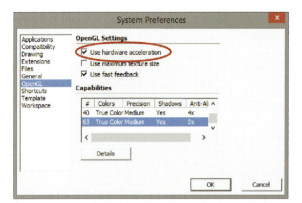

**Figure 7** | Be sure to check "Use hardware acceleration"

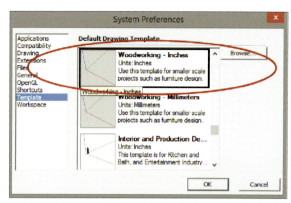

**Figure 9** | Choose the Woodworking – Inches Template to begin with

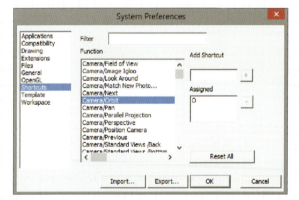

**Figure 8** | You can customize your shortcut keys on this page

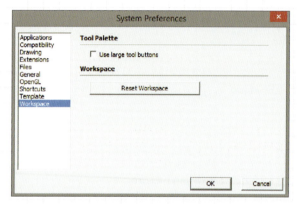

**Figure 10** | I leave "Use large tool buttons" unchecked to preserve toolbar real estate

## OPENGL

**Figure 7** shows the OpenGL page of System Preferences. This page shows the application's general settings. Be sure to check the "Use hardware acceleration" check box if you have one installed; all recently manufactured PCs, Macs and notebooks have a hardware accelerator. The other settings are best left as the default sets them.

## SHORTCUTS

**Figure 8** shows the Shortcuts page of System Preferences. On this page you can customize the shortcut key assignments to your preferences. Should you make changes you discover later you don't like you can get back to factory settings using the Reset All button.

## TEMPLATE

**Figure 9** shows the Template page of System Preferences. Use the scroll bar to choose the Woodworking – Inches template to begin. In Part One, you learned to create your own custom template with this template as the starting point.

## WORKSPACE

**Figure 10** shows the Workspace page of System Preferences. Toolbar real estate is a precious commodity in SketchUp; especially if you like to install a lot of extensions. For that reason I leave the "Use large tool buttons" unchecked. If you have less than optimal eye sight you may wish to use the large tool buttons.

# APPENDIX C

# MODEL INFO

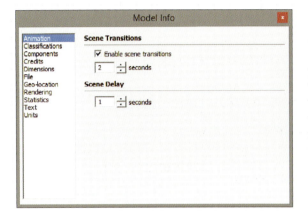

**Figure 1** | These are the default Animation settings, which I find acceptable

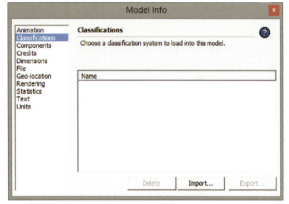

**Figure 2** | This is a Pro-only feature not covered in this book

The Model Info dialog box provides for model-specific attribute settings. Each model has its own settings, independent of other models, though the template used when beginning a model provides a starting point. Use the menu Window/Model Info to access the Model Info dialog box. On the left side of the Model Info dialog box is a list of pages contained in it. Each page is shown in this Appendix C section and you will find my recommendation for each Model Info page. Once you have finished this book, experiment with these settings to learn other options. You may find you have a drawing style that is substantially different than mine.

Remember, any settings or changes you make in Model Info are model-specific. If you wish to make application specific changes use the Preferences dialog box.

## ANIMATION

The Animation page, shown in **Figure 1**, can be used to enable scene transitions, set the scene transition

time and set the scene delay in seconds. These settings are used to customize scene animations which I don't cover except to mention it in this book.

## CLASSIFICATIONS

The Classifications page, shown in **Figure 2**, is a Pro-only feature not covered in this book.

## COMPONENTS

The Components page, shown in **Figure 3**, is used to customize the display environment during Component/Group Editing. The "Fade similar components" slider adjusts the shade of gray other instantiations of the same component are rendered. The Hide checkbox is used to hide other instantiations of the same component just like the Hide Similar Components tool. The "Fade rest of model" slider adjusts the shade of gray other entities in the model are rendered. The Hide checkbox is

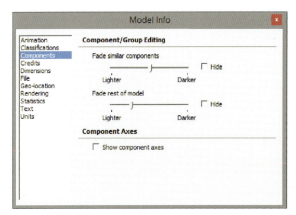

**Figure 3** | These are the default Components settings which I find acceptable

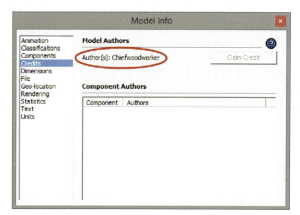

**Figure 4** | You can claim Author Credit for models your place in the 3D Warehouse

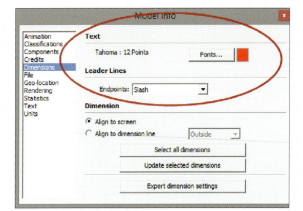

**Figure 5** | You can customize the way your dimension text and leader lines appear

used to hide other entities just like the Hide Rest of Model tool. The "Show component axes" check box in the Component Axes section is used to display the individual component axis in the entire model. The axes are displayed on all components when not in edit mode, but only the selected component in edit mode. I find the default Components settings to be acceptable.

## CREDITS

The Credits page, shown in **Figure 4**, is used to claim credit for a model. You must have a Google account and be signed in to claim credit and associate your

Google account identity with your model. If you used components in your model that you downloaded from 3D Warehouse component library you can see the author in the Component Authors section. If you claimed credit for your model and subsequently upload the model to the 3D Warehouse, anyone who downloads your model will see your Google account identity along with the name of the model.

## DIMENSIONS

The Dimensions page, shown in **Figure 5**, provides for customization of text, leader lines and dimensions. In the Text section you can specify the font and font size. The current font selection is shown. Change the font type, size and color with the Fonts button. Notice you can choose Points or Height for the size of the font. Height permits you to specify a scaled dimension for your text, just like any other dimensioned entity.

The Leader Lines section drop-down box provides a choice of leader endpoints. The choices are none, slash, dots, closed arrow or open arrow.

The Dimension sections provides for customization of dimension appearance. Choosing "Align to screen" allows the text to remain aligned with the screen view as you orbit the model. Choose "Align to dimension line" fixes the text to the dimension line and text will move as you orbit the model.

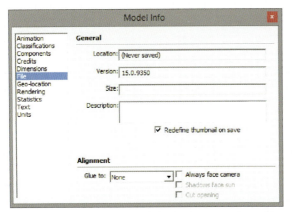

Figure 6 | The File page shows you the location, version and size of the active model file

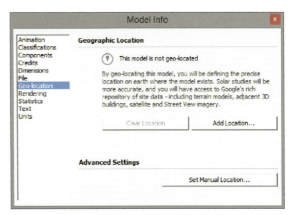

Figure 7 | The Geo-location page is not used in this book

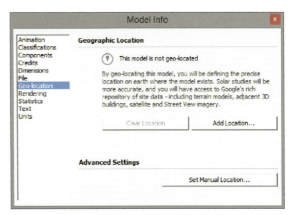

Figure 8 | Check "Use Anti-Aliased Textures"

To update or change dimensions you can use the "Update selected dimensions" button to update only dimensions you have selected. You can change or update all dimensions in the viewing area by first using the "Select all dimensions" button followed by the "Update selected dimensions" button.

## FILE

The File page, shown in **Figure 6**, provides information about the model's file. If the model has been saved it shows its Location. Version displays the version of SketchUp used to create the model. Size

shows the file size of the model. Description provides a place for the creator to add a description of the model. A thumbnail is created each time the model is saved, unless the "Redefine thumbnail on save" check box is unchecked.

Alignment provides the ability to specify the alignment of components loaded into the model from another model or source. It is not useful for the purpose of this text.

## GEO-LOCATION

The Geo-location page, shown in **Figure 7**, permits the user to specify a location on the earth where the model will be displayed in Google Earth. This page is not useful for the purpose of this text.

## RENDERING

The Rendering page, shown in **Figure 8**, provides a "Use Anti-Aliased Textures" check box to turn anti-aliased textures on/off. I suggest leaving it checked.

## STATISTICS

The Statistics page, shown in **Figure 9**, provides a count of all entities used in the model. When "Show nested components" is selected a count of all components used in the model is given. The Purge

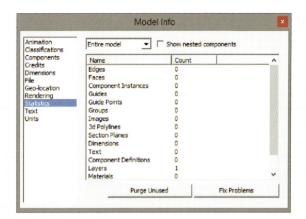

**Figure 9** | The Statistics page provides a count of all entities in the model

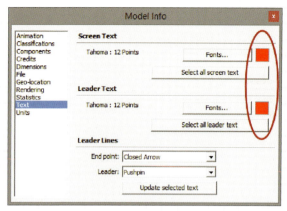

**Figure 10** | In this page you can customize the appearance of screen text, leader text and leader lines

Unused button will purge the model of all unused textures and components, hence reducing the file size of the model. The Fix Problems button will run a validity check on the model and attempt to fix any problems.

Problem checking is automatically performed each time a SketchUp file is opened, saved or auto-saved if "Automatically check models for problems" is enabled in the General page of the System Preferences dialog box. It is a good idea to enable this feature.

## TEXT

The Text page, shown in **Figure 10**, provides for customization of screen text, leader text and leader lines. The options are very similar to Dimensions discussed above. Screen Text is text that is not attached to another entity by a leader line and arrow. In the Screen Text section you can specify the font and font size. The current font selection is shown. Change the font type, size and color with the Fonts button. Notice you cannot choose Points or Height for the size of the font. Screen text Height is only displayed in points.

Leader Text is text that is attached to another entity by a leader line and arrow. In the Leader Text section you can change leader text font type, size and color with the Fonts button. Notice you can choose Points or Height for the size of the font. Height per-

mits to specify a scaled dimension for your text, just like any other dimensioned entity.

The "Select all screen text" and "Select all leader text" buttons selects all screen text and leader text respectively that appear in the viewing area. Used in conjunction with the "Update selected text" button, the user has a choice of updating only selected text or all text in the viewing area.

## UNITS

The Units page, shown in **Figure 11**, permits the customization of Length Units and Angle Units.

In the Length Units section you chose the Format of the length in a drop down box. Choices are architectural, decimal, engineering and fractional. Depending and the choice of format, you can choose between inches, feet, millimeters, centimeters and meters. The choices in the Precision drop-down box are contingent on both the choice of format and choice of units.

For the purpose of furniture design I highly recommend either of the following two choices:

### US/Imperial
Format: Fractional; Units: Inches; Precision: $\frac{1}{64}$"; "Enable length snapping": Unchecked; "Display units format": Checked.

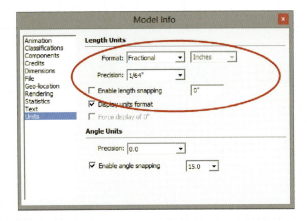

**Figure 11** | Check "Use Anti-Aliased Textures"

## Metric

Format: Decimal; Units: Millimeters; Precision: 0.0mm; "Enable length snapping": Unchecked; "Display units format": Checked.

It is very important that the "Enable length snapping" check box be unchecked. Leaving this checked could result in lines not meeting and creating difficult problems to find, such as why a face will not form in what appears to be an enclosed polygon.

## ANGLE UNITS

The Angle Units section permits customizing the displayed Precision of an angle and at what angles to snap to if the "Enable angle snapping" check box is checked. I recommend a precision of 0.0°unless you can discern less than a tenth of a degree with your eyes.

Check the "Enable angle snapping" checkbox to enable snapping to the specified angle increment while using the Protractor or Rotate tool. After defining your reference line, move the cursor inside the protractor. As you move, the angle will snap to the specified increments indicated by the tick marks. Move your cursor outside the protractor and you can select any angle. Of course you can always specify an exact angle by typing it in the VCB. Angle snapping does not create the same problem length snapping does.

# COMPONENT-RELATED DIALOG BOXES

There are three dialog boxes that are related and can cause some confusion if the user is not careful. They are Components, Create Component and Entity Info. They are described below.

## COMPONENTS

The Components dialog box, shown in **Figure 1**, shows all the components available in a library; in **Figure 1** I have selected the In Model library by clicking on the In Model 🏠 icon. You can select from several styles for listing and displaying the components: Small Thumbnails, Large Thumbnails, Details and List. In **Figure 1**, I have selected Details. You can also choose other libraries supplied with SketchUp or create your own and select it.

Once a component is in the Components library it cannot be destroyed without an explicit attempt to delete it. Even then it cannot be deleted unless there are no instances of it in the model. Realize that every part in a model is an instance of a component, not the component itself. So when you delete a part from the model you are not deleting its parent component. That component is safe in the library and another copy of it can be brought into the model at any time.

## CREATE COMPONENT

The Create Component dialog box, shown in **Figure 2**, appears when you select Context menu Make Component. You can enter the name of the component in the Name field. It is very important that you understand the component name you enter in the Name field in the Create Component dialog box is the same as the name that appears in the Definition field of the Entity Info dialog box. These

two fields, Name in Create Component and Definition in Entity Info, are the name of the component and must be unique. Unfortunately, the Entity Info dialog box also uses a field called Name, which is the instance name of a component, or part name. The instance name does not have to be unique, but I always try to make it unique by using adjectives such as right, left, top, bottom, front and back.

## ENTITY INFO

The Entity Info dialog box, shown in **Figure 3**, shows important characteristics and attributes about a selected entity or entities. The Layer drop-down shows the layer the entity resides on and can be used to change the layer an entity resides on. The Name field shows the instance name of the entity if it is a component or group. The Definition field shows the component name of a selected entity if it is a component. The Type field is used to assign classifications, which I don't cover in this book.

There are four check boxes. You can check Hidden if you want to hide an entity or entities. The Locked check box will protect an entity from any change if selected and it will change its selection highlight to red to indicate it is a locked entity. I don't cover Shadows in this book, but you can use the Cast Shadows and Receive Shadows check boxes – their purposes are obvious from their names.

An entity can be any entity in SketchUp including, but not limited to, edges, faces, dimensions, leader text, group or component. If you selected multiple entities the Entity Info box will only indicate those characteristics and attributes common to all that are selected.

**Figure 1** | The Components dialog box displays a list of all components in a library

**Figure 2** | The Create Component dialog box appears when Context menu Make Component is selected

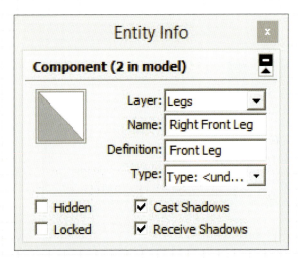

**Figure 3** | The Entity Info dialog box shows important characteristics about a selected entity

# APPENDIX E

# SKETCHUP VIEWERS

You may wish to share your model with someone who is not a SketchUp user, but who would like to view a model you created. SketchUp provides two viewers for this purpose. The viewers have no drawing or modeling capability, merely viewing. They are very simple to use. The best part is they are free, at least at this writing.

## SKETCHUP VIEWER

You can access the SketchUp Viewer by going to sketchup.com and clicking on the Products tab at the top of the page. Or you can access it directly at: sketchup.com/products/sketchup-viewer

From this page you can download either a Microsoft Windows or Mac OS X version. Once you have installed the viewer you can view any SKP file.

## SKETCHUP MOBILE VIEWER

The SketchUp Mobile Viewer is a little more limiting than the SketchUp viewer, which is essentially SketchUp Make with all modeling tools removed. The mobile viewer requires that you first upload a model to the 3D warehouse.

Any model in the 3D Warehouse can be downloaded and cached on your mobile device for viewing offline. The file format is specific to the mobile viewer and is a converted SKP file. Normal SKP files cannot be viewed on the mobile viewer.

You can access the SketchUp Mobile Viewer by going to sketchup.com and clicking on the Products tab at the top of the page. Or you can access it directly at: sketchup.com/products/sketchup-mobile-viewer

From this page you can download either an iOS or Android version. Once you have installed the viewer you can view any 3D Warehouse model.

# THE WAREHOUSE

You can use the Warehouse to Download SketchUp models, share models and components and get ruby script plugins. The 3D Warehouse has thousands of models and components you can download and use in your own models. The Extensions Warehouse similarly has hundreds of Ruby extensions you can download and install. Go to menu View/Toolbars, select the Toolbars tab and check Warehouse at the bottom of the list. This will open the Warehouse toolbar. You will need a Google account to access either Warehouse.

🐞 To Get a Model: Click on the Get Models icon, and it will take you to the library. You can do a search for what you want.

🐞 To Share a Model: If you wish to put your model in the SketchUp Warehouse, click on the Share Model icon.

🐞 To Share a Component: If you wish to share one of your components by placing it in the Warehouse, click on the Share Component icon.

🐞 To Get Ruby Script Plugins: If you wish to access the Warehouse to download a Ruby Script Plugin, click on the Extension Warehouse icon.

# INDEX

2-Point Arc, 45, 50, 94, 124, 136-139, 225-229
3D Warehouse, 26, 45, 46, 276, 283, 284

## A

Aprons, 59, 69, 74-79, 83-85, 89, 178, 185, 258
Arc, 9, 15, 33, 40, 41, 46, 50, 58, 89, 94, 118, 121 134, 136, 194, 229, 235, 257
Arch, 89, 217-235
Axes tool, 33, 52, 62

## B

Back Edges [definition], 34, 53, 55
Bézier curves, 46, 149, 194, 195, 202, 214, 235, 240, 242, 243, 247-257
Bracket feet, 242-255
Bullnose trim, 122, 138, 217, 221, 224-226, 235

## C

Cabriole legs, 9, 35, 47, 255, 256-269
Camera toolbar, 34
Center tooltip, 43-44
Circles, 9, 15, 43, 50, 58, 94, 136, 138, 206, 217-222, 227, 229, 235
Circle tool [definition], 41, 50
Cock bead, 97, 98, 122-139, 173
Component edit [definition], 47
Construction toolbar, 33
Context menu [definition], 16, 44-47
Copy, 46
Cove trim, 224, 227-235
Cursor, 35

## D

Delete Guides, 46
Dimension tool, 51, 52, 66, 154-157, 178, 200
Dovetails, 59, 83, 85, 95, 98, 100, 105, 106, 108, 113, 121, 167, 168, 178
Drawers, 95-139
Drawer pulls, 122, 123, 133-139, 158, 167
Drawer sliders, 92, 99, 100
Drawing toolbar [definition], 33

## E

Edit toolbar [definition], 33
Endpoint [definition], 39
Entity Info [definition], 48
Eraser, 33, 49, 55
Extensions, 12, 26, 45, 49, 140-149, 218, 271, 273, 274, 284

## F

Follow Me tool [definition], 33, 50, 125
French curves, 10, 194, 195
From Point tooltip, 41-44

## H

Half Circle tooltip, 41
Hide, 46-47
Hidden Line Style, [definition], 34, 53

## I

Inference Engine, 10, 27, 37-44
Intersection tooltip, 40-41
Instructor, 17,22,23,32,49
Import, 46
Iso, 25, 34, 35, 52, 54

## J

Joinery, 7, 34, 50, 52, 59, 63, 68, 69, 71, 73, 74, 84-94, 95, 100, 105, 121, 168, 173, 178

## K

Knowledge Center, 17, 49

## L

Layer Zero (Layer 0) [definition], 48, 58, 60, 63, 64
Layers toolbar, 34, 112
Layers Management tool, 138, 140, 141, 142, 143, 144, 145, 149, 150, 151, 156, 161
Legs, 58-72, 256-259
Line tool [definition], 16, 40, 41, 42, 44, 49
Lock command, 47

## M

Materials dialog box, 48, 170, 174, 271
Midpoint tooltip, 39
Monochrome style, 53
Mortise, 59, 63, 73, 77, 78, 79, 80, 82, 83, 85, 89, 94, 185, 192, 194, 200, 206, 210, 212, 214, 216, 218, 258
Move tool [definition], 15, 17, 50, 68

## O

Offset tool [definition], 50
On Edge tooltip [definition], 39
On Face tooltip [definition], 40
On Line tooltip [definition], 39
Orbit tool [definition], 52
Origin [definition], 35
Outliner tool, 69

**P**

Pan tool [definition], 52
Parallel to Edge tooltip, [definition], 41
Paste, 46
Paste in Place, 46
Perpendicular to Edge tooltip, [definition] 42, 44
Plugins, 9-12, 17, 26, 35, 37, 45, 48, 49, 138, 140, 141, 145, 146, 270, 271, 284
Principal toolbar, 33
Protractor tool [definition], 33,51
Push/Pull tool [definition], 50

**R**

Rails, 63, 82, 85-90, 64, 101-103, 122, 132, 133, 173, 217-221, 224, 229, 235, 236
Rectangle tool [definition], 50
Ruby script, 9-14, 26, 35, 37, 45, 49, 52, 59, 88, 94, 140-149, 150, 151, 160, 161, 271, 284
Rung, 192, 194, 200, 202, 208-216
Rung mortises, 200,210
Rotate tool [definition], 50

**S**

Scale tool [definition], 33, 50
Scene tabs, 47
Scenes, 49, 84, 94
Section toolbar, 33
Section Plane tool, 24, 34, 52
Select tool [definition], 33,49
Shaded Style, 53
Shaded With Textures Style, 53
SketchUcation Plugin Store, 147, 148
Standard toolbar, 34
Styles toolbar, 34, 53

**T**

Tape Measure tool [definition], 51
Tapered legs, 57-72, 73, 79, 82, 197, 257
Tenon, 26, 51, 76-78, 80, 83, 88, 89, 94, 185, 192, 194, 209, 210, 212, 213, 218, 222, 223, 258
Text tool, 33, 52

**U**

Unhide, 46-47
Unlock, 47

**V**

Value Control Box (VCB) [definition], 10, 16, 32, 33, 37, 38
View toolbar [definition], 34

**W**

Warehouse 34-35
Wireframe Style [definition], 34, 53

**X**

X-ray [definition] 34, 53

**Z**

Zoom tool, 52
Zoom Extents tool, 34, 52, 55

**SketchUp: A Design Guide for Woodworkers.**
Copyright © 2015 by Joe Zeh. Printed and bound in China. All rights reserved. No part of this book may be reproduced in any form or by any electronic or mechanical means including information storage and retrieval systems without permission in writing from the publisher, except by a reviewer, who may quote brief passages in a review. Published by Popular Woodworking Books, an imprint of F+W, A Content + eCommerce Company, 10151 Carver Rd. Blue Ash, Ohio, 45242. First edition.

Distributed in Canada by Fraser Direct
100 Armstrong Avenue
Georgetown, Ontario L7G 5S4
Canada

Distributed in the U.K. and Europe by
F+W Media International, LTD
Brunel House, Ford Close
Newton Abbot
Devon TQ12 4PU, UK
Tel: (+44) 1626 323200
Fax: (+44) 1626 323319

Distributed in Australia by Capricorn Link
P.O. Box 704
Windsor, NSW 2756
Australia

Visit our website at popularwoodworking.com or our consumer website at shopwoodworking.com for more woodworking information.

Other fine Popular Woodworking Books are available from your local bookstore or direct from the publisher.

ISBN-13: 978-1-4403-4201-1

19  18  17  16  15      5  4  3  2  1

Editor: *Scott Francis*
Designer: *Laura Spencer*
Production Coordinator: *Debbie Thomas*

## METRIC CONVERSION CHART

| | | |
|---|---|---|
| Inches | Centimeters | 2.54 |
| Centimeters | Inches | 0.4 |
| Feet | Centimeters | 30.5 |
| Centimeters | Feet | 0.03 |
| Yards | Meters | 0.9 |
| Meters | Yards | 1.1 |

a content + ecommerce company

# IDEAS • INSTRUCTION • INSPIRATION

## Receive FREE downloadable bonus materials when you sign up for our FREE newsletter at popularwoodworking.com.

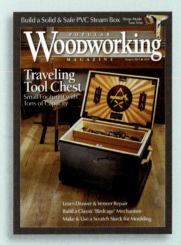

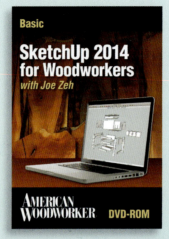

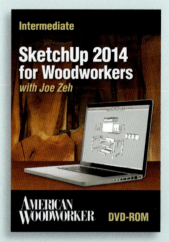

Find the latest issues of *Popular Woodworking Magazine* on newsstands, or visit **popularwoodworking.com**.

These and other great Popular Woodworking products are available at your local bookstore, woodworking store or online supplier. Visit our website at **shopwoodworking.com**.

## Popular Woodworking Videos

Subscribe and get immediate access to the web's best woodworking subscription site. You'll find more than 400 hours of woodworking video tutorials and full-length video workshops from world-class instructors on workshops, projects, SketchUp, tools, techniques and moare! **videos. popularwoodworking.com**

## Visit our Website

Find helpful and inspiring articles, videos, blogs, projects and plans at **popularwoodworking.com**.

For behind the scenes information, become a fan at **Facebook.com/popularwoodworking**.

For more tips, clips and articles, follow us at **twitter.com/pweditors**.

For visual inspiration, follow us at **pinterest.com/popwoodworking**.

For free videos visit **youtube.com/popwoodworking**.